ED VULLIAMY is the author of *Amexica: War Along the Borderline* and *The War is Dead, Long Live The War: Bosnia: the Reckoning*. He reported for the *Guardian* and *Observer* for thirty-two years and contributed to the *Sgt Pepper's Lonely Hearts Club Band* fiftieth-anniversary liner notes.

WHEN WORDS FAIL

A Life with Music, War and Peace

Ed Vulliamy

with illustrations by

Shirley Hughes

GRANTA

Granta Publications, 12 Addison Avenue, London, W11 4QR

First published in Great Britain by Granta Books, 2018
This paperback edition published by Granta Books, 2019

A CIP catalogue record for this book is available from the British Library

9 8 7 6 5 4 3 2 1

ISBN 978 1 78378 337 3 (paperback)
ISBN 978 1 78378 336 6 (ebook)

Typeset by Avon DataSet Ltd, The Studio, Bidford on Avon, Warwickshire
B50 4JH

Printed and bound by CPI Group (UK) Ltd, Croydon, CR0 4YY

MIX
Paper from
responsible sources
FSC® C020471
www.fsc.org

This is for Mum and Victoria

'Words fail. There are times when even they fail . . .
What would I do without them, when words fail.'

SAMUEL BECKETT, *HAPPY DAYS*

Contents

Overture

Sarajevo, 1 August 1993

Haydn, String Trio Op. 8 No. 6

The day before my thirty-ninth birthday, I was reporting on what came to be called the Dobrinje water-queue massacre in the besieged city of Sarajevo – people killed while waiting in line for drinking-water from an outdoor tap. I had arrived on the scene just as bodies were being removed, leaving a trail of plastic water containers neatly curved in a row, surrounded by pools of blood that men were hosing away, occasionally scurrying from the sniper fire coming at them.

On my birthday itself I felt like doing something else, in counterpoint to the killings: listening to a performance of Joseph Haydn's String Trio Op. 8 No. 6 in the city's blacked-out National Theatre. This was part of a 'Summer in the Chamber' series of lunchtime concerts – the kind of thing the citizens organized and attended not so as to belittle what was happening but to remind themselves they were still alive. The programme today had been intended for the Sarajevo String Quartet, but they had been reduced to a trio after the second violinist, Momir Vlačić, was killed by a mortar shell that hit a flight of steps behind the Conservatoire as he arrived for rehearsal.

The two movements in the key of C Minor – which Mozart and

Beethoven would later associate with struggle and intensity – were written as a piano trio, transposed this afternoon for violin, viola and cello. Outside the theatre, another brutal day: five civilians, one of them a child, were killed as mortars, one aimed at the main hospital, pounded the city. But here within the blackened windows, a mesmerized audience gathered around some residual hearth of defiant civilization.

During the three-year siege and torture of Sarajevo – capital of the stillborn republic of Bosnia-Herzegovina – the second-best-selling black market commodities after cigarettes were cosmetics; the women liked to look their best when, risking death by a sniper's bullet, they queued for bread or water, and today they wore careful makeup and best dresses. Like the music, it was a way of living, rather than just remaining alive. The men were wearing linen suits today, though soldiers and their commanders, back from the defensive trenches, wore combat fatigues and heavy eyebrows.

The trio began to play: every minor fall of the opening movement stirred some engraved though recent memory of blood and loss; while every major lift lit some glimmer of love or cautious hope, if only because it was so beautiful in contrast to the madness without. But as the music played, the shelling continued – ever nearer the theatre. Until at one point during the lilting Andante, one mortar crashed so close it caused a shudder that made the walls shake sufficiently to knock the viola player's music stand over, felling his score. An awkward silence descended over the 150 listeners. The trio stopped, unsure how to proceed – how to answer this outrageous interruption? Then the first violinist, Dzevad Sabaganić, made a simple split-second – but in its way momentous – decision: he waited for the stand and score to be picked up and reconstituted, raised his bow, then called the number of the rudely interrupted bar.

The trio played on.

Anyone who tries to write seriously will at some point become impaled on what the poet Vladimir Mayakovsky called 'the nail of words'. And I think I promised myself that afternoon in Sarajevo that I would one day attempt a book that would try to explain with words – the métier to which writers, but not musicians, are confined – why that moment and gesture said more about what was happening under siege than anything I could write. But what? Something about us – the best in us, hopefully but not necessarily – that converses with and interprets, expresses and intervenes in the world through music, as interlocutor, mystery, medium, language without and beyond words. That is how I have tried to listen to music all my life, and to those who make music – in wartime and in peace, in times of trouble and tribulation, mirth and occasionally exhilaration.

Every writer reaches that moment when they know the thesaurus and lexicon will fail them. The moment of haunting by Samuel Beckett's question: 'What would I do without them, when words fail,' spoken by his character Winnie, buried to the neck, in his play *Happy Days*. Among other things, we turn to music, its muse and alchemy. The reason for this is as primal as it is mysterious: the functions, meanings and non-meanings of music have baffled philosophers since the beginning of thought. Music is part of who we are, and we know its impact when we hear it: in the sublimity of Monteverdi's *Vespers of the Blessed Virgin*, throughout which tapestries of notes feel even more divine than the texts they proclaim. Or like a jagged, serrate viola through Shostakovich's last, Fifteenth, String Quartet – its abrasive intorsion like a barbed needle that speaks of desolation, exclusion from closure or repose.

We know it most familiarly with regard to love: words are 'all I have', according to a cheesy song by the Bee Gees whereby words are all you have to steal a heart. This is nonsense; they may help, but no words can speak the pulsating virility of a sinewy, sweaty and salacious James Brown song, or match the silken lure in a promise sung by Diana Ross. No words can speak the aqueous purity of love, resolved into sublime transcendence during a progression played by Gonzalo Rubalcaba on the piano. No words can pump love's adolescent pulse like Cherubino's aria 'Non so più cosa son, cosa faccio' in Mozart's *Marriage of Figaro*, or convey the cruelty of lost love like the Countess's lament soon afterwards, 'Dove sono i bei momenti?'

Conversely, when it comes to love's antithesis, no pacifist pamphlet or speech could match the onslaught of brass behind Edwin Starr's outrage at how war is good for absolutely NOTHING! Music is not necessarily neutral, and much of the music in my life – and in this book – has been an intervention in the world I grew up in during a period of tumultuous creativity in rock, blues, folk and jazz during the late 1950s, '60s and early '70s, during which a generation was forged on the anvil of an idea that music can change the real world. So there was the tangibility of what music *does* in the empowering glow of the organ, the unbowed pounding of the bass and the entry on guitar that opens 'Long Time Gone' by Crosby, Stills and Nash – the impatient beckoning of a better world.

It would appear an insane idea: if music could change it, the world would not be the worsening nightmare it is after so much great protest song and music for peace. The Haydn trio in Sarajevo did nothing to abate the slaughter. I see no impact by Woody Guthrie's union songs on today's sweatshop labour. Even less for the Beatles' 'Give Peace A Chance' on Iraq, Gaza, Mexico or Syria. I see no vindication of Pete Seeger's 'We Shall Overcome' on a servile populace voting for Brexit and Donald Trump. Can music change the real world? Probably not. Can a drop of water punch a hole in a rock? No. But can the Colorado River gouge out the Grand Canyon? It already did.

Even if music cannot change the world, might not enough good music be able to change the landscape? That was the question our music and most musicians asked when I was young, and in the main the answer was yes.

What follows is an exploration of my own experience, for what it's worth, of music in a world and life of war and peace: warfare, physical and mental; music for peace, and an ill-defined idea of justice and a better life. So *When Words Fail* is at once a musical memoir, a soundtrack to my life – at some moments exceptional, though not special. But it mainly lends a close ear to people talking about the music they make, why and how. It takes its title from Samuel Beckett, an exact contemporary of the composer to whose work three chapters are dedicated – Dmitri Shostakovich – and to whose music it was my fortune to become devoted at an early age. Both men, with much in common, were born in 1906.

The book tells stories of concerts that changed my life, and what might be called the 'id' beneath them – how we all got there, what was happening; interviews and recollections with musicians who play, or played, music that *does* something – plus a few intermissions, 7" singles and 'postcards' along the way. War has been the curse of my professional life, while peace, justice and freedom have been its failed causes. Music, however, has always been my great love, and here I attempt to bring all that together. Of course, it's a flawed enterprise because my tools are words, which have by definition failed, attempting to describe the indescribable, and therein lies the challenge.

I never met a decent reporter who did not use his or her ears more than their mouth, and I have tried my best, as a writer, to *listen*. Listen to people, and to whispers on the wind. Music is all about listening in the end, and in what follows we listen to the people who make it, to musicians talking about what they do, and why. I think the old have a burden of duty to the young to doubt most of what we believe, given the mess we bequeath them. But I'm still pretty sure that peace is better than war.

So what does – what *can* – music do in the real world, in our lives, in war, against war, for peace?

I

Hendrix Comes East

Isle of Wight Festival, 1970

The music had played all weekend at the foot of a hill that rises from the southern shore of the Isle of Wight – a long slope which by Sunday night had earned the name 'Devastation Hill', after Bob Dylan's song 'Desolation Row': a ragged, rugged multitude of mayhem – dirty, sleepless, listening to Miles Davis, the Who, the Doors . . .

But the two exhausting days of bombardment by talent were prologue, really, to one act above all for whom four hundred thousand people had packed the ferries from Portsmouth; one artist who towered above even all this. My friend and I had watched most of these other thrilling acts from afar, but we wove our way through the crowds to sit at the very front in time for the Jimi Hendrix Experience. An announcer stepped forward and said simply: 'Billy Cox on bass, Mitch Mitchell on drums, and the man with the guitar – Jimi Hendrix.' He came onstage around midnight wearing a bedazzling costume of many colours, and opened with a pair of tributes: the Beatles' 'Sgt. Pepper' – which he had first performed in London even before the album had been released three years previously – and a rendering of the Bob Dylan song Hendrix had made his own, 'All Along The Watchtower'. Then something extraordinary happened: 'Machine Gun', searing cry of my generation against war and the masters of war.

It was inevitably, in the ears of the beholder, a song about America's war in Vietnam which outraged those years. But introducing it during a concert at Berkeley, California, Hendrix had said: 'I'd like to dedicate this song to soldiers fighting in Berkeley – you know what soldiers I'm talking about,' and of course everyone knew: the peace soldiers. 'And oh yeah,' he added, cryptic as ever, 'and dedicate it to other people that might be fighting wars, but within themselves.' So 'Machine Gun' was and remains rock and roll's war symphony – but goes beyond Vietnam, from the fields scorched by napalm to the wars in people's minds. As music, it is a combination of impenitent aggression, yearning, lyrical rage and ravaged peace – a double entendre.

Hendrix opens with a suggestive guitar line reminiscent of the more famous 'Voodoo Chile', into which crashes a drum roll of rat-a-tat machine-gun fire. A fusillade from Hendrix on guitar, then a slow descending riff that moves like an armoured vehicle pushing forward, harvesting life, interrupted by bursts of gunfire. The figure builds into a merciless, driving theme, relentless repetition of a minor fall from which Hendrix's opening solo breaks free, giving way to a 'second movement' – a slow blues, each note crying, crystalline. He calls out: 'Hey hey, Machine Gun!', and there's a bitterly ironic quotation from 'The Star Spangled Banner', the torn, broken flag.

Hendrix has finished. It has been so overwhelming, so loud, the silence pierced my ears. Joan Baez followed, radiant, to soothe the night, then Leonard Cohen, who told about a time his father took him to the circus as a boy, where a clown had asked everyone in the audience to light a match – and he bade Devastation Hill do that, so that a sea of little flames illuminated the night along the escarpment, as far as the eye could see from among the grime, the sweaty sleeping-bags and the euphoria. As the candles and lighters faded, so the eastern sky quickened, and a red sun climbed into morning – and thereafter back to school.

I was born in 1954 on the London street Lansdowne Crescent in the then shabby Notting Hill, where Jimi Hendrix died on 18 September 1970, eighteen days after that Isle of Wight performance. I read the news of his death on my way back from school in the *Evening Standard*, and a cutting of that cover story still marks the apposite page in my diary. I returned home, had the usual cup of tea and ginger biscuit, and waited for darkness to fall. Once it had, I walked the necessary minute to pay homage. The street – oddly, on reflection – was deserted. I had brought a piece of chalk, with which I wrote on the pavement outside the hotel in which he had died: 'Kiss the sky, Jimi', from that outrageous line in 'Purple Haze'. I stood around a while; nothing happened until I heard the latch drop, so I slipped into a doorway. A man emerged with a bucket of water and mopped my tribute away.

Notting Hill was a special place to grow up. My parents moved there in 1952 because – ironically, today – it was among the few places in London they could afford: Dad from the Wye Valley in Wales, via the Second World War; Mum from Merseyside, via art school. A contemporary glossy magazine called *The Hill* describes the now changed neighbourhood of my youth as 'a no-go area for sure'. That's not how I remember it. There was a well-established white working class, many of whom lived in grinding poverty. But Notting Hill had been built largely by the Irish, who had begun arriving in the mid-nineteenth century and continued to do so. It was settled in the 1940s by refugees from the Spanish Civil War, and later by those arriving from the West Indies to provide a cheap workforce. Then came Portuguese, Moroccans ... All these people amounted to a whole greater than the sum of its parts, infusing Notting Hill with vim and vigour, a unique sense of community and *mélange*, into which came young arty professionals of the postwar jazz generation, like my parents.

We used to play on a bombsite where the Kensington Hilton hotel now stands; among my first memories are the race riots of 1958, Teddy boys streaming out of Ladbroke Grove station to attack our local black people. I recall my mother going up to four of them setting on a young black boy at the then scrappy Holland Park station, and saying, rather imperiously: 'What on earth do you think you're doing?' The assailants slunk off. This was the worst of it, though, the rest far better. The fascist Oswald Mosley's attempt to cash in on the riots and contest the seat of North Kensington in 1959 was catastrophic for a reason: there had been genuine conviviality between the peoples of Notting Hill long before anyone invented the words 'multicultural' and 'diversity'. In those days, we really did – it's not just an old wives' tale – leave the front and back doors unlocked. Mothers would swap children around for daycare when they needed to work.

I became vegetarian at the age of eight, the first serious – and best – decision I ever made; I haven't eaten meat since. It was a sudden conversion while walking with my father John Sebastian Vulliamy one day in Sussex, watching lambs frolicking around their munching mums, though I stuck to my choice for a different reason: my mother would make me a packed lunch for school each day, and each day it would be kicked across the floor by jeering pupils. The headmaster wrote to my parents to suggest a common approach to my 'non-conformist attitude'; Mum and Dad replied that they were happy with my choice, and that's how I learned who my parents were, and who I was – in the world.

There were no musicians in my family, though we all learned instruments: only my brother Tom played well, on the flute; I sang in a school band, but gave up the clarinet. But the house was full of music, mainly jazz and blues. When I was sick, home from school, Mum – a children's book illustrator – would be downstairs, drawing. And drifting over the banisters: Billie

Holiday, Bessie Smith, Louis Armstrong and Edith Piaf, whose songs Mum would play, voices that sang of pain, defiance – and danger. My mother later went on *Desert Island Discs* and chose Billie Holiday's 'I Must Have That Man', first heard during the war when a neighbour introduced this import that had arrived along with the American GIs into Liverpool. 'It was a sound of thrill and danger, things I didn't know,' said Mum. Dad bought tickets for a concert in 1965, when I was eleven, to see Bessie Smith's greatest accompanist on trumpet, Louis Armstrong, play Hammersmith Odeon. 'Satchmo' was still emperor of jazz then, at the age of sixty-four. 'Play it again, old man!' people shouted, demanding an encore of the indelible 'Hello Dolly', which had recently topped the charts.

That night, and on those days with flu, I became fixated on the blues and jazz, and only two years later, aged thirteen, went to the same theatre with a friend to hear a line-up of acoustic Delta bluesmen that seems unbelievable when I recall it now: Son House, Bukka White (B. B. King's uncle), Sonny Terry and Brownie McGhee. Bukka sang 'Parchman Farm', about a prison farm – voice like sandpaper from the back of his throat, from way down inside, way back in time, fingers sliding up and down the frets like mercury. Son House was the frail main attraction: his voice at once eerie but rhetorical, his touch lighter on the guitar. I was hypnotized.

On one level, this music was all so distant from life as a London schoolboy; yet relevant to a political awakening that had put Martin Luther King and Che Guevara on my pubescent bedroom wall. Here was music to go with those posters: what attracted me to the blues was their *edginess*, their testimony, their authenticity, in contrast to most of what I understood (or failed to) of what was happening around me on the 'progressive' music scene. The oddity was that people like Son House and Bukka could in those days fill a theatre with white blues fans in Europe, while barely able to breach the plantation hedge or ghetto walls back home in America.

My mother's playing jazz and blues taught me things about her family too; it was a while before I found out how different her childhood had been from mine. Her father, who had founded the Liverpool department store T.J. Hughes, had taken his own life, jumping off the Dublin ferry when Mum was five after realizing that he had been swindled out of the ownership of his own shop. Mum then endured the Luftwaffe's blitzkrieg, as did her mother and sisters Brenda and Valerie. I liked my aunties, kindly Bren and mysterious Val, intrigued as I was by the latter's left-wing politics – she too committed suicide when I was young. I could hear all this in Billie Holiday's voice and Louis Armstrong's trumpet. Then came the Beatles, filling the house with a different sound, and vindication for Mum, whose hometown, hitherto regarded as a distant joke in London, was now the centre of the universe.

I had a Dansette record player and a Grundig reel-to-reel tape recorder. I'd stay up late playing 45 rpm singles of the Beatles, the Hollies and the Spencer Davis Group (six shillings and eight-pence each, they cost) on the Dansette, while on the Grundig I transferred LP records lent by schoolfriends onto tape – 'progressive' albums by Buffalo Springfield, Jefferson Airplane, Nina Simone, Johnny Winter and Velvet Underground. The first LP I bought for myself was Bob Dylan's *Blonde on Blonde*, which I heard in 1966, just turned twelve, at the home of the writer Michael Rosen, whose father my parents were visiting. I was told I probably wouldn't understand Dylan, because it was 'grown-up music'. But the words Dylan sang, and the sound his voice and his band were making, compelled me utterly. I gradually added – at thirty-two shillings and sixpence of saved-up pocket money each – *Bringing It All Back Home*, then *Highway 61 Revisited*. I'd lift the needle to transcribe the lyrics longhand, line by line, onto sheets of paper cut a foot square to fit into the album sleeve.

As we reached our teens Notting Hill's spinal cord, the Portobello Road, became the Haight Ashbury of Europe. Pink Floyd rehearsed in a local church; *Oz* and *International Times* set up shop, as did the Mangrove Café, epicentre for a new black soul culture. The anarchist Angry Brigade plotted in the shadows and squats along Freston Road declared independence from Britain – the republic of 'Frestonia' – beneath a new skyscraper called Grenfell Tower.

The backdrop to all this was insurgency: against capitalism in Paris, Rome and Berlin, against Britain in Ireland, against communism in Czechoslovakia, against militarism in Mexico, and against everything in Chicago and San Francisco. I had turned fourteen in May 1968, and collected artwork by the Atelier Populaire of the Paris uprising's posters. When the Prague Spring was crushed by Russian tanks, I painted nerdy posters supporting the dissident Czech president, Alexander Dubček.

I was an avid reader of books that tore me between contradictory views of the world, and still do. The first, from Samuel Taylor Coleridge, was the pantheist idea that Mother Nature is divine; the second, from the Italian Renaissance and directly countering Coleridge, was 'Man is the measure of all things.' But I preferred a darker side to the Renaissance that seemed prescient of the third notion, existentialism; I read in Albert Camus' novel *La Peste* (The Plague) the idea that humankind is alone and accursedly free. The fourth came from Émile Zola – the view that naturalism is the opposite of the 'progress' in which most of my political 'comrades' of that time believed; the inevitable disintegration of all things, including human endeavour. And my favourite writer was Percy Bysshe Shelley, for whom art was political and vice versa, as were myth and muse.

So I was a conscientious teenager, smitten by alternative culture but enjoying schoolwork, wary of ubiquitous drugs and timid towards girls. In summer 1969 I took myself to hear the Rolling Stones in Hyde Park, but left early to do my history homework. In October that year I went alone to my first real gig in Notting Hill, to hear Group X, later Hawkwind; they were feral, superb, but I was as freaked out by the people dropping LSD as they were by the acid, and again left early. By summer 1970 I'd plucked up courage to attend the Bath Festival with schoolfriends and sit in the rain for Jefferson Airplane and the Byrds, unsure where to look when a woman next to me in the mud started masturbating in time to the beat. I somehow slept through Led Zeppelin. That same summer, Steppenwolf played the Albert Hall in London, unforgettably, and Pink Floyd premiered their album *Atom Heart Mother* back in Hyde Park; it was magnificent, and this time I stayed. CBS records promoted a 'Sounds of the 70s' series of their artists at the Albert Hall, and over they came from America: Santana, the Byrds, Johnny Winter, Taj Mahal. All the while, though, I'd been waiting for two things to happen: the return of Jimi Hendrix to Britain; and the fulfilment of my dream – to go to Chicago and buy blues records by those people I'd heard at Hammersmith and that I couldn't get in the UK.

Hendrix's music scared and enthralled me. It came from the other side of some checkpoint along the road of experience I had not crossed. Hendrix's first album was entitled *Are You Experienced?*, an audacious question. I wasn't. Hendrix was to me what Billie Holiday had been to Mum, with his intensity, savagery and soaring beauty at times – like the moors beyond the garden walls in *Wuthering Heights*, it transgressed the boundaries of my world.

Hendrix first arrived in Britain on the morning of 21 September 1966 from New York – a black American musician from a poor home, barely known in his own country and a stranger to England. Of course I never met him, but I resolved to find and hear out those who knew him well. Hendrix shared an apartment with only one woman during his life, 'the only real home I ever had', at 23 Brook Street, London W1, the address at which another great musician had lived, George Frideric Handel. That woman was Kathy Etchingham, now living in Australia. 'I want him to be remembered for what he was' is her first point, when we first meet in 2010, 'not this tragic figure he's been turned into by nit-pickers and people who used to stalk us and collect photographs and "evidence" of what we were doing on a certain day. He could be grumpy, and he could be terrible in the studio, getting exactly what he wanted – but he was fun, he was charming.'

When Kathy met Hendrix (that same day he landed in London), he had already lived an interesting, if frustrating, twenty-three years. John Allen Hendrix was born in Seattle to a father who drank more than he cared and a mother he adored but barely knew – she left the family home when Jimi was a child and died when he was fifteen. Lucille Hendrix is said to be the inspiration for two of his three great ballads, 'Little Wing' and 'Angel' (the other, 'The Wind Cries Mary', was for Kathy). Hendrix's father James, known as Al, was black; his maternal grandmother was full-blood Cherokee.

On the fiftieth anniversary of that landing in London, in September 2016 Jimi's brother Leon arrived, visited the beautifully reconstructed replica of Jimi and Kathy's bedroom (now part of the Handel House Museum), and played guitar at the London club, the Scotch, at which Jimi jammed that first night. We talk in Jimi's flat. Leon's eyes have it: immediately, the same as those staring out from the portrait of Jimi on the wall. While Jimi's features are more Afro than Cherokee, Leon's are vice versa: Cherokee, slender, intense. 'Jimi looked out for me,' he recalls, 'I never missed a meal. He made me what you English call "tea" and made sure I was OK. And sometimes, we used to sneak off to Mom's for dinner.'

But where did the music come from? 'It's called inspiration,' says Leon, almost scolding. 'As in "spirit", "*in-spirit-ation*". It's in the wind.' So he talks like a Cherokee too. 'When Jimi was a boy, he'd play with a broom, his first guitar. And Pa would come home and see the straw and shit from the broom on the floor, 'cause Jimi'd been doing acrobatics with his broom-guitar, and Jimi'd get a whuppin'. But the music came from nowhere. Music has no body, and I remember when Jimi was playing, he'd try to conjure up the sound with his fingers – where is it? [as he later did, famously, on stage]. Once, when we were little, Jimi took a radio apart, trying to find the music inside it. We lost the screwdriver behind the sofa and couldn't put it back together, so that was another whuppin'.'

Leon adds, poignantly, of Hendrix's soft vocal timbre: 'It came from always being told to shut up as a kid. Jimi went inside with his music, and when he got on stage, that was his time.' Later at the Scotch, Leon sang a cover of 'Angel'. And of course, this was written for Leon's mother too; he took his hands from his guitar, removed his glasses and wiped a tear.

Books about Hendrix abound, but in only one – *Starting at Zero*, edited by Alan Douglas and Peter Neal, friends of Jimi – does he speak for himself in a collection of notes and *pensées* that confound the stereotype of the reckless genius who played himself into an early grave. Timid Hendrix who, when not working, preferred to stay home listening to records. Schoolboy Hendrix, persecuted not for being black but for being Native American: 'Indians are bad,' insisted his teachers; peers bullied him for wearing ponchos made by his 'groovy mother'. His childhood poems were about 'flowers and nature and people wearing robes', and his early love was the 'primitive guitar sound' of Elmore James and Howlin' Wolf on radio. Hendrix was romantic, rejecting what he called 'the everyday mud world we're living in'.[1]

When he was eighteen, he was offered a chance to enlist in the military as a way to avoid conviction for car theft, and took it, training for the 101st Airborne Division of the US Army. Hendrix recounts, 'I hated the army immediately,' with its ritual sadism and punishments. His report read: 'Individual is unable to conform to military rules and regulations. Misses bed check: sleeps while supposed to be working: unsatisfactory duty performance.'[2] Paul Gilroy, in his book on the 'moral economies' of black music, insists that we must see Hendrix as an 'ex-paratrooper who gradually became an advocate of peace' and his music as a series of 'transgressions of redundant musical and racial rules'.[3] He engineered his discharge in time to avoid Vietnam and worked as a backing guitarist for Little Richard and the Isley Brothers. But here begin the transgressions: arriving in New York to establish himself in his own right, Hendrix found he did not fit – not black enough for Harlem, which he found 'cold and mean', nor white enough for the Greenwich Village scene dominated by his next great influence, Bob Dylan.

Hendrix is fascinating on race: subject to abuse and segregation, yet his life and music occupy a place beyond race or even, to use an expression of Gilroy's, 'against race'. 'There is no such thing as the colour problem,' Hendrix insisted; 'It's a weapon for the negative forces trying to destroy the country. They make black and white fight each other so they can take over at each end.' And later: 'Race isn't a problem in my world. I'm not thinking about black people and white people, I'm thinking about the obsolete and the new.'[4] I sat one afternoon in 2009 with Tony Garland, who became a general factotum for Hendrix's management company Anim, on his barge at Maida Vale in London. 'White America was listening to Doris Day,' said Garland, 'while black American music got nowhere near white AM radio. Jimi was far too black for white radio, but too white for black radio.' Thus Hendrix began something rare in American history hitherto: transgression across the lines of racial segregation. This was something surprisingly few groups were ready to undertake – mixing not only their music but their personnel. In America, there were only four at the top level: Sly and the Family Stone, the Paul Butterfield Blues Band, Mike Bloomfield's Electric Flag and most importantly, the Allman Brothers Band.

The Allmans illustrate the depths of Hendrix's transgression even better than he or any of the others do, because they came from the segregated South. The band developed a cult following in the US and across Europe for their blend of blues, jazz and unfettered improvisation, but what also distinguished the Allmans was the fact that they had a black drummer and, later, numerous other black musicians – and this in the Deep South. Here was extreme transgression, mixed music in a brutally divided world. I interviewed Gregg Allman about how, as little boys, he and his brother Duane slipped into an Otis Redding concert while visiting an aunt in Tennessee, and vowed: '"This is what we need to do. This is for us," and from then on I learned to play mostly from black people. We used to listen to a station that called itself "The black spot on your dial",' said Allman. 'It played Muddy Waters and Howlin' Wolf, and it hit Duane and me like spaghetti hitting a wall. The DJ used to play romantic music too, and speak to his girlfriend on air, saying: "I'm on my way over, baby – so get on that black negligee." He'd play *The Sermon!* by Jimmy Smith and a track called "Flamingo", and it sent us right across the tracks because that's where the music was.'

Allman and I were speaking before a concert in Kent, England, forty-eight hours after the death of his mother, in 2015 (and boy, did his voice convey his feelings). 'The clubs we used to go to on Daytona Beach – the Surf Bar, the Paradise – were all black dudes,' he recalled. 'One time, Ma came in while Hank Moore was taking us through a song called "Done Somebody Wrong" [it became an Allmans classic] and she says: "Come into the kitchen; I want to know what you doing with a nigger in the front room?" But she was just having a bad day. We were raised not to hate black people, and Mother did a good job.'

After bringing black friends home, the brothers crossed to the forbidden side. Their first real work was with the Floyd Miles blues band: the first white boys to back a black blues singer in the South. Once the Allmans were formed, the brothers brought in Jai 'Jaimoe' Johanny Johanson from Otis Redding's band to play drums – the Deep South's first major mixed-race rock band. The odyssey of the Allmans' greatness and tragedy is unmatched in rock and roll: Duane was killed in a motorcycle accident in 1971, the bassist Berry Oakley exactly one year later in another motorbike crash, drummer Butch Trucks committed suicide in 2017, and three months later Gregg died. But the line had been crossed: once Hendrix arrived in London and the Allman Brothers formed, music – entwined with the civil rights movement – was the battering-ram against segregation not just in its proclamations, but in its actions.

In England, things were different. A generation of white musicians were eager to hear and play blues, led by John Mayall, who explains, on tour in Frome, aged eighty-one: 'It happened here rather than in America because in Europe – not just England – black blues began to be heard by an audience that was not listening to them in America. We discovered Elmore James, Freddie King, J.B. Lenoir, and they spoke to our feelings, our life stories and that was it. Hooked.' 'People here felt a certain affinity with the blues, music which added a bit of colour to this grey life,' said Keith Altham, then of the *New Musical Express*, who would later become an embedded reporter with the Hendrix entourage.

Altham and I met at a café in Kew; he wore a flaming orange jacket and a fedora, in defiance of a heart attack only a few days before. Music in London, says Altham, had reached a 'tumultuously creative moment' when Hendrix arrived, and was 'perfectly poised to receive him'. One night, Cream and Eric Clapton asked Hendrix to join them for a jam at Regent Street Polytechnic, for which Hendrix blew into a version of Howlin' Wolf's 'Killing Floor' – 'at breakneck tempo', recalls Tony Garland. Altham remembers Clapton leaving in the middle of the song, 'which he had yet to master himself. I went backstage to find Clapton furiously puffing on a cigarette, saying: "You said he was good but you never told me he was *that* fucking good."'

An initial tour saw Hendrix open for the Walker Brothers and Engelbert Humperdinck; something was needed, thought his then manager Chas Chandler, for Hendrix to blow the ensuing acts off the stage, and Altham had the beginnings of an idea: 'Pity you can't set fire to your guitar.' There was a pregnant pause in the dressing room, then Chandler told Garland: 'Go and get some lighter fuel.' Garland remembers: 'So I went out to buy lighter fluid. It didn't make sense – there were too many things going on to worry about lighter fluid – but it all became clear in the end.'

After a tour of France in support of the French rock star Johnny Hallyday, Hendrix played around working men's clubs and theatres in northern England. 'That's when I remember him at his best,' recalls Etchingham, 'and at his happiest, desperate to make a name for himself, but playing for himself. In working men's clubs they just wanted some music while they drank their beer, and in the theatres people came to hear him for the first time. That was his best music, none of these crazy expectations, no one hanging on.' But what was this music – uplifting, menacing, exotic and erotic? 'Hendrix was a magpie,' says Altham. 'Only Coltrane could play in that way – he would take from blues, jazz, and Dylan was the greatest influence. But he'd listen to Mozart, read sci-fi, and it would all go through his head and come out as Jimi Hendrix.' 'And don't forget,' says Tappy Wright, roadie at first, then joining the management, 'we were using the cheapest guitars – Hofners we bought for a few quid, not Fenders or Strats, and a Marshall amp. Very basic, but stretched to the fucking limit.'

There's more precious insight from Kathy Etchingham: 'People often saw Jimi on stage looking intense and serious . . . I remember him, sitting on the bed or floor at home in Brook Street. Sometimes he'd play a riff for hours, until he had it just right. Then this smile would creep across his face or he'd throw his head back and laugh. Those were the moments he had it right for himself, not for anyone else.' When Hendrix realized he was living in the house that had also accommodated Handel, he went to HMV on Oxford Street to buy the *Messiah* and *Belshazzar's Feast*. Kathy recalls him playing these records, jamming along. But there was science behind the magic. 'Hendrix knew exactly what he was doing,' says Garland. But what? The answer begins with a man called Roger Mayer.

'We call this the Surrey Blues Delta,' says Mayer, with a wave across suburban Worcester Park, in the southwest London suburbs. 'Eric over here, Keith down the road, Mick from over there.' Mayer was a sonic engineer for the Admiralty, a civil servant in the Ministry of Defence, when he met Hendrix and his life changed. He had been working on what he called 'the "Octavia" guitar effect, a unique "doubling" – an echo, an octave up. Jimi said the moment we met: "I'd like to try that stuff."'

Mayer, who describes himself as a 'sonic consultant' to Hendrix, explains: 'In his case, the basis was the blues, but their framework was too tight. We'd talk first about what Jimi wanted the emotion of the song to be. What's the vision? He'd talk in colours, about what he felt, about war and peace, sensations, personal memories. And my job was to give him the electronic palette which would engineer those colours into sound, so he could paint the canvas as music . . . The electronics we used were "feed forward", which means that the input from the player projects forward – the equivalent of electronic shadow-dancing – so that what happens derives from the original sound and modifies what is being played. However, nothing can be predictive – this is speed-forward analogue, a non-repetitive wave form, and that is the definition of pure music.'

He adds: 'What I did with Jimi was therefore the diametric opposite of digital. Digital is a loop, a predictive repetition, and pure music cannot be repetitive.'

Mayer is disdainful towards 'digital remastering' of Hendrix, let alone 'downloading'. 'It just isn't Hendrix. Look, if you throw a pebble into a lake, you have no way of predicting the ripples. It depends on how you throw the stone, or the wind. Digital makes the false presumption that you can predict those ripples, but Jimi and I were always looking for the warning signs. The brain knows when it hears repetition that this is no longer music. Hendrix is pure music pushed to the limit, to paint the canvas of colours in Jimi's mind – in sound. It expresses what he felt, what we feel, scares us, makes us happy. It took discussion and experiment, and some frustrations, but then that moment would come, we'd put the headphones down and say, "Got it. That's the one."'

'One of my favourite memories of all,' says Etchingham, 'is Jimi and Roger huddled together over the console and instruments, talking way over my head, and then this glorious *thing* happening.'

But, says Mayer: 'I take none of the credit, in case you're wondering. You can build a racing car like that which won the 1955 Grand Prix, but if you can't drive like Juan Manuel Fangio you're not going to win. Jimi Hendrix only sounds like he does because he was Jimi Hendrix.'

Hendrix is often portrayed as a tragic figure, but people who knew him give no hint of this: Kathy remembers him enjoying *Coronation Street*, with an amused fascination for Ena Sharples. Altham remembers Hendrix tuning up to 'Teddy Bear's Picnic', and 'his way of saying things that made you do a double take: "Did he *really* say that?" Such as, just before he went on to play with Clapton, "I want to see if he is as good as he thinks I am."' Altham talks about Hendrix 'saying nothing to reporters, or contradictory things, on purpose. He would pat his fingers against his lips mid-sentence and go, "etcetera, etcetera", in order to say, in effect, nothing. He wanted the music to speak.'

Nor does he bear out people's suppositions about his tastes. 'I don't want anybody to stick a psychedelic label around my neck,' he wrote, '– sooner Bach and Beethoven. Don't misunderstand me, I love Bach and Beethoven, I have many records by them, also by Gustav Mahler.' His record collection, reassembled at the Handel House Museum, shows an eclectic taste in blues and jazz. What he called 'freak-out psychedelic' music didn't interest him; Hendrix loved to be called 'the Paganini of the guitar', but when voted the world's greatest guitarist by *Melody Maker* readers, he responded: 'That's just silly.' The Experience rehearsed little: most of the time they practised, he writes, they were 'thinking about it'; he describes his work as trying endlessly 'to make the note come out a little different'. 'Don't forget about the music,' he urges his public, 'we don't.'[5]

In 1968 Hendrix returned to America to record, in particular, *Electric Ladyland*. The album sails towards a distant nautical horizon as described in the lyrics to 'Moon, Turn The Tides ... Gently, Gently Away', with something like a waltz, of which the producer Eddie Kramer told me: 'Hendrix always wanted to improvise, to see what would emerge from the mood between those assembled in the studio – and suddenly, out of whatever he had in his mind, this waltz emerged, as though he and Steve Winwood [on keyboards] were literally dancing around the studio.' One project was dear to Hendrix's heart: Electric Lady Studios in New York, which opened with a party on 26 August 1970, the night before he returned to England to play the Isle of Wight.

Much rubbish has been written about Hendrix having a 'death wish', but death was the last thing on his mind that summer. Tired of being treated like a workhorse by his English management, he wanted to stretch himself so as to create 'something else, like with Handel and Bach and Muddy Waters and flamenco' – hardly musings springing from a death wish. He was shy to appear at his own studio's launch party, and retreated to the steps outside, where he met a young singer-songwriter also too timid for the fray – Patti Smith. 'I was just young then, a street punk on the edge of the scene, learning what I could, and Hendrix at the centre of it all,' she remembers in conversation decades later. 'The studio party was all too much. All the stars there, everybody needing to be seen. So I thought, "I'll just sit awhile on the steps", and soon afterwards out came Jimi and sat next to me. And he was so full of ideas; he talked about all the different sounds he was going to create in this studio, wider landscapes, experiments with new musicians and soundscapes. All he had to do was get back over to England, play the festival and get back to work.'

But Hendrix never returned. After the Isle of Wight, he went on a brief tour of Scandinavia and Germany. Back in London, he booked into the Cumberland Hotel and gave his last interview, to Altham, who recalls that 'he seemed better than I'd seen him previously', though there was a 'dodgy woman in the room who dealt him drugs'. On Altham's tape, Hendrix jokes and discusses an idea to re-form the Experience.

Then, on the night of 16 September, he went to Ronnie Scott's club hoping to jam with Eric Burdon's band, War – but Burdon considered him unfit to play. The following night he did join his friend on stage, and proceeded to a party with a German woman, Monika Dannemann. 'I was with him that night,' recalls Jon Brewer, maker of music films, including one on Hendrix. 'Look, one tab of acid is quite enough to deal with – you can't take *eight*.' Hendrix accompanied Monika back to her room at the Samarkand Hotel in Lansdowne Crescent. Most accounts converge on the fact that he had drunk wine and taken drugs and some of Dannemann's sleeping pills. He vomited during the ensuing sleep, insufficiently conscious to throw up; Dannemann panicked and telephoned Burdon, who urged her to call an ambulance. The greatest guitarist of all time was dead upon arrival at St Mary Abbots Hospital, aged twenty-seven. Dannemann took her own life in 1996.

Douglas and Neal's book of *pensées* ends with a fitting epitaph, Hendrix's own: 'When I die, just keep on playing the records.' And we do, and not just because of the wizardry. There's a reason why Hendrix epitomized his time, why his music encapsulates the wars that hung over it, the pity and the sound of war. The writer Susan Sontag was asked at an event in New York during 2002: 'What does war sound like?' 'Thank you,' she replied, 'that's a good question. War is very loud.' If I had been asked the same question in 1970, I would not have known how to answer. Now that I know warfare, I know that 'Machine Gun' is not just what war sounds like, it's what war *feels* like.

Among the audience at one of those early Hendrix concerts in London, sitting behind the Beatles, was Graham Nash, destined to make a major contribution to the American music scene. 'There I was,' recalls Nash in conversation, 'listening to a sound of a kind I'd never heard before. I was thinking what a lot of other people were thinking: *What on earth is going on?*' It was a very good question. What indeed?

2

What on Earth Is Going On?

Origins and Essence

Carlos Santana talks about music like he plays it: with disarming serenity, from some higher ground. And no wonder: 'I've always thought that God is in everything and everything potentially divine,' he tells me. 'I'm talking about universal spirituality. Look at the cherry blossom in Washington this time of year – it's beautiful, it knows how divine it is, and it pleases the divinity.'

Finding Santana at his hotel room in DC had involved a code: asking for Huddie Ledbetter, better known as Leadbelly the blues singer, in whose name he was registered. Leadbelly was a convicted murderer; Santana is of a different cast, for whom music plays a special role in this 'universal spirituality'.

'I first started listening to music when my family moved from Jalisco in southern Mexico, to Tijuana,' he recalls. 'My father played the old Tijuana sound, a mariachi musician, and music was in my blood. I started learning the violin when I was five, and playing bebop on the strip in Tijuana, right on the US border, people crossing in either direction.' When Santana moved to California, though, 'something happened in my head, I was in a poor area, with a lot of people telling me I was unworthy. It was hard at school being Latino, and I felt my identity questioned. But I had my dad, who was charismatic, and everyone respected his music, and I grew up like my mother, questioning everything.

'So after being discriminated against at school, I found who I was in music. Then it all fused together during that flowering in California at the time. There was not a great deal of Latino influence on the rock scene, and we injected a new sound into that, which drew on my own Latino roots plus the roots all the others brought: soul and jazz, blues and funk. You know, some people took and take drugs,' he says, 'but I could never understand that. You don't need drugs to get high. You can get high by getting into the music. What is it that music does?' he asks himself. 'It does something no other force can do. It cuts right into your subconscious, speaks right past your head and into your soul. It sublimates the whole process of communication like no other language. I find it hard to talk about, but it's the level I live on. Why is it that you can play one note, and it can make people cry?'

So what is going on? Like Santana, the ancients believed the origin of music to be divine. The words 'music', *musica*, *musique* and *musik* come from the Greek word μουσική, *mouzikē*, meaning 'of the muses'. In ancient Greece, μουσική could signify any art inspired by the nine muses – daughters of Zeus and Mnemosyne, who represented memory. But even during Hellenistic times, μουσική came to refer specifically to what we call 'music', pivotal to civic and spiritual life. To ancient Greeks, not only was music a gift from the gods, but instruments were attributed to specific deities: the *aulos* or flute (the oldest instrument, first made from bone, possibly some forty thousand years ago) to Athena, the lyre to Hermes, the pipes to Pan. Apollo was master of the lyre, and Orpheus, with his, became the symbol of music.

The most important ancient Greek contribution to the philosophy of music came from the mystical mathematician Pythagoras, who is said to have equated pitch with sonic waves while noting the sound made by different hammers on a blacksmith's anvil. This led him to examine mathematical ratios at work within intervals between harmonious sound frequencies, and to advance the theory of the 'harmony of the spheres' whereby the sun, moon and planets emit their own particular 'hum'. Followers of Pythagoras thus saw music as expressing the cosmos; as a harmonious paradigm for mathematical truths, which were the closest thing to reality humans were capable of understanding. Plato accordingly regarded music and astronomy as inseparably 'twinned', but both the Pythagoreans and Plato were also interested in the potency of music in human life, its expression of and impact on human emotion, its mimetic cogency. Proclus divided music up into three categories: music for the gods, music for humans and music for both gods and humans.

We can have little idea what ancient Greek music sounded like, though we do have accounts of music-making, clues as to structure, rhythm and form, and we know that music was intimately entwined with dance, poetry, costume and drama. Texts on harmonics date from the sixth century BC – among the earliest is that by Aristoxenus, who considered pitch, consonance, dissonance and other musical elements as combining into what the Greeks called *melos*, the musical whole. Music is important in the *Iliad* and the *Odyssey*; in Book One of the former, emissaries sent to the island of Chryse spend a day upon arrival singing a paean to Apollo, to whom hymns were sung in quintuple rhythm, while passionate songs known as 'dithyrambs' were sung to Dionysus.

Odysseus is warned by the goddess Circe, from whose throne dawn breaks, how to deal with the most mysterious musical allegory in literature, that of the Sirens – usually depicted as winged maidens – whose song is so beautiful it lures men to their deaths. Man can survive only by blocking his ears to this music; in a translation of Homer's *Odyssey* by T.E. Lawrence, 'the thrilling song of the Sirens will steal his life away'.[1] And in E.V. Rieu's version: 'No seaman ever sailed his black ship past this spot without listening to the honey-sweet tones that flow from our lips and no one who has listened has not been delighted and gone on his way a wiser man.'[2] But Circe has already warned the mariner: 'There is no homecoming for the man who draws near them unawares, and hears the Sirens' voices.'[3] Odysseus does as bidden by the goddess – he fills his sailors' ears with wax and has himself tied to the mast so that he may 'listen with enjoyment to the Sirens' voices', and survive to tell the tale.

As the Sirens suggest, ancient Greece was aware of subversive potential in music: Sophocles warns against excessive innovation, urging that 'one must be cautious changing to a new type of music, because this risks a change in the whole. The modes of music are never moved without movement of the greatest constitutional laws.' And Sophocles' notion was irresistible to a champion of the idea that music can change the real world, and communicate at a level no other form of creativity can: that champion was Richard Wagner. Wagner regarded the Greeks as having laid philosophical foundations for music in their time and his time, and for all time – in their elevation of music above other arts, but also in its integration with them to produce the *melos*, which he called *das Gesamtkunstwerk*, 'the total work of art'. Wagner also hauled the Greek notion of divine music into our world, giving it a pantheistic meaning, and – as we shall explore later – a psychological one.

Wagner was a follower of the philosopher Arthur Schopenhauer, who believed that when man observes the natural world, its essence 'makes itself known to him as *Will*'. The Will thus connects us to nature, but is something no words – only music –

can describe. 'Music,' wrote Schopenhauer, 'gives the innermost kernel preceding all form, or the heart of things.'[4] Both Jean-Jacques Rousseau and Charles Darwin concur in their different ways: both believed that human beings communicated musically before the formulation of language. But 'it was Schopenhauer', wrote Wagner, 'who first defined the position of music among the fine arts with philosophic clearness, ascribing to it a totally different nature from that of either plastic or poetic art'. Wagner likens the way we understand music, rather beautifully, to a sort of dreamland: 'Besides the world that presents itself to sight, in waking as in dreams,' he writes, 'we are conscious of a second world, perceptible only through the ear, manifesting itself as sound; literally a *sound world* beside the *light world*; a world of which we may say that it bears the same relation to the visible world as dreaming to waking.'[5]

According to Wagner, when the poet tries to reach the heights of expression, his words fail – even Shakespeare's, whom Wagner called 'the mightiest poet of all time'. And what shall we do when words fail thus? His conclusion, in a pamphlet called *The Artwork of the Future*, is dramatic and decisive: 'We have seen the poet driven onward by his yearning for a perfect emotional expression, and seen him reach the point where he found his verse reflected on the mirror of the sea of harmony, as musical melody: unto this sea he was compelled to thrust; only the mirror of this sea could show him the image of his yearning.'[6] The composer Hector Berlioz drew a variation of this conclusion with regard to painting, sculpture and architecture, as explained in his wonderful memoir. When he arrives in Rome, overwhelmed by the richness of architecture and painting, Berlioz observes, upon hearing music in the Vatican: 'Yes of course – these paintings and statues, those great pillars, all this giant architecture, are but the body of the building. Music is its soul, the supreme manifestation of its existence. Music is the sum of all the other arts; it is music which gives utterance to their eternal hymn of praise, uplifting its song.'[7]

The notion that music has divine origins and essence is fundamental also to African, Mesoamerican and Native American societies and their religions.

The society of the Mexica – better known as Aztecs – echoed Greek thinking. In their splendid imperial capital of Tenochtitlan, now Mexico City, the Mexica honoured what they called in Nahuatl 'tlamatini' – literally 'people who know things', philosophers to us. One of them, also a poet, called Ayocuan Cuetzpaltzin, suggested that truth was by its nature beyond human experience but could be expressed metaphorically by the song of the coyolli bird. 'From whence come the flowers that enrapture man?' he asked. 'The songs that intoxicate, the lovely songs? Only from ... the innermost part of heaven.' The Aztecs made beautiful flutes and pipes which imitated birdsong. In most ancient American and African cultures, music, chant and drumming are primal means of communicating with the deity, and specifically so in shamanic rites. I was, in 2017, present for dancing, singing and chanting at the 'hidden village' of the Zuni nation in what is now New Mexico; on one evening, the music was of deep spiritual significance, but on the next, it was a comic farce. This was comedy accompanying a game of tag played by clowns – but a comedy conjoined and carefully presided over, however, by elders and shamanic spiritual leaders – the profane and the sacred inseparable – and bonded by music.

Wagner's idea of music as having origins in dreams had a deep-rooted precedent in Native North American culture, as expounded in the remarkable work of Frances Densmore, who tirelessly recorded and investigated American Indian music at the beginning of the twentieth century. Densmore explains that to many Native and First Nations, dreams were expressions by divine elements of tasks to be accomplished, and songs were performed to describe them to the group, as part of the passage from the dream to the task's fulfilment. In her book on the Teton Sioux of Standing Rock – people later famous for a protest against an oil pipeline being installed through their sacred land, affecting their water supply – Densmore describes a song bidden by the wind, sung by a chief called Lone Man: 'The words of the song require some explanation. From the time of the dream until the time when the dreamer has fulfilled its requirements he regards himself as belonging to the elements and under obligation of obedience to them . . . So in this song, the elements are said to be "wearing" the singer, who has not yet fulfilled his obligations to them.' The word for 'wind' changes as versions of the song progress towards that fulfilment.[8] Of all the symbols that endure from Native American culture, none is more familiar than Kokopelli, trickster and spirit of music, whose flute-playing keeps evil spirits at bay and heralds the advent of spring. The figure echoes through ancient rite: in Paul Gauguin's mysterious – almost hallucinogenic – Tahitian painting of 1894, *Mahana No Atua* (Le Jour du Dieu, Day of the God), an imposing deity is summoned by a seated hunched piper similar to Kokopelli.

The idea of divine music also infuses Western Christianity – the shamanism of the Mass and the rite of Holy Communion. Though 'musicke' plays no great part in the Bible, Joshua's army fells Jericho's walls with blasting trumpets, David's harp is the reason for his calling and Christ's birth is hailed by 'choirs of angels'. Musical accompaniment of the liturgy dates back to Apostolic times, and in the Judaeo-Christian tradition the words 'psalm', 'hymn' and 'song' are sometimes interchangeable. The Greek word πνεῦμα, pneuma, meaning both 'breath' and 'spirit', was adopted in the Middle Ages for the notation of plainchant, which had flourished in ancient Rome and became the music of Christian liturgy with the conversion of Emperor Constantine I in AD 313. The simplicity of 'Old Roman' plainchant was elaborated by the addition of what we now call Gregorian chant, with its sequences and tropes, textual or musical extras – for purely *musical*, rather than liturgical, effect – and here the trouble began.

Some corners of Reformation Protestantism banned music altogether, for its distraction from the Word. But even for the more mystical Catholic Church music was not a spiritual end in its own right; quite the reverse – it was a means of conveying the Word. In the early sixteenth century, the ambitions of composers in pursuit of sound texture led them to experiment with polyphony – the simultaneous entwinement of two or more independent parts – to achieve musical messages beyond the adornment of scripture. So began the first serious discussion in the West of the relative impact of words and music, and the insistence of authority upon the primacy of the former. Polyphony signalled the death of the unadorned melody, or *cantus firmus* (Latin: 'fixed song'), and the beginning of what we call 'modern' music, attempting to integrate 'conflicting' parts to achieve a whole greater than their sum.

But the Roman ecclesiastical authorities decreed that multi-part polyphonic settings obscured the scriptural message. Accordingly, some of the period's greatest writers of choral music failed to have their works cleared for performance, until a breakthrough in 1567 when Palestrina's glorious *Missa Papae Marcelli* was deemed to strike the balance between musical sophistication and verbal (and thus doctrinal) clarity. Polyphonic music was thereby freed to flourish during the latter half of the sixteenth century; its composers include such figures as Carlo Gesualdo, a kind of musical Caravaggio who, like the painter, was a murderer (finding his wife and her lover in flagrante, he killed both). And in England, Thomas Tallis, author of mystical music, whose motet *Spem in Alium* (composed in the same year as Palestrina's Mass) is a waterfall of sound, combining forty parts over a mere seven minutes.

I first heard this music properly during the mid-1980s at the Church of St Thomas Becket in Salisbury, performed by the Tallis Scholars. Led by their founder Peter Phillips, the choir not only pioneered a revival in polyphonic music but also made startling revelations in their careful editing and reconstruction for performance of pieces unsung for centuries. This concert was of a Mass by the Flemish Josquin des Prez, sung beneath a 'doom painting' of the Apocalypse, called *Missa La Sol Fa Re Mi*, deriving from the five-note phrase, but also a play on the old Italian *Lascia solo fare mi* – 'Leave me alone'. The phrase is sung hundreds of times in 'imitative counterpoint', passed around the choir at different pitches, note lengths, upside down and backwards – to create glorious sonority, a perfectly balanced crystalline structure. Phillips explained afterwards: 'The minute you get equal polyphony, you get tremendous individuality in each of the voice parts, but at the same time, a knitting of all those parts into a complete work of art.'

Although the text is liturgical, this is also music of the humanist Renaissance. As Phillips points out: 'The Renaissance development of perspective in painting led to canvases in which everybody and everything had their space, and therefore individuality. At the same time, the overall composition is enhanced, and the analogy of this with Renaissance music is thrilling. At about the same time, musicians were moving towards the same thing: equal voice polyphony gave the overall its unity, and counterpoint gave each part its individuality.' Like a Piero della Francesca painting, he says, 'everything has its precise place in the picture – just as every part and note has its precise place in this music'. With polyphony begins the double entendre: just as Renaissance painters depicted biblical narrative to assert 'man, the measure of all things', and in effect tear down God, so music as expression of divine design became also that of humankind's sense of itself.

But though polyphony was the mind of Renaissance man at

work, Berlioz makes a striking classical suggestion: that polyphony exists in a world entirely unto itself, as a truth independent of the composer who writes it. Upon hearing Palestrina sung in the Sistine Chapel, he says: 'The music's purity and tranquillity lull one into a state of suspended animation which has a charm of its own. But the charm is in the style, in the harmony itself, and is quite independent of the alleged genius of the composer.'[9]

The baffling figure of Wolfgang Amadeus Mozart had, as a child, 'made such progress that in his fifth year he already composed little pieces which he played for his father', wrote his sister Marianne to Andreas Schachtner, a trumpeter and family friend.[10] There is no evidence that Mozart considered this a divine inheritance, but his father Leopold did, and Albert Einstein's biography goes some way to endorsing his view: 'Leopold has been reproached with having forced his son's talent like a hothouse plant, but was not being altogether hypocritical, or indulging solely in self-justification, when he emphasised repeatedly that he held it to be his duty before God and the world to further the inconceivable talent of Wolfgang as a gift sent from above.'[11]

The notion of divine music found foothold in the twentieth century through the French composer Olivier Messiaen. Messiaen was a devout Catholic in an age that tended to reject God, and he saw divinity in musical syntax. One writer on Messiaen, Paul Griffiths, finds his work 'powerfully stimulated by the most marvellous events and imaginings of the Judaeo-Christian tradition: the Nativity, the Transfiguration, Resurrection and Ascension of Christ, the glories of the resurrected existence and the affiliation of all humanity to God'. But, more than this, Griffiths continues: 'The basic truth enshrined in all these is a truth particularly amenable to musical expression; it is the presence of the eternal in the temporal, the unmeasurable within the measured, the mysterious within the known. It is the truth of everything Messiaen has written.'[12]

The idea continues into our day, as not only Carlos Santana demonstrates. Ireland's leading harpist, Anne-Marie O'Farrell, is also a priest ordained into the Church of Ireland. During a conversation about Irish music in a café above a bookshop, she said: 'I had wanted the idea of the divinity of music to be my PhD but was unable to find supervisors from both the theological and music departments to go ahead with it. Interestingly, I did eventually find a professor of theology who was prepared to incorporate the musical element, but not the other way round.' O'Farrell added, with poetic and mystical straightforwardness: 'There is also something very symbolic about the harp itself: flesh stretched across wood.'

Though differently from the Christian tradition, folk music is brimful with the idea of divine muse: music as the sound of nature in a pagan, occult sense, a folkloric adaptation of Greek celestial music. A song by the English–Irish band Steeleye Span entitled 'Harvest Of The Moon' narrates the story of country people singing an apparently devout harvest thanksgiving song. However, children present hear a different tune emanating from the harvest moon itself and carried on the wind shaking the barley. One of the number, Bridget, starts to sing it too, whereupon a mysterious harmony fills the air, entrancing those assembled. This notion has gratifying roots in literature: consider the two fauns in Shelley's *Prometheus Unbound* questioning one another about animating forces in the universe, one of whom asks: 'Canst thou imagine where those spirits live / Which make such delicate music in the woods?' Or Prospero's lines in Shakespeare's *The Tempest*: 'Be not afeard, the isle is full of noises, / Sounds, and sweet airs, that give delight and hurt not. / Sometimes a thousand twangling instruments / Will hum about mine ears . . .'

But not everyone sees benevolence in a divine origin of music. 'My music hellish jarring sounds to banish friendly sleep', went a song attributed to John Dowland and published in 1610, 'In Darkness Let Me Dwell'. I am not alone in thinking Thomas Mann's *Doctor Faustus* (published in 1947) the finest book ever written on music. Here, musical genius is anything but divine – or rather, it is, but inverted and diabolical. Mann's book is erudite on music to a degree that is almost overwhelming, but has at its core the bargain struck between his principal character, the composer Adrian Leverkühn, and Mephistopheles. Mann's story contains some wonderful definitions of music, such as 'that strangely cabalistic, simultaneously playful and rigorous, ingenious and profound craft'.[13] 'Music is ambiguity as a system', posits Leverkühn; 'Music was song long before it was anything else', Leverkühn's first teacher, Wendell Kretzschmar, reminds us.

Mephistopheles' suggestion to the talented composer is that 'every better composer bears within him a canon of what is forbidden, or what forbids itself'. The demon posits that 'the illusion of emotions as a compositional work of art, music's self-indulgent illusion, has itself become impossible and cannot be maintained'. Leverkühn is pledged the chance to overcome this impasse by writing music

> [that] will break through the laming difficulties of the age – you will break through the age itself, the cultural epoch, which is to say the epoch of this culture and its cult, and dare a barbarism, a double barbarism, because it comes after humanitarianism, after every root-canal work and bourgeois refinement . . .[You] will raise yourself above it to the most dizzying heights of self-admiration and make such things that a holy horror of them should come over you . . . What raises you up, what augments your sense of energy and power and mastery is the truth, damn it.[14]

In return, Leverkühn submits his soul to eternal damnation.

Actually, the idea of a pact with Faust in exchange for the gift of music was not Thomas Mann's. Long before *Doctor Faustus*, the blues had been regarded as 'the Devil's music', whose most influential early master, Robert Johnson (1911–38), had – according to his own legend – sold his soul to Satan 'down by the crossroads' in Clarksdale, Mississippi, in return for an uncanny ability on guitar and a haunting, haunted voice. Johnson was the most famous, but not the first, bluesman to claim this particular diabolical pact: his namesake Tommy Johnson had apparently done so in the 1920s. Tommy was famous for singing a descending line against an ascending accompaniment, and vice versa – as well as for drinking cooking fuel, shoe polish 'and almost anything else that could provide a kick'.[15]

The idea plays on a dichotomy in the blues. Namely, that they originate in a continuation, or resurrection, of West African magic among slaves and tended to be played by people with un-Christian lifestyles, but they were also related to gospel song – there was even a genre called 'Holy Blues'. And it was yet another Johnson, Blind Willie, whose gospel blues hits included such songs as 'Jesus Make Up My Dying Bed'. 'Don't let the devil steal the beat from the Lord!' pleaded the singer Mahalia Jackson.[16] What these Johnsons, the blues and Leverkühn shared was a yearning for Armageddon: Leverkühn writes an oratorio about the Apocalypse, capturing both its epic horror and its terrible beauty; of the many slave songs that begat the blues, one beseeches the sun to 'go down, Moses' and not rise again unless it bring the Judgment Day. Blind Willie Johnson was arrested for 'incitement to riot' for standing outside the New Orleans customs house and singing his ferocious 'If I Had My Way I'd Tear The Building Down' (covered by the Grateful Dead), with all its biblical implications; the sentiment re-emerged with Bob Marley and reggae, Rastafari's curse on 'Babylon', Jah's vengeance.

But the notion of music as divinity or its opposite is largely unpalatable in our time. Its antithesis is intelligently argued by Wolfgang Hildesheimer, who prefers to see the music of Mozart as just the reverse, something 'fallen' from the purity of nature. Hildesheimer assails the claims of those for whom Mozart's music is 'a kind of redeeming miracle', adding that 'of course, he himself did not have the remotest suspicion of his posthumous power to bring such fulfilment'.[17] Great music, says Hildesheimer, 'does not originate from any mystical obscurity; rather it is *made*, in the interaction of unconscious ideas and conscious methodology. It is, therefore, not as natural as nature and certainly not as "innocent", if we may indeed credit nature with attributes such as innocence and guilt.'[18]

In 2017, the Royal Opera revived a production of Mozart's fourth opera, *Mitridate, Re di Ponto*, written when he was fourteen. The staging was as psychedelic as the notion of Mozart writing such erudite music at that age – hooped skirts that made the male characters look like the Queen of Hearts in *Alice in Wonderland*. And one kept hearing – one thought – citations from *Così fan tutte*, or *Figaro* – only of course it would be the other way round.

I spoke to the man who more than any other performs and records child Mozart, Ian Page, with his ensemble Classical Opera. Page acknowledges both Einstein and Hildesheimer: 'When we play this music, I can bank on half the critics pointing out that it's not as good as *Figaro*. But what matters is that Mozart could and would not have written *Figaro* had he not written these early pieces in the extraordinary way he did. There are so many crucial opposites at work in early Mozart,' he argues. 'On the one hand, the idea of some God-given talent is so palpable; on the other, this comprehension of what was being composed around him by grown-ups, and improving on it with incredible inventiveness of technique. The more I dissect and re-dissect the very early pieces, the more staggered I am by Mozart's ability to turn a phrase, to do something nobody else would have thought of.'

Hildesheimer develops arguments on Mozart of further importance, among which is his insistence on the element of the unknown in a composer's impulse: 'To express it musically: we have before us a score consisting of two staves – the melodic line (Mozart's music) and the bass (his external life). The connecting middle voices are missing – his unconscious, the dictates and impulses of his inner life, that which governs his motives and behaviour.'[19] We go 'behind the scenes' of Mozart's life to place these unknown 'middle voices' in their time. Hildesheimer writes:

> *Doubtless he, too, was possessed by a tendency of his time, one which others followed more consciously and collectively: the spirit of rebellion. Mozart experienced it as an urge to freedom, a freedom no one had deemed possible a few years earlier . . . Mozart never commented on the political upheaval of the French Revolution and probably did not recognise it as the beginning of a new age. As far as we can determine, political events never penetrated his consciousness. How should he express his thoughts other than in his music? His response to the spirit of the age was* Figaro, *a work whose story he did not create, but whose possibilities he exploited to the full, as was his custom.*[20]

The Marriage of Figaro was Mozart's setting, to a libretto by Lorenzo da Ponte, of Pierre Beaumarchais' play of the same name, a droll comment on the outrage that was aristocratic power, and its demise. The play was initially banned by King Louis XVI, was thereafter successful on stage, and was then brought scintillatingly to life by Mozart. But if *Figaro* was Mozart's reflection of the 'spirit of the age', our point here is that the spirit of the age, by being expressed in music, becomes universal; the work is brimful with what Hildesheimer calls 'possibilities' of rebellion, in essence rather than rhetorically.

Hildesheimer devises a useful term, 'thinking in music':

> *In contrast to the verbal thought, which painfully encounters its own limits, language being insufficient . . . musical thought is constructed exclusively on its own material, not upon an abstraction lying outside the discipline, but upon the supply of musical tones, infinitely enriched by timbres. It formulates with the greatest possible differentiation and precision. But what does it formulate? We will of necessity come across this question many more times without being able to answer it for Mozart.*[21]

Indeed we will, and not just in Mozart; 'thinking in music' is what this book is largely about.

Hildesheimer's argument is a variant of that of the great eighteenth-century Italian poet and all-round philosopher Giacomo Leopardi, though Hildesheimer neither cites nor refers to him. It was Leopardi who coined one of the wisest remarks ever written about music, in his extraordinary set of reflections, *Zibaldone*: 'The other arts imitate and express nature, from which feeling is drawn, but music imitates and expresses only feeling itself, which draws from itself, not from nature.'[22]

Although Leopardi and Hildesheimer move us towards a 'modern' – whatever that means, perhaps just 'non-romantic' – idea of where music comes from, our age demands additional scientific explanations. Philosophers and scientists have for centuries distinguished between the mind and the brain, but now much work has been done on the neuroscience of music, on the electrochemical activity going on when we listen. In his book *Musicophilia: Tales of Music and the Brain*, the physician and writer Oliver Sacks cites cases in which music played some role in a neurological, rather than psychological, problem.

An extraordinary one is that of Tony Cicoria, struck by lightning via a telephone line. A man of casual interest in rock music, Cicoria is suddenly seized with an 'insatiable desire to listen to piano music', and later even to play and compose it. Sacks posits that 'patients with degeneration of the front part of the brain, so-called frontotemporal dementia, sometimes develop a startling release of musical talents or passions'.[23] He identifies what he calls 'musical circuits' or 'networks', and finds patients who exhibit 'a "phonographic" memory ... as some people may be said to have a photographic memory',[24] adding that 'the anomaly is not in the skill itself, but in its isolation – its unusual and sometimes prodigious development in a mind that may otherwise be markedly undeveloped in verbal and abstract thought'.[25]

Daniel Levitin, a former rock music producer, now neurologist studying the science of music, wrote a book called *This Is Your Brain on Music: The Science of a Human Obsession*, which to Sacks's collection of cases adds instances of Williams syndrome, defects in the formation of the cerebellum – the 'brain within the brain' – due to missing genes. The syndrome can impair the ability to count, read or judge whereabouts, and among Levitin's cases is a boy called Kenny who found it hard to eat, button his cardigan or get upstairs, but who played the clarinet.

Levitin cites a neurologist called Isabelle Peretz who 'discovered that the right hemisphere of the brain contains a contour processor that in effect draws an outline of a melody and analyses it for later recognition, and this is dissociable from rhythm and meter circuits in the brain'.[26] In his laboratory, Levitin finds the cerebellum 'involved in tracking the beat' of a piece of music, while showing no particular activation when the patient is listening to other noise. He further finds that 'the brain's music system appears to operate with functional independence from the language system', but that 'the close proximity of music and speech processing in the frontal and temporal lobes, and their partial overlap, suggest that those neural centres that become recruited for music and language may start out life undifferentiated'.[27] On music and visual processing, Sacks writes that 'attributes of musical imagery and musical memory have no equivalents in the visual sphere', a discovery which 'may cast light on the fundamentally different way in which the brain treats music and vision'.[28] He is intrigued, as we all are, by the musicality of blind people.

But Sacks's separation of music and vision only deepens, rather than explains, the mystery of music once the science is then re-subjected to the artistic muse, which often insists on convergence, like Hendrix 'playing colours'. Goethe proclaimed that great architecture was 'frozen music'. Rimsky-Korsakov claimed to see musical keys in terms of colour, as did Scriabin, who associated human moods with both, anticipating our term 'the blues' (in his schema, blue is B). Scriabin's *clavier à lumières*, which he invented, equated sound and light. Kandinsky painted canvases with the generic titles *Composition* and *Improvisation*. Most remarkably, the poet Charles Baudelaire was intrigued by what he called 'correspondences' between apparently separate sensual experiences. The poem entitled 'Correspondances' – from his collection *Les Fleurs du Mal* – stipulates that 'Perfumes, sounds and colours correspond' and expresses our experiences of nature in terms other than nature itself, including musical ones. In a forest, for instance: '*Il est des parfums frais comme des chairs d'enfants,/ Doux comme les hautbois, verts comme, les prairies*'.

Baudelaire's notion was fundamental to French music of the period, markedly that of Claude Debussy and Maurice Ravel, whose compositions were in turn integral to the painterly movement of Impressionism. In an essay of 1902 entitled 'Musical Painting and Fusion of the Arts' the critic Camille Mauclair compared Debussy's compositions to landscape paintings by

Monet. 'The landscapes of Claude Monet are in fact symphonies of luminous waves', he wrote. Debussy's music, 'based on the relative values of sounds in themselves, bears a striking resemblance to these pictures'. According to Mauclair, 'Harmony, value, theme, [and] motif' are 'employed equally by musicians and painters.'

Paul Gauguin saw his vision as musical, as he departed to paint in Tahiti: '*Mon rêve ne se laisse pas saisir, ne comporte aucune allégorie: poème musical, il se passe de libretto*' ('My dream cannot be grasped, it is not an allegory: it is a musical poem that needs no libretto'). The jazz composer and saxophonist Oliver Nelson entitled one of his albums *Blues and the Abstract Truth*, and in the jazz film *Round Midnight*, the protagonist, played by Dexter Gordon, likens what he is trying to do with a saxophone to what Monet did with painting – 'breaking it down' to a quintessence. Bob Dylan likened the texture of his album *Blonde on Blonde* to 'bright gold, whatever that conjures up'.[29] Dylan's song 'Lay Down Your Weary Tune' equates a morning wind to the blowing of a bugle against dawn's drumbeat; the wild ocean plays like an organ, while waves crash ashore like cymbals. Irish music has a sense of landscape like no other; Christy Moore performs a song that goes: 'I sing the spring of well water /I sing the field of standing stones' – the visual landscape is the music, and vice versa.

Such notions take us back, in turn, to science. Isaac Newton believed the seven colours of the spectrum correlate to the seven notes of the diatonic scale. It was Newton, however, who first posited that light had no colour – that colour occurs inside our brains. Similarly, Levitin argues that waves of sound are not necessarily notes in themselves: they impact our eardrums, triggering a series of electrochemical and mechanical events along various neural pathways to create the pitch of a note in our heads. So here is an argument apparently against Pythagoras's: the action happens within our brain, not in the spheres, or on the wind that shakes the barley.

Giacomo Leopardi does not so much connect music with other sensual experience as classify it as a phenomenon outside the aesthetic realm altogether – even outside ideas and theories of beauty. He puts his point in a rather convoluted way, worth unscrambling:

> *That the miracle of music, the force which it naturally exerts on our affectations, the pleasure which it naturally gives us, its power to arouse enthusiasm and imagination, etc., consists in, and is chiefly proper to, the harmony of sounds and voices, insofar as it is a combination of sounds and voices which is naturally pleasing to the ear; that it is not proper to melody; and that consequently the main point of music and the consideration of its effects, do not strictly speaking belong to the theory of the beautiful, any more than consideration of smells, tastes, primary colours, etc. does, for the delight of music, insofar as its main and most essential part is concerned, is not produced by its propriety.[30]*

The talent of a 'good singer', Leopardi writes elsewhere, is about 'engaging' us:

> *this attribute which we don't even know how to express, nor what it consists of, is entirely characteristic of the voice alone and wholly independent of harmony, whose qualities we do know how to define and express and distinguish clearly and mathematically. It therefore has no more to do with beauty than does a soft colour that appeals to the eye and pleases it on its own account, or a flavour, or an odour, etc. Sometimes this quality resides in something affectionate, tender, expressive, etc. This too is independent of beauty.*

'Even barbarians and animals are so delighted by music', Leopardi tells us, 'despite their not being accustomed to our melodies.' He writes about the pleasures of music to the ears of Saul and King David in the Bible as having occurred in 'most unsophisticated times'; and 'the fact of not having been used to hearing music for such a long period of time also caused many wonderful effects'. He posits – relevantly to our purposes in this book, for sure – that 'If Alexander, after being engaged in military matters all day, when he sat down to dinner in the evening was so wonderfully affected and dominated by the music of Timotheus (if I am not mistaken), this is for the reason [of] . . . the wine, which naturally exalts the mind particularly in a body that is tired'![31] Leopardi is spot on about wine at the end of a long day's warfare, as I've come to know, and about animals: the little stray cat who often keeps me company is always partial to Bach partitas and Neil Young, but dislikes Wagner and is unsure about the Grateful Dead. A French friend of mine has a cat who listens carefully to her practising the piano, greeting the end of a piece with a miaow, unless there's been a serious mistake. When an error is corrected, there's a louder miaow.

Music speaks to the unborn brain. Alexandra Lamont at Leicester University discovered that a foetus in the womb can hear music, and that a year after birth, babies recognize and prefer music they heard while *in utero*.[32] I vividly recall an evening my four-month-old daughter Elsa was especially and volubly vexed, and I put on a record of Mendelssohn's Violin Concerto in E Minor Op. 64, played by Yehudi Menuhin. Elsa stopped crying and listened with rapt attention, eyes wide open. Elsa's mother Louisa and I had played that same recording numerous times while she was pregnant; other music had failed to have the same effect that rainy night in Dorset, however soothing. (Sacks had an experience with the same piece, playing it while in hospital and – in a reverie – moving to switch the CD player off, only to find that it *was* off; he was playing Mendelssohn in his head.)[33] Moreover, Levitin provides neurological evidence for the fact that music we absorb during adolescence has a greater impact than that heard or learned later in life.

Hildesheimer addresses a further point: how can pure music – unaccompanied by lyrics or commentary – be *about* anything? How can music acquire meaning? Sacks asks:

> . . . *why this incessant search for meaning and interpretation? It is not clear that any art cries out for this . . . Music, uniquely among the arts, is both completely abstract and profoundly emotional. It has no power to represent anything particular or external, but has a unique power to express inner states or feelings. Music can pierce the heart directly, it needs no mediation. One does not have to know anything about Dido and Aeneas to be moved by her lament for him; anyone who has ever lost someone knows what Dido is expressing. And there is, finally, a deep and mysterious paradox here, for while such music makes one experience pain and grief more intensely, it brings solace and consolation at the same time.*[34]

The music not only 'means' something, it says and does two things concurrently.

How is it, then, that we come to understand what a piece of music is 'about'? Especially if we have no idea of the composer's intentions, or even who the composer was. Paul Lewis is his generation's greatest interpreter of Franz Schubert's piano music, having played across the world over two and a half years every piece Schubert wrote for piano after he discovered he was dying from syphilis. Lewis has an unusual background for a classical soloist of his standard (we'll hear the story later).

During his epic tour of Schubert's valedictory music, between 2011 and 2013, Lewis arrived at a startling theory about the theme of *inconsequentiality* in Schubert's music. At one point he played his Sonata in A Minor D784 to a group of children of about the age at which he himself had started borrowing records from the library. 'It was a concert for seven- and eight-year-olds, and I played a passage from the A Minor . . . the "syphilis sonata" as I call it, bleakest of all. Why am I playing them this? I wondered – but no going back, it's the last movement, a cry of distress. They weren't prepared: I said, "I'm just going to play this to you, tell me what you think it means." And I couldn't believe what they came up with – "He sounds scared of something", "He's running away", "He's remembering another time." It was exactly what I'd spent years discovering. They'd never heard of Schubert, but knew what he was trying to say. They understood the emotion, they *heard* it. In order to hear and identify with something, do you have to have experienced it? What is it that we engage and identify with, at any age? I'm the last person who should have been surprised by them, having started music the way I did. But I don't know what was going on – whatever it is, you don't have to have caught syphilis in the nineteenth century to understand what Schubert is saying.'

Lewis's point invokes another made by the historian Eric Hobsbawm, who wrote as a jazz critic under the pseudonym Francis Newton, appealing to the idea that music expresses something neither divine nor natural, nor only of itself, but something essentially human; he writes of jazz that 'if it is moving, it is because men and women are moving: you and I. If it is a little lunatic and out of control, it is because the society in which we live is so.'[35]

The brain apparently enjoys 'thinking in music', as well as change and complex dynamics, and becomes bored by monotony. Sacks finds we get neurologically excited when a regular beat is subverted. As Leopardi says: 'A very simple harmony or melody, no matter how lovely, would very soon prove tedious, and would not produce the varied, multiple, rapid, and rapidly changing sensation that music does.'[36] (It's a variation on the theme of Samuel Beckett's question in his novel *Molloy*: 'Might not the beatific vision become a source of boredom, in the long run?')[37] In this way, much of Leopardi's endeavour in his writing on music is to distinguish between music and just 'sound', the world of difference between melody and din.

In 1974 I attended the loudest rock concert of all time, the Who at Charlton Athletic's football ground in London – Levitin cites the event as having delivered decibels way above levels that inflict pain, yet I recall only adrenalin and inspiration. Since working in war zones, however, I have developed PTSD – though I prefer the old-fashioned term 'shell shock' because it is specific – and as a result cannot bear loud noises, sirens, fireworks or drilling. But shortly after Bosnia, I secured a pew rear-stage at Glastonbury for the opening power-chords that ignite Radiohead's 'Planet Telex', so loud I felt my intestines quiver – it was thrilling.

So unless one is a cat, music as din is obviously different from just din. Why? Why would we want to listen to music when it captures and expresses the sounds of bedlam, discord and dysfunction in our lives? Why do we love jarring noises with which composers like Alban Berg – even Richard Strauss – experimented at the dawn of the twentieth century? Conversely, why were there riots after the premiere of Stravinsky's *Rite of Spring* in 1912, and why do we love it now? What are extreme dissonance, punk and contemporary 'industrial' music doing? What is music when it is not music at all, but made up of sounds taken from everyday life?

The most famous early champion of what came to be called 'Whole World Music' was Gustav Mahler, who infused his symphonies with cowbells and kitsch, as well as folk tunes in the way that Schubert and Dvořák did. The critic Tom Service wrote that Mahler, 'by incorporating everything from the sounds of the world around him, in nature and on the street, to his latest poetic and philosophical obsessions . . . wanted his symphonic journey to encompass the whole world. It's the most crazily ambitious symphonic project in the genre's history.'[38] A generation later, the American Charles Ives – in whose New York apartment I lived for six years, by happy coincidence – did the same thing in one piece, *Independence Day*, including the sounds of two marching bands playing different tunes (Ives's father was a bandleader). A programme note for a performance by the San Francisco Symphony Orchestra describes how

> *as a child [Ives] had delighted in the effect, observed on the Fourth of July and other such occasions, of hearing two bands in two marches, each in its own rhythm and key, coming at him from different directions, and in motion. Much later, his knowledge of Mahler, whom he admired during his years at the New York Philharmonic and Metropolitan Opera, confirmed Ives's idea of the expressive possibilities of the collage and collision. Again like Mahler, he loved found objects, particularly hymns and marches. He couldn't see why . . . if there could be a polyphony of lines, there couldn't also be, by extension, polyphonies of whole worlds.*

I asked David Gilmour of Pink Floyd about what the SFSO programme called 'found objects' in his music: the alarm clock on a track called 'Time' from *Dark Side of the Moon*, or the Liverpool Kop singing 'You'll Never Walk Alone' on *Meddle*. Gilmour responded with a wonderful story about what he terms 'found sound'. We both recalled a sequence of notes heard in loudspeaker announcements at French stations during the 1970s, at Avignon in particular. It was like a four-note version of the five-note Kodály Method phrase, accompanied by hand signals, for teaching music to deaf people – adapted by Steven Spielberg to communicate with aliens in *Close Encounters of the Third Kind*.

Gilmour played the recording he had made on the station platform, immediately recognizable when slowed as the introduction on guitar to 'Shine On You Crazy Diamond'. So where does the tannoy end and Pink Floyd begin? What's the difference between sound and music? What's happening in our head so that one is the preface to a station announcement, and the other is music?

Few people know more about how and why we listen to music than Joe Boyd, who produced Bob Dylan's first and famous electric performance at the Newport Folk Festival in 1965, then came to England to produce Pink Floyd, Eric Clapton's early recordings, Fairport Convention, the Incredible String Band and more. 'Music,' he says, 'is something I was drawn to at an early age and I don't know whether it's because my grandmother used to play to me and I used to sit at the piano when I was three. She didn't like pop or jazz, but I love the fact that she was taught by Lechititsky, who was taught by Liszt who was taught by Czerny who was taught by Beethoven. So that makes me five generations from Beethoven.'

On the origins of music: 'The thing that seems most likely to me is that bushmen were sitting round the fire on the eve of the hunt, and would probably do a dance imitating the sound of the animal they were after. But there must have been a point at which music was made that did not have a function, music made for its own sake – that's the bit that interests me, because it's a conversation about who we are . . . I believe that the essence of music is texture, and the sonic signals it contains are about who you are, where you come from. There are subliminal signals in all music,' Boyd continues, 'that become almost anthropological. Subtle signals that involve texture, harmony, vocal decoration, and send messages to people.'

He has for many years researched and recorded music across the planet, immersed in 'World Music', as it is called in the West

– from Africa, Asia, the Americas and Europe. The vinyl collection at his apartment in Maida Vale in London is forbiddingly wonderful, collated by country in alphabetical order, so that 'Iceland' goes on a fair while, after which 'India' and 'Indonesia' are substantial and 'Ireland' interminable. 'For me,' he says, 'real music comes from the earth. From the land, be it of Cuba, Jamaica, Congo, South Africa, Albania, wherever. Music that lasts tends to be the most unselfconscious music, music that is not top-down but bottom-up, drawn from experience often rooted in a tradition of place. It's "What do we have in common?" A commitment to place, culture, father-to-son music.'

Boyd makes a point about the modern urban reaction to classical music that would be comic if it weren't awful: about the police and shopping-mall managers using baroque music to disperse gangs of young people – initiated in America, copied in Birmingham, UK. 'It's literally fleeing from Telemann!' says Boyd. 'These malls, they became too popular with kids hanging around, black mainly. People who wanted to spend money were unhappy about this and they had to figure out how to get rid of them. First they tried a dog-whistle-like note, at a pitch that the young could hear but older people couldn't. But it was ruled illegal. Then someone had a brilliant idea: baroque music! And it worked. The kids couldn't bear it. This stuff was just too white, strange to the template, just didn't fit into the space or experience of those young people – they couldn't stand it, and stayed away.'

The studies of the Finnish entomologist Olavi Sotavalta were aided by the fact that he had perfect pitch, and was able to discern the note made by the frequency of an insect's wingbeats. The sound made by the moth *Plusia gamma*, for instance, was a low F-sharp. Not for nothing did Judy Collins entitle an album *Whales and Nightingales* and incorporate the songs of both. Nikolai Rimsky-Korsakov wrote his most famous fragment of music trying to encapsulate 'the flight of the bumble-bee'. One of the most extraordinary pieces of baroque music was the *Sonata Representativa* by Heinrich Ignaz Franz von Biber, in which he stretches the capacity of the violin to unprecedented limits to 'represent' sounds made by animals (the passage representing a frog is especially bizarre). The piece often regarded as the genesis of American music after the genocide against Native Americans was written by Dvořák during his early-morning sessions composing by the banks of the Turkey River near Spillville, Iowa: the 'American' String Quartet No. 12 in F Major incorporates negro spiritual chromatics and Native American rhythms – but above all the sound of birdsong that Dvořák heard around him.

Leopardi likened the power of song over us to that of birdsong over other birds: 'Nature,' he says, 'has given to human singing (I mean independently of harmony and modulation) a marvellous power over the soul of man, one greater than that of sound. Likewise it will have given it to the singing of birds over other birds of the same species, and other analogous species, then proportionately over other birds and other analogous species, and even over us.'[39] For all his Catholicism, no composer tried harder than Olivier Messiaen in the apparently pagan and pantheistic endeavour of scoring birdsong. And many musicians believe that our first attempts to make music out of 'found sound' came from the urge to imitate nature: the singer-songwriter Graham Nash agrees with Leopardi and others in thinking that birdsong and the voices of animals are where music began. 'Do I believe that music is the product of early man listening to the music of waterfalls, the sounds of animals and birds, and wanting to imitate them?' Nash asks himself during a conversation. 'Yes, I think I do. And trying to communicate like them? Yes, I believe that's where it all began, and it comes out as music.'

I asked the Irish singer Christy Moore: Why did we as a species start singing? 'Agh Jaysus Ed,' he replied. 'As a *species*!? I know why I start singing every morning, and that's as far back as I'm going. It soothes me, it's my meditation, my medication. It tickles me, allows me to express my feelings, if only to myself. It helps me feel useful, it's the only thing I'm good at. My mother sang to me in my first hour and I wanted to continue the comfort she gave, the nourishment of the human voice in song. It's about soothing the troubled soul, beating some ancient rhythm, lightening some constant load, momentary respite from some gnawing pain, reminding of some precious time, rekindling an old fire – that kind of thing.'

3

Double Entendre: Shostakovich Goes West

Fifth Symphony, Leningrad Philharmonic,
Jansons, BBC Proms, London, 1971

During the deep freezes of the Cold War, on the afternoon of 13 September 1971, I walked through Hyde Park to queue for six hours and ensure my place in the front row of that season's climactic BBC Promenade Concert: the Fifth Symphony by Dmitri Shostakovich – still very much alive at the time – performed by the Leningrad Philharmonic Orchestra.

It was the third and final concert by the visitors from the USSR – a rare and exotic circumstance in those days – under the baton of the deputy principal conductor, Arvid Jansons. Jansons was familiar to British audiences, having also led the Hallé Orchestra as guest conductor; he would later die on the podium in Manchester while conducting Mahler's Fifth Symphony. But now he appeared with his illustrious Soviet co-citizens (he himself was Latvian), who played at another level of power, with intuitive understanding of Shostakovich; they and their predecessors had premiered most of his symphonies. Jansons emanated purpose and reverence for what the Leningrad Philharmonic was about to play, bowed to his audience, turned to temper the applause and set about the work in hand. He raised his baton, and dived into the music.

Shostakovich's Fifth opens without relent, before two contrasting

moods combine: a sense of recollection, with another, impatiently turbu-
lent. There is reticence, then attack – one feels acutely and uneasily aware
that two things are happening at once: acceleration and deceleration,
tension rising but held back by reflection in the woodwind, until this
opening abstract rises to a first great crescendo, and the piece is launched.
A second phase is ushered in by a rhythmic throb from the cellos, over
which violins play the theme: a sense of loss, seeking tranquillity, uneasy
calm. But all reflection is swept aside by blasting trumpets, a martial
march, accelerating to a gallop. A plateau is reached, and the throb
returns, above which the flute plays a mellifluous tune as though through
parted thunderclouds, the storm come and gone; the flute varies its call,
answered by solo violin like a high-flying bird, bringing the movement to
an uneasy close, eerily picked out on xylophone.

The symphony's Largo has been described as Shostakovich's requiem
for the victims of Stalin's Terror, and whether or not he intended it as
such, this is how his audience at the premiere heard it. It opens mournfully,
through a weave between low and high strings. There's a sudden flurry,
a woeful oboe, a lone clarinet, a shimmer among the violins; flutes
wander as though through darkness across a wasteland. The pressure
intensifies and builds into an outpouring of grief – if the common
interpretation is right – as the symphony gathers forces for its denouement.

An opening salvo ignites the final movement, and the march goes on.
A cascade, breathtaking, but we cannot be sure whether this is the sound
of relentlessness or resilience. For a while it is both, until a second phase
of the movement gathers strength, only to be followed by a barren
interlude, until the resilience struggles to reassert itself. The kettledrum
whips it down, but the theme finds muscle in the strings, pronouncement
in the brass; and critical mass, ratcheting up notch by notch, to release a
climactic hurricane of sound, at once uplifted and devastated – so that
in the end there is defiance and there is defeat.

Shostakovich outlived Jimi Hendrix by five years; that is how
close he is to our lives, and contemporary within them. The year

after the Prom concert, Shostakovich arrived in Dublin to accept an honorary doctorate from Trinity College. A friend of mine went to the ceremony, and wrote: '... it's like having a visitor from another time'. But it wasn't, it was our time – that's the point.

Shostakovich survived the performance of the Fifth Symphony, but an axe fell on his life nonetheless, not to end but to bifurcate it, forcing him to work in a masked world of dichotomy, treading on splinters in order to both express himself and survive, writing music which had often to communicate two things simultaneously. Along with Hendrix's transgressions, this was my first lesson in serious music – that it could do this: be of the world and its wars, but commenting at a diagonal, independent of it.

Dmitri 'Mitya' Shostakovich was born in St Petersburg to an educated family with origins in Siberia. It was a musical household: both Mitya and his sister Zoya were assigned to learn the piano after their ninth birthdays (Shostakovich recalls putting up 'stubborn resistance' until realizing that 'I had perfect pitch'). 'Although we were not very rich, we lived a comfortable life', recalls Zoya in the definitive biography of Shostakovich by Elizabeth Wilson.[1]

Shostakovich graduated young from the Conservatoire and worked to keep his family by playing piano at a silent cinema, a job he loathed; his embellishment of accompaniments led audiences to complain the pianist was drunk. The 1920s in Leningrad into which Shostakovich made his first incursions as a composer were a time of outrageous cultural innovation. The slipstream of revolution ignited foment among artists: experiments in theatre, graphic art, poetry – and in music, for a while free of the constraints and oppression to come. Young Shostakovich was timid but also mischievous, funny, with a keen sense of the absurd, and his favourite author was Gogol; his setting of Gogol's story *The Nose* as opera turned modern life into a bitter but psychedelic absurdity. He collaborated with the experimental theatre director Vsevolod Meyerhold, composing music for his stage adaptation of Vladimir Mayakovsky's *The Bedbug*. Meanwhile, Shostakovich's acquaintance the philosopher of language and literary critic Mikhail Bakhtin was working on what he called 'the polyphonic novel' and 'dialogism' – a notion crucial to Shostakovich's composing: namely, that different contrapuntal narratives could coexist in the same text.

In 1934, Shostakovich premiered the culmination of his avant-garde period: his opera *Lady Macbeth of the Mtsensk District*, about a woman bored and oppressed who takes revenge by conspiring with her lover to murder her husband and father-in-law. The work bursts with lust, ennui, defiance – and the politics of freedom. I bought the records in 1973, a Soviet triple-LP recording of a later reworking of the opera as *Katerina Izmailova*, the leading lady's name. She is a truly modern heroine, honest to herself and the world, demonstrating her erotic defiance of oppressive social surroundings, conventional morality and the law. *Lady Macbeth* was hailed as a masterpiece, confirming twenty-eight-year-old Shostakovich as the USSR's leading composer. Until the night of 26 January 1936, when Stalin himself stormed out of a performance of the opera in Moscow, appalled by what he had been listening to.

For Shostakovich, that moment was the delivery of a life sentence to purgatory. He wrote to his friend the critic Ivan Sollertinsky: 'The show went very well. I was called out by the audience and took a bow. My only regret is that I did not do so after the third act. Feeling sick at heart, I collected my briefcase and went to the station.'

Stalin's verdict appeared across page three of *Pravda* some days later, in an article Shostakovich happened to see while awaiting another train at Arkhangelsk, entitled 'Muddle instead of Music'. He had written, it said, an 'ugly flood of confusing sound . . . a pandemonium of creaking, shrieking and crashes . . . unadulterated cacophony'. Upon publication of *Pravda*'s article, a hail of bigotry was unleashed against Shostakovich. A special meeting of the composer's union formally condemned the work and its author, while fair-weather friends rushed to ingratiate themselves with Stalin by berating Shostakovich in articles and letters; only a bold few stood by him. 'As I visited Shostakovich every day, we read them together', recalls one of them, Isaak Glikman. But, Glikman adds, 'We reacted differently. I with disgust, irritation and sometimes indignation, whereas Dmitri Dmitryevich remained silent and made no comments.'[2]

For thirty years *Lady Macbeth* vanished from public view, but not so Shostakovich, and the story of what came next is a complex and powerful fable of what happens to music in a world of war and terror. He had begun writing a fourth symphony in the autumn of 1935 – his reputation high after the initial success of *Lady Macbeth* – and continued while the furore broke. The symphony is a thrilling climax to Shostakovich's early period: massive, volatile, dissonant and technically complex, alternating between attack and rumination. He later wrote to Glikman: 'The authorities tried everything they knew to get me to repent and expiate my sin. But I refused, I was young then. Instead of repenting, I wrote my Fourth symphony.'[3] Bold and challenging, 'it is an incredible monster in many ways,' said the conductor Bernard Haitink in an interview, 'it is incredibly powerful and moving . . . At times, impossible to play loud, because it's already louder than loud. There are huge passages of immense struggle; then everything comes to rest; and there are reflective passages of beautiful writing for what becomes no more than a chamber orchestra.'

But by now these were years of tremor and masks in Leningrad: Shostakovich and his circle lived in fear of the foot on the stair, a knock at the door. He was himself summoned for interrogation by the NKVD regarding his friendship with one Marshal Tukhachevsky, a military commander and accomplished amateur musician who defended *Lady Macbeth* and thereby came under suspicion. Shostakovich was asked about having supposedly witnessed talk of a plot to assassinate Stalin in Tukhachevsky's presence. When Shostakovich insisted he had no such recollection he was told to return the following Monday with a clearer memory. He did, expecting to be arrested, only to be saved by the arrest, meanwhile, of the interrogator himself.[4]

But his position remained precarious; family, friends and people with whom he had worked vanished, interned by the Gulag, or were executed. His elder sister was internally exiled, as was his favourite uncle, Maxim Kostrikin, a Bolshevik militant. His brother-in-law Vsevolod Frederiks, a physicist, was sent to a labour camp. In such a climate, Shostakovich withdrew the Fourth Symphony; it is a matter of conjecture whether he was pressurized, or did so of his own accord to keep the Leningrad Philharmonic as well as himself out of danger, having been made to understand that to proceed would jeopardize even the musicians who played the work. (It was not performed until 1961, during a relative cultural thaw in the USSR. 'When Shostakovich heard it after four decades,' says Haitink, 'he said he hadn't known it was such a good piece!')

Then came one of the great moments of Shostakovich's mercurial genius at work on the dais: his Fifth Symphony, begun in April 1937. It was finished by July and premiered on 21 November by the Leningrad Philharmonic under Evgeny Mravinsky. If Shostakovich had intended a double entendre, he achieved his aim. Hovering authoritarian vultures hailed the composer's return from decadent modernism to heroic classicism. But the audience heard a different symphony, and were released by it into an outpouring of emotion, a cathartic greeting to Shostakovich's first public requiem – so they thought – to the victims of Stalin's Terror or, as shall be argued here, all terror. During that long Largo men and women wept, and as the work surged towards its finale, people rose spontaneously from their seats. Mravinsky responded to the applause by holding the score above his head, as though to deflect praise (and perhaps liability) to the composer, who took twenty bows on stage.

For the Moscow premiere in January 1938, Shostakovich published a curious article entitled 'An Artist's Reply' which – typically of him – appears to be an explanation, but isn't. 'The birth of the Fifth Symphony', he wrote enigmatically or perhaps ironically, 'was preceded by a protracted period of internal preparation.' He continued: 'I saw man with all his sufferings as the central idea of the work, which is lyrical in mood from start to finish.' He wonders 'whether tragedy is even a legitimate genre in Soviet art', arguing that 'the contents must be suffused with a positive inspiration like, for instance, the life-affirming pathos of Shakespeare's tragedies'. He cites the requiem masses of Mozart and Verdi as being able to 'fill the human soul not with weakness or despair, but courage and the will to fight'.[5] As so often, he seems to be saying everything and nothing, both affirming and contradicting himself and his work, which is full of tragedy, but also full of the humanism of Mozart and Verdi. The symphony was packaged in Moscow – without Shostakovich's approval, but without his opposition either – by a fawning description coined by a journalist: 'A Soviet artist's creative response to just criticism', referring to the fusillade against *Lady Macbeth*. Sphinx-like, Shostakovich added that the symphony 'contained all my hopes and fears'.

I was captivated by this man and his music. This symphony was the beginning of my understanding that you can think two things at once, and that music can express both. Aged sixteen, I wanted to find out what else Shostakovich had written, before and after that premiere. And here the story complicates: the range of compositions that follows the Fifth Symphony is various, eclectic and mercurial. Shostakovich had written some magnificent music for film already, including to *Counterplan* – about uncovering the sabotage of industrial targets – premiered in 1932, and 'The Song of the Counterplan', which became a popular hit. But in 1936 came a soundtrack for *Girlfriends*, featuring one of the composer's most remarkable innovations to date, never discussed.

To make this point, let's revert to Jimi Hendrix. Everyone who loves Hendrix's music reveres the suite that closed his set at (and ends the film about) the Woodstock Festival, with its pastiche of 'The Star Spangled Banner'. However, for once, Hendrix is not the pioneer – Shostakovich had been there, done that. *Girlfriends* is a propaganda film about three friends who go off to work in rural Russia, tend the war-wounded and support an agricultural productivity drive. At one point, the music accompanies a scene in which a train rattles along, camera tracking along the sleepers and the steel rails beneath it. What we hear is a version of 'The Internationale' morphed into a strange, soaring, swooping melody performed on what sounds like a saw but is actually the first ever electronic instrument, a theremin, designed by and named after Lev Theremin, an acquaintance of Shostakovich in Leningrad who patented his instrument in the USA in 1928. It uses a radio-wave processing technique to generate an audio signal, transmitted through an amplifier, with pitch dictated by the distance of the musician's hands from its antennae. Each piece of music is a double entendre: Hendrix seems to simultaneously mock but reappropriate the anthem; Shostakovich's 'Internationale' accompanies footage of the bold march of progress, but mocks it too.

In 1938 came a turn in his direction as a composer: his First String Quartet. It is often said that while his symphonies are his public posters, his quartets are like confessional letters. They become progressively introspective and intimately dark, but the first is an exception. 'Don't expect to find special depth in this, my first quartet opus,' he wrote. 'In mood it is joyful, merry, lyrical. I would call it "spring-like".' For all the tribulation over *Lady Macbeth*, Shostakovich appears to be in higher spirits than one might expect, and certainly higher than we are usually told by those who write about him. He had taken up a teaching post by this time, but his talent and personality as a teacher interest Western writers little, though the children of his close friend Sollertinsky give this role illuminating prominence in their memoir and in the editing of their father's letters. Shostakovich, they wrote, spent 'hours poring over a student's compositions', producing his own only as examples of 'how not to compose'!

One student called Yevklakov tells a touching story about how, after he had fallen ill, Shostakovich had handed him money for medical treatment, saying that it had come from a union fund at the Conservatoire. Only when Yevklakov had recovered and went to thank the union did he find out the gift had come from Shostakovich himself. The composer urged another pupil: 'Study polyphony, look at how the old masters wrote. For example, look at Haydn's bass lines, look at the shape of them. But the main thing', he added, 'is to learn to express what you want to say directly and tersely, in the appropriate language. There should be no meaningless music.'[6]

But Shostakovich was himself anything but 'direct and terse' – from now on, he kept his public guessing. He hinted in 1938 that his next symphony would be the tribute to Lenin planned for some time; but any member of the Establishment expecting this was in for a disappointment. Premiered on 5 November 1939, the symphony could not have been further from the promised tribute. Fittingly, I first heard the Sixth conducted by Arvid Jansons's son Mariss at the Proms of 1987. The finale is a breathless gallop presented by Jansons at head-spinning speed, as though it were the end of one of the film scores – such are the drama and drumfire. Surprisingly, Shostakovich himself found this – not the famous climax to the Fifth – to be the perfect ending: after playing a piano version to Glikman and Sollertinsky, he said: 'For the first time, I think I've written a successful finale.' Glikman recalls musicians joking that it had the end-to-end action of a football match; Glikman found the analogy 'vulgar', though Shostakovich, an avid football fan, would almost certainly have accepted it as a compliment.[7]

Shostakovich's final piece of 1939 was most surprising of all: music to an animated film called *Silly Little Mouse*. One can feel a sigh of relief as he turned his attention to this popular children's story by Samuil Marshak, about an infant mouse who refuses his mother's pleas to sleep, then resists lullaby after lullaby sung by a series of animals. Unfortunately, the cat's turn comes around, who lulls the mousekin only to steal it away for mealtime – and a dog saves the day.

The need to score animal noises presented Shostakovich with an opportunity to experiment and play with those primal origins of music – and there was that challenging precedent, von Biber's weird *Sonata Representativa*. Shostakovich clearly rose joyfully to the occasion, producing a soundtrack full of quirks and wonders. I took my youngest daughter Claudia, then seven, to see the film at a festival of Shostakovich soundtracks during his centennial year, 2006. But the Barbican cinema was less than a quarter full, suggesting that *Silly Little Mouse* didn't fit the idea of Shostakovich that people require of him. Indeed, his film scores are often dismissed by 'experts'; some insist he turned his hand to them for work when he had no other, or in order to keep sweet with the authorities. But, says John Riley, who curated that Barbican festival, given Stalin's personal fascination with film, 'cinema was no place to hide: writing for film was more exposed to Stalin's personal attention than any other music'.

*

So: there is no summarizing the music contained in this slice of Shostakovich's oeuvre on the slipstream of the Fifth Symphony. And rightly so: he defies summary, just as his music defies compartmentalization. Like Hendrix, it is 'transgression' – that's the point. It is about the world of power, fear and violence, but also about vernacular intimacies and ironies; it is about both the severe and the quotidian. Neither is there any categorizing the coexistence of Bach-like intricacies in the piano quintet he also wrote during this period, nor the endearing flirtations of a girl called Yanya selling tickets in a cinema booth, heroine of another film, *The Adventures of Korzinkina*.

What are we to glean from this period in Shostakovich's life? Again, everything and nothing. We can infer that when faced with an assault such as that on *Lady Macbeth*, music can speak at the epic level of a people's soul, delight children, and give an absurd account of an absurd world. We can infer that, as with Shostakovich's exact contemporary Beckett, lack of meaning has meaning; that it is futile to categorize the musician's response, or paraphrase what is happening; to define or fix that which is immanent in music. But in the West, this is exactly what happened; Shostakovich's music was about to be subject to commentary and ventriloquism from which it has yet to recover.

First, though, I was interested in how this music was viewed on the other side of the Iron Curtain. I studied cover notes that accompanied vinyl recordings on the Soviet Melodiya and Czech Supraphon labels at a shop on Charing Cross Road called Collet's, run by a communist family and Trust. I read what I could find in nearby second-hand bookshops: those in English then were translations of Soviet criticism, such as that published in 1959 by David Rabinovich, who regarded *Lady Macbeth* as an instance of 'erroneous tendencies' inspired by 'modernistic trends' and

'naturalistic crudity', while the Fifth Symphony marked Shostakovich's 'liberation from the fetters of modernism'.[8] 'The ex-
pressionist opera', hack Rabinovich had written, 'proved to be a
foreign body in Soviet reality.'[9] A critic called Ivan Martynov
found Shostakovich's work in the 1920s and early '30s 'daring
and interesting', but was obliged to conclude that '*Lady Macbeth*
was a warning of the danger that menaced his development as a
composer and also a harmful deviation existing in Soviet art as
a whole.'[10]

I found a less depressing book, *Dmitri Shostakovich: The Life
and Background of a Soviet Composer* by another Russian, Victor
Seroff, written with backing from Shostakovich's aunt Nadeja
Galli-Shoat but published in America during the Second World
War when the USSR was an ally, and therefore unfiltered by the
Cold War lens. Here was tantalizing information, including the
judgement of a critic called Victor Belyaev writing on *The Nose*,
which he called 'the musical equivalent of a great literary work'
involving 'the development of a new style in our music for which
we have not, as yet, the performers'.[11]

I was enthralled: here was a whole unwritten chapter, it
seemed, of the composer's work, significant to our contemporary
musical life. Seroff also quoted Shostakovich as raising something fundamental about music and the real world: music's claim
to purity versus its reflection of the age – themes which in those
days ran beneath the emergent experiments in rock, jazz and
blues. 'I consider that every artist who isolates himself from the
world is doomed,' said Shostakovich. 'I find it incredible that an
artist should want to shut himself away from the people who, in
the end, form his audience.' He then added, cryptically: 'I always
try to make myself as widely understood as possible, and if I
don't succeed, I consider it my own fault.'[12]

So said the composer who would write in riddles for much of
his life, but the point stands: he hoped the masses would

understand the riddles, and at that premiere of the Fifth Symphony, and again and again, they did.

In 1980 came the English translation of the book by Sollertinsky's children Dmitri and Ludmilla. Here were details about the young Shostakovich enraptured by the visits of a hurdy-gurdy man turning the handle 'on his brightly-painted box'; about his lifelong fondness for animals; the adolescent Shostakovich's crush on a girl called Tanya Glivenko at a sanatorium for musicians in Crimea; and pages on his love of football. My mind gawping, I thus developed my idea of this great composer.[13]

For all this, however, Shostakovich was suddenly straitjacketed during the fifteen years between Arvid Jansons' performance of the Fifth Symphony in 1971 and his son's of the Sixth in 1987. A year before the Sollertinskys' book, another was published which would, unlike theirs, irrevocably forge the Western 'legacy' of Dmitri Shostakovich.

Testimony: The Memoirs of Dmitri Shostakovich was written by Solomon Volkov, a Russian scholar recently arrived in America who had, he said, been the confidant of the dying Shostakovich; and to him, apparently, the composer had dictated a valedictory confessional. Volkov the confidant claimed to relate a secret history behind the music; the mystery of Shostakovich was here explained, the enigma decoded. Shostakovich as dictated to Volkov is a composer of specific music to address specific circumstances in a specific time. Almost no claim is laid to universality; every note is commentary – emitted in code, now broken – on the Soviet narrative, a record of the composer's struggle with the insidious totalitarian intimidation of his muse. No less, but certainly no more. The music is picked apart, and what Volkov claims to be the authentic accompanying narrative provided. Shostakovich reveals his own guile and emerges like a musical counterpart to the formidable Alexander Solzhenytsin – dissident composer of a haunted but heroic depiction of the Soviet regime, and by implication an embodiment of Western values that countered the dark Red night. No less, but no more.

The impact of Volkov's ventriloquism was felt everywhere, and still is. It led to an even more extreme 'decoding' by another paraphrast called Ian MacDonald in *The New Shostakovich*, which insists, for instance, that an ascending scale in the Fourth Symphony represents NKVD agents climbing the composer's stairs, and that every two-note motif says 'Sta-lin'. Volkov inspired a film starring Ben Kingsley based entirely on *Testimony*'s account of Shostakovich; more recently, a fictionalized account of three episodes in the composer's life by the novelist Julian Barnes is openly based upon Volkov's commentary.

What has happened here is what criticism calls 'reduction'. This enables Volkov to say, for instance, that he knows the second movement to the Eleventh Symphony refers not to 'Bloody Sunday' in 1905, as the programme says, but to the crushing of the Hungarian uprising in 1956. The wonder of music is that there is nothing to prevent Volkov from inferring this or any other interpretation – there is no proving him right or wrong because there is no right or wrong. In 1933 Shostakovich himself counselled against this kind of 'reduction': 'When a critic in *Worker and Theatre* or *The Evening Red Gazette* writes that in such-and-such a symphony Soviet civil servants are represented by the oboe and clarinet, and Red Army men by the brass section, you want to scream!'[14]

We are left with a stereotype: Shostakovich as featured in almost every concert programme – unsmiling, depressive Shostakovich, brilliant and revered two-dimensional dissident victim, a great artist confined by 'legacy' to having written merely a soundtrack to his time and circumstances. We are invited to listen to music that is a product of its time and only that, by a man defined by his time, rather than a composer who wrote music for all time. It is ironic that this posthumous Shostakovich should be moulded by those wishing to critique a Marxist dictatorship – the anti-Marxists have out-Marxed Marxism! – by reducing the composer's work to the sterile Marxist principle that art must be defined by, and can have little significance outside, its historical circumstances. From this interpretative manacle complexity is banished, along with wit and humour, the potency of the absurd, the delight of *Silly Little Mouse* and the weirdness of the 'Internationale' on the theremin, alongside the mighty Fifth Symphony and the famous story of *Lady Macbeth*.

Also missing is Shostakovich's hollow laugh, his penchant for alcohol and football (and to these we shall turn later). He was certainly *not* the 'Soviet artist' the awful official literature claimed, but nor was he this stereotype on which Volkov and the Zeitgeist insist. The ventriloquizing of Shostakovich should serve as both starting point and cautionary tale about the didactic packaging – and claims of ownership – of music, in Shostakovich's case, by the hacks in Moscow and the dissidents in New York. Neither Moscow Shostakovich nor New York Shostakovich is the real man or the real music, and at this point the discussion thus breaks its banks and becomes about how we listen to all music – music not just era- and place-bound, but music for all time.

4

State and De Soto: 'Down to the Crossroads'

B.B. King, Indianola, Mississippi, 2013

The fat red sun settled against the horizon, throwing a last honey-sweet light across the humid evening and over a small crowd on the lawn beside a railroad track that cut through the cotton fields beyond. A quarter-moon was rising and a chorus of cicadas serenaded the imminent twilight, now joined by the sound of the band; the drummer caught the backbeat and the compere announced: 'How about an Indianola hometown welcome for the one and only King of the Blues – B.B. King!'

And on he came, to applause from people who knew him well and claim him as their own – last of the blues masters, a few weeks short of his eighty-seventh birthday. 'Nice evening, isn't it?' he said, and introduced his nephew on sax. Some of his fifteen children (all by different mothers) and innumerable grandchildren were in the audience, though one of his daughters had died recently of diabetes, giving added poignancy to the occasion. 'I guess you can look at me,' he said, 'and tell I'm the old man. My name is B.B. King.' Backed now by a lilac glow in the western sky – and looking east towards the village of Itta Bena where he was born – B.B. sat down and started the show. He reached a song called 'Key to the Highway', and there it is: that one long, trembling note, hanging there in the wafts of barbecue smoke, like only B.B. King could play it. He rolled his eyes, stared out into the crowd – and there's a collective gasp, a ripple of applause, a mutual bond of affection.

This was a huddle, not a crowd, really. The town had come to hear its famous son: mostly black people – in families, many with a picnic – plus a few white enthusiasts like me. There were people here like Alfred Knox – one of eleven children with eight of his own (and twenty-one grandchildren) – who left Mississippi for Milwaukee when he was nineteen and had now come back with his nephew Gervis to hear B.B. The usual jocks and suits who wave bottles of Bud and shout in the B.B. King tourist clubs in Memphis and Manhattan were not present for this annual homecoming concert – oddly, but thank God. Nor, indeed, were some of Indianola's good citizens. A girl called Latunya and her friend in the post office had earlier explained how 'We're real excited B.B.'s coming back. Gee, I'd lo-o-ove to go see him play. But I don't go out Wednesdays, I only go out Fridays.' There's no arguing with that logic.

This was the thirty-fifth homecoming concert, staged in memory of Medgar Evers, civil rights activist and friend of B.B.'s assassinated by the White Citizens' Council, founded in this town as the political wing of the Ku Klux Klan. The maestro's sonority on guitar was inimitably perfect. After another long, clean but poignant note during 'The Thrill Is Gone', B.B. King darted a clown stare right into the front rows, as though to say: 'How about that!?' But it was his voice on the warm breeze that stopped a heartbeat – that feeling behind and between the words that is the quintessence of the blues.

When B.B. left the stage, the night was just beginning. Not just on the wrong side of those railway tracks – where juke joints and rural slums are hopping to life – but also for B.B. himself. Two hours after bidding farewell in the park, he was due to take the stage again at one of the most historically charged venues in America: Club Ebony, founded in 1907, where as a boy Riley B. King would gaze through a gap in the wall, wide-eyed, at Duke Ellington, Charlie Parker, and the 'jitterbugging, snake-hipping', as he'd described it when we talked earlier. The place was owned by B.B.'s first wife's mother.

Sure enough, around 11 p.m. B.B. King appeared onstage again, in the heat and sweat and exhaled beer of Club Ebony. Much of his audience was one over the eight, but mellow, ready for the experience of a lifetime. The master who had played to stadia and venues across the world settled on a tatty old chair as if in his own living room, which in a way this was. There's a power problem with the lights and amplification: 'Guess I didn't pay my electric bill on time,' B.B. chuckled. Then he picked up his guitar 'Lucille' and played those notes, impossibly stretched, at moments crashing into some zone Hendrix might have navigated. He greeted his hometown audience and bantered – 'Well, sweet ol' Indianola!' – but he was in a world of his own now, less the showman than the musician listening hard to his own alchemy.

Outside in the sauna of night, poor young men gathered to watch those with tickets coming and going; there's a buzz around the big event as well as at it – loose joints for sale, police bundling someone into a van, guards patrolling the visitors' parked cars and lads eyeing up the ones whose owners have not paid the 'tip' to have them watched over.

B.B. swung through his all-time greats as the air filled with whiskey fumes and a surprising level of chatter: cusses were exchanged with a redneck family, one of whom was blind drunk, unsteady on his feet, blocking people's views and trying to steal an elderly man's trilby hat. For 'Every Day I Have The Blues' B.B.'s voice was an instrument, at once guttural but velvet, Lucille singing back to the singer. He ended with a rendition of 'See That My Grave Is Kept Clean' – that blues dirge about the imminence of death that makes the blood run cold: but tonight it had a chunky-rolling feel to it, pierced by the defiance of King's guitar, and the nearest he gets to a field holler this evening. 'Not bad for an eighty-six-year-old,' he said, signing off the night that has now become early morning in cotton country.

To behold this encounter between music and race – and this feast of music beyond race – was something I had promised myself since my teens, when my father had been working with an architectural firm based in Chicago and befriended a colleague, Jack Turley, as underwhelmed with corporate life as Dad was. Jack was a frequent guest in London during the late 1960s, and I would pump him for information on the insurgencies of '68 – and blues music. Then in 1969, Graham Nash wrote a song that went: 'Won't you please come to Chicago . . .'. I resolved to save up and by 1971 had the requisite £67 for the fare, plus $35 to spend on blues records. It was my first and formative solo adventure abroad, turning seventeen in a sleeping-bag on the floor of a (deconsecrated) church at the junction of Ashland and Lake Streets, where the Quakers were holding a weekend-long 'seminar on peace'. That was also the night I lost my virginity.

The Turley family gave me rope to explore; Mrs Angela Turley was a Catholic activist in the peace movement, and secured me a job with the (Quaker) American Friends Service Committee's draft-resistance centre. I also got to work with Joan Baez's husband David Harris, recently released from jail, in the anti-war campaign. But there was this other, principal, quest in Chicago: the blues. I spent whole days walking for miles around the city centre and the black South Side, where some had urged caution. Having grown up in Notting Hill I felt nonchalant enough to wander the ghetto, and there was this imperative: seeking out records that I could only find here, by Son House, Bukka White, Elmore James, Otis Spann – and of course the three Kings, Albert, Freddie and the king of Kings, B.B.

I toured the South Side record shops, with few people blinking an eye at the sight of a white boy with long hair, but was warned twice by people along South State Street that I was not really supposed to feel safe. One was friendly advice from a woman who urged me to 'get yo' *white* ass in a *green* bus outta *black* town'.

Another encounter could have gone wrong, after four older boys stopped me on the street to ask if I was 'carrying any bread'. For reasons that escape me, I steered the discourse round to telling them that I had seen the late Jimi Hendrix just before he died, which caused a consternation of curiosity. One of the lads even called over to another across the street, urging him to 'meet this Limey white kid who done seen THE JIMI HENDRIX!' I gave them some, but not all, of my money and walked safely north to the city centre Loop.

From that summer on, I assembled the best collection of blues on vinyl of anyone I knew, apart from my best friend from school, the aforementioned Paul Gilroy, who played – and plays – a mean blues guitar. I came to understand why the blues sound the way they do: about the 'blue scale' – there's an ordinary major scale with the third and seventh approximately flattened (the 'blue notes' – possibly an adaptation of European scales to African ones), used for melody, while the major European scale is used for harmony. There's conflict between the two, like a subliminal 'science', in the way we hear the blues.

Over decades, I heard bluesmen play concerts I'll remember all my life: Otis Rush at Tramps in New York, Albert King at the New York Palladium in 1981, Muddy Waters at the Checkerboard Lounge in Chicago during the same year. Mighty Joe Young in Milwaukee in '86; Buddy Guy in 1996 in London, bringing Clapton out to jam – then in San Diego twenty years later aged eighty, and Paris the following year. Taj Mahal: in London 1971, then Paris 2016. Cross-eyed albino Johnny Winter was my favourite 'white bluesman' (he's also B.B. King's); I heard him play his first-ever UK gigs in 1970 in Bath and a year later at London's Albert Hall – and his last: at Frome in 2012 and Shepherds Bush in 2013.

But there was one towering figure I had always, somehow, missed – more important than any: B.B. King. The last of his generation to call himself the great-grandson of slaves, then make the big time, who started life in a cotton field. The man of peace who fought against the race war, and won his own battle to the point of having a day of the year named after him – 1 September is B.B. King Day – in the former slave state, Mississippi, in which he and the blues were born.

Finally, in the autumn of 2012, it happened. A message to my *Observer* newspaper on a Monday afternoon from the office of the film director Jon Brewer, who was making a documentary about the master: if I could get to Indianola, Mississippi, by nine o'clock on Wednesday morning, B.B. King might – *might* – talk to me. He was inaugurating a pavement along B.B. King Street in his hometown at that hour. Brewer's PR agent, a heavy-metal connoisseur called Duff Battye, and I took a delayed flight, missed a connection and drove through the night, found a motel in Indianola, slept a couple of hours and took up our position on B.B. King Street.

B.B.'s bus arrived right on 9 a.m.; his manager from New York knew nothing about our supposed appointment. And no, we couldn't talk to him on the bus while he waited for the ceremony to begin. It was a fine occasion: tributes, a little speech from B.B. before he sat down to sign records and chat with the small crowd. But how to talk to him at length, seriously? Two local reporters occupied the seats next to him, until one got up to take a call. That's my seat, I thought, sat down in the shade of a pecan tree and introduced myself. 'I don't do this,' B.B. smiled back, 'but I heard you come all the way from England.' 'Got here a short while ago,' I replied, 'two hours' sleep. I never thought I'd see the day, when I was sixteen and bought this' – it was a copy of his album *Indianola Mississippi Seeds*.

While B.B. laughed and signed the record, I asked my first question: I saw your uncle Bukka White play in London when I was thirteen years old. And I heard that he tried to teach you slide guitar, but you couldn't play it, that's why you play the butterfly. Is that true? B.B. looked at me askance. 'You play guitar?' 'No, I just love the blues.' I'd got him: he leaned forward and began to explain the butterfly style that became his and his alone – the vibrato that is instantly recognizable, after a single note, as B.B. King's.

He was staying with Bukka when he first came to Memphis, he said, and 'Bukka used to play slide using a bottleneck, or just a piece of pipe. I wanted to do that, and he showed me how – but I got stupid fingers, see, and I just couldn't do it.' However: 'The sound Bukka made went all through me, and I devised my own technique for producing the tremolo without the slide.' B.B. 'called it the butterfly, 'cause I swivel my wrist from my elbow, back and forth, and this stretches the string, raising and lowering the pitch of the note rhythmically. With my other fingers stretched out, my whole hand makes a fluttering gesture, like a butterfly flappin' its wings.' Thus the B.B. King sound was born – a sound that expresses mood, feeling, blue or otherwise, like no one else's.

There's a turn off the main road into town that leads through the low-slung fields to Itta Bena. The season was waning by now, autumn-time. Just north, around Clarksdale, little clouds of cotton had burst forth 'like popcorn', as John Steinbeck once remarked; but here the white puffs remained enclosed in their pods. When he was a boy, B.B. King used to drive his mule through these fields while his uncle Jack, up front, sang 'the holler', the descendant of slave chants and responses wherein the blues began and where, he thinks, all music began. 'I remember the holler,' he said, under the pecan tree, 'holding the reins of a mule pulling a hoe through them there cotton fields.'

The holler is a lament, he explains, sung in a minor scale by a single voice. It functioned as a communication to alert others in the field that the boss was coming or that water was needed, but it goes further back than that. 'The holler . . . I think it's in all of us . . . The holler of a man tryin' to say something he didn't have no words for; talkin' without words to his fellow man the way the animals did. Hollerin' to get through the day, to get food, to warn his fellow men and women that danger was near. Just like the animals, birds and bees. That's blues music, and that's how all music began long, long time ago, that's what music *is*.'

Riley B. King was born on 16 September 1925. He moved soon after with his mother to Kilmichael, in hill country, where he later worked as a child farmhand and listened to his aunt's Blind Lemon Jefferson records. Uncle Bukka would visit from Memphis – play and sing. Picking cotton for 75 cents a day, B.B. coveted the local preacher's guitar and was even allowed to 'play a few chords he taught me'. He then made his own instrument, he says, 'with wire, the kind you use to make a cotton bail, and tied it to a broom handle. Clamp it down, the sound changed and I'm playin' music.' Later, his employer, a white man called Flake Cartledge, advanced him the $15 he needed for a real guitar.

First B.B.'s mother died, then the grandmother in whose care he was placed. 'The blues', he would later write in his memoir, 'was bleeding the same blood as me.' There followed an unhappy period with his father's family further south in Lexington. There, B.B. witnessed the lynching and castration of a black man by a white mob – his crime had been to wolf-whistle at a white girl. Soon afterwards, little Riley King fled Lexington and his father's new family, cycling alone 'like a bat out of hell' back to Itta Bena. The nine-year-old already worked the fields, picking 'Delta Pinelet' (Delta and Pine Land) cotton. Cotton, he later wrote, 'was a force of nature. There's a poetry to it, hoeing and growing cotton.' He added: 'Though it didn't make none of my people rich. I figured out that I must have walked around the world, all those days and weeks and months behind a mule.'

On Saturday nights, workers left the fields for town. 'I was peeping through the slats at a place I'm playing later tonight they call Club Ebony,' B.B. remembered, 'to hear Count Basie play, Charlie Parker, too – and see all those beautiful women in tight dresses jivin' away.' Young Riley sang gospel on the street corners of this town, Indianola, and soon learned that 'the church folks that liked my singing didn't slip me a dime much as the other folks did when I changed sidewalks to the other side of town and changed the words praising the Lord to praising a lady'.

Another thing King learned early: it is not just the words of a song, it's the mood that matters, conveyed by the larynx, as instrument. This is what defined, and defines, B.B.'s voice. Then there's the other instrument, the guitar. B.B. said it this way: 'I tried to connect my singing voice to my guitar an' my guitar to my singing voice. Like the two was talking to one another.' He admitted that he could not sing and play at the same time. B.B. called his guitar Lucille after someone else's fight in a juke joint knocked over a container of kerosene that fuelled the heating system. The place caught fire, the crowd fled, but B.B. realized he had left his guitar inside and ran to get it. Chastised for his recklessness, he discovered that the fight had been over a girl called Lucille. 'I named my guitar Lucille,' he said, 'to remind myself not to do something like that again, and I haven't.'

After the mechanization of the cotton plantations, the blues went north from here with the great migration in pursuit of work in the cities, and plugged in. Each musician from the new, urban golden age mutated the acoustic Delta sound to form their own electric style – Elmore James, Muddy Waters and Howlin' Wolf – in burgeoning Chicago. But B.B. King chose a different scene, on Beale Street in Memphis, closer to home up the Mississippi reach, where Uncle Bukka sang. B.B. came to forge a more rounded, less feral timbre than Muddy or the Wolf, with a bigger band including brass and rhythm sections. Blues Boy King –

shortened to B.B. – became a radio star at WDIA, the Memphis blues station. He built his band, ensured that he toured on a bus, made lifelong friends. He indulged his love of women and released his first hit, 'Three O'Clock Blues'.

In Brewer's film *B.B. King: The Life of Riley* Calvin Owens, trumpeter in the original B.B. King band, recalls those days on the segregated Chitlin' Circuit – named after chitterlings, pig and cow intestines, supposedly preferred by black people in America. 'Though,' says Owens, 'I never called it any Chitlin' Circuit. The road,' however, 'is home,' he adds, and it remained B.B.'s home for the rest of his life; sometimes he did 350 performances a year. 'I like my job,' he said, under the pecan tree.

B.B. married Sue Carol Hill, daughter of the owner of Club Ebony. Their marriage, while it lasted, was lived on the road. Staying, of course, in segregated black hotels, eating at segregated black restaurants. 'I've put up with more humiliation than I care to remember,' King wrote in his autobiography *Blues All Around Me*. 'Touring a segregated America – forever being stopped and harassed by white cops hurt you most 'cause you don't realise the damage. You hold it in. You feel empty, like someone reached in and pulled out your guts. You feel hurt and dirty, less than a person.' One night at the Gaston Hotel in Birmingham, Alabama, where B.B. was staying at the same time as Dr Martin Luther King, 'they bombed the place. The bomb rocked my room.'

Last time I'd been in this area it was to report on poverty, and in Mississippi that means black poverty even now, half a century after the assassination of Dr King. But first, there was a pilgrimage to make – a blues pilgrimage. At the junction of Highways 49 and 61 at Clarksdale there's a gas station on the northeast side, a laundry to the northwest. A clue that the intersection between State and De Soto Streets – as the two are named as they converge in Clarksdale – is no ordinary crossroads is the electric guitar atop a pole in the southeast corner. This is the crossroads where, according to his song 'Crossroads Blues', the blues singer who sounds like no other, Robert Johnson, sold his soul to the Devil in exchange for his otherworldly wail and the ghostly guitar-playing with which he defined the Delta blues and much of the blues beyond.

The crossroads in music is associated with disobedience of the Christian God; the New International Edition of the Book of Jeremiah reads: 'This is what the Lord says: "Stand at the crossroads and look; ask for the ancient paths, ask where the good way is, and walk in it, and you will find rest for your souls." But you said, "We will not walk in it."' Papa Legba, a popular Loa in Haitian and Louisiana Voodoo, stands at and rules over a crossroads, and a Haitian Voodoo band called Boukman Eksperians made an album called *Carrefour Dangereux*.

I had had a nasty car accident at dawn on a crossroads in North Dakota in 1988, colliding with the only other car for miles around (my fault, failing to see a stop sign). But nevertheless, that morning back in 2000, I awoke early at the hotel where I was staying on what is still the black 'wrong side' of the railway track in Clarksdale, and drove off in homage to Robert Johnson's crossroads. A few minutes north up Highway 61 I pulled up at the stop sign, then eased my rental car out across the junction, acutely aware of the importance of the moment. Just then, a car coming at speed along Highway 49 slammed into me from my left. There I was, right in the middle of the crossroads – *the* crossroads – seeking the help of a lady police officer to push my damaged car over to the gas station and make my statement. The situation was resolved easily enough: the other driver towed me back to my accommodation – which guarded its secret well.

Rooms at the Riverside Hotel were dank, and darkened by net curtains that seemed fixed at closed. The manager, Mr

Thomas, told me how his mother had opened the place way back when. Most of his clients were black workers on their way from one casual job to another. But not all. A look through the visitors' book indicated several from Europe, and flicking through, I came upon the name of John Kennedy Jnr. These people came to the Riverside Hotel for the same reason: it was right here, down by the crossroads, that Bessie Smith was brought after her – more serious – car accident, and died.

Many folks around here feel that not much has changed since then. The day after my crash I sat with old Ruby Walker on her porch, most of her twenty-two cats frolicking around her. The next few days would be particularly hard for the Walker family, since they were to have marked the nineteenth birthday of Ruby's granddaughter Sandra. But there was a different anniversary to be observed: 'She was just crossing the railroad line on her way home this time last year when a bullet hit her right in the head.'

There's a macabre intimacy to the murder. Ruby gestures towards the house behind her, folks hanging out their washing in the muggy heat: 'It was their boy done the shooting. He only got ten years and it's hard to look at them every day.' He was, she added, 'one of the gangbangers, fighting for territory; Sandra done got caught in the crossfire'. Like B.B. King's, Ruby's great-grandparents were slaves working these cotton fields. 'And so was I, after a fashion,' she reflected. 'We worked from sun-up to sundown, and the money was cheap.' Her daughter Mary became the fifth cotton-picking generation until she found work in a local school. But, added Ruby, the furrows deepening across her brow, 'I sometimes wonder if they ever really did do away with slavery. I don't know what's happening round here no more. All I know's it were better in the forties than it is now.'

During that same visit I met a relative of the Fair family who had shared a plot with the young B.B. King. Shirley Fair was the owner of a flower store in Jonestown called Ooh So Pretty Flowers, where a meeting had been arranged with President Bill Clinton when he blew through on his poverty tour of 1999. But, said Mrs Fair, 'nothing's gotten any better. There's nothing here to grasp on to. The railroad's closed, the good folks move on and gangbangers take over the streets, and that makes it mighty hard for business. The president wrote me a letter saying I could apply for a grant and employ ten people. But there were so many rules and regulations I couldn't understand nothing. Always something to slow and stop you.'

Nights around here are different when B.B. King is not in town. Down at the Club Sugar in Jonestown – a ramshackle brick cabin beside the railroad track – lads like Q with his blue bandana were arriving to drown their real world in the barrage of rap music, while Q's friend Icy Man pulled hard on a tube of 'rocks'. It was like stumbling upon the old 1970s Bronx in the middle of a twenty-first-century cotton plantation. My host was a man called Clee, who disliked rap and dreamed of setting up a blues club in town. He added, of this crowd: 'They're not local, they're County, and they're serious trouble.'

B.B. King knew all this, when we talked. He was not as self-satisfied as one could have expected him to be with 'progress' since the bad old days. Sure, he had jammed at the White House with a black president, and there really is a B.B. King Day in the Mississippi calendar – but there's also the confederate ensign in its state flag. 'We've come a long, long way,' he said as we sat there under the pecan tree, 'but we ain't come far enough.' I asked if he was aware of his own role in that 'long, long way' since he saw a man lynched and shared a bombed motel with Dr King. 'I'd like to think I made a li'l footprint in the sand,' he replied, and put his arm around a boy next to us, on his right. 'This here little boy's the same age as me when I was holding the reins of a mule. He won't never know those times, but I wonder what this boy will grow up to do. I wonder . . .'

However, 'The racists couldn't legislate musical taste', he writes, of my white generation and the blues. In Brewer's film, B.B. describes his arrival at the Fillmore West, the music venue in San Francisco, where queues of white hippies line the street. At first B.B. thinks he's in the wrong place, but confesses that he was so moved by several standing ovations he 'cried back up the stairway'. In our interview under the pecan tree, he called it 'my breakthrough moment. It was an unusual situation. You had all these white people playing the blues' – and he leans forward as if to impart some secret: 'They had something, these kids. They introduced us to a whole new world. We learned a lot from people like Johnny Winter and Peter Green [of Fleetwood Mac]. I ain't gonna tell you what it is,' he whispers, 'but we learned something, as well as the other way round.'

B.B. King once wrote: 'Lucille was singing the blues better than me.' But now he said something intriguingly different: 'You've heard me call myself a bluesman and a blues singer. I do call myself a blues singer, but you ain't never heard me call myself a blues guitar man. Well, that's because there's been so many can do it better'n I can, even some of these white boys. But they just ain't me, that's all. They're not B.B. King.'

I'd had B.B. to myself for forty minutes now, surrounded by people who'd known him for decades, and I'd started to feel bad. With his old friends and family gathered around, and young fans come to behold him for the first time, it felt like a levee was about to break – to unleash not the Mississippi backwaters but this throng of good people. B.B. King ended our interview with an observation that hallmarks true greatness. In the film he had said: 'When I hear what I want to hear, I'll have to stop.' Now, for all the accolades, he elaborated: 'I think I've done the best I could have done. But I keep wanting to play better, go further.

There are so many sounds I still want to make, so many things I haven't yet done. When I was younger I thought maybe I'd reached that peak . . . if I make it through to next month, I'll be eighty-seven. And now I know it can never be as good enough as I want to be, never exactly what it should be, so you got to keep going further, getting better. The time I tell you "I was good tonight," that's when I gotta stop. Not until then.'

On the subject of women, B.B. King's autobiography is candid. And he says now: 'I never met a woman I didn't like. I love 'em all, in their different ways.' Just then, a lady demanded his attention. 'You know,' he mused in my direction, 'if I find myself a nice wife who'll give me a chance, I may just come back to Indianola!' He turned to the lady in her splendidly coloured dress: 'Are you married?'

'No sir,' she replied.

'You shouldn't be telling me that kinda thing,' he confided – and I ceded her my seat.

B.B. King died two years later – those forty stolen minutes were his last major interview.

7" Single: Viva Verdi! Una Vita Italiana

I left school in the winter of 1972 and headed straight for the music: to Vienna, with a schoolfriend. We went to Austria specifically to queue in the snow for *Stehplätze*, standing places, at the Vienna State Opera – and for the education of a lifetime. Through bitter January afternoons we'd line up from three o'clock for the little blue ticket that admitted us, slush slithering from our boots, past elegant Austrians who could afford full-price seats, to five rows of red-velvet-topped bars beneath the overhang of the grand circle, against which to lean. Night after night, to hear *Figaro, Don Giovanni, Tristan und Isolde, Salome* – the works.

But by deep February we'd run out of money. We'd been living on a diet of bread dipped in red wine, in digs with a sole electric cooking-ring for heat. These were days long before ATM machines and anyway, neither of us had a bank account. We had just plucked up the courage to tell our fierce landlady, Frau Gmeiner, that we had to depart ahead of time, when I spotted a notice on a board in the university *Mensa* (canteen): an advertisement for *Komparsen*, whatever that meant. 'It means "extras",' said my friend Simon, 'they want extras for the *Staatsoper*.' We couldn't believe our luck. A date and time were specified for anyone interested to turn up; what on earth was this about? Well, the State Opera wanted bodies, basically: young men to stride on and off stage and back again as two circular columns, giving the impression of an army for the triumphal march in Verdi's *Aida*, the story of love between the Egyptian hero Radames and Aida, the Ethiopian princess bound as a slave by the Pharaoh.

The 'audition' was a perfunctory affair: we were lined up in order of height so that staff could count down the line until they reached a certain number, take those they needed and dismiss the shorter candidates. There were about a hundred of us, divided up, according to instructions I could barely understand, into two groups: the *Erste* and *Zweiter Gruppe Soldaten*. Little did I know, preparing for my operatic debut at the Vienna Opera, that my life in Austria was about to end and a life with Italy about to begin.

There were rehearsals during which we marched round and round – *Links! Rechts!* – to the accompaniment of a piano. For a bunch of itinerants and music students we weren't bad. We collected our payments in cash from a little window on the way out. Then came the dress rehearsal, and an immediate bonus: having manoeuvred ourselves into synthetic gold armour and helmets, the time came to get sufficiently bronzed so as to appear Egyptian. This involved makeup girls applying fake tan to our bodies – a good thing. The provision of *ein roter Speer*, a red spear, was a final touch as we headed towards the stage.

The conductor was a young Italian called Riccardo Muti, and Radames was sung by Placido Domingo. Muti called the rehearsal to order, raised his baton, and the trumpets began their fanfare. In comes the march on strings and wind, and with a swoop of Muti's baton the choir launches *fortissimo* into 'Gloria all'Egitto', shivers down every spine. Then, behind our *Gruppenführer* – a man with wild hair and shaggy beard – on we march – *Links!*

Rechts! – until we take the places rehearsed. Mine was front of stage left, third soldier in, with a fantastic view of the orchestra, Muti and Domingo. On streamed the ballet dancers, a flowing mist of fairies turning their arms to wings, grace and beauty swimming past my eyes, *roter Speer* held tight. The soldiers' task is to remain as still as possible while the tableau unfolds: the slave princess Aida recognizes her father among a group of prisoner-slaves and the scene builds into a statement of love pitched against terrifying power, accelerating into our march again – *Links! Rechts!* – for which Muti seemed to brake the tempo to monumental effect. I expected to hear a burst of applause as the crescendo came to an end. Instead, Muti tapped his baton on the music stand before him, and dismissed us.

Opening night was a national news story, as demonstrators assembled to protest against the cost of the production at a time of housing shortages – probably with reason. But never mind all that tonight – I was in *Aida*, watching the soloists not only sing but breathe and catch one another's eye. I obeyed Muti from the same distance as Domingo did, and kept my marching time. But the most intense feeling of all, in this gilded dream come true, was the music itself, its power and its story: defiant Radames against the Pharaoh, love against might, liberty against enslavement – the music and vision of Giuseppe Verdi.

So: having come to Vienna to immerse myself in the Austro-Germanic tradition in music, I now resolved to become immersed in the world of Verdi. On the last night, the opera house threw a party for us all – there'd be more work and there was every reason to stay. But my plan had changed: I had decided to leave Vienna for Florence, to learn Italian, learn about the Renaissance, get involved in radical politics and hear Verdi whenever possible.

My life with Italy – with the happiest years of it living in Italy – has been as much to do with ancient stones, painting, sculpture and architecture, friends and football, food, wine and landscape as with music. But it all began with Verdi, for his music's passionate, compassionate cry of liberty, and its human dimension. After the liberation fable of *Aida* I quickly found 'Va Pensiero', the chorus of the Hebrew slaves, and anthem for freedom anywhere since Verdi wrote it for inclusion in the opera *Nabucco*. I got to see *Don Carlo*, his greatest work, invoking the revolt of the Netherlands against the darkness of Habsburg Spain as a metaphor for his time. I heard his terrifying *Requiem*, not devotional music so much as a human cry against the outrage of death. It was composed for the writer Alessandro Manzoni and inspired by his masterpiece of nineteenth-century Italian romantic literature, *I Promessi sposi* (The Betrothed), a book about love and liberty pitched as one, as in *Aida*, against the brutality of armies and empire. This was Verdi's world and his calling: he was the radical conscience of the unification and liberation of Italy from – ironically – Austrian dominion; the cultural icon of nineteenth-century radical romanticism.

Verdi was a deputy in Italy's first parliament, a fourth figure to add to the triumvirate of Mazzini–Garibaldi–Cavour which liberated and unified the country. '*Viva Verdi!*' was a rallying cry for unification, and it helped that the initials of the King of Savoy who wished to lead the unified nation were VERDI (Vittorio Emanuele, *Re d'Italia*); so that by acclaiming the composer – '*Viva Verdi!*' – the crowds could also swear their loyalty over the heads of the Austrian troops. Not that this would have necessarily pleased Verdi: when a rift opened between the Constitutional Monarchist and Republican wings of the independence movement, he sided firmly with the Republicans. Giuseppe Garibaldi said: 'We owe a major part of this Italy to the poets,' and his red-shirted troops sang Verdi's choruses as they marched – just as every Italian knows them, and his arias, today. During the five days between the composer's fatal stroke and his death, the entire country came to a halt to hear the latest news. His funeral cortège passed among the largest crowds ever convened in Italy's history.

But the matter cuts deeper: to a little-known manifesto by Giuseppe Mazzini on music and liberty. Mazzini's revolutionary pamphlet of 1836, *The Philosophy of Music*, urged that opera become a means of political expression, voice of the 'individual collective'. It's a wonderful booklet, a romantic Mediterranean precursor of Wagner's *Gesamtkunstwerk*, even of Marx's *Das Kapital* – and more convincing than either. One of Verdi's biographers, Max Bruschi, writes of Mazzini's urging 'that melodrama ... should become the means to inflame a love of the nation, among both noblemen and the people. And though [Mazzini] lacked the composer to meet his needs, it occurred to him to imagine one. The dedication of his little work is to "an unknown youth, who maybe in some corner of our land, is readying himself".'[1]

Mazzini's ideas were theoretical, not just polemic: operatic arias in romantic music, he argued, should reflect individual expression within the democratic whole, and therefore be fluidly connected by seamless, continuous recitative, not split into detachable numbers as hitherto in 'classical' opera. In an occupied Italy on the verge of liberation, his booklet inspired young Verdi's early operas. The composer was working in Paris during the European uprisings of 1848, having written *Nabucco* in 1841. *I Lombardi* of 1843 concerned the struggle of the Lombards against Austrian domination; *Attila* (1846), the Nordic Hun repelled by Italian warriors. Verdi even slipped an aria called 'La patria tradita' – 'The Homeland Betrayed' – into his setting of Shakespeare's *Macbeth* in 1847.

The role of Verdi's operas in the Italian insurgency is illustrated by a description, in Mary Jane Phillips-Matz's huge biography, of the dress rehearsal for the Rome premiere of *La Battaglia di*

Legnano at Teatro Argentina in 1849: crowds wearing liberty rosettes and chanting '*Viva Italia!*' insisted on their right to be there, until

> *the Argentina was virtually in a state of siege* . . . La Battaglia di Legnano *was intended to inflame and it did* . . . *The new opera matched and may even have heightened the fever that infected Rome, for [Verdi's] music rallied the people like no music could. Patriots' harangues and leaflets proved not nearly as effective as dramas accompanied by music in an hour when Italy's situation could be interpreted on stage. When it was a crime to agitate openly for freedom, the people found that music offered them a way to defy the authorities. A labourer or shopkeeper cannot walk through the streets declaiming . . . an excerpt from a pamphlet; but to sing a piece of music from an opera score is another matter.*[2]

Verdi's work was of superlative artistic merit too. An article by the journalist Francesco Regli in 1843 examined how and why his music circulated in this way: 'The important melodies are passed along from one person and one group to another. The Milanese public went around and is still going around singing the main themes. When an opera becomes *popular*, so to speak, it must of course possess supreme merits. Everyone will not be touched, will not be moved, will not feel rapture unless there are good reasons for this to happen.'[3] Thus, says Phillips-Matz: 'Like Mazzini, Verdi became a prophet of a people, of the force of nationalism that was carrying Italy in its tide. When he composed music to patriotic phrases in his librettos, he evoked a cultural and philosophical idea that was to become a political reality in his lifetime. Words like "liberty", "the people" and "Italy" were not mere catchwords.'[4]

But in his grand opera *Les Vêpres Siciliennes*, written in Paris in

1855, Verdi complicates even his own cry of liberty with subtleties and dilemmas of great significance to the twentieth century and the present one too. In this mighty work, the metaphor of occupied and occupier is that of late-thirteenth-century Sicily in its struggle for freedom from France. There are two revolutionary heroes, Henri and the patriotic Sicilian Procida, and one heroine, Hélène, whom Henri loves. But Henri finds out that he is the bastard son of the French governor Montfort and a Sicilian woman he raped, and comes to believe that the only route to peace is to collaborate with his father's occupation against Procida, who plans to assassinate Montfort and massacre the French troops. Henri is cursed by a furious Procida, the Guevara figure with whom we also sympathize, and who launches the massacre just as Henri and Hélène are married in order to secure peace – though their effort is in vain.

So what price peace? What price liberty? Questions that would dominate the century after the opera was written. At the end of this work, for once, Verdi leaves it for us to decide.

There's irony here: Verdi is probably the most widely popular composer of all, his arias sung in baths and at weddings the world over, especially and rightly in Italy, where his operas are folk music, embedded in the country's consciousness. Yet outside – and even within – Italy, the engagement of his music is barely considered, and very rarely as an expression of romantic revolutionary politics and his role in them – to the detriment of our understanding of it. It is a little bewildering to go to the Royal Opera in London or La Scala in Milan and see well-heeled, expensively dressed stalwarts of the Establishment paying vast amounts (or billing their corporate entertainment budget) for a seat from which to listen to revolutionary music, with no idea that this is what they are doing. Of course, today's reactionaries will always feed on the creative power of yesterday's revolutionaries, air-brushing context and content, but with Verdi this ignorance is extreme.

With Shostakovich, however, the diametric opposite is true – to the equal detriment of our understanding of his music. While Verdi is sapped of historical context, Shostakovich is confined within – and defined by – his circumstances. Both wrote music specific to the abuse of power and to causes of freedom in their time, but it was music for all time. That is the point in both their cases. The oddity lies in the extreme contrast between how each is perceived: Verdi being seen as having little or no significance within his context, Shostakovich all but shackled within it.

In 1990 I finally moved to Rome, by which time my intense relationship with – and love of – Italy had been changed, forged and defined by a serendipitous nightmare, nothing to do with music – but it all comes together.

Two friends and I had cultivated an estimable tradition of convening for the European Cup Final each year, and spending more than we could afford on doing so – match and dinner, wherever, which in 1984 happened to be Rome. The following year we met in Brussels, for the most exciting final imaginable – between dazzling Liverpool and the mighty Juventus of that time – among the best teams ever to play football. But instead, we watched a massacre – of decent, innocent Italians (many of whose stories I would later write) by a drunken, charging hoard of British fans – they killed thirty-nine in all. Wearing – and this was part of the shame – the colours of my grandfather's team, from my mother's hometown. In the aftermath, all that followed at the British end, in the media and at Liverpool FC, was denial and feeble excuse bordering on an attempt to justify.

I spent that summer of 1985 in Turin, as if on a pilgrimage of penance, and joined the Juventus fan club Primo Amore (First Love). The day after the carnage, back in London, I wore a

Juventus scarf to a café in Notting Hill Gate where one wall was decorated with Juve memorabilia (the other, Napoli), ate a bowl of spaghetti and returned home – to play Verdi's *Requiem*. Within five years, I was at last living in Italy.

My passion for Verdi has intensified ever since, and continues to do so, though less complicatedly than my love for his country. Along with Shostakovich, if there is one classical composer whose work speaks louder at this time of writing, 2017, than ever, it is Verdi. The movement that spawned Verdi and his music was for a Europe that entwined the values of the Enlightenment and the Romantic movement: enlightened in its view of liberal, republican government based firmly upon the rights of man; romantic in its oath to the struggle for liberty until death, sworn by Rodrigo and Don Carlo; and insistent on the purity of art, as Verdi wrote in a letter of 1878: '... if we let fashion, love of innovation, and an alleged scientific spirit tempt us to surrender the native quality of our own art, the free natural certainty of our work and perception, our bright golden light, then we are simply being stupid and senseless'.[5]

Verdi rails also against the apathetic acceptance of power, as with Rodrigo's retort to Philip of Spain in *Don Carlo* when the emperor claims to have brought peace to his territories: 'a terrible peace,' thunders Rodrigo, 'the peace of the sepulchre'. And in his most popular opera of all, *La Traviata*, Verdi invokes Mazzini's instruction: 'Love and respect woman. Look to her not only for comfort but for strength and inspiration and doubling of your intellectual and moral powers. Blot out from your mind any idea of superiority, for you have none.'[6]

His was a vision of Europe that flowered in the mid-nineteenth century, an era ironically called 'nationalist' but which was actually liberal and tolerant in a manner true to the democratic origins of those words. During that century nationalism had two faces, which we would now call 'right' and 'left'. The twentieth century either turned the liberal, or 'left', Verdian idea of nationalism – which took its last stand in Ireland in 1916 and in subsequent anticolonial insurgencies – on its head, to mean the opposite of these things, or else endorsed only its 'right' wing. In Verdi, the causes of nation, liberty and tolerance are synonymous and universal, advanced as parallel values, equally applicable to any people; they do not signal the domination – or separation – of one by or from another. They are also romantic and moral causes, rather than defined by economic structures alone, as with the parallel Marxian rebellion of Verdi's time. And they are as cogent now as they ever were: the tenets of human rights charters enshrined in law out of the ashes of the Second World War – including the European Convention of Human Rights, rejected by Britain – may have their political origins in Tom Paine's *Rights of Man* and the French Revolution, but their moral genes come in no small part from Verdi.

Verdi's music expresses exactly the opposite sentiment to the abomination of 'Brexit' and other xenophobic challenges to European unity. Verdi speaks against the dismissal and alienation of 'the other', as depicted in *Il Trovatore*: a production at Covent Garden in 2017 was timely for its sympathetic depiction of the Gypsies – the other – as in our time, with their caravans, flotsam and jetsam. In August–September that same year a music festival was held in the 'Golfo dei Poeti', the Bay of Poets on the Ligurian coast, to make Verdi's point – and performed his music like I've never heard it before. The festival included the opening of the house in which Percy Bysshe Shelley was living, in the port of Lerici, when he drowned: Shelley who, during his four years in Italy, forged with his poetry an inspired and inspiring – presciently Verdian – coming together of morality, culture and politics, a vision of art intervening in society that propelled the Suoni dal Golfo festival.

Gianluca Marcianò was the festival director, and the conductor of its young Orchestra Excellence, which brings together musicians from all over the world. Marcianò has nurtured music across conflict and post-conflict zones – the Caucasus, former Yugoslavia, Lebanon – building orchestras and staging festivals in places where musicians from formerly warring communities are 'reading off the same page, making music for a purpose, music as a mission'. A committed Verdian, he believes that 'we need to think that music *matters*. And musicians should try to understand they can be part of change for the better. Because music has a power that needs no intermediary element – it addresses the soul directly. Politicians know that, and have tried to use and abuse music. But they cannot really touch it. You can imprison a dissident, burn a book or ban a speech – but you can never destroy music. We should not do politics, we have to do music, but with a mission.'

The 'great composers', says Marcianò in conversation, 'had a message, I believe ... If you take the poetry of some of Verdi's operas, like *Il Trovatore*, it is actually not especially inspiring, even weak. But the libretto is underpinned by the music, which makes it powerful, it gives energy to the words ... it moves you, it makes you tremble, it mesmerizes you. It brings everything to another level, stays with you after the event and so brings the message.' Verdi, he continues, 'appealed to Italy as a nation – but in a nineteenth-century way that called itself nationalism but was not nationalist. His music is about values – values which have no borders, and are universal and contemporary.' One concert, played for free to citizens of Lerici packed into the Church of San Francesco, ended with Verdi at gale force: we did not just *hear* arias from *Nabucco*, *Aida* and *Il Trovatore* – we were blown over by them.

Two soloists, the soprano Cristina Ferri and the baritone Damiano Salerno, acted and sang their roles as though on stage, so that every gesture and emotion in their voices, sufficient to fill a theatre holding three thousand, was delivered at point-blank range – as was the message, the cry of liberty, 'universal and contemporary'. The inward gaze of Salerno's eyes seemed to gouge the notes from within him. Never mind Hurricanes Harvey and Irma that were blasting the American South that week – there was Hurricane Cristina Ferri hurling the music of Leonora's passion with an artful, often wrathful drama, eyes ablaze, *décolletage palpitant*, a voice of rage and beauty. Among the audience were San Francesco's priest flanked by two nuns, and one wondered whether such overtly profane music had ever been sung in this lovely church before – sanguine it certainly was, but not *Sanguis Christi*, for sure: rather, something deeply, primally uplifting.

After the fifth and final performance of *Aida* in Vienna back in 1972, washing off the perma-tan cream, I had found myself at the basins next to my intimidating *Gruppenführer*, to whom I had not spoken. I needed the soap, and dared ask: '*Kann ich die Seife* borrowen *bitte*?' He replied, in Dublin brogue: 'I can't understand a feckin' word you're saying, mate.' This was Seamus McArdle, with whom I exchanged addresses, telling him that I was leaving Vienna for Italy. Seamus had been on the road long enough, and was heading home. 'When you're through with Italy,' he said, 'come to Dublin.' That July, though by no means 'through with Italy', I did – and another adventure in music, and a first in war, began.

5

'No Time for Love'

Planxty: National Stadium, Dublin, 1973
Christy Moore, Knightsbrook Hotel, Trim, County Meath, 2016

Round-and-round, up-and-down, around-again and spin-around, never ending – at least, never supposed to end. The giddy, whirling, reeling reels and jigging jigs of 'Raggle-Taggle Gypsies', played on uilleann pipes and mandolins, in an eternal circle, into the air of a Dublin summer night thick with rebellion, grog and grime. It had been four summers since Loyalist Protestant mobs and a sectarian police force torched the Catholic Falls Road in Belfast; eighteen months since the British Army killed thirteen innocent civilians on Bloody Sunday in Derry, and a year since the IRA hit Belfast city centre with twenty-two bombs on Bloody Friday. And now we were here, round-and-round, raggle-taggle Gypsies.

This was Ireland's best young group, Planxty, at the National Stadium in Dublin – the band whose music, whether they intended it or not, had become soundtrack to those events in the North for anyone who called themselves the movement for Ireland's hopes and trauma, as they erupted in tandem from 1968 onwards. In Ireland, the stakes that year had been higher than elsewhere – more to win and more to lose. Ireland's 1968 had morphed into something else entirely from the uprisings in

Paris, Prague, Chicago – into vicious, if not open, warfare. But whatever was true to the original rebellion found its voice in music, in interesting times that had become a little too *interesting. 'Planxty' is itself an interesting word: according to some accounts, it means a melancholic, lachrymose air, to others a more animated melody; or a fellow of those qualities.*

Planxty's audience was mostly young, plus a few older folk in Donegal tweed come to see what these long-hairs were doing with their forefathers' music. This was student Dublin, hip Dublin, rebel Dublin closely following – and attached to – what was happening in the North, on the continent and in the Americas.

The band started studiously. Spindly Dónal Lunny on guitar wearing a hooped sweater; Andy Irvine on mandolin, dark-bearded; seated Liam O'Flynn on pipes, master of his art, with side-parting. And vocalist Christy Moore every bit his planxty self, larger than life, sweet-toned but wild-eyed.

Some three or four numbers in, O'Flynn began playing jigs and reels: round-and-round the music swirled – we stamped, clapped, and filled the air with steam, devil may care; and swigged whiskey from hip flasks, me and Mary Mullan from Dungiven in the North, whom I loved and who loved me, I hoped – but who was forbidden by her family and religion to sleep with me, more's the pity. But then Lunny and Irvine play the first notes of the next song and Christy sings the opening lines of 'Raggle-Taggle Gypsies'. One of the oldest stories in the world: His Lordship's lady deserts him for the travellers and tinkers, horsemen and horse thieves; the story of the Irish, scattered and shattered around the world whether they wanted to be or not. The instrumental coda twirls like Celtic mystic knots that signify Trinity and infinity – crowd on its feet, Mary from Dungiven kissing me.

Then Christy Moore bade us all shut up, somehow, with a gesture, and stillness fell, in anticipation. Lunny picked the opening progression, and although everyone knew the song, very few clapped in recognition. Christy sang the opening line: 'When apples still grow in November . . .'

Then shut his eyes to sing the rest, sad but strong: 'If only her rivers run free.' So went the song, and all it laments, all it claims, invoking the wild Atlantic seaboard, peat smoke on a pluvial wind, the brightness of the green criss-crossed with drystone walls; but also plastic bullets and the crack of a live round, the stench of CS gas and charred masonry, the Free Derry gable end; Janus-faced Erin, two stories entwined by that of land.

When O'Flynn took the solo on his tin whistle each note carried with it the narratives of pain and hunger: the arrival of overlords against crofters and cutters of bog; of harsh capital against obscurantist faith; of Empire, which demanded cleared land and, to get it, famine. But in those notes too: sacrifice and struggle, vengeance and liberty, one day. All this in the flow of notes – and a hush descended, the audience spellbound, and when the last chord sounded there was silence for a moment, then applause which began as a ripple, and I closed my eyes, unable to put my hands together, that the spell not be broken.

Having missed the last bus, Mary from Dungiven and I walked forever to the Stoneybatter quarter of town – then poor, nowadays quite trendy. She was studying at University College Dublin and shared digs there. So I walked Mary from Dungiven back to the front door of her bedsit, kissed her again against a cold stone wall and repaired to a narrow single bed at Mrs Riordan's B&B and its sweaty nylon sheets that gave me mild electric shocks. I was too tired and buzzed to read, so I put down my book, switched off the naked lightbulb and listened to Planxty echo around the inside of my skull, missing Mary from Dungiven and planning my return to Belfast next day – after Mrs Riordan's breakfast (cardiac arrest within twenty minutes or your money back) – back to my nerdy thesis on the Troubles, back to my first war.

Ireland accounts for half my DNA (both grandmothers) and was always around the table at Christmas lunch in the form of stories my great-aunt Sheelah Hynes would tell; she was the younger sister of my father's mother Eileen who died in 1943, and she

lived with third sister, Gladys. I dimly remember Gladys – she
died when I was five. With the help of another glass, Sheelah
would tell us about Gladys: 'a bit of a one', good artist, friend of
Ezra Pound and illustrator of his *Cantos*. One of Gladys's best
works was a picture done in 1941 depicting a grotesque masked
figure in a pinstriped business suit and holding a hand grenade,
behind whom decorative winged angels shed tears; it bears her
inscription: '*Penny for the Guy – the thought that all war is caused by
the faceless money men of the City*'. Eileen, Gladys and Sheelah were
clever women, avowedly Catholic, socialist, suffragette – and
Irish Republican.

I came to know details behind this ancestry when my father
collated letters his mother had written him while he was a soldier
during the Second World War. That had in itself been quite a
story, and a relevant one: the Hynes sisters managed a version of
pacifism that applied to everywhere but Ireland and Spain. My
father was also a conscientious objector for two years until 1941
when, aged twenty-two, he wrote to his mother: 'I came to the
conclusion that my doctrine of pacifism is not a complete conviction and that I would join a combatant unit . . . One thing I am
sure of: this war must be won by the allies if any trace of decency
is to survive in Europe.' Eileen, to whom both Hitler and the
British Army were anathema, replied:

> At your age, convictions simply cannot be fixed. The best
> all of us can do is to follow our convictions as we go along.
> I believe war to be an evil. But I also know that men can
> muddle themselves, or sin themselves, into situations
> when they have only the choice between greater and
> lesser evils. And when the muddlers and sinners are in
> high places, they involve the innocent masses.
>
>   Love to you my son, and fine adventures!
> Mother

And off Dad went to war, hating every moment apart from the chance to see and sketch Renaissance architecture during the Allied advance through Italy.

Perhaps because Dad was now wearing the uniform of the hated British Army, his mother chose this time to write about his flamboyant lineage: from 'a solid body of yeomen … fiercely Catholic, fiercely national, uncouth, wild, adventurous, reckless', who 'fenced, fought, drank and were incredibly tough', 'smuggled Spanish wines' and dined from 'Waterford glass and Dublin silver … usually, I'm afraid, on a dirty tablecloth of lovely linen'. And about the patriarch Patrick Hynes, of whom I am terribly proud: educated in France, wrote my grandmother Eileen, he 'joined the rebellion of 1796–8' by Wolfe Tone's United Irishmen 'as a very young man, probably with a following of tenantry. The French let them down … and Patrick fled the country with a price on his head, having first, almost in the dark, fought a duel to which he was pledged. He went to France to join the Bonapartists either as a soldier or more probably as a spy.'

Eileen recalls a story told her by her grandfather – Patrick's then infant son James Lewis Hynes – about how 'the battle of Quatre-bras found him at an inn nearby. And the three-year-old James was – to his indignation and lasting memory – put to bed with *all* his clothes on … and told that if the French won, he could go to bed properly, but if the English, the hated English, won they must go a long way in a carriage.' The hated English did win, at Waterloo two days later, and Patrick went to India to fight them there: '… he entered the service of a Rajah, and details of this part of his career are sparse, my mother presuming that they may not have been suitable for small girls to hear … But there are accounts of these Irish adventurers fighting, intriguing and acting as propagandists against the English East India Company all across India.'

From my grandmother's sister Sheelah we mostly heard stories about Gladys's close friendship with Desmond FitzGerald, whom we think she met through Ezra Pound. FitzGerald had trained the Irish Volunteers in County Kerry, and with his wife Mabel had been among those to take and defend the Dublin General Post Office during the Easter Rising of 1916; he was charged by its leader Pádraig Pearse with the evacuation of the wounded. Gladys and FitzGerald maintained a correspondence over many years; he became Minister for Propaganda in the provisional government during Ireland's war of independence. The letters are a revelation, showing how these people combined waging war with intellectual prowess. One letter from FitzGerald looks back on a visit by a Labour Party envoy, Alfred Davies, sent to liaise with FitzGerald's Sinn Féin. FitzGerald refers Davies to an event at the National Gallery in Dublin, but laments: 'Unfortunately I wasn't there most of the time as the great W.B. Yeats hauled me out to tea.' One moment, drilling a guerrilla army; the next, cucumber sandwiches with the greatest poet of the age.

FitzGerald became Ireland's first Minister for External Affairs; he had disagreed vehemently with Aunt Gladys and even his own wife over the treaty that founded the Free State, and the civil war that followed it. Gladys had supported – and, our family papers indicate, aided – the IRA's war against both, and against Britain. They diverged again, but remained friends, as the Hynes sisters sided with the left and the Spanish Republic, FitzGerald with Mussolini and General Franco – such were the varied shades that claimed their roots in Ireland's 1916 Rising.

I did not need these origins, however, to identify with Ireland when the 'Troubles' began in 1969; when I got to Oxford on an open scholarship, I felt an affinity for what Gladys had written to another of her circle, Dorothy Carter, in 1921: 'At times I cannot keep my obsession out of the conversation, then I see the politely bored look come into their faces . . . they are thinking – "Ireland again!"'

*

So in 1973 I was glad to have found Mary from Dungiven and Planxty in Dublin; there appeared to be little music in Gladys's and FitzGerald's revolution, though they corresponded endlessly about Irish culture – but this one under way in the 1970s certainly had a soundtrack, and not just at the National Stadium. One way to remain a diligent Oxford student but spend time more interestingly in Ireland was to embark on an undergraduate thesis on the Troubles, which I did; in what would turn out to be a lifetime of reporting conflict, this was my first war. And when in Ireland to research, I'd drink in places that invariably 'locked in' for the night and the music session – another town, another pint, another whiskey, another song. I got into all kinds of scary scrapes on this principle, but the musicianship was bedazzling, from people who were van drivers and postmen – or gunmen – by day.

But this music – Planxty's or in the bar – was not just about politics and drinking, though there is no overstating the importance of either. What *is* Irish music, and what is so Irish about it? The harpist Anne-Marie O'Farrell combines in her work traditional Irish music with baroque airs, which feels like the most natural thing. O'Farrell finds a pivotal moment: the Belfast Harpers' Assembly of July 1792, during and after which a young classically trained musician, Edward Bunting, was commissioned to note down the airs played. 'It was the first attempt to write down a music that had been played in stately homes – a first real canon of Irish music.' And in Irish music, says O'Farrell, 'one can detect those classical influences – the gavottes, and baroque dances from Europe' – as of course one can, once pointed out.

We talk in the bay window of a café above a favourite bookshop. And, O'Farrell suggests, add to what Bunting wrote down 'the airs of Thomas Moore – like "Minstrel Boy", and the traditions of an itinerant music sung by balladeers and musicians who wandered around the country. And you have this unique rhythm and metre, which we'd now call "Irish".' O'Farrell talks about how this music from a rapacious range of sources then proceeds through 'the session in the bar. That's where Irish music really happens, when people join together, sometimes without talking very much, and play off and with one another. A totally spontaneous music, but based on a common sense of what it is and where it came from. The session has its own special etiquette, an understanding of when to come in, when to cede to someone else. So that the music we call "Irish" constantly evolves, in variations on that rhythm and metre, of those airs and ballads, but with points of reference dating back to Edward Bunting's writing down what was played at that harp festival in 1792.'

'Irish music has a grammar,' says Philip King – film director and organizer of the Other Voices festival in the southwest – 'which makes it instantly recognizable. Firstly, it is dance music: jigs, reels, slips, mazurkas – usually played on a fiddle, a concertina and cheap wind instruments. But although a dance, it's shot through with longing and lonesomeness, even in its wildest abandon. Whether played in Ireland for those who have left, or by those who have left for Ireland. It's lonesomeness, rather than loneliness – wistful, less austere than loneliness. It's a simple grammar, but enormously varied in the ways it's expressed. You take the dance, add the ballads and sessions in the pub, and you end up with music that was a help when there was nothing else – something that is as essential to Irish identity as the blues are to the African American, because Irish music is a kind of blues.'

King introduces the idea of *idir eathrú* – the 'in-between'. 'The Irish,' he says, 'always moved between this and that. Between Ireland and exile, Britain and our own country. The Irish story has been through so many confused identities fuelled by hunger, emigration, despair, violent struggle and postcolonial hangover: are we Irish or British? Do we speak our own language, or

English? Who are we? The music is a partial answer to that question, because it runs so deep in our DNA – it *is* us.'

King quotes the poet Moya Cannon and her notion of 'carrying the songs'. 'The grammar of Irish music translates,' he says, ' – have grammar, will travel. Because the songs are like seeds, and the wind takes them. They're literally carried, from place to place, around the country and into exile by people who knew they were never coming home. You close your eyes and open your mouth to sing – and in your mind's eye you are back home. If I'm in New York, busy with jazz or rock, and I'm walking down a street and hear a reel coming out of a pub – that does it for me. I know deep down: that's *mine*. It's something that happens with Irish music – it collapses time and space.'

There's no argument over who is 'the voice' of Irish music in my – our – time: the man who sang that night in 1973, Christy Moore. The man who brings the struggles of the world to Ireland, and takes those of Ireland to all corners, though he himself travels little these days. 'I have a feel for this country,' says Christy, 'and I've been happy here.' There's nothing unadventurous about this; it's just because 'I like the Irish – they're straight, they have a canny intelligence and they're fun.' Nor is it parochial or myopic; no Irish singer has a repertoire that draws so much from around the world. Christy sings about the Spanish Civil War, then the murder of the journalist Veronica Guerin by the Dublin mafia; the Chilean coup in 1973, then teenagers killed by a fire at the Stardust Club on Valentine's Night 1981 – a song banned by a court of law.

Moore grew up in Newbridge, County Kildare, and went to London in 1966 – not for the reasons of frustration with Ireland that sent Edna O'Brien to England and Beckett to Paris, but only 'because I wanted to sing, and I couldn't get any gigs in Ireland'. There, Christy encountered the charismatic singer and writer

Dominic Behan – brother of Brendan and son of an IRA volunteer. With Behan, Christy released *Paddy on the Road* in 1969, just as the Troubles erupted. 'My Irish Republicanism grew from boyhood,' he says. 'My maternal grandmother Ellie Power shared stories and fables of brave men who fought and died for Irish freedom; my mother sang rebel songs, her feelings ran deep.'

'I returned to Ireland,' he says, 'in 1972, and whatever dormant feelings I had while in London were awoken by Bloody Sunday in Derry. By then Planxty was in its infancy. The band never had a collective political viewpoint; occasionally we had short talks about certain songs, and it was decided that we would perform songs provided all four of us were in agreement.'

Christy and I are talking now in 2016, driving out of Dublin towards a gig in the ballroom at a hotel in Trim, County Meath, birthplace of Christy's mother Nancy Power, for whom he adapts the anonymous words of 'Singing Bird': 'None can sing', it goes, 'so sweet as you'.

Before we get on to rebel stuff, it seems right to ask Christy what's so *Irish* about Irish music? 'My answer is an uneducated one,' he replies. 'The Irish music I know and love stirs my spirit, a stirring that began when I heard the Clancy Brothers in 1962: old reels, jaunting jigs, slow airs and "traditional" songs that touched me as nothing ever did. Then in London, Irish music in exile consolidated my growing obsession.' And as an expression of Irish identity? 'I feel part of a continuing tradition, a ballad singer who carries the news. I feel very Irish and want for nothing else. Our trad music and our folk songs are more mainstream than in other countries known to me; many singers of folk songs have become household names on the island.' The closest to a memoir Moore has written is done song by song, with notes to each. And in those to a song called "Billy Gray" he writes: 'There must be 50,000 exceptionally good singers in Ireland, and ten times that number able to hold a good song.'[1]

Rebel politics are integral to Irish music like no other. Even longing for home is invariably set against a backdrop of flight from famine, challenge to the colonial invader by the rebel outlaw, or other tribulation. Can Irish music exist without (direct or indirect) reference to and infusion by the struggle against Britain? 'It's in our DNA,' says Christy again, as we drive through the wind, 'eight hundred years of oppression by our longest-ruling colonizer. It's in the very mixture of music and lyric, and the instruments used; plus the love of the craic, distrust, and scheming against all forms of authority.'

This music unites rebel and joker, hard times that beget good times. The struggle and the 'craic' come what may, what the hell, and to hell with it all. Christy Moore laughs, and his songs make people laugh, as well as cry. 'I remember a night thirty years ago, when playing to five thousand people at the Point Theatre in Dublin, a lone voice rang out, stark and clear: "For Jaysus' sake Christy, lighten up!" And I did. I believe if it gets too heavy for too long, the audience just switches off. I like for people to exit the room feeling good. At the end of the day I'm a song and dance man' – as Bob Dylan said in 1965.

We pull up at the Knightsbrook Hotel in Trim, wrapped in drizzle. 'I like these hotel gigs,' says Christy, 'eight hundred people out for the night in a place they'll have been for weddings or whatever.' When he comes on to play – a hefty, powerful presence – he flexes his muscles and says: 'There's a wonderful scent of perfume and after-shave in the room tonight – I'm already high on it.' There are four nurses from Liverpool here for a sixtieth birthday bash; plus studious young people, elderly men with cloth caps and skin like tanned leather. Everyone is here – although, Christy says, 'I think ambitious councillors and politicians have given up on me. They find all this repugnant.' He plays the song for peace in Ireland, 'North and South of the River', written with Bono and the Edge of U2; he sings his song of rage at apathy and subservience to a lousy lot, 'Oblivious', wondering what it takes to generate some anger. He sings a tribute to the Chilean singer Víctor Jara, murdered during General Pinochet's coup. He sings about people who survived the ravages of famine to reach 'The City of Chicago' – 'As the evening shadows fall . . . dreaming /Of the hills of Donegal'.

Christy had talked in the van about song and exile: 'Everyone here has been touched by emigration across the centuries. Whether forced or chosen, we all still instinctively understand that sense of separation from where we come from. It's complex: it's the air that exists between those who stay and those who go. The feeling exists in every immigrant ghetto around the globe and in every homeland left behind – it's not peculiar to Ireland, it's just that we're better at singing about it.'

Then, the other of the two ballads Christy sings for his mother – 'Yellow Furze Woman': in the notes to it he writes about Nancy Power's 'enormous and beautiful deep soprano voice' when she sang in church, and how 'when she sang the old songs . . . It would be in a small, quiet lonesome voice that often stilled my night.' The song over, Christy was shaking, visibly.

'Viva la Quinta Brigada' is about Irishmen who fought for the Republic during the Spanish Civil War. You can feel your blood pump in time with every beat. What is it about the pulse of song? 'It's love, it's obsession, it's emotion,' Christy had said, 'but it's also show business. It's standing before lamps and putting on a show. It's all part of the bundle, going out there, with a basket of songs and sharing them out into that dark emotion-filled room. Everyone with a different expectation, but the music brings us all together, the listener creates the atmosphere that enables the singer to reach it.'

A triad of songs ends the evening: each with its own poignant resonance. 'Back Home in Derry' is about an Irishman exiled to Australia, but that is not its significance: it was written by the

IRA hunger-striker Bobby Sands, the first to die during the protest-to-the-death in H-Block at the Long Kesh prison camp during 1981. Then comes a Jack Warshaw song, which in Christy's rendering is the most powerful of them all. If our parents' generation had 'We Shall Overcome', so mine has this, about the universal police siren, the timeless knock at the door, the quintessential protest song, marked and marred by the appalling notion of its title, 'No Time for Love'. It's about Ireland and about everywhere – Christy often adds his own ingredients: apartheid and partition, the Chicago trials and *Solidarność* in Poland (or it could be the Warsaw Uprising) in the same breath as Bogside and Belfast, Vietnam alongside the Easter Rising. The encore – 'one for the road!' Christy called it – is 'The Time Has Come', written after Christy had befriended Peggy O'Hara, mother of Patsy O'Hara of the Irish National Liberation Army, fourth of the ten to die on hunger strike in 1981.

(I met Peggy – and Patsy, after a fashion – when making a film for my then employer, Granada TV's *World in Action*, in 1981, which included a shot of O'Hara in his coffin, surrounded by a masked INLA honour guard. It was a famous case: the Independent Broadcasting Authority demanded the frame be cut, but my editor refused and the film was banned. Decades later, back in Derry, I told the story to a man organizing a peace-building history project I was working with. 'Oh aye,' he said calmly, 'my brother was in that picture.' What ?! Er, he wasn't one of our crew, he wasn't in the coffin . . . I later greeted him, Tony the taxi driver, back then one of the INLA guards. I said: 'I think we've met, we weren't introduced . . .')

Inevitably, Christy and I talk about these things in the van back to Dublin. He's walked a high wire: singing in deference to sacrifices by, and struggles of, the IRA, but distancing himself vociferously from its outrages. Since 1969, he says, 'there've been different levels of ideas and methods. Some of it has been just plain thuggery, some of it has been to forward the original ideals.' Of the O'Hara song: 'I recorded it in 1982, the year after the hunger strikes. It was played on the radio as a love song, and very popular until [the Republican Socialist] Eamonn McCann inadvertently mentioned what it was actually about – Patsy O'Hara's death. It disappeared off the airwaves after that.'

In an insightful film portrait made for RTÉ television by the director Mark McLaughlan, Christy explains how he felt himself part ways with the IRA decisively after the 'Poppy Day massacre' in Enniskillen on Remembrance Sunday in 1987, when a bomb killed eleven people and injured sixty-three. 'I think it's a matter of just telling the truth,' he says now. 'If you're asked a question, give an answer, don't beat around the bush. There are people who hate what I do, that I still sing for those who died. But I've always done it, and I always will.'

Irish music is almost always set in landscape; Irish songs are like Romantic paintings, giving rivers and mountains, villages and towns, a poetic significance little other music does. One song that night in 2016 was 'Gortatagort' with its line 'I sing The Field of Standing Stones'. What is it about the landscape in Irish music? The pipes evoke it, rebel songs call upon it for justification. 'I was back in Kildare,' replies Christy, 'in the graveyard among the dust of my father's people. I met old neighbours, some of whom I've not seen for years. We remembered the previous generations, spoke of old times, shared some laughs and sorrows. It's a very deep bond that I don't understand, but that I cherish. I love going down boreens, into old farmyards and haggarts, across bogs and up hillsides. That's where I hear the stuff that turns me on.'

Christy's car drops me off, late autumn leaves blowing in the cold wind across a driveway. The rain has stopped, the sky cleared and there's a 'supermoon' on the rise, nearest we'll see in our lifetime, apparently. 'Ach, no,' says Christy, 'there's another in 2036.' That would make me eighty-two and him ninety-one. One more time, Christy: why is singing so essential to the Irish narrative? 'We sing,' he replies, 'so as the musicians can take a piss, get a drink.'

6

Floating Anarchy Radio 'You Can't Un-ring the Bell!'

You Can't Un-ring the Bell!
Planet Gong, Rougemont Gardens, Exeter, 1977

Not one of those wearing cloaks or robes, long hair and lambent colours had paid for their patch of grass in Rougemont Gardens, Exeter, to hear a band that usually played for free, and did so for its Live Floating Anarchy tour of 1977. An event promoted, said the posters, by Radio Gnome. On stage was one of the variants of a group that was more institution than band, really: Planet Gong, with its founder and leader Daevid Allen, billed today as Dingbat Alien, and the musicians calling themselves Here & Now.

Planet Gong was an international roadshow drawn from Australia, Britain and France, the quintessential hippie band, part of that vast peace movement which expressed itself above all in music during the 1960s. The range of instrumentation was sophisticated, timecodes even more so. Planet Gong was stage madness, jazz-acid-rock with a cult following and some epic comic storytelling. A trilogy of albums unfolded the narrative of 'pothead pixies' communicating advice to earth – through music – on how best to ascertain the meaning of life. Planet Gong was hippie music-theatre of the absurd.

I remember little about the running order of the songs in Exeter that day. There was the driving power of the occasion's title track 'Floating Anarchy', and a spirited number called 'Opium for the People' that mocked sheep-like acceptance of the system by its subjects, with a subplot of poppy product as a means towards liberation from it. Planet Gong's music has a sinewy complexity, especially in a number today called 'Stone Innoc Frankenstein', with Allen's guitar gliding over a vehement jazzy bass played by Keith the Missile Bass. We ended, as dusk fell, with a rock-jazz 'symphony' drifting on the sweet summer air entitled 'Allez Ali Baba Have You Any Bullshit', and with 'Mama Maya Mantra', with Arabic chromatics and a proto-techno pulse on synthesizer which would define the music of the ensuing decades.

The reason for my crystalline reading of the music but hazy grasp of its ordering was that one of my company had provided psilocybin – or psychedelic – mushrooms to eat. 'Fungi', as we called them, were the drug of choice in the West Country at the time, free and natural – the only hallucinogen I've ever tried. Drugs were the diet of 'peace music', and fungi were a means of interesting escape for a small number of us on a journalism training scheme operated by the tabloid Daily Mirror *in a grim Portakabin on the outskirts of Plymouth.*

One night, after a day practising shorthand, by way of antidote a fellow trainee called Tim Minogue and I went to Plymouth Hoe for a few fungi. Somewhere along the water's edge I watched thousands of creepy-crawlies emerge from the brine to climb the concrete walls of the reach, like an Escher drawing animated in fast-motion. But here's the twist: 'Do you see what I see?' I asked Tim. And he did, the same hallucination as me – telepathy, or was it real?

For the Floating Anarchy gala there'd been salad with fungi, and when the music was done we headed for Exeter Cathedral to sit on the cobblestones. Someone with a guitar was playing riffs from 'Mama Maya Mantra'. But before long I found myself talking to a police officer and later at a police station making a statement. After a night in the cells, I was released without charge along with my fellow anarchy-

floaters, and obliged to arrive at the Mirror's *Portakabin in Plymouth with a document accounting for my absence. It was a copy of my statement, headed (wrongly) 'Overdose of Marijuana', and containing my verbatim explanation in earnest: that I had been 'watching Planet Gong and waiting for Exeter Cathedral to take off'.*

Planet Gong were just a particle in the carnival that was the hippie uprising they epitomized: in England, along with Pink Floyd, Hawkwind, Traffic, King Crimson; in America, the Grateful Dead, Jefferson Airplane, Buffalo Springfield, the Byrds; in France, Magma; in Germany, Kraftwerk; in Holland, Focus. And in the aftermath of shattered idealism and war in Vietnam these wise clowns bore a standard through the 1970s: a standard of something precious, funny and feral on the one hand, pretentious, myopic and egocentric on the other; while the imminent hegemony of materialism prepared to obliterate the carnival with what the Chilean writer Roberto Bolaño called 'the abominable '80s'. Planet Gong were serious about peace, and very serious about war, but they were also jesters at the court of society. There is anger and escape in Planet Gong's music, mirth and wisdom – a wisdom whereby the ostensibly mad laugh at what is really mad – the system.

I returned to Exeter in 2013, for the first time since the concert. The cathedral was still there.

The fact that the US president Donald Trump and Britain's 'Brexit' prime minister Theresa May can both take the stage to the sound of the Rolling Stones – 'You Can't Always Get What You Want' and 'Start Me Up', respectively – might say as much about rock and roll as it does about them. Ergo, that rock music can, like everything else, be infinitely commodified and has no intrinsic moral or democratic ingredient.

Tony Blair can enthuse about playing in his band at Oxford after waging war with still unfathomable consequences in Iraq, then harvesting a few consultancies with J.P. Morgan et al. On another level, in 2003, I interviewed friends and relatives of the

French actress Marie Trintignan, who had been beaten to death by her lover, rock star Bertrand Cantat of Noir Désir, who opposed global capitalism, environmental abuse, etc. After the murder, some fans melted down their CDs and laid flowers at screenings of a posthumous film starring Trintignan and attention was drawn to the wider horror of domestic violence against women. But Cantat's record sales soared as he acquired a grotesque, tragic mystique. At the time of writing, Cantat was recently freed and touring with a new album to rapturous applause, though some municipal authorities had cancelled concerts in outrage. No one can *own* rock and roll, even those who want it to be inherently radical, or 'alternative'. In 2016, when the Grateful Dead played their final concert in Chicago, their democratic attitude facilitating bootleggers back in the day was hailed as prescient of Internet marketing.

It is part of capitalism's genius that it can take any culture pitched against it, then absorb, neutralize, and make it profitable. Just as the medieval Vatican's answer to St Francis's rebellion of 'holy poverty' was to give the Franciscans an order, so the super-wealthy attended the Dèsert Trip festival of October 2016 at the Empire Polo Club near Palm Springs to hear Bob Dylan, Paul McCartney, Neil Young and Roger Waters of Pink Floyd. This appropriation and commodification of rock is made easier by the fact that, as E.J. Hobsbawm (writing as Francis Newton) says, 'a crucial distinction between jazz and rock was that rock was never a minority music . . . rock was the opposite of a minority taste'.[1] It's the process whereby Dylan becomes a multimillionaire after writing 'The Lonesome Death Of Hattie Carroll'; Johnny 'Rotten' Lydon advertises British butter and stars on *Celebrity Big Brother* after composing 'Anarchy In The UK'; Flavor Flav becomes star of the TV series *The Farm* after posing as Public Enemy No. 1.

I have always resented this process and – I have to say –

spotted it early. When I was eighteen in 1972, I was fined for criminal damage after paint-spraying a slogan on a small independent record store in Notting Hill Gate called Virgin Records, the hip place to be – but there was something that didn't convince me; this was a business pastiche of the ethos it claimed, and was selling. In those days the world was divided, quite usefully on reflection, between 'hip' and 'square' – whatever the definitions, we knew what they meant. And in between was 'pseud' – people who looked or thought they were hip but were actually square. I thought Virgin Records was pseud. The owner, who had long blond hair, came to my trial at Marylebone Magistrates' Court, curious as to who would want to damage his lovely shop. Richard Branson recognized and stopped me on Ladbroke Grove shortly afterwards and asked me why.

But the premise of the 1960s was that music targeting the Establishment develops a life of its own – just as the Colorado River did indeed gouge the Grand Canyon, drip by drip. Colonel Oliver North of the US Army, later disgraced for his role in arming paramilitaries in Nicaragua via drug profits and deals with Iran, was a proven liar but said something true: that war in Vietnam was lost not in Vietnam but on the campuses of America. It's hard for a country to wage war with such a drain on its national morale as a peace movement that has music at its core. Overtly, music by people like Joan Baez, Jefferson Airplane, Crosby, Stills, Nash & Young and Steppenwolf; and less didactically, Joni Mitchell, Velvet Undergound – and the rest. Black rights and the relative end of American apartheid would not have been won without B.B. King, Aretha Franklin, Nina Simone, Marvin Gaye and the others. Conversely, it is perhaps no coincidence that the creed of greed during Bolaño's 'abominable '80s' took root without a protest song screaming in its ear.

It had begun as a subdued explosion, when a generation of bohemians and the Beat poets – Jack Kerouac et al. – installed themselves on North Beach, San Francisco, during the late 1950s. A singular city on America's edge – literally and meta-phorically – San Francisco had a history of counterculture, and while the convergence of rebellions, energies and experiments of the early 1960s erupted variously in New York, Los Angeles, Chicago and across Europe, San Francisco went its own way as the nascent hippies adapted the Beat lifestyle into a phenomenon of music, psychedelic drugs, politics, anti-politics, art, sex, rebellion, celebration, squalor and calamity that reached what was for some its climax, and for others its nadir, during the 'Summer of Love' in 1967.

During the previous four years, in and around the cheap Victorian housing of Haight Ashbury, something akin to what Bob Weir of the Grateful Dead calls a 'little renaissance' had occurred. On a diet of LSD, a core of bands played with each other, for each other, for free, and at the Avalon Ballroom and Bill Graham's Fillmore: Jefferson Airplane, the Grateful Dead, Quicksilver Messenger Service, Country Joe and the Fish. Artists illustrated the sound: Stanley Mouse and others. Revolutionary activists called the Diggers endeavoured to demonstrate a new way of reorganizing (or disorganizing) a society without money. And there was a 'look': costume was pastiche, often mutating some Edwardian or Victorian fashion gleaned from thrift shops – tie-dye came later – and hair was long. Music was the strongest current among these tributaries of the alternative river; music, as intervention in the world, is what the age will be remembered for. Like many people my age, I have listened to it ever since, and so went in search of some of those who played it, to listen to them too.

As shafts of early sun strike the precipitous streets of San Francisco's North Beach, just before 7 a.m. in spring 2007, a gathering of bearded folk sip espressos at Caffe Trieste on the corner of Vallejo Street and Grant Avenue. And up the hill into this huddle arrives a man with long grey hair beneath a beret, jacket and scarf against the cold of early morning, but no socks – only slippers. This is Paul Kantner, engine behind the first superstars of hippie music, Jefferson Airplane. He lights an unfiltered Camel, the first of about eight he will devour over the next ninety minutes. 'One cigarette closer to Jesus!' he laughs. 'Might as well die of something I like.'

Airplane forged the sound of psychedelia; their early albums welded a new texture: metallic, dissonant, bluesy, with an intensity that reflected the violence of the system that waged war, but also the rage and vulnerability of those who challenged it in the name of peace. 'I was brought up Catholic,' Kantner explained, 'but lucky enough to have been educated by the Christian Brothers, who gave me books on the forbidden list: *Tom Sawyer*, *Lady Chatterley's Lover*.' He immersed himself in folk music and read science fiction, which 'opened my mind to what was beyond the possible'.

'By 1965 in San Francisco,' he says, 'music was just another thing to do at the concert. Sometimes it was the least interesting thing – everything was exploding: a challenge to the establishment: *Don't trust these people.* There was a nexus of intelligent folks; costume had changed and there was this window between the invention of the contraceptive pill and sexually transmitted diseases. People call it hedonism, but it wasn't. It was: "We will break your laws at our leisure." For me, the music was part of that and therefore political, a way of conveying a revolutionary idea in a way that pamphlets or speeches could not. You create a sound that is radical, against what the ear is accustomed to from too much shit on TV and too many lies from politicians, and you subvert that with the sound you make – with dissonance, unpredictability. You break the frame, expand the horizons. For some people, this is an end in itself, but for me it was for a social reason.

Some of the band got irritated by this – they were like the Grateful Dead, just musicians. They didn't want all this revolutionary shit.'

Most surviving pioneers of hippie music now live over the Golden Gate Bridge in Marin County – an idyll of coffee houses, meditation and natural beauty. Kantner recalls: 'I tried living in Marin County, like that island in the *Iliad* where everyone is so fucking happy all the time. It was like an old-age home; I thought I'd died and gone to heaven. I couldn't take it, came back to the city.'

In 1981, I had driven down Pacific Highway One from Big Sur to watch what was now called Jefferson Starship at Santa Barbara. We had cheaper seats high up in an amphitheatre with a view of the city as well as a distant one of the stage, on which Kantner and Grace Slick belted out their anthems about tearing down walls and revolution on the streets. But the view was of sleepy streets, a luxury marina and everything that new president Ronald Reagan, whose ranch was nearby, stood for. I also saw Kantner's last performance in the UK, at the 100 Club on Oxford Street in 2008, while Iraq was ablaze. So I ask Kantner: How can the music claim an impact? 'Obviously the influence was limited to a degree,' he concedes, 'a lot more has gone worse than better since then ... [this was before the election of Donald Trump; Kantner died in 2016]. But we're still there, we people, saying: "Get out of your fucking SUV! Put down that cell phone!" A good idea is a virus, it catches and spreads like a virus, and,' he says unforgettably, 'you are not going to be able to un-ring the bell! Once it has rung, it has rung. Thank you for your time.' And off he went into the morning, cigarette in hand.

'Give us an F!' shouts Country Joe, one of the instantly re-cognizable faces and voices of Haight Ashbury '67. 'F!' they reply, then 'U', 'C', 'K'. 'What's that spell?' demands Joe. 'FUCK!' they retort. And Joe McDonald strums the opening chords to his anthem, broadcast to the world from Woodstock, 'I-Feel-Like-I'm-Fixin'-to-Die Rag' by Country Joe and the Fish. But this is not Woodstock, it's Anna's Jazz Island in Berkeley in 2007 – Joe in his mid-sixties and many in the audience no younger, apart from a few children, including Joe's son, in charge of merchandise which includes 'Fuck Bush' badges for a dollar.

Earlier during the day, Country Joe sits in his modest home in Berkeley to discuss what he calls 'the Aquarian Age'. He produces a box-set of protest songs and observes: 'But there aren't many jokes in there. I love this music, but was delighted to become a hippie. Some people were in Haight Ashbury just for the fun and games. Others here in Berkeley wanted to be Bolsheviks.' But Joe 'was from a Bolsheviky family, *and* wanted to have fun, free-style. So we brought a political message wrapped in a psychedelic package.' Saying what? 'Untranslatable, really. The only metaphor I can think of is map-making. For centuries, the greatest minds thought the earth was flat. And when someone comes along and says it's round, there's always going to be a guy with a map store full of flat maps saying, "This is going to be bad news" – he's going to have to keep saying, "No it's not, it's flat!" But we found that it was round, and that was a language that the flat-earth people will never understand. They'll call us crackpots for saying the earth is round, and we'll take that as a compliment.

'That's where the music comes in,' he continues, 'like cool beer on a hot day. It delivered that round-earth message for the people to hear and drink.' I ask McDonald about a photograph of him playing with Jerry Garcia of the Grateful Dead. 'I was never a Dead Head,' he replies. 'I mean, they weren't only non-political, they were anti-political. But hey, the music, Garcia and Bob Weir – wow . . .'

Over time, the Grateful Dead have become the enduring icon of hippie peace-music: an adventure in sound hallmarked by boundless improvisation and crystalline lyricism – there are few moments in all rock music like Weir's rhythm and Garcia's lead guitars imitating the peel of church bells on a famous live account of 'St. Stephen / The Eleven'. Half a century later, the album on which it features, *Live Dead*, is beautifully performed in its entirety by a kind of 'Dead family' touring band led by the original keyboards player, Tom Constanten, with the parts of now deceased Garcia and very much alive Weir taken by Slick Aguilar of Jefferson Starship and Mark Karan of Weir's current band Ratdog. And now, I'm driving along a road winding through Marin County from the untroubled town of Mill Valley towards Bob Weir's house in the Arcadia that Kantner likened to Homer's happy island, the scent of jasmine, shafts of sunlight through the eucalyptus. Weir duly appears wearing baggy trousers, and barefoot. The chairs in his studio have no legs, so we sit cross-legged on the floor to talk. There are statues of Shiva among the guitars. 'We found the classical spiritual practices later,' says Weir. He has an intense stare and speaks with a deep, singing voice. 'Haight Ashbury,' he says, 'was a ghetto of bohemians who wanted to do anything – and we did, and I don't think it's happened since. Yes, there was LSD, but Haight Ashbury was not about drugs. It was about exploration, finding new ways of expression, being aware of one's existence.' In contrast to what he saw as the political ideologues, 'we wanted everyone to be their own leader. Ideology never meets reality with any grace.'

I saw the Dead play a number of times; always hypnotic. At an airfield near Manchester, twice in London and memorably in Salinas, California, for which crowds arriving several hours before the concert included circus acts and 'touch and love' circles. But Weir is scathing about the 'cult' of the Dead. 'The only other person it happened to was Dylan,' he says, 'that notion that we're up to more than we actually are.' The Dead's chronicler Dennis McNally – in a book entitled *A Long Strange Trip: The Inside History of the Grateful Dead and the Making of Modern America –*

cites a line in the solitary 'Black Muddy River', about how dark night lasts seemingly forever' – which some Dead Heads, says McNally disdainfully, 'take as an instruction to keep the party going'. Weir cites the droll 'Casey Jones', about a freight train driver high on coke. 'People don't realize,' he says, 'that this is a cautionary tale about cocaine.' And he starts singing his own line (which is rather thrilling) about having two eyes, yet seeing nothing, adding: 'It gets very annoying, being misunderstood.'

What is the music doing? Weir's eyes light up as he leaves the subject of the 'scene' for the music itself. 'We were folk musicians unable to resist the array of electric guitars in the music store where we were working, and the possibilities, tonally. There was also classical music and jazz, Stravinsky and Coltrane. Let's say the ultimate goal was to find something like the first movement of Stravinsky's *Rite of Spring*, but free-form. We would take LSD and work around, say, a two-step programme; find a key, open up a room of possibilities and explore them. There was a thread to it all, and the idea was to find the thread, something heaven wants you to do. And when it happens, everyone in the audience knows. It's palpable. It's about peace, inner peace, the thread that winds through the music itself as an expression of the thread that winds through everything – but it isn't about politics.' Surrounded by his Shiva statues and Indian shawls, Weir reaches for a box of Skoal Bandit chewing tobacco, the hallmark of blue-collar working-class America, and inserts a pouch beneath his lower lip.

'You'll know which house belongs to the Native American,' come the directions in spring 2007 by phone. 'It's the one with the hulk of a car kinda propped up, auto parts piled up, and big dogs.' Gary Duncan – half Pawnee, quarter Cherokee, the rest mixed-Native – played guitar for Quicksilver Messenger Service along with John Cipollina, who died in 1989. Quicksilver were huge, playing triple bills with the Dead and Airplane; their suite 'The Fool' was among the most adventurous pieces, 'certainly the longest', says Duncan. His house is a Pandora's box of statues, plants and what he calls 'junk', just uphill from the gangland-gunland of Richmond, on the East Bay. 'It's dangerous around here and I've got the bullet wound to prove it', he says, showing his scar and telling a scary story about crossfire and ricochet.

Duncan is the salty dog of rock 'n' roll (literally: he has sailed the Atlantic) – white beard, pulling on his pipe, shotgun beside his bed. We sit on toolboxes and sip Guinness as he tells how it all began for him: born in Oklahoma, working the canneries of California's fruit-growing plains – Steinbeck for real. Then San Francisco, hooking up with David Freiberg and Cipollina to form Quicksilver. By which time, he says, 'the Beatles had screwed it up for any rock 'n' roll musician because they had taken rock music to its limits of innovation – there was no point in attempting anything like them, which is why the San Francisco sound had to be invented, entirely new. That was the time when if you knew the right address, you'd find the right people. It was in part about politics, the peace movement, being against the war and against "The Man", as we called the machine of power. But we didn't *talk* about all that, we played against it. What we had to say, we said with music.' But 'something went wrong. Then came the "Human Be-In" in January 1967,' he recalls. 'We saw more and more people. And I said to David [Freiberg], "This is the end of it." And it was. ABC News, NBC News, all the kids came for the Summer of Love, and all I saw were victims. Kids getting hooked on the wrong kind of drugs, people coming in to exploit it all.'

One major band, Steppenwolf, founding fathers of heavy rock, stood apart from all this, and for that I identified with them. Their roots were entirely different: the band's name was inspired, appropriately, by Hermann Hesse's novel, since 'the Wolf'

himself, John Kay, was born Joachim Fritz Krauledat in East
Germany. Kay's mother smuggled herself and her son to West
Germany in 1948 (of which more later); after ten years, they
emigrated to Canada.

Kay sang the anthem of the road rebels, 'Born To Be Wild',
written by Mars Bonfire – brother of Steppenwolf's drummer
Jerry Edmonton – and soundtrack to Peter Fonda's *Easy Rider*,
part romance, part nightmare. Although he howls the song,
Wolfman Kay turns out to speak with a firm courtesy and a
marked command of the English language, offering such counsel
as: 'I think you may be well pleased by spending a couple of
evenings with this book ...' He also wrote the rock oratorio
Monster, a scathing history of America, although 'I am an American
by choice.'

So, Kay's history with the American dream is fascinating. Born
Joachim Krauledat and smuggled to the Western side of the
Berlin Wall when he was four, he was taken by his stepfather
to 'America House' in Hannover. Here, he recalls, 'were things to
read and short films about America. I learned a lot about how
America looked, but also about some of its founders, the progressive thinking that went into the Declaration of Independence,
the Constitution. Then, a few years later – I was twelve, I guess
– I came across the Armed Forces Radio network, and Little
Richard. It was instant chicken-skin time, goose bumps head
to toe. I had no idea what he was singing, but it became an
adolescent daydream that some day I would be on the other side
of the ocean – and this music is something I would play.'

By the summer of 1958 the boy now renamed John Kay was a
'kid on the block' in Toronto, listening to radio from Buffalo,
New York, across the border. 'Because of my bad eyes, I couldn't
play team sports, I became inward, focused, banged around on
my guitar and found other people who were into music.' The
Yorkville quarter of Toronto was 'in its first few years of becoming

a scene, always something going on'. But something else was going on too: close to Kay's heart after he had watched the insurgencies against communism as a boy. Only, now, the uprising was the other way round, in the land of his dreams. 'There was a landlord in a flat we were renting and we sat there and realized we were both weeping as we watched: dogs and fire hoses in Birmingham, Alabama, attacking civil rights activists. This was not what I learned about America, this wasn't liberty and justice for all.'

Still, Kay then moved to Buffalo and 'the main library, where they let you take LPs home. I immersed myself in the folk music of this country, mountain music, Cajun music, prison chain-gang songs and Delta blues. They spoke to me on a body level, very strong emotions. I saw the great Son House,' he says, 'then I thought: Let's apply this sound to the here and now. To the civil rights movement, to what is happening in Vietnam. And the Wolf duly became part of all that.'

By 1968, Steppenwolf 'was out there on the road when America was literally exploding. The assassinations of Martin Luther King and Bobby Kennedy, the Chicago convention riot and the uprising against the war in Vietnam.' But 'I felt outside that whole flower power "trip" thing. Maybe ... because I'd grown up in Germany watching those newsreels, and that was my world.' Other things set Steppenwolf apart, including an insistence against easy answers: at the heart of the drug culture, here was Kay's protest, in 'The Pusher', whom Kay damns to hell. A song of which he says now: 'When I look at today's world of meth labs and tragic consequences – internal displacement in Colombia, the opium fields of Afghanistan, war in Mexico, and the havoc they wreak – I do think of 'The Pusher' as a justified statement. The hippie dream was too unrealistic and cut off for me,' he reflects. 'I needed to be connected to the world, and the political world.' And he adds, in his guttural but rounded tone: 'There just seemed to be too many serious things going on to be dancing around with flowers in the park.'

Kay's view is durable at a different level from that of the Summer of Love's other stars – certainly closer to my own feelings, then and now. What Kay stood and stands for lasts: with his German wife Jutta Maue, whom he met in Toronto back in the mid-1960s, Kay now runs the Maue Kay Foundation, which supports carefully chosen 'defenders' of environmentalist and human rights causes around the world, with a special project defending elephants from extinction. 'It's the thought that I can put a few ducats in the direction of achieving something, rather than concentrating on what has not been achieved, that keeps me from the abyss,' he confesses. 'The main reason the Wolf still plays is that doing so keeps the Maue Kay Foundation funded. I operate on the dictum of the young South African Aids victim, Nkosi Johnson: 'Do all you can, with what you have in the time you have in the place you are.'

And there was this: by the time I made his acquaintance, the daily news was of killing in Iraq, and 'Monster' had returned to the stages of America. 'Now we are fighting a war over there. /No matter who's the winner, /We can't pay the cost /'Cause there's a monster on the loose' – written in 1969, and now on the loose again in Babylon. 'That song,' says Kay, 'has grown to become even more apposite now than it was when I wrote it. And the more that war in Iraq drags on, the more the audiences respond. It says now what it said then: this war is insane, and there's no winning it. This is the turning wheel, history repeating itself, and that's why I repeat the song, at every gig, more intense each time. The Monster come around again, but we're come round again too, older, maybe a little wiser, singing that same song.'

In the event, the original Gong split up fairly acrimoniously, and carried on gathering and shedding a huge cast, while the only composer of music on all the 'Flying Teapot' trilogy, Tim Blake, went off to apply his pioneering work on synthesiser and theramin to solo projects. Blake, who moved to France during the 1970s, says that he 'listens mostly to classical music these days. The thing about music, war and peace,' he says, 'is that love-and-peace music usually ends up in war between the musicians.' Be that as it may, Britain had its own Haight Ashbury, and I grew up in it, where Hawkwind, the band which overlapped with Blake and Gong in the many fractious mutations of each, like a double helix through the British underground, played for free under the Westway flyover on Saturdays. Hawkwind also played each summer solstice dawn at Stonehenge, where the dancer Kris Tait (now married to the band's leader, Dave Brock) would have to 'go and find seven vestal virgins in the audience, but their boyfriends weren't too pleased,' she said. Police ended the Stonehenge ritual by attacking and evicting the pagan faithful at what became known as 'The Battle of the Beanfield' in 1985. Hawkwind's music connects the inner city to the wilds, the ancients to sci-fi technology; it's 'peace music' with both severity and humour. They're impossible to pigeon-hole; as punk, metal, dance and trance come and go, all pay tribute to the enduring Hawkwind, because Hawkwind impacted on them all – thereby rendering the term 'genre' meaningless to their own music, and hence the need for a 'genre' of their own: space rock.

The approach to intergalactic headquarters, in 2009, runs along narrow Devon lanes, under the bridge of a long-closed railway and through gates with signs warning 'Our Dogs Bite'. There's a totem pole in the garden, and a studio like Dr Who's Tardis – apparently a small shed, but an electronic wonderland within – banked up with equipment and posters for concerts spanning decades. This is the epicentre of the band that became a tribal gathering, the tribe that became a British institution. The continuity and essence of Hawkwind rest with the band's founder and sole original member from 1969, Dave Brock, who quells his barking dogs at the last gate – long hair flowing from beneath a straw hat, and puckish smile that belies his seventy-five years. 'We always kept that down-to-earthness,' he says, 'that's what kept us sane and in touch with our people. Eating in cafés, kind of thing, so we never got big-headed.'

It began on Eel Pie Island in the Thames outside London, where Brock, born in 1941, began busking. He was influenced by blues, but working with other forces too: visiting Holland, investigating psychedelic visual effects and electronic experiments prevalent on the continent. So that by the time it came to that debut gig as Group X, Hawkwind had fused blues and folk, with very British symphonic rock pioneered by Pink Floyd and, 'using LSD, tape loops, colours and lights', a driving electronic pulse.

The band became the beacon of the 'benefit circuit', playing free for Friends of the Earth, the anarchist White Panthers, striking miners – so much so that Brock would tire of band members forever promising his time: 'We had to do *something* for money, dammit.' And they did: Brock and bass player Lemmy Kilmister – who later departed to found Motörhead – wrote 'Silver Machine', among the most played hits of all time. One crusade, against heroin, including a concert featuring Britain's wartime darling Vera Lynn, led to 'all kinds of things we don't talk about,' says Brock, 'like getting shot at and making enemies' among motorcycle gangs and drug dealers. But also winning very important friends, 'including my mum and dad, by including Vera Lynn, and that meant a lot to me. The Second World War was my childhood.' Hawkwind now underwrites a militant seafaring, anti-whaling and environmental organization, Sea Shepherd.

But what is Hawkwind's music, and why? 'It's as complicated as you want it to be,' says Brock, as we embark on a tour of the effects in his Tardis studio, 'and musically rather more than meets the eye.' The band is about live performance above all, the studio a place to prepare for the stage act. I've seen them scores of times: at Stonehenge, at the Astoria in London for an annual winter solstice event until the historic theatre was demolished, at their own festivals around midsummer, and at Eastertide when tepees are erected in bitter cold above the sea, as the tribe converges on Seaton in Devon for the annual 'Hawkeaster'. 'Ultimately, it's optimistic music,' says Brock. 'We do believe in some kind of deliverance for our flawed, fucked-up species. We believe in nature, and a duty of care for the planet and its creatures, however goofy that may sound.' 'Hopefully with a sense of humour,' adds the wizard on theremin and synthesiser, Tim Blake, formerly – unsurprisingly – of Gong. But then Brock the sci-fi reader smiles: 'Mind you, forget the idea that aliens are going to arrive from some other planet and rescue us – they're not!'

'For me, the music is the politics and the politics is the music,' says Richard Chadwick, drummer and longest-standing member apart from Brock. 'Which means not becoming "stars", but playing music that could only be Hawkwind. We stay on the edge, create a sound which is our own, so we survive with decency. I've seen Dave turn down opportunities time and time again, this supergroup or that.' 'They wanted me to get back together,' says Brock, 'with Lemmy and Paul Kantner, but I thought: Oh Christ, please no. What the fuck would I want to do that for? I've got strawberries to look after here, and seven puppies.'

Joe Boyd, who produced and mixed Bob Dylan's first electric set at Newport, has seen the hopes of the peace movement and its music ebb and flow. Now, in January 2017, he stands behind the mixing desk of a studio in Manor House, North London, at which also sits his German wife Andrea, perfecting an album Mr and Mrs Boyd recorded in Albania. It is rich music, passionately sung, gypsy chromatics, the timbre melancholy, instrumentation dense. 'It's about a young boy watching a girl,' explains Andrea, 'growing prettier and prettier than everything else around him – then he notices: "How big your tits have become!"'

Boyd's expression suggests a coyote listening out for some far-distant sound; even his eyes seem tuned. This is the man who pioneered recording techniques from eight tracks on one-inch tape to twenty-four on two-inch tape, then realized that the optimum sound needed sixteen tracks on two-inch tape; the man who champions vinyl over anything digital, because digital 'hurts my ears after a while, my head gets tired; it's the difference between metal and wood'.

The track recorded in Tirana comes to an end. 'The instrumentation is kind of what I had in mind,' he judges, 'but the voices are a little too roomy, a little much in the room, especially the upper voice; it needs to come down towards the other, and they both need to go back a short distance . . .' Boyd takes time out to think back on that day plugging Dylan into an amplifier, and what we've termed 'peace music', 'hippie music'. He should know: he tells a wonderful story about how a band he was introduced to agreed to play a benefit gig for the alternative 'free school' at which he was working in Notting Hill. He recorded a demo tape for the head of Elektra Records in London, for whom he worked. But 'not only did he not sign them,' says Boyd, 'he fired me for spending too much time looking for bands and not marketing the ones we already had'. The group was Pink Floyd.

Boyd had begun as assistant to Elektra's producer in the USA, Paul Rothchild, initially promoting Big Joe Williams and Muddy Waters. In his early twenties, Boyd was travelling across Europe with Coleman Hawkins and Roland Kirk. Back in the USA, he worked the Newport Jazz and Folk Festivals, the latter with Pete Seeger and Alan Lomax, archivist of folk. At the 1965 festival, Boyd saw Lomax 'scowling' as he hauled amplifiers onto the stage for the Butterfield Blues Band; that was the Saturday, and on the Sunday, the hitherto troubadour Bob Dylan plugged in his guitar for the first time – Lomax and Seeger were 'furious', recalls Boyd. In the crowd, 'some loved it, some hated it, most were amazed, astonished and energized by it', he later wrote.

Boyd made his home in London, where he founded the UFO Club, with Pink Floyd as resident band until they 'outgrew' it. After which, he signed Hendrix and the Who to Polydor, before founding his own record label and becoming the driving force behind Fairport Convention and others. But there's a surprise, in conversation these decades later. 'I look back at it as a tragedy, a story that is rather sad,' he says. I'm amazed, please explain. 'In a way,' he begins, 'the musical accompaniment to the peace movements of the 1960s, the connection of the whole thing to music, began with "We Shall Overcome" in 1959, with Guy Carawan at the Highlander folk school in the South – which became Pete Seeger's song quick enough, soundtrack to the civil rights movement. Seeger's was a communist vision, using music for the purposes of equality, peace and unity; it was something to be done together, even in the concert hall, but ideally round the campfire – to stiffen the spine – and it works. I don't think that what ensued during the 1960s would have made the difference it did without that song, and the likes which followed it.'

But 'then along comes Dylan, "Blowin' In The Wind", "Masters Of War". A kid, a genius, hoisting a sail that had already got wind in it, and he gave it a push. Here were the seeds of a disconnect that culminated at Newport in 1965. Dylan always took the view that the protest movement wasn't necessarily his fight. He dovetailed into it, wrote some great songs, but he was a careerist, unapologetically so. He always disappointed people who wanted him to be "one of us", and still does. And when the palette changed, and hard rock became the sound of the day,

Dylan wanted to broaden his own, write different stuff, sing it in a different way.

'So there he was, with half the Butterfield Blues Band, playing rock and roll. It was a defining moment: Pete Seeger left in the middle of Dylan's set, he was appalled. I met him later in New Orleans and he said what bothered him were electric guitars, the way the texture of the sound changed the dynamic of what was happening. Dylan, who had until now been playing *with* the audience, was now playing at it; Seeger felt that the music was no longer participatory. And I think it's right to see that night as the beginning of the rock era,' says Boyd. 'It changed everything. Until then, you'd had protest folk, and pop songs about boy meets girl. Suddenly, there's this "third rail". You can sing about anything, about "Maggie's Farm", a parallel politics which is personal, songs about psyche and drugs – it turns into a personal rebellion. That's one thing – then there's the texture, the disconnect.'

What 'disconnect'?

A single story haunts Joe Boyd. 'It's in *Dispatches*, by Michael Herr, his book about Vietnam. There's a story about a pilot who has been bombing and strafing the Vietcong, and he's on his way back and has a few bullets left, and he sees a farmer with his oxen, strafes and kills them too – why not use up the payload? But here's the thing: while he's doing this, he's listening to Dylan and Hendrix. I've . . . come to think that Pete Seeger was right. It's about texture. If the texture is memorable and singable-together, it can help save the world. Maybe. But if the texture is head-banging and thumping, it can be played as background to killing a farmer and his oxen, even if the words are about saving the world. And in that instance, maybe the music loses its ability to have that function – again, maybe. When you play an electric guitar, you emit a power charge. Most of the alienation inherent in that sound is between the performer and what you do, the

Michael Herr moment. You can be singing whatever you want, it doesn't matter. It's a good soundtrack to strafing a farmer.'

Boyd's observation is borne out by the systematic use – or is it abuse? – of rock music by the American military since Vietnam. Heavy rock was deployed as a means of bombarding Panamanian drug-lord ruler Manuel Noriega into submission on Christmas Day, 1989. And by way of a horrific twist to Boyd's theme, music by Metallica and Queen was used at high volume to accompany the torture of inmates at the Guantánamo Bay internment complex, as was – to make his point with bitter irony – even a song by the left-wing anti-war band Rage Against the Machine. Songs including Nancy Sinatra's 'These Boots Are Made For Walkin'' were part of American troops' torture routine at the Abu-Ghraib jail in Iraq.

Boyd pleads that he is not *against* heavy beat, but 'I'm coming round to a view which is Seeger-like ... that hard rock and electronic beats in clubs bring a coarseness to our urban lives, and even rural lives. There's something about being in a pounding club or listening to heavy music on a stage that may be easy to dance to or punch the air, but it coarsens our lives, whereas singing along, or singing together, does make people nicer to each other.

'One has to resist being a musical version of King Canute; sometimes what Dylan did to his songs in 1965 made the music better, but it did pull him away from something that started in the late 1950s, which was warmer, more human, communitarian and convivial. If you ask me what does music do in the real world, that's how I see it, during the arc from that time. It shows that somehow, with the application of electric music and harder and harder materials in the performance of music, you have a reduction of humanity ... I would say that a lot of what you see in the coarseness of modern life is not unconnected to music ... When you reduce the differences between various forms of music, and put it into an amplifier or digital box, you do a similar thing to the audience: you make it a little harsher, less personal.' He uses a phrase in his memoir *White Bicycles*, during discussion of Alan Lomax: 'tainted by Mammon'.[2]

This is, says Boyd, 'the argument which fits into my own trajectory', as he roams the planet researching and recording 'World Music'. He has already talked about music that 'comes from the earth'; his passion now is for 'traditional music that belongs to a people'. But there is something else happening here, to do with past and future. Boyd puts it this way: 'For middle-class people who love World Music, the ideal holiday is to go somewhere unspoiled where Grandma cooks fish and there's some music. But now a KFC has opened in town, and that's where the young people want to go, to hell with Grandma's fish. We are people who grew up in the 1960s, and now with Trump and Brexit, and the fact we know we are destroying the planet, we take a look at the future and we don't like it. But these young people do like it: the past is a place where people were poor, and the future offers the possibility that they might not be.'

It's the same in music. Boyd tells of a band he saw in Ghana 'playing traditional music, a high-life band, wonderful. But they weren't just booed off, they were thrown off stage. And on comes a Ghanaian hip-hop guy with a ghastly Casio drum machine, and I was talking to a seventeen-year-old who told me: "I hate tradition. What did tradition ever do for me? I love the sound of a Casio, I love how cheap and tinny it sounds."' I wonder if there'd been a similar exchange at Newport in 1965, though it's unlikely anyone would have thrown Pete Seeger off stage.

I heard Seeger play three times and met him twice. The first concert was at a church on Clinton Street in Brooklyn during 1984; he had just reached retirement age, but it was not a nostalgic evening: the support act was a young, edgy African-American duo called Serious Bizness, singing about race and food stamps.

Seeger was born in New York in 1919 with red genes and folk music in his DNA. His father, Charles Louis, was a musicologist and a communist. With Aaron Copland he formed the Composers' Collective, and took Copland to meet coalminers in West Virginia – then red, now Trump, heartland – where folk and contemporary 'classical' musicians were taking up labour and gospel songs sung by strikers – thereby inspiring Copland's *Fanfare for the Common Man*.

Young Pete won a scholarship to Harvard, but dropped out. He tried to make it as a newspaper reporter, but as a member of the Young Communist League could not find a job. Then in 1940, he met two people who would change his life: Alan Lomax and Woodrow 'Woody' Guthrie. Lomax wanted Seeger to transcribe a collection of protest songs for a book, *Hard Hitting Songs for Hard-Hit People*, with notes by Guthrie (it wouldn't find a publisher for twenty-seven years). Then Guthrie, seven years Seeger's senior, took his friend to another world, Oklahoma, and they hit the road and the radio stations. Seeger recalled, when I met him later, how 'I puzzled Woody, because I didn't drink, smoke or chase girls'.

A joint appearance on CBS in 1942 would provoke the headline 'COMMIES TRY TO TAKE OVER THE AIRWAVES': it was the last time Woody Guthrie was allowed to broadcast. Seeger toured the Pacific front during the Second World War, serenading the wounded; and upon demobilization, New York's 'subway circuit'. He founded the Weavers, who came under investigation by the House Un-American Activities Committee and were blacklisted. Seeger refused to testify to the committee and was sentenced to ten years' imprisonment. He served one of them and was released on appeal. By the time of 'We Shall Overcome' at Carnegie Hall in 1963, his time had come.

In 1994, Seeger turned seventy-five; there was a round of tributes, including a National Medal of Arts presented at the Kennedy Center in Washington. Bill Clinton's America had grappled with sufficient demons to make yesterday's troublemakers today's national heroes, an irony not lost on Seeger: 'The whole situation is hilarious,' he said. 'I've usually come down to Washington to picket the White House and now I'm coming to get a medal! I'll have to be careful not to shoot my mouth off.'

Seeger was telling me this four years later, when he played another night at Carnegie Hall to mark the fiftieth birthday of Folkways Records, a Lomax creation of May Day 1948 at the insistence of Albert Einstein. Now, he recalled days when 'Woody and I were goin' around singing to striking oilfield workers'; he called himself 'still a socialist' just as 'bombs still come down and kill innocent women and children'. But, he thought, 'It's going to happen on a local scale, chipping little cracks in the system.' He explained how he had 'gone green' – long before environmentalism became mainstream. Seeger had formed the non-profit Hudson River Sloop Clearwater organization, launching a replica seventeenth-century sloop of that name as a campaigning vehicle for cleaning the Hudson in particular and the planet in general. 'I think it's the next great cause – not so much the material issues of the twentieth century, but the relationship between us and our wider environment,' he said with prescience, 'and in real life, that means your immediate environment.' The project increasingly absorbed him, so that when we met a second time, in 2009, it was all that mattered.

That year, the summer rain poured down, sadly, on the Corn Festival of folk music – and, well, the corn – at the Hudson riverside town of Beacon. Seeger, for all his frailty, was chopping wood. I think I wanted to talk about 'bombs still raining down', about Woody, about Dylan plugging in his guitar, about Iraq – as well as the climate crisis that now vindicated him. But Seeger wanted to talk about the ingenuity of his team in devising the right kind of mesh to create swimming pools in the now cleaner Hudson. And a great deal about how to properly cook corn. 'I don't think people can think big,' he said.

I did not want to think him right, but maybe he is.

I spent a day with Michael Herr back in 2000, on a garden bench at his home in Upstate New York. In that book *Dispatches*, published in 1977, Herr invented a new way of writing about war. As a war reporter myself by then, I visited him rather like a student of the cello would approach Mstislav Rostropovich. Herr's reporting was the first to bring rock and roll firmly into the narrative of war. In one section he writes:

> *There was no way of stopping their fire, no room to send in a flanking party, so gunships were called and we crouched behind the wall and waited. There was a lot of fire coming from the trees . . . when I suddenly heard an electric guitar shooting right up in my ear and a mean, rapturous black voice singing, coaxing . . . I turned to see a grinning black corporal hunched over a cassette recorder. 'Might's well,' he said. 'We ain' going nowhere till them gunships come' . . . That's the story of the first time I heard Jimi Hendrix.*

Michael Herr died in June 2016, and I wish he was alive so that I could put Joe Boyd's point directly. But I did ask him about rock and roll at war. 'It kind of deprived me of the ability to believe in what was called the "anti-war" thing back home,' he replied, 'the fact that everyone over there was listening to it. War separated me from rock culture. You saw my music down there in the office: it's classical, and if it's not classical, it's jazz. Rock music was there in the war, same as it was back home; the guys liked it before going out and killing people, same as peaceniks on the vigils in Washington. That's the bit that freaked me out.

Sometimes they'd get themselves into gear to kill people by listening to rock and roll. It belonged in the war, just as much as the "anti-war" thing.'

Herr worked in a bat cave, a tiny room in a spacious house amid rolling hills, piled with music and books. Wagner, Mozart, Coltrane and Monteverdi climbing one wall, Kierkegaard, Cicero, Nietzsche and Russian classics opposite. 'And you know what?' said Herr with a grin, 'I could throw it all away tomorrow and not notice. I am cleaning it all out. Cleaning everything out.' But he was not only cleaning out his music; by the time we met, he said: 'I've cleaned all *that* out also. People keep asking me to go and write about war. I say: "Haven't you read my fucking book? What the fuck would I want to go and do that for?" Publishers send me books about Vietnam; I wish they'd stop.' (I had recently left Bosnia, and I agreed entirely, determined never to return. Later I did a volte-face and could not keep away; now I'm back in accord with Herr. This shit changes our lives, not in a good way.)

Why, Michael Herr, are you not crazy? He stared out across the lawn and answered with a naked honesty that was almost scary: 'I did go crazy. The problem with Vietnam is that if your body came back, your mind came back too. Within eighteen months I was on the edge of a major breakdown. Real despair for three or four years; deep paralysis. I didn't see anybody because I didn't want anybody to see me. Then I decided to look the other way and went back to my book.' I kept those words close, as a warning.

In 2012 Bruce Springsteen played in Hyde Park, and again five days later in Dublin. The tour was to promote the only album made by a star of Springsteen's standing in reaction to the economic carnage wrought by the financial crash of four years earlier: *Wrecking Ball*, a magnificent achievement, a tirade. For the London concert, Springsteen was joined by Tom Morello of Rage Against the Machine for a duly enraged account of Springsteen's tribute to Steinbeck, 'The Ghost Of Tom Joad'. Another song, 'Death To My Home Town', lambasted the banks' 'robber barons' who destroyed communities without a cannonball being fired. In London, I heard these superb songs and more like them standing behind an outing of lads, rocking out and punching the air with their plastic glasses of lager, all wearing the same branded anoraks announcing 'Aberdeen Private Wealth Management'.

'The genius of capitalism,' says Joe Boyd, 'is its ability to co-opt anything. Dylan, Hendrix, anything. That is what it did, and has done, to 1960s rock and roll, and most of that has to do with texture', beginning with Dylan and 'confirmed with the "Michael Herr moment" . . . Look, I'm not against rock and roll. I produced that sound for Dylan, I was rooting for Dylan, I brought Pink Floyd to my UFO Club and rooted for them and Syd Barrett [founder member], I was influenced by the avant-garde ideas. We were not especially political, but . . . we were certainly counter-cultural. So bless them all – bravo Roger Waters for reviving *The Wall*.

'But there he was, with Dylan and the Stones, playing near Palm Springs at the Desert Trip festival, for all those hedge-fund managers paying $10,000 a ticket so they could punch the air – "Hey Roger, cool, man!" – my idea of a nightmare. It's a visceral thing. Who cares what was nobly intended by the author of the music? That's why I call it a tragedy. Because I care, because I was there, in the thick of it.'

7" Single: Rock Against Racism

I got my first proper job in 1978, as researcher for a music impresario called Tony Wilson who ran a company called Factory Records and a venue, the Hacienda, in Manchester. The subject of a film called *24 Hour Party People*, Tony created and managed Joy Division among others, while my work involved missing out on all this. Wilson was also a presenter on Granada TV's nightly local news programme *Granada Reports*, covering events of the day, and my job was to set up filmed stories for Tony to report on. Many nights, after the show had aired, he would invite me to the Hacienda to hear one of his big names or recent discoveries, and I would have to remind him that my day began at 5 a.m. in Liverpool, ahead of the rush hour into Manchester, to read the papers in time for the 9 a.m. editorial meeting. I was certainly not a twenty-four-hour party person, more interested anyway in a different scene, Rock Against Racism.

My friends, my brother Tom and I were never really part of the 'hippie' thing. In the early 1970s we formed a proto-punk group called the Keith Bender Band (after the lead guitarist's name, me on vocals) and played local fetes and parties. I wrote and sang a high-octane number about a 'greasy-fingered acne floozy' called 'Saveloy Suzie, fish bar queen / From Shepherds Bush roundabout to Willesden Green', name-checking local haunts and Queens Park Rangers football club – 'Saveloy Suzie, *manger à la mode* / And they don't 'arf pile on the ketchup down on Latimer Road' – kind of thing. We wore lab coats and I think we were the first group to spit into the audience (1974, before the Sex Pistols or the Clash). And on Christmas Eve 1978, Tom and I were enjoying our traditional drink along Ladbroke Grove when a rumour went round the pub: anyone prepared to miss Christmas lunch next day could hear the Clash before an 'invited' audience (ergo, anyone in the right boozer at the right time).

The Clash – from roots around here – had become one of the biggest bands in the world; we proffered apologies to Mum and made our way to Acklam Hall, off Portobello Road. And there they were: at full tilt in a tiny space to an audience of about 150, a warm-up for what the band called its '16 Tons Tour' of the world. It lasted two loud hours, after which – back in time for mince pies.

The Clash were among the groups emerging from a significant political time in British music. Bob Marley had burst onto the scene and across the planet; spellbound, I saw him twice – unforgettably – at the Lyceum Theatre and Hammersmith Odeon. Marley's colossal presence and driving influence were everywhere, not least in fuelling Rock Against Racism – RAR – which was just that, initially: a retort by musicians to remarks made by Eric Clapton and David Bowie. 'Vote for Enoch Powell!' urged Clapton during August 1976 from a stage in the West Midlands; 'Stop Britain from becoming a black colony!' Bowie had a year earlier proclaimed. 'I believe very strongly in fascism ... Adolf Hitler was one of the first rock stars ... You've got to have an extreme right-wing front come up and sweep everything off its feet and tidy everything up.'

The response was music, as explained by a fanzine published on Mayday 1977 called *Temporary Hoarding*. 'We want rebel music,' it demanded. 'Crisis Music that knows who the real enemy is. Rock Against Racism.' The publication was for circulation at the Roundhouse in London but quickly spread through streets and sweaty pubs and clubs throughout the land. Within months, the ratchet would turn and the temperature rise on both sides of an already raging street war. The 1976 Notting Hill carnival ended in a riot, young blacks chanting 'Soweto, Soweto' as they claimed vengeance against the police; the National Front won significant success at local elections in 1977 – there had been violent demonstrations and counter-demonstrations between the NF and anti-fascist groups. Then, that summer, came the battle royal, after the NF announced a march through the largely immigrant area of Lewisham in London. We beat them back that day with rocks and reckless courage – student politicos, RAR fans, the local black population and much of the local white one.

Thus, the political wing of Rock Against Racism was born: the Anti-Nazi League, initiated by the hard left but with the intention of something broader. The other response was the movement that culminated in Rock Against Racism's 'carnival' in London during April 1978, attended by tens of thousands and headlined by the Clash and Steel Pulse, a reggae band from the Handsworth ghetto in Birmingham. There followed other RAR carnivals in Manchester and Cardiff. RAR spawned a boom in what would be called 'two-tone' music: racially mixed bands playing ska, adapted not from the emergent heavy reggae sound-systems with their ponderous unrelenting beat, but from the light-footed, upbeat tempo of late-1950s Jamaican music. The originals came back into vogue: Toots and the Maytals toured Britain, then the Heptones – like blues masters in the 1960s, to their own disbelief – inspiring black and white alike to imitate their rock-steady beat, but powered by the voltage of the Clash.

Among them were Special AKA from Coventry, whose founder Jerry Dammers organized a huge music rally at Wembley demanding the release of the jailed South African Nelson Mandela. There was UB40 from Birmingham, named after an unemployment benefit form, most daring for its song entitled 'Burden of Shame' – a bold reference to the British passport.

Also from Brum were the Beat, whose music hopped like a cat on a hot tin roof. This was a time of grungy parties in dank rented houses, of pouring the dregs of bad red wine into used polystyrene cups – and it was the Beat that got everyone dancing, or staggering about. The band had on saxophone a Jamaican veteran called Saxa and a rapper called Rankin' Roger; the lead singer was a thoughtful white Brummie, one Dave Wakeling, with whom I spent time walking through the ruins, literally, of industrial Britain, staking out locations.

'It's the destruction of the country my father thought he was building at the end of World War II,' said Wakeling as we stood in what was once a tool-making factory, now a shell. 'He lived through the dream of the Welfare State, but what we're living through now is the end of industry, and of all that. I think it's connected with the end of empire – self-destructive madness, and sadness. The music is part escape from it, part comment on it. The Beat takes the sound from one corner of that empire, the Caribbean, from where Jamaicans came to play it here in Birmingham, so we grew up with it. Now we're doing it together, black and white – and that's something important to me in and of itself.'

7" Single: Diamonds and Rust: Joan Baez and Bob Dylan

In 1987, Joan Baez and I sat opposite one another drinking coffee in a suite in London where she was staying. I had always adored her, seen her at the Isle of Wight, and had met her, drop-jawed, while working for the Quaker draft-resistance centre in Chicago in 1971, as an usher for a benefit concert she gave. Now, sixteen years later, was a good moment to talk. This was now the time of cruise missiles in Europe and America's murderous 'dirty wars' in Central America. Baez had turned her attention to these: to tens of thousands disappeared in Chile and disappearing in Argentina, and massacres of indigenous peoples in Guatemala and of eight hundred civilians at El Mozote, El Salvador, in 1981. In the Place de la Concorde in Paris, she had sung to a rally of 120,000, 'dedicated to non-violent struggle'. 'It gave me the feeling,' she said, 'that sometimes the courage can be as contagious as the fear.'

'All this,' she continued, over coffee, 'just makes me especially grateful that I can still fill a reasonable-sized hall with a relatively simple message of peace.' Yet Baez berated what she called 'the nostalgia I see rampant for the 1960s. It won't come back as it was, and neither will I. I don't miss those times, and I don't go to "'60s parties".' She cites an example – 'a "Twenty Years After Avalon [Ballroom]" show: Mick Jagger and stuff. And I thought: Where was I during all this? I was in jail. My husband was in jail. And except for the intensity, which we lack now, I don't have nostalgia for the detail of what went on in those years, and my general grimness. Now is fascinating, now is important.'

Baez called the 1980s 'the meantime years'. Her radical pacifism was, it seemed, sitting out a siege by what she called 'Ramboism'. 'I think that what we have to keep doing in the meantime years can be anything from organizing on a visible scale to simply keeping sane, especially if one lives in the States under a constantly heartless [Reagan] administration. Just keep any values at all against what people tell you to believe . . . how we have conducted ourselves during these times will determine the future of the next movement, if there is one. It won't come out of a vacuum. It will be built on the structures that people manage to hold together, and even build a little during these times.'

As between music and the cause, Baez takes the cause, she says. 'If I had to choose between a room full of people singing songs and jamming, and another where there's a meeting of the Mothers of the Disappeared, I'll choose the Mothers of the Disappeared.' For all her love of jewellery and skirmishes with luxury, Baez has shed the profits of her career with a willingness that contrasts with many at that level. Most of the money goes to Humanitas International, her own creation, the Californian offshoot of Amnesty International. It concerns what she describes as 'the constant business of getting people to see with both eyes that oppression is oppression, wherever it is'.

In 1979, after years of protest against America's war, Humanitas received and sponsored a group of Vietnamese 'boat people' fleeing the victorious Vietcong – and Baez found herself derided by erstwhile supporters. 'People from the Left thought I'd betrayed them. I just replied that there were hundreds of thousands of political prisoners in Vietnam, and as many more in flight as refugees. A refugee is a refugee, whatever.' Humanitas worked with the Greens in Germany and for political prisoners in Latin America and Eastern Europe, 'wherever possible fusing a human rights issue with disarmament'. In the UK, it was involved in the Greenham Common peace camp against cruise missiles, and in Ireland with Women for Peace.

Three decades after our meeting, the day of the women's march against Trump, she said: 'There's not enough [songs] right now. There needs to be more. It's terribly important, because that's what keeps the spirit . . . The problem right now is we have no anthem, we have to keep redoing "Blowin' In The Wind" and "We Shall Overcome" forever. We need new things, we need fresh songs.'

If only it had been that straightforward for Joan Baez herself. She confided that she had been in analysis for twenty years, 'building up to combat that craziness, building up an adult within me which was strong enough to reason with that fear of disappearance, and death'. For her *Desert Island Discs*, she said, she'd include Wagner's *Tristan und Isolde*, 'so I'd have years to figure it out, particularly the last movement [Isolde's 'Love-death'], and die happy. Listen, the way I've conducted my life, I've got to find a link between love – and beauty – and death.' She was disarmingly clear about saint and queen: 'I suppose I would have fewer demons if I worked out a relationship between these elements. Demons come from guilt and fear mostly, and the guilt around being "Queenie" is always giving me problems, so then over into the other camp.' It was a relief for her to find out that even Martin Luther King got drunk and had a woman in his room one night when they were on the campaign trail together.

'It kind of cleared the air, it meant that we could go on in that way without having to be saints.'

Baez was raised a Quaker, and was in the 1980s as religious as ever. But, she said, 'it's a curious relationship with God'. She derives from a religious ancestry: 'Look, there were two grandfathers who were ministers, and there were ministers beyond that – all varieties of churches in Spain and Mexico. On my father's side, Catholics, on my mother's the Victorians – she was always being told by her mother: "You're a worthless human being and sex is wicked" – so thanks for the legacy everybody!' She tells me how Odetta and Big Bill Broonzy were her first inspirations, about being taken to a Boston coffee-shop folk concert by her father, and getting hooked, playing her first gigs for $10 a turn. There was a first performance at Newport in 1959 – at which 'the audience went crazy, I was surprised' – and an audition with Vanguard Records in a damp hall otherwise used for bingo, for whom she first sang not a protest song but the Scottish folk ballad 'Mary Hamilton' – it has remained in her repertoire ever since.

Queen Joan Baez sometimes comes across as a leaf content to blow around on the breeze, but zephyrs can become gales, and the most forceful of those was, famously, Dylan. Her autobiography, *And a Voice to Sing With*, affords some insight into this 'royal marriage' on the New York folk scene, into Dylan's behaviour – sometimes ludicrous, sometimes callous, sometimes brilliant and always self-indulgent – and into Baez's clinging on regardless. Dylan two-times her, refuses to let her on stage, drinks, shrugs and shambles through his enigmatic genius haze. There's a bizarre scene of Dylan, hopelessly drunk, attempting to cut his wrist with a filthy blade so he and Joan can swear blood brother-sisterhood. Baez exchanges the blade for a clean one, and goes along with it. The pair related to the 'movement' differently, from the beginning. 'He didn't do what he wrote about – I did what he wrote about, after a fashion,' she says. 'I was politically active, he wasn't. But I was not writing songs in the early days, and he was – and to have it in song was miraculous.'

In the book, she's harsh on Dylan, in conversation more reflective. 'Don't you think that if someone is just out of reach, you keep grabbing for them? Even the most stable person has that defect, even without whatever intricacies I had in my nature. You think: *Damn*, that's the one who got away. I suppose I'd say now: "It's not that I was in love with you, it's just that nobody had ever been able to kick me around like this." Basically, I just kept wanting to go back, and wanting to stand up and prove that I was – I don't know quite what – as good as, as big as. Because it certainly wasn't any fun being there. But that's what couples are like, you just share and shred the thing to death, and when you look at it, there's nothing that makes you want to be in the room with that person. It's just that you can't bear having them walk out of the room first.'

It was for Dylan that Joan Baez wrote her best and most bitter love song, 'Diamonds And Rust'.

Along with diamond Joan's, Dylan's rusty voice was for me, as for so many, an entwinement of poetry with music that expressed and expresses ideas about ourselves and the world. Those records I bought after first hearing Dylan – *Bringing It All Back Home*, *Highway 61*, *Blonde on Blonde* and *John Wesley Harding* – have accompanied me through the half-century since. When I fell in love, I'd send them as gifts – an odd choice on reflection, because they tend to contain the end of an affair as well as its lovestruck beginning.

As Boyd and Baez attest, Dylan was politically nonplussed. Yet he had written the greatest song-poem of them all against the military machine, 'Masters Of War', the prayer for peace, 'Blowin' In The Wind', and the anthem that linked the victims of war with the poets and prisoners: 'Chimes Of Freedom'. He wrote the song about nuclear Armageddon that hung over our childhoods, 'A Hard Rain's A-Gonna Fall' – sung by Patti Smith in lieu of his arrogant non-appearance to accept the Nobel Prize for Literature, fifty-four years after it was written. Dylan's a bit like the Bible and Shakespeare, inasmuch as for everything there is a season: he could be merciless ('Like A Rolling Stone', 'Positively 4th Street'), downright funny ('Leopardskin Pill-Box Hat'), desolate ('Just Like Tom Thumb's Blues'), seductive ('Lay Lady Lay'), apocalyptic ('When The Ship Comes In'), spiritual ('I Dreamed I Saw St. Augustine'), surreal ('The Ballad Of Frankie Lee And Judas Priest'). Or epic, as in the best *tour d'horizon* of the world we live in ever written: devastating 'Desolation Row'. There's no 'owning' Bob Dylan.

By 1987 I'd seen him play a number of times, and he returned to London not to sing but to promote an awful film called *Hearts of Fire*, alongside Rupert Everett and Fiona Flanagan. Aware of my enthusiasm, the news editor at the *Guardian*, Paul Johnson, kindly sent me along to cover a press conference with Dylan and the insipid Flanagan, during which a pompous journalist from the *Sunday Times* challenged the bard to come clean about what interested him. 'I got a monkey-wrench collection in my garage back home, and I'm mighty interested in that,' came the reply.

Moments later, the air was filled with a screech of electronic feedback – Dylan had taken off the microphone clipped to his shirt and was dismantling it. Afterwards there was a photo-call, Dylan slouched against a wall with the Thames as backdrop, Fiona pouting. A cleared zone of flagstones separated them from the assembled press, across which I now ran, staving off the security guards. I just happened to have a felt pen and my copy of *Bringing It All Back Home* with me, and duly asked Mr Zimmerman to sign it. There was a squint from behind the sunglasses, and Dylan spluttered: 'This is supposed to be for journalists.' 'I *am* a journalist,' I replied. 'You don't look like a journalist,' mumbled Dylan, scribbling 'Bob' across my album cover. It ranks among the highest compliments I've ever been paid.

In April 1989 I found myself singing 'Blowin' In The Wind' to a crowd of 250,000 people in Hong Kong. Yes, there was a rally there in protest against the massacre in Tiananmen Square. The speeches and traditional music were starting to bore the crowds, and I said to one of the organizers: 'This needs some Bob Dylan.' 'We don't know any, do you?' he replied. Next I knew, someone had shoved a guitar into my hand and was pushing me up towards the stage, giving me a view across a sea of faces and a papier-mâché Statue of Liberty staring north towards Beijing. I took a deep breath and did all I could to remember the words, in concert! – and for an audience of a size I'd never had before for anything, nor since, nor will I again – so thank you, Bob.

7" Single: Dvořák in Iowa

In 1988, I won a fellowship to work on the *Washington Post*, which dispatched me to write a series of articles on a drought in the Midwest – visiting farms and Lakota Native land on which it had not rained in years. The trail, through locust clouds and across distances that film directors measure in telegraph poles, brought me to Bob Dylan's birthplace – Hibbing, Minnesota – and within tantalizing distance of another fountainhead in the history of American music: Spillville, Iowa. Not many people detour to Spillville – and if they do, it's for the same reason I did: this was where Antonín Dvořák spent the idyllic summer of 1893 and wrote what was, in its way, the hinge between ancient and modern American music.

Spillville, settled by Czechs in 1854, is tucked away in the northeast of Iowa, where the plains, flat as a snooker table, give way to undulating hills reminiscent of the land the newcomers had left behind in Bohemia. 'It is a completely Czech village,' Dvořák enthused. He had been in New York, working on his famous 'New World' Symphony (No. 9 in E Minor), when he heard of this remote community from Josef Kovařík, a friend whose hometown it was. Here, in the early morning hours, Dvořák would take a pail of beer down to the Turkey River and, while making his way through it, score the sounds he heard around him and from which he composed his 'American' String Quartet No. 12 in F Major. To call this piece a seminal work of American classical music is a subjective and outrageous claim, not least because it overrides the question 'What does *classical* mean?' – especially in relation to Native American song and flute music. But that is precisely the point: Dvořák realized the importance of this tradition, and that of black music, to the American narrative, and hence to any 'national' music that might emerge from it.

In New York, his presence and the 'New World' Symphony had caused a sensation. As one of the founders of what is considered the 'national' music of Czechoslovakia, replete with folk music and dance, he set about advising Americans on how to forge a 'national music' of their own, and in part demonstrated how it might be done in the symphony's invocations of African-American spirituals and Native American music – or, as he put it, in 'original themes embodying the peculiarities of the Indian music'. In May 1893, an article had appeared in the *New York Herald* entitled 'Real Value of Negro Melodies', subtitled 'Dr. Dvořák Finds In Them the Basis For An American School of Music'. In them, said the composer, 'I discover all that is needed for a great and noble school of music'. The 'new American school of music', he insisted, 'must strike its roots deeply into its own soil', rather than transplant from Europe. Dvořák's bold claims detonated an outcry and a rally of support advocating financial aid for the recruitment of black students to the National Conservatory of Music of America.

Now, Dvořák escaped the stress of the limelight he found himself in, to arrive in Spillville at a brick-built house on the main drag leading down to the river. One moment in the quartet recalls his first morning in town, when he is said to have woken its people with a blast of the Czech hymn 'Boze Pred Tvou Velebnosti' (O God before Thy Majesty) on the organ of St Wenceslas' Church, whose priest Father Tomáš Bílý had been his point of contact.

Dvořák's feeling for nature and the countryside infuses his Czech music, and he was no less responsive to the vast prairies of Iowa, where he was so relieved to arrive after the hullabaloo of New York; he was especially irked by the fact that without a rail ticket he was not allowed on to the platforms of Grand Central Station, to pursue his love of train-spotting. The 'American' Quartet is a pastorale in every sense, but one that all but banishes the European tradition – even 'decidedly anti-European', according to the critic Hartmut Schick. Germanic 'counterpoint and dialogue between the instruments are replaced by drones and ersatz drumbeats', writes the musicologist Michael B. Beckerman.[1]

I think the flowing, shimmering progressions of the second, *lento*, movement evoke, perhaps more than any piece of music, that sense of *space* that is the eternal American landscape. But not just these notes, hovering in the heat: as he walked, sat and worked, Dvořák was entranced by the birdsong around him and annotated it musically, so the call of the scarlet tanager finds its way into the quartet.

And there's this: during Dvořák's Iowa summer, a troupe of Native Americans arrived in Spillville. Their musical performances are thought by historians to have been fairly kitsch, but clearly they impacted Dvořák. In her book *Spillville*, sold at the local museum, Patricia Hampl recalls: 'Toward the end of summer, a small band of Kickapoo Indians came to Spillville, to sell medicinal herbs . . . There was a show every night – dancing music, the sale of snake oil and blood medicine . . . There was a minstrel show as well, several blacks playing banjos and guitars, singing. Dvořák went every night . . . He even had the snake oil headache treatment, administered by Big Moon, the leader of the Kickapoos. An Indian drum rhythm appears in the scherzo of the E-flat quintet.'[2]

Not long after these performances in Spillville, Dvořák composed his String Quintet in E-flat Major, the *largetto* of which contains a variation on a Kickapoo song he had heard, and the scherzo the influence of what he called the 'rhythmic monotony [of] Indian music'. There's an unsubstantiated local story of scandal, which tells of Dvořák's daughter 'riding out' with Big Moon's son.

Dvořák was a butcher's son, and the Spillville butcher's name was Dvořák too; in New York, the composer was known as 'Doc Borax' because no one could pronounce his name; here, to avoid confusion, he became 'the Master'. On his fifty-second birthday, 3 September 1893, the Master 'passed out cigars to the towns-people who gathered for a celebration in his honor'.[3] When he wasn't listening to the Kickapoo making music, Dvořák would usually spend his evenings playing the Czech card game *darda* with Father Bíly, and occasionally there was chamber music. Or else he could be found in one of the taverns with the farming folk whose descendants were facing drought when I came through in 1988 and the town, according to one local headline, was contending with an 'Invasion of the Spider Mites', bugs the size of pinheads.

The mayor in 1988, Ed Klimesh, lived in a sort of wooden igloo; more interested in playing the Byrds on his guitar than listening to Dvořák, he admitted, although 'I've certainly read the biographies'. In Cathy's Minimart, Dvořák was venerated for his music and another keen interest: 'Oh yes,' said Lennie Senkep, behind the counter, 'he put this town on the map, and he liked his suds. Bit of a town drunk so they say.'

Spillville remains almost 'completely Czech'. An otherwise peaceful Saturday afternoon was interrupted by the growl of

Harley Davidsons, as the Bo-Hunk Club ('Bo' as in 'Bohemia') revved up in the park where stands a modest monument to Dvořák. Lyle Klimesh (no close relation to the mayor), wearing a Czech-flag bandana, says: 'Sure I know who Dvořák was. Got some of his albums at home. Used to play organ in the church and stuff, used to drink a lot too, but everybody here does that.' A room in the little museum is dedicated to the composer, but it's mostly concerned with carved wooden clocks made by the Bíly brothers, Frank and Josef, probably from the same extended family as the priest of Dvořák's time.

Back in New York, Dvořák missed Spillville, which he loved, writes Beckerman, 'precisely because all the things that intimidated him elsewhere were absent. There were no reporters around, no high-society types to make him feel brutish, no critics to scrutinize him, no crowds to avoid. Just farmers drinking in pubs, simple folks to chat with, and a card game always in progress.'[4]

On my last evening in Spillville, the Szczecin University Choir from Poland came through for a concert at St Wenceslas' – and to connect the community with Eastern Europe. My story from Dvořák's Iowa appeared on page three of the *Washington Post* on 22 August 1988, while the front-page lead carried news from Poland, where the banned *Solidarność* union had extended a wave of strikes; and from Prague, where thousands had filled Wenceslas Square the previous day to observe the twentieth anniversary of the invasion of their country by the USSR. I had never, at this point, been to Czechoslovakia. However, while I sat in St Wenceslas' Church, the plates were shifting back there in Bohemia, where Dvořák's music still seems to drift from every meadow and silver-birch wood. The roots of the 1968 Prague Spring had never been removed; now they were about to come to life again, and into bloom.

7

Fuck the Wall!

*Berlin, 1989, and Plastic People of the Universe, Uničov,
Czech Republic, 2009*

*The Plastic People of the Universe are summoned for a rehearsal in an
outlying quarter of Prague called Radlická, but stop off first for a breakfast of soup and beer round the corner – there's a Plastics song called
'Fly In The Morning Beer'). Staff at the café know and love the band,
and the walls are lined with posters for concerts from before the Czech
'Velvet Revolution' of 1989. 'An archive,' I offer enthusiastically. 'A
graveyard,' the clarinettist and saxophonist Vratislav Brabenec clarifies,
flapping his arms like wings: 'We are all like bats, flying blindly through
the dark, towards our creator, the God who does not exist.' For Vratislav,
'there is no such thing as time. Only the moment – what Germans call
the* Augenblick.' *This is hardly political talk, but it is the kind of
observation that once put Brabenec in jail. Many rock musicians have
preached revolution, but few can claim to have sparked one.*

*The Velvet Revolution was so called partly because it was peaceful,
but also because of the band that unwittingly drove it – the Plastic People
of the Universe, who were influenced by the Velvet Underground.*

*The rehearsal was due to start at 10.30 but it is now past eleven, and
Brabenec is pouring himself a fourth beer. 'Perhaps we'll not rehearse*

*after all,' sighs Eva Turnová, the bass player whom bearded Brabenec
has greeted with a kiss on the belly button. 'Perhaps not indeed!' he
agrees, accepting a brandy chaser from his host. 'The important thing
about this band is our friendship, our relationships – and the music is
born of them' – Brabenec turns to me – 'so we're having what you might
call an emotional rehearsal.' But Eva worries that the other members of
the band, Josef Janíček and Jiří Kabeš, who are hard at work, will take
a dim view of this warm-up going on round the corner. And another
problem: the Plastics have been invited to perform at the fortieth-
anniversary Woodstock Festival, 'only we don't think we can do it,
because Josef says he cannot miss the school lunch delivery he does. We're
trying to persuade him, but he insists he can't let them down – the children
call him "Uncle Lunch".'*

Tonight's concert is in Uničov, over the mountains, and a plan for me
to travel with the band falls through because the Plastics are taking only
one vehicle, another having lost its exhaust pipe. This entails me taking
a fine iron horse through Bohemia, and eating lunch in the dining car
with lace curtains at the windows. Also aboard is an economics student,
David Doubek, he too heading for the concert. He says he *'learned about
the Plastics as part of my school curriculum'.* In which subject? *'Czech
history, our national institutions: King Wenceslas, Kafka, Dvořák,
Václav Havel – and Plastic People of the Universe!'*

Because of rain, the concert's venue has to be switched from a baroque
courtyard to the local kino – a cinema in communist style. There's a
bewitching sound check, for which the musicians depart from the necessary
technicalities to engage in elaborate improvisations of pastorales
punctuated by jagged edges. Then, before the performance, they adjourn
for beer, cigarettes and chats with fans on the cinema steps. The Uničov
audience is aged eight to eighty, with every vintage in between. Some, like
Ludmila Polednová, a maths teacher, have come because *'[the Plastics]
were part of my youth, a mixture of having fun and being frightened.
They woke me up to what was happening, but made me happy'.*

The Plastic People's sound is very much their own, an ingenious *adaptation of jazz, underground rock and electronic music with folk chromatics from Janáček and Martinů. The music is sinewy, combining unavoidable darkness with playful dance – very Bohemian dance too, complex and hard to place, not polka or waltz, for sure – I was reminded of a wonderful article Leoš Janáček wrote for the local paper in Brno in 1905, saying: 'In Moravia we have about 300 dances, and so neither the waltz nor the polka were really our folk dances . . . We can dance to any kind of music' – and play it too, here and now.*[1]

They launch into a long, bold exploration called 'Krešt', which starts as a chunky-rolling number but departs on magical mystery detours, wayward sax by Brabenec, flurries on violin from Kabeš – both solos as wild as their hair – and doom-laden vocals from Janíček at the piano. There was a poignant doff to the song's origins: 'Toxika', from the band's first album – published in France and distributed clandestinely in Czechoslovakia – of music set to words by the banned dissident writer Egon Bondy: fits and starts on the instruments, and moans rather than cries of pain – dark times spoken in music, and satire: jumpy sounds to express jumpy bureaucrats at work against the song itself.

Three tracks into the second half of the evening the guitarist, Joe Karafiát, leaves the stage, and Eva Turnová discards her bass and sits cross-legged, leaving the 'Central Committee' of original players – Brabenec, Janíček and Kabeš – to play an improvisation that sends shivers up the spine. Janíček, on synthesizer, plays a sequence like the surface of a lake lapping in the breeze; Kabeš scales the range of sounds on his violin with both sensuality and venomous attack, while Brabenec, who has attached the reed and the barrel of his clarinet to only the lower half of the keys, plays something simultaneously cacophonic and lyrical, tragic and comic, that could only be played by this band.

And so it feels OK to walk away early into the night to catch my train back to Prague. I wait a while at a small railway halt for the last branch-line service, then connect at Olomouc onto the rattling night train, through the hills of Bohemia now illuminated under a fruity full moon.

*

As Roberto Bolaño's 'abominable '80s' drew to a close, the political night neared its end not in our Western orbit of Thatcher and Reagan, but with a quickening in the Eastern skies of Europe. I had, for work, been to Poland in 1981, when a strike by shipyard workers gave rise to the *Solidarność* trade union and ultimately the fall of communism. A world familiar yet utterly strange: brushed denim buttoned against the cold, the moustached figure of young Lech Wałęsa held aloft on the broad shoulders of dockers and shipbuilders, beneath blue corrugated iron and the sign: *Stocznia Gdańska*, Gdansk Shipyard.

Eight years later, in November 1989, I was at a performance by the Welsh National Opera of Richard Strauss's *Salome* at the New Theatre, Oxford. My lady friend and I repaired to a station hotel, switched on the news and there it was: a breach in the Berlin Wall through which thousands were surging – incredulous crowds hacking the concrete with pick-axes. I called my brother, and we were in Berlin by the end of the following day – in packed bars along the Kurfürstendamm amid tough folk in more brushed denim, who had waited all day for the two hundred Deutschmarks Chancellor Helmut Kohl had decreed for each. Some spent it on fluffy toys but most on lager, which was flowing and flying across the biggest street party of all time. It was the longest I've ever gone without sleep – three days and nights, one of them spent dancing in a packed bar to an appalling band called Euro-cheque, to which elderly East Berliner couples were two-stepping through the early hours. Everywhere, Trabant cars belching black exhaust.

What a way to live – why feel compelled to be here? Is this voyeurism, tourism, or what? There's a journalistic imperative and a need to bear witness ingrained in my nature. But I was not writing here in Berlin – in fact I was 'missing in action' at the office. It's some urge that dictates: if possible, be there, see it, put faces to the news, humanize the historic moment, preferably with a soundtrack. I've had it all my life; it's what took me from Oxford, gleefully, to Falls Road, Belfast.

A few weeks after Berlin, the pack of cards that signalled the end of communism began to tumble: an uprising in Romania toppled the dictator Nicolae Ceaușescu. It being Christmas, no one on the paper really wanted to go, but I volunteered like a shot – to smell that charred masonry, see tanks and shrines in the Bucharest winter, behold those scenes that looked like black-and-white newsreel of yore – except they weren't, they were real. As I get older, it's about memory: I took no photographs in Berlin or Bucharest, this was all about storage for the memory-bank in later life, when it is too late to see more.

On the last evening in Berlin, Tom and I wondered: What about the other side? We took the *U-Bahn* to the junction at Friedrichstrasse – beneath East Berlin but closed to it for decades – through 'ghost stations' that had not functioned since the Third Reich – Gothic lettering on the tunnel walls. That day, gates to the street from the Friedrichstrasse connection had opened for the first time since 1946, and out we went along the dark boulevard. It took a while to find a bar, but eventually we came upon a hole in the wall where the sole other customer had collapsed forward onto the table; the barman said that ours were the first Deutschmarks he'd ever taken for a beer.

One figure on the American rock scene had a special connection with the fall of the Wall: the man who sang 'Born To Be Wild' and who 'felt outside that whole flower power "trip" thing': John Kay of Steppenwolf. Kay had written a song called 'The Wall', about 'Crossing the line in the dead of night', aged five and on the run; being warned 'This ain't no game . . . don't make a sound', 'watch that man with the gun'. And this was autobiography. Kay was born in Tilsit, East Prussia; his father was killed during the Reich's retreat from its Russian front. He writes in a song called

'For the Women In My Life' about how Daddy has gone away – to the front – and will not return. And in another, 'Renegade', that his 'birthplace would be hard to find' – it has 'changed so many times' that the boy is 'not sure where it belongs'.

Kay and I spoke again soon after the Wall went down; he recalled his origins on its far side, and his return there. 'When the Second World War drew to a close, and the Red Army advanced on East Prussia,' he said, 'my widowed mother took me as an infant and headed west, by train. We came to a halt at Arnstadt, due to the tracks having been bombed; Mother found herself in the middle of the night in a strange place and got off the train . . . We wound up staying for the next four and a half years – in this family's home, who had lost three sons in the war, and had extra room.'

The Europe of Kay's childhood was a continent across which waves of people wandered, in flight from what was behind them, in fear of what lay ahead, searching for the missing. Arnstadt, in the event, was not far west enough: 'Shortly after the end of the war, the Americans moved into Arnstadt,' he remembers, 'but they pulled back out, and the Russians came; all of a sudden, we were behind the Iron Curtain.' His mother had another problem – a domestic one: 'She discovered I would squint, and my eyes were bad. The doctor said if there was any chance of getting my vision improved, West Germany had the opportunity for treatment. My mother decided to get us out.' To a child, it was a terrifying flight. 'There were dog patrols, searchlights and that sort of thing, and I had a nasty cough . . . I had a little knapsack and – well, then I was told: *Run!*' 'Renegade' recalls: 'Just you run like hell / . . . Don't you look around, please, don't make a sound' because 'The Man will shoot you down'.

'Once in West Germany we made it to Hanover, and being refugees from the East, lived in the attic of a building that had been bombed and repaired.' Romance blossomed for widowed

Frau Krauledat: 'Shortly after, my mother met a fellow who had just been released from a prisoner-of-war camp in Russia and had made it home.' As often happened between camp survivors and others bereaved, 'those two hit it off', says Kay with a chirp, 'and got married'. He was eight years old in 1953 when the first uprising against communism took place, in East Germany. He remembers the radio broadcast: '"Russian troops pour into East Berlin" – German citizens were attacking Soviet tanks with Molotov cocktails, and it was an incredibly galvanizing experience – I became politicized at that early age. It became something that's part of me to this day.'

Kay's stepfather, a kindly man, 'saw I wanted a guitar, and from photos of Elvis, tried to build me one out of fibreboard'. The instrument was never quite finished, and never played. '"We are going to Canada,"' he told us suddenly. '"We got some letters from your aunt and uncle, they bought a house, they got good jobs and we're going." So we left the half-built guitar behind.'

But until the Berlin Wall came down, says Kay, 'I was unaware that I had such strong emotions about my homeland,' although he had by then married Jutte Maue. Steppenwolf travelled to Germany to play soon after the fall of the Wall, 'and after playing in Berlin,' Kay tells me, 'I got a call from someone in Arnstadt where I had spent those five years growing up. He said: "Would you consider doing a benefit concert for our orphanage?" I thought: I was half orphan; my father was dead already when my mother first stepped into this little town, and we were given shelter by a family here, and by this community. What an appropriate way to pay back.

'No sooner were we in the hotel than the mayor and other dignitaries of the town arrived and gave me the grand tour. When we were walking past the church, he told me how this square was where one of the first candlelit vigils started before the Wall came down. About a dozen people were being protected from the secret police by the Protestant minister, hiding them in the basement of that church … The Stasi were above that cinema, with cameras taking pictures of everybody,' but what at first had been a very small group turned into two dozen, then five dozen, then three hundred. 'Across East Germany, the same thing was happening, and eventually in Leipzig and Dresden there were a hundred thousand – but it started right here.'

The mayor of Arnstadt told Kay: '"There are two people who came through this town and made a name for themselves in music, and one of them is you. The other was an organist here for about three years." "Who was that?" I asked. "Johann Sebastian Bach," replied the mayor.'

Communism was toppled in Czechoslovakia six weeks after the fall of the Berlin Wall, and in that narrative the story of the Plastic People of the Universe is probably the weirdest ever to combine politics and rock.

It began in 1969 with the naming of the group after a song by Frank Zappa, 'Plastic People'. The band are dismissed by Zappa's biographer Barry Miles as 'loud, surreal, irreverent and not very good', but they ended up having an infinitely greater impact on the real world than Zappa.[2] The Plastics set out as a communist-approved group playing Velvet Underground covers in dance halls. They gave their shows a theatrical emphasis, with 'happenings', costumes and psychedelic effects, and co-opted the art historian and poet Ivan Martin Jirous as muse and publicist in a role not unlike Andy Warhol's. However: 'We were not political,' said Josef Janíček, on keyboards. 'We insisted on playing a certain kind of music, dressing and performing in a certain way. And in Prague in 1968 and 1969, if you wanted to play your own music you became political, whether you intended it or not, because the authorities deemed that you were a threat to their "official" culture.'

In 1970 the Plastic People were effectively banned, their licence to perform revoked. But they continued playing for private occasions, which were thereby transformed into subversive countercultural events. With the arrival of Vratislav Brabenec, a former gardener, in 1971, the sound and the project changed. Brabenec insisted they play only original material and sing in Czech, while his saxophone and clarinet added textures from avant-garde jazz, Slavonic dances and klezmer. Brabenec also arranged for the release of that first record in France, based on lyrics by the outlawed writer Bondy. The album was entitled, wittily but in earnest: *Egon Bondy's Happy Hearts Club Banned*.

In 1975 police intercepted fans heading for an unofficial music festival, headlined by the Plastics, in the city of České Budějovice, beating and arresting scores of them. 'They feared us,' says Brabenec, 'because it wasn't an organization; we were part of, more like, a circus of a few thousand people, and they couldn't manage us. What could they do to us? The worst was in '77, never-ending interrogations – constant battering, making our daily lives hell. We would sometimes sit for two or three interrogations a day, from three to ten hours.' Brabenec was jailed for eight months; the rest of the band, for various periods. 'They wanted to wear us down,' he says. 'They didn't.'

'In the 1970s,' reflects Janíček, 'before the concert in Uničov, people used to go to hear the Plastic People to be with each other, as well as hear us. People of like mind, with some free spirit. We became a focal point; it was social resistance, not political. And the pressure became extreme – [the authorities] wanted to jail us, or kick us out of the country – they must have seen us as a threat, because now we know how much effort went against us. And not just us, our fans too.'

After the state's attack on České Budějovice, the band's mentor Ivan Jirous wrote a manifesto entitled *Report on the Czech Musical Revival*, setting the Plastics in the tradition of Dvořák and Janáček. 'One of the highest aims of art', he wrote, 'has been the creation of unrest. The aim of the underground here in Bohemia is the creation of a second culture that will not be dependent on official channels of communication or a hierarchy of values laid down by the Establishment.' At the same time, coincidentally, another document – an 'open letter' to the General Secretary of the Communist Party, Gustáv Husák – was published by Czechoslovakia's celebrated samizdat playwright and future president, Václav Havel. Jirous met Havel and played him some of the Plastics' music, after which they adjourned to a bar and drank all night. Havel agreed to come to the next festival at which the Plastics intended to play. But it never happened.

Soon afterwards, on 16 March 1976, the secret police were unleashed on the music underground. Most of the Plastics and many other musicians were arrested. In July, the Plastics were charged with – and Brabenec and Jirous imprisoned for – 'organized disturbance of the peace'. But the impact, says Brabenec now, 'was different than the authorities expected. They expected people to say: "Ooh, horrible drunks, idiots." But whether people liked the music or not, they identified with what we were doing.' The outcome, thanks to Havel's seizure of the band's cause, was the celebrated Charter 77, genesis of the Velvet Revolution. The music underground, wrote Havel, 'was a challenge that was all the more urgent for being unintentional. It was the challenge of example.'

The Chartists were brutally assailed. Havel's country home, where he lived under house arrest, was among the few places the band could play. The houses of others, recalls Janíček, 'were burned down. It wasn't easy to play in a place belonging to someone, if you knew the concert could get their house burned.' Havel was jailed, Brabenec fled to Canada, the band split up in 1988.

But Czechoslovakia could not un-ring the bell, either: the

regime was doomed, and by the winter of 1989 it was spring again in Prague. 'They were such happy times after the revolution,' Janíček reflects, but as though of something lost. 'It was a golden age, full of hope. But those hopes have not been realized; we're still the same people, trying to offer something that makes people think about the world in which they live.' In 1997, the twentieth anniversary of the Charter, President Havel pleaded with the Plastic People to come out of retirement and re-form for a one-off celebration at Prague Castle. 'We didn't play very long,' recalls Jiří Kabeš, the violinist, 'five or six songs. And it was a bit weird seeing these people in suits dancing around, the Interior Minister jumping about with a beer.' But enough of an experience for the band to realize that, as Brabenec says, 'we couldn't live without each other'. So the Plastics re-formed, and have remained on the road ever since. 'It was to make this music with these people that I came back from Canada,' Brabenec adds. 'No other reason. My wife is still there, my children are still there, but these musicians are here, so I am here.'

A moment of limelight came with Tom Stoppard's play *Rock 'n' Roll* – but Brabenec is unimpressed: 'This play might be interesting for people outside, but Czechs see it as rather pathetic.' Why? 'Because it makes us out to be heroes, and we are not.'

Here we are, in 2009, back from Uničov, in the bar that is Brabenec's court, the Shakespeare, on Krymská Street in funky Prague 10. 'Ciao, bambino,' he says, by way of greeting to those who enter, holding his skinny arms wide like a rangy urban fox. 'I am no less dissident now than I was then,' he says. 'Why should I be? Our identity as a band was to do with poetry, not politics. Our cultural, not political, actions were sufficient to make me subversive. It was the politicians who made us political, by being offended; I don't know how many musicians in modern times have been imprisoned because their music offended the authorities, but we were among them. And although it's more comfortable for us now than it was then, we're still artistic dissidents.'

He points out, gleefully, that criminal charges against the band were not dropped until 2003. I think he's joking. He's not: 'I have not found that their behaviour could be considered criminal', ruled the District Attorney for Prague West, Ondreij Smelhaus, on 2 April that year, twenty-six years after the charges were brought.

Outside, evening shoppers pass on the cobbled street; the buildings are glories of the Austro-Hungarian epoch, paint peeling like parchment, floral mouldings unrestored. I thank Vratislav for bringing me away from the tourist-infested centre to a place with old wooden tables, lined with interesting books, and serving beautifully kept Plzeň beer. 'Fucking tourists,' he says. 'Once it was Russian soldiers, now it's tourists. I can't decide which is worse.' Women with tattoos and tatty flowing dresses enter, Brabenec kisses each of them as some old wizard might greet a princess arriving at court – only, in each case, she is betrothed to some young prince, to Brabenec's disgust. 'They're so beautiful,' he says warily, 'I love them all, but they're too young. I also love my girlfriend, but she is with her boyfriend this evening. Behold, the hero of the revolution!'

And he adds: 'I hate it when people talk about 1989 as a "revolution". A revolution is supposed to change things. But what's changed? I don't consider myself any . . . less a traitor to a society of shopping than I was to a society of socialism. It's all still shit, only different shit. Communist Party, mobile phone party – what's the fucking difference? The poets are still the poets, the shits are still the shits, politicians still politicians, the Plastic People still the Plastic People. You must remember one thing above all others about this band and our so-called revolution: none of us ever got anywhere. This is what matters most.'

8

Through the Wire

Music from Terezín, Nash Ensemble, Wigmore Hall, London, 2010

The music had ended for the evening, but few people dared speak. Although beautiful, it had been hard to take at times.

There'd been a weekend of it, every piece on the programme composed in Terezín concentration camp; the concert was organized by the leading chamber music group the Nash Ensemble. The Nazis called Terezín, near Prague, by its German name, Theresienstadt. It has a grotesque and unique place within Holocaust history: at any given time it housed sixty thousand people, almost all to be transported to Auschwitz. Yet it was also where, surreally, the musical life of inter-war Czechoslovakia was permitted to continue and thrive; where great music was written and performed by the condemned. Among the inmates were fine composers whose music had been played over various concerts this weekend at the Wigmore Hall in London: Pavel Haas, Viktor Ullmann, Hans Krása and Gideon Klein – their pieces were shoots of genius, harbingers of a school of modern European music that never was, annihilated in the ovens.

We heard songs and a piano sonata by Ullmann, who said of life in the camp: 'We did not simply sit down by the rivers of Babylon and weep, but evinced a desire to produce art that was entirely commensurate with our will to live.'

Ullmann was born on the Moravian–Polish border. He had so impressed Arnold Schoenberg that the Viennese master recommended the young Czech to his brother-in-law Alexander Zemlinsky, director of the German Opera in Prague. Ullmann's most acclaimed work for that house had been an opera called Fall of the Antichrist, *but we had this weekend heard selections from another, composed in the camp:* The Kaiser of Atlantis – *apparently slapstick music-theatre which was actually a parody of the Third Reich, even containing a pastiche on 'Deutschland über Alles'. But the Nazi censors were so stupid they spotted the caricature only when the piece reached dress-rehearsal stage.*

We heard a string quartet with percussion and settings of Chinese poetry by Haas. Born in Brno, Haas had studied with Janáček at the State Conservatory there, and thereafter infused his music with folk song; in Janáček's wake, his quartets pushed the frontiers between folk melody and modernism. We also heard a string trio by Gideon Klein, considered his masterpiece. Klein had been influenced by the poetry of Charles Baudelaire and wrote choral works, including a song cycle, The Plague *(a few years before Albert Camus' novel). The organizer of concerts in Terezín, Rafael Schächter, had been at the centre of the Prague music scene; and the conductor of most major performances in the camp, Karel Ančerl, would go on to become one of the greatest of his generation with the Czech Philharmonic. Ullmann said that 'the urge to play in Terezín was the urge to live'. But in vain: with the exception of Ančerl, they all perished.*

We heard a suite from a children's opera, Brundibár, *composed in about 1941 by Hans Krása, just before the 'transports' to Terezín began, in collaboration with the poet and novelist Adolf Hoffmeister. About a group of children and an organ-grinder, it was first performed in an orphanage, the director of which had commissioned the work for his fiftieth birthday. Little could anyone at the premiere have known that* Brundibár *would soon become a favourite in the camp, but that it would be subject to a repulsive propaganda exercise. One performance in Terezín was presented for the International Committee of the Red Cross during an inspection visit. The charity's delegation was impressed, perhaps touched, by the singing of the children, who had been specially fed for the event; all but one of them were dispatched to Auschwitz within days of the show – there's a picture of them. The Red Cross gave Terezín a clean bill of health.*

Then the Nazi propaganda department made a documentary entitled The Führer Gives a City to the Jews, *for which Terezín was cleaned up and sequences filmed in which apparently happy inmates, in fact condemned to die, play football and cultivate market gardens. And of course there is music: the Nazis' cameras filmed the Terezín Orchestra playing under the baton of its founder, Ančerl. What the film conceals is that none of his musicians are wearing shoes.*

So, immersed in this music for a weekend, one realized that within the human horror of Terezín a major school of great twentieth-century music was obliterated in its prime. Ullmann's music was experimental in the way of the Viennese Secession movement: angular, innovative. Haas's quartets evoked that romance in the Bohemian landscape reminiscent of Dvořák, and later of Janáček in his more radical way – but took it a step further, infusing the folkloric melodies with modernist sensibility. Klein was the Impressionist of the group, his music fluid, translucent – but with a darkness missing from the French composers who inspired him and to whom he is likened, Debussy and Ravel.

At one point during the programme an artist and camp survivor, Helga Weissová-Hošková, took the stage for discussion and questions, during which she was asked, from the floor: 'Were any babies born in Terezín?' She replied, in her deep Czech-Jewish accent: 'I do not remember, but I do recall a baby born on the ramp at the concentration camp of Mauthausen, when we arrived by cattle train from Auschwitz. A German soldier took pity and found a doctor in the camp, I don't know why, or what happened to the baby.' Silence followed; a woman stood up and said, quite matter-of-factly: 'Could I just say: I am that child.'

*

'How many of you know what a milliner is?' Eva Clarke asks students gathered at Long Road Sixth Form College in Cambridge during winter 2012. No one raises a hand. 'Well, I'm talking about a time when women wore hats, and my mother was apprenticed to a milliner, someone who made hats.' Eva stands beneath a projection showing the gulag of death camps operated by the Third Reich, for this latest in her tireless series of presentations on the Holocaust. She talks about how her German-Jewish grandfather – awarded an Iron Cross for valour during the First World War – left his native Berlin, thinking Czechoslovakia to be safe: 'It wasn't,' says Eva, 'but if he hadn't come, he'd never have met my grandmother.' Eva is the woman who stood up at the Wigmore Hall that night, the baby born on the ramp at Mauthausen.

She shows the students pictures of her newlywed parents before the war in Prague, smiling, wearing yellow stars and with 'no idea what that would mean for them in the future'. Eva's father, Nathan Bergman, was 'transported' – the Nazis' word which survivors also use, for want of another – to Terezín first, and her mother Anka followed him, taking with her a box of doughnuts, to which he was partial. Men and women were segregated, yet Anka 'managed to get pregnant by my father', as Eva Clarke puts it. 'Which was an extreme danger,' she explains. 'Other women, hearing for the first time a new word, "euthanasia", had been forced to sign a document agreeing to surrender their babies once born.' There was a place known in Terezín simply as 'the East', to which people were transported, to disappear for ever. 'Once in Auschwitz,' says Eva, 'to be pregnant was to be sent straight to the gas chambers.'

Eva Clarke concludes her talk. And now, to meet her mother Anka herself at Eva's home in Cambridge, where Anka moved not long before, from Wales. It is ninety-six-year-old Anka's turn to tell her own story. In mind, she is razor-sharp; in body, a frail miracle of carefully expended energy.

She recounts how she left Terezín for Auschwitz, 'knowing I was pregnant, to follow my husband'. She recalls asking the question, 'among the brick chimneys, "When will I see my parents?"', and the hollow mirth that greeted it among those in her berth. '"We'll all go up in smoke," they replied, "you'll never see them again."' She became, she says, 'thinner and thinner, while my stomach became bigger and bigger,' but was transferred to a factory near Freiburg where V2 'buzzbombs' were manufactured 'and where we were delighted to find bedbugs, which meant food and warmth'.

Six months later, Anka was moved on to Mauthausen, where she went into labour. 'You can carry on screaming,' said one German soldier, but another fetched a Jewish doctor from within the camp: 'And I gave birth to a healthy girl. I was in Mauthausen, but also in heaven.' Mother and daughter escaped certain death only because Anka arrived as the approaching US Army was so close that the Nazis had dismantled the gas ovens: 'The war was lost,' she says, 'but if we had arrived just a few days earlier, we would not be here.' She tells also of 'the most terrible moment of all', when bedraggled survivors 'returned to Prague, which we had once called home, like ghosts – begging even the fare for a tram'. But members of her extended family had also survived, 'and treated us like gold; they knew there was a baby coming'. After annexation by the Soviets, Anka fled again – to arrive as a refugee, 'happy and lucky, in Cardiff'.

But there had been this other story, back in Terezín, of the music. 'Czechoslovakia had been one of the most culturally vibrant nations in Europe,' remembers Anka. 'Prague between the wars was on a level with Vienna, Berlin or Paris. It was indescribable: music in the air, and a level of culture among the people you wouldn't get nowadays. You never expected to meet these great musicians and composers: but suddenly there they were – in the camp, putting their talents to work. It distracted us, to hear the performances – it connected us to the lives we had lived, and lost. Looking back, it's amazing to think how much pleasure they gave, under the most horrific circumstances.' It has baffled historians why, exactly, the Nazis encouraged music in Terezín; but they made good use of their scheme: grotesque propaganda films showing talented and apparently contented Jews playing their – and the Germans' – music. Many among the Nazi high command were cultured, and appreciated the talents of those they were in the process of mass-murdering.

Anka preferred traditional Czech music: 'My favourite performance in Terezín was *The Bartered Bride* [by Bedřich Smetana] – our Czech opera. There were so many people there, and the part of [the bride] Mařenka was sung by an eighteen-year-old, beautifully.' She also attended a famous performance of Verdi's *Requiem*, conducted by Schächter from a harmonium. 'Every time he rehearsed the choir, more people had gone, transported east,' she recalls, 'but the *Requiem* was sung, and when the music stopped, total silence. We were shattered – until the German officers started clapping, in the front rows.'

Anka knew the conductor, Ančerl; her memories are at once intimate and epic. 'I distributed milk in Terezín, and would see Ančerl with his wife and child,' she continues, on the sofa in Cambridge, making this unimaginable story surreally tangible. 'I knew his wife from Prague and him by name – he had begun to make his reputation as a conductor. So I would give them a bit extra, and more milk for the boy – we became the best of friends. He was a modest man, quite stern and pensive, but affectionate, loyal to his friends and family, with a love of our music that ran deep inside him.'

Of his leading his own doomed musicians in the propaganda

film, she says: 'He could not do otherwise.' Ančerl's career had begun in an atmosphere that embraced both Czech and German traditions – and that was logical. The Austro-Hungarian Empire had existed astride the Germanic and Slavonic worlds, nurturing the forces of each. The new Czech composers, Ančerl and Schächter, were acutely aware of this dual heritage, so the fact that Terezín's guards and jailers were German was no reason to exclude German music from the repertoire: Bach, Beethoven and Brahms are staples on the beautifully crafted handbills. 'Beethoven,' says Anka, 'never lived under the Nazis – he had nothing to do with them, nor they with him. There was a German opera [house] in Prague, a German theatre – it was part of our culture, and we were part of theirs.'

As a teenager, I went with my father to hear Karel Ančerl conduct the London Philharmonic playing Beethoven's 'Eroica' Symphony at the Festival Hall. Ančerl had by then become one of the world's most celebrated conductors, his name synonymous with the prowess and power of the Czech Philharmonic; he was a leading interpreter of Mahler, but mainly of his country's music, conducting Smetana and Dvořák with a poignancy that bordered on the unbearable.

There was something palpably *different* I will never forget about watching and hearing him, and this was to do with his story, as related by Dad: that this man had survived Auschwitz and another camp of which I had not then heard, 'Theresienstadt'. The reason for Ančerl's conducting feeling different in some way was as obvious as it was intangible; if we read Sylvia Plath's *The Bell Jar*, does it make a difference if we know that she took her own life? When we are looking at Van Gogh's late paintings, does it matter that they were done inside a mental hospital and just before his suicide? The knowledge is not essential, but even someone who did not know the story of Ančerl, Plath or Van

Gogh might detect some extra, inexplicable element at work in the 'id' of what is happening.

It cannot be a rule of thumb, but in circumstances such as these the narrative of the artists' life inevitably impacts upon how they work, and that impact is there for the beholding. So we need to navigate, carefully, some track here for which there is no definitive map: the story of ventriloquizing Shostakovich teaches the perils of entrapping his music within its context, yet the experience of music at the Festival Hall with Papa, then at the Wigmore Hall over that weekend was inevitably charged with the circumstances under which it was composed. The former is a claim of 'ownership' of the music for a particular interpretation; the latter simply accepts and respects what Krása said about art being 'commensurate with our will to live'. For that reason, hearing Ančerl conduct was like few other experiences in music, because I knew that he was an Auschwitz survivor conducting German music – ergo placing the music above the history of which his own appalling narrative was, *in extremis*, part – at the hands of those who elevated 'German art'. And at that time I knew only a small part of Ančerl's story; I had yet to meet the woman who told me the rest.

A train arrived at Auschwitz from Terezín on 15 October 1944 carrying Ančerl, Hans Krása, Viktor Ullmann, Gideon Klein and Rafael Schächter. Also aboard was a twenty-three-year-old who had played the lead female role in cabarets and plays at Terezín: Zdenka Fantlová, with her mother and little sister. Schächter produced a tin of sardines from his bag. 'He was sitting opposite me,' says Ms Fantlová. 'He took out his sardines and a piece of bread. Sardines were the highest currency in Terezín; with sardines, you could buy cigarettes, anything. Now, Schächter mixed them with bread, saying: "This will be my last supper." I thought it odd, how did he know? But we got to Auschwitz – and it *was* his last supper.'

The transport lined up before Dr Josef Mengele himself, the 'Angel of Death' in Auschwitz, directing the arrivals towards either forced labour or the gas chambers. Ullmann, Klein, Krása and Schächter went first, to the ovens. Then came Ančerl, and behind him young Zdenka, her mother and sister. Ančerl, says Ms Fantlová, was 'with his wife and child, carrying the little boy. At one point he fell, with the child, and a German soldier hit him, shouting "Up! Up!" We reached three SS officers, boots polished, badges like mirrors. The one in the middle I only later learned was Mengele. And without any emotion, a wave of his white glove, he sent Ančerl's wife and son to the left, and Karel to the right. We didn't know what it meant – and he disappeared into the crowd, looking back at them.'

Then came Zdenka's turn, 'and there was Mengele. He motioned my mother to the left, and she disappeared into the crowd. I didn't wait, I grabbed my younger sister and joined the line to the right, I don't know why. That is the last I saw of my mother.'

Seventy years later, Zdenka talks beside her window in Bayswater, London, overlooking Hyde Park; coincidentally, a plaque on the building identifies it as the location where the plot was hatched by exiled Czechs to assassinate the Third Reich's emissary to Prague, Reinhard Heydrich. In the corner of the room is a piano; papers are carefully organized around a typewriter; even the dust seems to have been transplanted from a household in central Europe. Young Zdenka learned the piano and became the protégée of an older man in Prague, who would take her to concerts and plays. Among the last things she did in the household of her later childhood, as the family packed for transportation to Terezín on 20 January 1942, was to play Dvořák's Waltz in D Major.

Much of the time in Terezín, Zdenka was, as she puts it, 'dancing under the gallows' – performing in plays such as *The*

Last Cyclist by Karel Švenk, an allegory of the Holocaust. She heard the performances of *Brundibár* and Verdi's *Requiem*. 'We were in a camp, but seeing friends, holding discussions and rehearsals. I remember the concerts and plays, but I don't remember sleeping. I think the quality of the music was so high,' posits Zdenka, 'because people were playing only for love of music, in such a place. There was no money involved, no jealousy – everyone equal, playing to the best of their ability in the moment.' She remembers Ančerl again: 'We'd be twenty-five people working, mixing ersatz soup, and Karel would be right next to me. He'd made his name with the Radio Orchestra before the war, and we'd talk about Brahms and Dvořák while making this watery soup.' Zdenka remembers that during rehearsals of the *Requiem* 'almost half the huge choir vanished, transported to the East. People urged Schächter: "Give up on this," but he wouldn't. He wanted it performed, and it was.'

The Germans would invite distinguished guests from Berlin, and once Adolf Eichmann himself came. When the music ended, Schächter bowed to the singers but not to the audience, which included German officers. 'I suppose the Germans thought: Let them play, they'll soon stop smiling.' Zdenka's fondest memory of music in Terezín was not a formal concert, but a moment with Gideon Klein. 'It was late, in the Dresden Barracks as they called it; we had finished our duties and rehearsals, I was dawdling and last to leave, and there was a piano. And Gideon said: "Don't go, I'll play you something." So I sat there, on a wooden bench in the front row. And he played a Chopin étude in C Minor, to an audience of just me. It was so beautiful, and so romantic. That was just a few months before we took the train to Auschwitz together.'

On the Death March from Auschwitz, 'colder and hungrier than can be imagined', says Zdenka, Klein – who had perished in the ovens – remained with her after a fashion: she accompanied his sister Elisa. 'And when Elisa and I reached the river Oder, it was frozen. The Germans said: "Those who can will go on, those who cannot must stay." Elisa Klein said: "I'll stay," and we thought that would be the last of her. But she was found by the Russians, and after the war I met her in Prague.'

Ančerl flourished as director of the Czech Philharmonic, among the greatest orchestras in the world during the 1960s and '70s. After the Soviet invasion of Czechoslovakia in 1968 he left for Canada, and died in Toronto in 1973. Zdenka was meanwhile taken to Belsen and after liberation moved via Sweden to Australia, where she pursued her career as an actress. In 1966, Ančerl visited Melbourne on tour with the Czech Philharmonic. 'I was in the front row,' says Ms Fantlová, 'so that now there was no Iron Curtain between us. And there he was, an elderly man. I thought: No one can see what I can see: my last picture of him, separated from his wife and son. He conducted Dvořák's Ninth Symphony [the 'New World'], and I cried so much I had to leave, climbing over people in their seats.' However: 'Next morning, Karel came to see me. It was so wonderful, I almost cried again but I didn't – we talked about music, we drank coffee, twelve thousand miles from home.

'I could hardly believe we were the same people who had known one another in Terezín, been together on the ramp at Auschwitz, witnessed the last of his wife and child, of my mother. But of course we were the same people, who had shared music and were now reunited by music. He could not stay long, however, and I never saw him again.'

The story of music under the Third Reich – of music *and* the Third Reich – has, accursedly, left a trail of questions. How and why did the Nazis not only permit, but attend, concerts at Terezín? How and why did the commanders of the Holocaust possess, apparently, good taste in music? Niklas Frank, a writer living on the northwest coast of Germany, keeps a photograph of his father in his wallet: dead, with a noose still round his neck. Hans Frank was Adolf Hitler's lawyer and in 1939 became Governor General of Poland, to which he promised: 'We bring art and culture.' And he guaranteed that 'the Jewish problem will be addressed'. Frank was hanged after his trial at Nuremberg in 1946, for the murder of three million people.

But Hans Frank was also a talented pianist and friend of Richard Strauss, who even wrote an ode to him. A book by his son Niklas, *In the Shadow of the Reich*, is a visceral challenge to the father, whom the text addresses in the second person singular, like an open letter.[1] 'You could play Chopin so beautifully. You loved Beethoven', writes the son. As the Red Army rolls back the Wehrmacht's conquests, 'even in the chaos of battle, culture and the arts maintained their same important place on your scale of values'. When the Reich crumbled, Hans Frank is chastised by Heinrich Himmler for 'gluttonous and inappropriate behaviour, with those theatre and opera performances of yours'. Niklas quotes from his father's diary: 'This evening I was . . . at the great festival concert which [Wilhelm] Furtwängler conducted at the Philharmonic Hall for the German People's Winter Benefit for the Needy.' Hitler, Hermann Goering and Joseph Goebbels were also there. 'It was a powerful, profound, thrilling experience', writes Frank Snr, 'to hear this true giant of a conductor recreate the Overture to Weber's *Der Freischütz*, Brahms' Fourth Symphony and Beethoven's Seventh. A magnificent evening of consecration. With indescribable emotion, I felt the years I have experienced pass before me, accompanied by this glorious music.' Upon which his son asks: 'What's going on, Father?' What indeed.

The trial of Hans Frank lay at the centre of a research project by the human rights lawyer Philippe Sands, which culminated in a book, a film and a stage performance. Among the surprises in this last was the premiere, with reconstructed music, of that 'hymn' written to Hans Frank by Strauss, the text for which had appeared in Niklas's book. 'We became immediate friends,' says Sands of Niklas, in conversation, 'after an initially strange handshake with the man whose father murdered my grandfather's family, and three million other people.' Sands discovered that Hans Frank was prosecuted by one of his own professional inspirations, the Polish-British lawyer Hersch Lauterpacht, who grew up in the area from which Sands' own family came, now in Ukraine. Lauterpacht, who lost most of his family in territory under Frank's authority, studied law in Vienna, then taught at Cambridge, where he promoted the term 'crime against humanity', laying foundation stones for our 'laws of war'. In his forties, he was drafted to prosecute Frank and others at Nuremberg.

There were strange connections between the two men facing one another across the courtroom. As the trial proceeded, Lauterpacht would repair after court to listen to his favourite music, from which he took inspiration for this task: the *St Matthew Passion* by J.S. Bach. Meanwhile, Frank was taken to his cell, where he discussed music with the prison psychologist and summoned up in his head – seeking not only solace but affirmation – the same piece: Bach's *St Matthew Passion*. Each man heard in Bach's masterwork an entirely different, indeed contradictory, message; two opposed promulgations in the same score, two contrary messages in the same edifice of beauty. Lauterpacht heard an assertion of the individual, the endorsement of his legal task.

This raises questions about music after the Third Reich, and all music by implication: what did those who exterminated millions of Jews and others hear when they listened to music of great beauty? How did such elevated music compute through minds capable of such monstrosity?

Before we turn to the minefield of Richard Wagner, let us start with the Bach. What did Hans Frank the war criminal and Hersch

Lauterpacht the human rights lawyer hear in Bach's *St Matthew Passion*? 'I'm an amateur enthusiast,' says Sands in conversation, 'and not even that, in Bach. But I've read and thought a lot about this, and there's an interpretation whereby Bach used the passion of Matthew to register a Lutheran affirmation of the creativity of the individual against Catholic commitment to the centrality of the whole. It's about the direct relationship between the individual and God in which, one may infer, Lauterpacht found an inspiration for his idea of individual human rights.' Meanwhile, 'I wonder about Frank,' he muses. 'Frank may have heard in these glorious chorales an assertion of the collective, the rights of nation over those of the individual, which was the basis for his defence, such as it was.'

For the stage performance of his work, Sands presented the French baritone Laurent Naouri, a leading interpreter of Verdi's Falstaff and Mozart's Figaro. Naouri notes in conversation:

> *Hans Frank was a great pianist, and when he had to make a decision, he would play a while on the piano – something beautiful to help him with his thoughts. And it comes as a shock to think of Frank doing this – that he was a mass killer with sensibility, a soul, apparently. But the meaning of music is wide open. Most music moves between tension and release. Everything is built around the dominant seventh and the tonic, building pressure and the orgasmic conclusion. And this is primal, it affects all beings whatever their ideology. Why would the same music move Lauterpacht and Frank? Because they are both human beings. They both need food; they both experience these moments of tension that need to find rest. This has nothing to do with morality – it's physical.*

And the *St Matthew Passion*? 'When Hans Frank hears "Erbarme dich" [an aria that goes, 'Have mercy ... regard my bitter weeping']', says Naouri, 'it may release within him the guilt he seems to have felt. I don't actually think that feeling has anything to do with religion – it's more: "How can I get away with what I've done, live with it, die with it?" If it were only a prayer book rather than a piece of music, the words would not have had the same effect.'

Why should Frank and men like him not love beauty? They were not the foot soldiers who herded Jews into the ovens, or torched villages during the Barbarossa offensive; these were cultured Germans who loved German art for the same reasons Thomas Mann loves his heritage in *Doctor Faustus*. And not only German art, nor even only that which the Nazis prescribed as ideologically 'healthy'. Niklas Frank is surprised to find, among the music promoted by his father, experimental and modern pieces considered 'decadent' by the Nazis, many of them by Slavonic composers. 'I was astonished to find them', he writes. These were intelligent but evil men – and they loved the same music as we do. And why not? Hans Frank and his kind demonstrate that music cannot belong to anyone.

'I think,' posits Sands, 'that we find this story unsettling because we want to hope that beauty, the notion of beauty, only makes us better people, that great music is good for humanity. This story shatters that illusion – it illuminates how bad people too appreciate beauty.'

As between Krása, Ančerl and Hans Frank, we are trying to demonstrate a dichotomy: to sever the artist from the art, but also to connect the two. Both sever and bind the piece of music from and to the circumstances under which it is composed or interpreted. We want it both ways. On the one hand, we insist on Bach's distance from Frank, who loved his music. On the other, we know that Krása's music is infused with the circumstances under which he wrote it, and that Ančerl's conducting is so powerful because we know who he was. We want an apparent compromise – and, I think, with reason: I want to insist on the separation, to a degree, of Shostakovich from his historical narrative, but on the inevitable connection of Ančerl to his. To suggest, once again, that no one can be said to *own* music; it is what it is, separate from humanity and from inhumanity. But to acknowledge that art is made in the world, in spite and because of it.

We must proceed along this precarious path as the Third Reich throws up two further towering figures, giants of German music. One is Wilhelm Furtwängler, who directed the Berlin Philharmonic throughout the war, sometimes with the Führer in attendance.

Furtwängler interpreted German music with unparalleled insight and passion. Recently remastered recordings of his wartime performances, of Beethoven especially, are the most electrifying ever made. Also the eeriest – one wonders: Who is that coughing in the front row? There are probably no Jews playing this music with such devastating power as there would have been a decade before, and constituting a significant proportion of the orchestra.

There is much debate, a mirror image of that over Shostakovich, about Furtwängler's relationship to Nazism. He never joined the National Socialist Party, and there is copious evidence that he assisted the escape of many Jewish musicians. His biographer Fred K. Prieberg even discusses Furtwängler's 'goal of reversing Nazi policy towards the Jews' during the 1930s. On the other hand, when the pursuit of the 'Final Solution' was irreversible, Furtwängler kept the baton. Just as Shostakovich accepted an invitation to Stalin's birthday celebrations, so Furtwängler conducted a birthday gala for Adolf Hitler. One argument holds that he remained on the podium not for reasons of ideology but through an absolute commitment to German culture, and music in particular, of a kind shared by Thomas

Mann in his passages on the rise and collapse of the Reich in *Doctor Faustus*. An adhesive fidelity to something described by John Le Carré when recalling his German teacher during the war: '. . . the Germany he knew was still there somewhere'.[2]

One senses from the literature on Furtwängler that it was this passion, rather than subscription to Nazi doctrine, that kept him in place; an unwillingness to face the consequences of what Mann, again in *Doctor Faustus*, calls 'replacing the intellectual dream of a European Germany with the albeit rather terrifying, rather flawed, and as the world sees it, so it would seem, quite intolerable reality of a German Europe'.[3]

There was also the more intimate but salient drama of Furtwängler's loathing of an ambitious young rival, Herbert von Karajan, who joined the party not once but twice. One historian of the Berlin Philharmonic during this period, Misha Aster, details 'Furtwängler's machinations' and even a 'vengeful pathology' which 'went some way to explaining the limited opportunities made available to Karajan' – along with the preposterously arrogant demands of Karajan himself.[4] A play on 'the Furtwängler question' – *Taking Sides* by Ronald Harwood (1995) – shows the composer, interrogated by a boorish American philistine, wanting to retain his position at any cost of principle so long as his presence keeps Karajan out of it. The Nazis manipulated the older man's jealous insecurity.

After the war Furtwängler struck up one of the most fruitful of all musical partnerships, with the Jewish prodigy Yehudi Menuhin. There is something defiantly poignant about the quality of music made together by Hitler's former conductor and the bedazzling Jewish talent, which puts their understanding of one another, and thereby their love of music, somehow above the horrors just past. Their recording of Brahms' Violin Concerto in D Major is unsurpassed – even the LP cover is moving: fresh-faced Jewish Menuhin staring in awe at the apparently troubled elderly German.

The other figure looming over any reflection on music and the Third Reich is Richard Wagner, who died six years before Hitler was born. Along with Verdi and Shostakovich, Wagner is arguably the most important composer to any discourse on music in the world, and brings us to some kernel of the matter of music and evil; his vision became a totem for the Nazi high command. But we have to confront the question: what was it in Wagner the Nazis admired, and why? Again, where does the music end, and claims to its 'ownership' begin? How and why can the Nazis have tried to 'own' Wagner in this way?

During late 2006, I did something not easily arranged: my partner Victoria and I sat through the entire cycle of Wagner's *Ring des Nibelungen* on four consecutive nights. Total immersion in fifteen hours of oceanic music as dangerous as it is beautiful, penetrating the subconscious, by design. The Wagnerian sage Bryan Magee once observed how the composer's music has a tendency to appeal to 'the unhinged, indeed the downright insane'. But also to a range of people including Émile Zola, August Strindberg, Edgar Degas and Odilon Redon, all members of the Wagner Society in Paris at the close of the nineteenth century. Bernard Shaw, Thomas Mann and James Joyce were Wagnerians too – as was Hitler.

Now here we all are for the *Ring*, including venerable Magee – like a tribe gathered for this epic 'unhinging' experience. The cycle was a coup by the Wales Millennium Centre in Cardiff, where the Mariinsky Opera of St Petersburg would perform this marathon under the baton of one of the few men alive with the stamina to undertake it, Valery Gergiev. Over some thirty-five hours in the theatre, including long intervals and discussions, we were cocooned in a womb of music. Although exhausted, we found it hard to sleep after performances that finished beyond eleven, Wagner's motifs swirling around in our heads. There is a distinctively Wagnerian sound, uncomfortable and dangerous. Mysterious but at the same time oddly familiar, even if you've never heard it before; it seems to come from a long way back and a long way down. It is almost exhaustingly direct; seems to be talking straight to our feelings, bypassing reason, and that is not a sensation we necessarily enjoy. Sometimes the music is erotic, sometimes heroic – and often a blend that is not always to our taste. Thomas Mann recalls a conductor saying to him: 'This is no longer music.'

'Mark my new poem well', Wagner wrote to Franz Liszt in 1853, 'for it contains the world's beginning – and its destruction.' Only Wagner could have written something so pompous to introduce his latest endeavour to a friend. And only Wagner could have then produced a masterpiece that matched the pomposity. The 'new poem' was *Der Ring des Nibelungen*. In *Doctor Faustus* Thomas Mann calls the work 'cosmic metaphor', through the voice of Leverkühn's teacher Kretzschmar, in which Wagner was 'equating the basic elements of music with those of the world itself. For him, the beginning of all things had its music – it was the music of the beginning, and likewise the beginning of music, the E-flat triad of the surging depths of the Rhine' that opens *Das Rheingold* and the entire cycle, 'the seven primitive chords like cyclopean stones hewn from primeval rock, out of which the fortress of the Gods rose up'.[5]

There are passages in the *Ring* which seem to plant themselves far inside us, and we respond intuitively. Sometimes it is just too much and we become bored, preferring to get back outside ourselves again. 'What'll we do tomorrow, when it's all over?' said a lady with a strong accent from the Valleys, as the last act of *Götterdämmerung* approached – 'Catch up with the ironing, I suppose.' But who was this composer whose music this lady loved and whom the Nazis turned into a poster boy? What was it they admired in Wagner, and why?

Very few who listen to Wagner remain indifferent; in between those devoted and those repelled are others forcefully drawn in, but uneasy about the music's magnetism as though it were telling them something about themselves they would rather not know. Wagner is as passionately adored as he is reviled; 'Wagner has been fought', wrote the critic Eduard Hanslick, who loathed his music, 'but he has never been denied.' Methodologically, Wagner was an unrelenting modernist; emotionally, he is the quintessential nineteenth-century Romantic, celebrating the creativity of the irrational. Claude Debussy called him 'a glorious sunset, mistaken for a dawn'. Extreme reactions to Wagner's music reflect the reactions of his contemporaries to the man himself. He seldom enjoyed ordinary friendship: he had only disciples, patrons, enemies and lovers. One awestruck associate, Carl Glasenapp, noted: 'His ability to see through people, particularly strangers, seemed demonic . . . Often, even when he had no wish to cause offence, he touched people's raw nerves.'

Perhaps the reasons for this discomfort, and these extreme reactions, lie in Wagner's direct line to the irrational; his music is about the subconscious and unconscious, about dreams and common experience; it is an attempt to elucidate underlying truths general to human motive. He wrote in his essay *Opera and Drama* (1862) that it was the function of the artist to 'bring the unconscious part of human nature into consciousness'. Also: 'In the instruments, the primal organs of creation and nature are represented. What they articulate can never be clearly determined or stipulated because they render primal feeling itself . . . The human voice is quite different from this. It represents the human heart.' So that half a century before Carl Jung and Sigmund Freud, Wagner's music envisaged constructions of the mind advanced by psychoanalysis. Magee says: '. . . one might put all this in Freudian language by saying that the singer's is the voice of the Ego, whereas the orchestra is the voice of the Id'.[6] Wagner, he argues, handles 'universal attributes of the human psyche with proto-Freudian and proto-Jungian insight'.[7] The interior *Ring* is about what we do with the 'shadows' in ourselves that we choose not to see; this much the Nazis might have intuited.

Wagner's technique for depicting and addressing the subconscious is the leitmotif, or musical signpost. The leitmotif is a phrase that accompanies an idea or point of character. For instance, there is no absolute 'Wotan motif' to define the god of gods, Nordic Zeus, in the *Ring*, but there are a number of phrases associated with aspects of his character. The *Ring* contains thousands of these motifs, developing and re-emerging in different forms. They are thoughts behind words, the presence of forces unseen, ideas beneath the action cutting like rip tides, pointing the music back and forth to make associations across the entire cycle, so that we in the audience build up a subconscious musical memory of these things, of which we are not necessarily aware.

Such a 'siege of truth' could only be located outside history; somewhere that is nowhere, but nevertheless a place we all recognize: the world of myth and legend. 'The incomparable thing about myth is that it is true for all time', wrote Wagner. The Jungian writer Robert Donington brings these ideas together, to unpick Wagner's leitmotifs in the *Ring* with commendable obsession, treating each as a symbol arising from the myth. 'If we take myth literally', he argues, 'we get the pleasure of a well-told story we do not believe. If we take it symbolically, we add to this pleasure a distillation of human experience.' And 'a musical motive is a symbolic image', writes Donington – so that Wagner's genius was thus to 'distil' human experience in music by recourse to myth.[8]

Another theme prescient of Freud is the overt sexuality in Wagner's music. It is everywhere: the Venusberg in *Tannhäuser*, from *Die Walküre* to *Siegfried*, Kundry in *Parsifal* and 'all *of Tristan und Isolde*', says Laurence Dreyfus. In his book *Wagner and the Erotic Impulse* Dreyfus affirms that Wagner 'more than anyone else in the nineteenth century made plain his relentless fixation on sexual desire', though it is possible to see him as a musical pioneer of sexuality in the work of Gustave Moreau (who also entwined Eros and myth) and Auguste Rodin – as well as in that of Odilon Redon, John Collier and Arthur Rackham, all of whom depicted Wagner's operas. And compared with the writing of Baudelaire, and ultimately the weird Marquis de Sade, Wagner's sexuality is not *that* revolutionary. Like the ancients, he luxuriates in incest; as in many medieval Catholic and baroque texts, he revels in the (unconvincing) renouncement of sex – in *Parsifal*, for instance; and in *Götterdämmerung* and *Tristan und Isolde*, in the romantic trope of the 'love-death', written eighteen years after *Wuthering Heights*.

After a performance of *Tristan* in New York in 2016, however, my friend Judith Thurman pointed out astutely that Wagner, unlike Emily Brontë, tempers his own fixation with the lovers' death-wish in an enlightened plea from King Marke to the hero and heroine, bent on their own doom, to stop this madness. Take my bride then, he tells his errant knight, and live. This did not, however, deter Clara Schumann, the most talented female composer of the time, from her splendid reaction: 'In the evening we went to see *Tristan und Isold*e. It was the most repulsive thing I have seen or heard in my life. To be forced to see and listen to such sexual frenzy the whole evening, in which every feeling of decency is violated.'[9]

Wagner treated women – apart from his second wife Cosima, Franz Liszt's daughter – with a mixture of adoration and contempt. He asked Mathilde Maier to 'see to my study . . . and spray it with perfume. God how I long to relax with you at last! The pink panties are ready I hope?' He courted women who were already romantically occupied; his lover Mathilde Wesendonck's husband was paying for the *Ring*, and the husband of the woman who later became Cosima Wagner was a distinguished musician and friend. Cosima bore Wagner three children – Isolde, Eva and Siegfried – before they eventually married (on which occasion Mathilde Wesendonck sent a bouquet of wild edelweiss).

This revolution in music came from a flamboyant mind. Wagner was a cultural idealist who explained his enterprise in pompous theoretical texts. The idea of Wagner 'in the world' was something he himself was unhappy about; he wrote about what he called the 'outer world' – a shadow, he said, through which his legs carried him, but it was the 'inner world' that interested him. Yet he was a dynamo, and even when he had given his all to work there was plenty left to unleash into the 'outer world', in great schemes like the theatre at Bayreuth devoted to performances of his work in exactly the radical way he demanded – lights dimmed, orchestra in a pit, as is now standard.

Wagner's conduct was bewildering. According to his first wife Minna's daughter Nathalie, Wagner would shout at her mother until she cried, then crave her forgiveness. During his flirtations with Mathilde Wesendonck, Minna wrote: 'We were just having breakfast when another hefty letter came from that Wesendonck tart. I kept silent, but Richard again began to shriek himself into a mad rage, ranting for three-quarters of an hour.' After visiting Wagner, Liszt recorded that his friend 'wept and laughed and stormed with joy for at least a quarter of an hour at seeing me again'. The French musicologist Édouard Schuré said Wagner's company was like 'a flood bursting its dykes . . . His gaiety flooded over in an exuberant foam of comical fancies and extravagant compliments, but the slightest contradiction provoked in him a terrible anger.' Wagner was forever romping with children and animals. To lighten his singers' long rehearsals, he would entertain them by standing on his head; his assistant August Roekel, describing the *Tristan* rehearsals, recalled that 'if a difficult passage went well, he would spring up, embrace the singer warmly, or – out of pure joy – stand on his head on the sofa, creep under the piano, jump up on to it, run into the garden, and scramble up a tree'.

Wagner was fond of animals. They 'were given to us purposefully by a benevolent power', he wrote to Mathilde. And he told Minna: 'Once, when I woke from a restless doze, I heard a nightingale in the park. It brought a flood of tears to my eyes. If nature could move me no longer, I would not want to live among people. You feel like this too, and your love of animals pleases me greatly. Yes, they are our only comfort.' One of Wagner's pamphlets proposed enlightenment through vegetarianism, another assailed vivisection. His pantheism is admirable: Parsifal's compassion begins with his remorse at killing a swan, and the work's most moving moment is when Kurwenal the old knight points out to Parsifal the resplendent beauty of the meadows, the flowers, and 'all creation that blooms and breathes, lives and lives anew'.

So why did the Nazis admire him? The Third Reich's cult of Wagner was one of the most effective and poisonous acquisitions of music by any regime or political movement – more resonant in history, even, than the USSR's claiming of Shostakovich as the great 'Soviet artist'.

The evidence does, but does not, support the Nazis' claim. Young Wagner's rebel causes would seem to give them little to identify with. He was involved with insurrectionary political causes; he argued that money and property were the root of society's evils. He knew the anarchists Pierre-Joseph Proudhon and Mikhail Bakunin, joined the Dresden uprising of 1848 and was a member of the provisional rebel government. Of the *Ring*, he wrote: 'With this conception I break decisively with the formulas of the present time . . . I cannot think of a performance until after the revolution.'

Yet the contents of Wagner's library in Dresden show it to have been a monument to cultivated taste – Greek and German literature, Shakespeare, philosophy, theology, history – but no politics. Wagner's revolution was for art, and about art in the Greek mould: the *Gesamtkunstwerk*, 'the total work of art'. One can see here in the nineteenth-century nationalist movements those dual roots of what we would now call 'right' and 'left', as shown by my aunt Gladys and Desmond FitzGerald reaching opposite poles from their experience of the 1916 Irish Rising. As Gianluca Marcianò said, Verdi's Italian 'nationalism' demonstrated the reverse: values without borders; while Wagner's German 'nationalism' spoke to the Third Reich, as well as to the anarchists whose company he kept. But then Wagner's art – unlike Verdi's – was never actually in the 'real world', but that of myth, and thus more open to appropriation. As Thomas Mann wrote, 'in the realm of politics, fairy-tales become lies', which happened when the Nazis adopted Wagner. Wagner's argument that myth was the collective memory of a people – *ein Volk* – was of course attractive to them.

But the *Ring* is brimful of foreboding political allegory, commentary on the inevitable abuse of power and the moral compromises entailed by a system of political law. Wotan – god of gods, the Führer – has laws engraved on his staff, but then embarks on a series of deals to secure his divine palace, Valhalla, the Nordic Olympus. The bargaining and calculation are his undoing. His mortal children Siegmund and Sieglinde fall in love and conceive a child, Siegfried, whose birth Wotan is determined to prevent by instructing his faithful *Walküre* – one of a band of demi-goddess warriors – Brünnhilde to kill them both.

But Brünnhilde defies her master, securing Sieglinde's flight, for which she is condemned to sleep surrounded by a ring of fire atop a mountain, to be woken only by a hero who deserves her. Meanwhile, baby Siegfried is raised by a dragon and re-forges

the shards of his dead father's smashed sword. There is a moment
of confrontation at the foot of the mountain: Wotan stops
Siegfried in his tracks, but the youth cuts his staff of law and
authority in two. 'Pass on, for I cannot stop you,' cedes the god of
gods, which Siegfried does; then he climbs the mountain,
traverses the flames and kisses the girl, thereby awakening her
for a sumptuous love duet. In the end, Valhalla burns; the Führer
is revealed a fool, his Reich doomed – strange themes for the
Nazis to admire.

At one level, this could be envisaged as a fascistic denunciation
of political complexity, a raw appeal in sound akin to that
visualized by the choreographers of Nazism, Albert Speer and
Joseph Goebbels. Thomas Mann, as so often, cut to the quick
when he wrote that Wagner displayed 'a downright anarchic
indifference to political structures, as long as German intellectual
and spiritual values – German art – are preserved intact' – and
the Nazis would have appreciated that too. But the notions of
authority and obedience are quintessential to Nazism, and
Siegfried is if anything anarchist, not fascist, and *dis*obedience is
a major and recurrent theme of the *Ring*.

Bernard Shaw, Fabian socialist, believed Wotan personifies a
political establishment living on borrowed time. 'The world is
waiting for Man to redeem it from the lame and cramped government of the gods', he wrote; and the redemption comes from
Siegfried, the free man before whom obsolete laws crumble.[10]
Yet Siegfried's fearless anarchism is also his downfall. He brings
the old order crashing down, but not until he is trapped and
betrayed. Which begs a further possibility: that Wagner and his
Ring allowed the Nazis the decadent perversion of revelling in
the prophecy of their own destruction. Goebbels' diaries show
him to have been almost diabolically aware of the absurdity of a
'thousand-year Reich' long before he and his wife killed their
children, then themselves, in 1945, his own Valhalla in ruins. Yet

Goebbels knew as well as any the power of Wagner's music over the human mind.

Obviously attractive to the Nazis was Wagner's poisonous anti-Semitism. The Nazis loved *Die Meistersinger von Nürnberg*, its elevation of German art and its ridicule of the odious town clerk Beckmesser, presumably Jewish. The Wagnerian Barry Millington writes that 'anti-semitism is woven into the ideological fabric of *Die Meistersinger*, and the representation of Beckmesser incorporates unmistakable anti-semitic characteristics'.[11] Wagner wrote about what he saw as threats to the purity and integrity of German art: threats from France, Italy – and especially from Jewry. He may well have been half-Jewish himself, born less than nine months after his mother married her Jewish second husband Ludwig Geyer, after the death of her first spouse Carl Wagner. Unlike Herr Wagner Snr, Geyer was a man of letters and music.

In 1850 Wagner published 'The Jewish Spirit in Music', a repugnant tract arguing that Jewish culture was not rooted in the *völkisch* tradition and was alien to Germany – proto-Nazism to the letter. But while Wagner's outbursts scandalized his liberal acquaintances and his homosexual patron King Ludwig of Bavaria, they tended not to drive away his Jewish acquaintances. The conductor Hermann Levi wrote to his father, a rabbi, to plead that 'Wagner's crusade against what he calls Judaism in music stems from noble motives'. Wagner distanced himself from the political anti-Semitic movement, but Bayreuth had already attracted a dilettante, racialist right wing, among them the English philosopher Houston Stewart Chamberlain, who married Wagner's daughter Eva. By the 1920s, there were moves to ban Jews from Bayreuth – the festival site for Wagner's music drama, which King Ludwig had built to his specifications – leaving the unfashionably liberal Siegfried Wagner to respond: 'I have to tell you that I cannot share this view . . . If the Jews are willing to lend their support, they deserve our special thanks, for my father's writings offended them.' (Jewish admiration for Wagner continued beyond the Holocaust: Leonard Bernstein recorded a bewitching *Tristan und Isolde* in Bavaria; Daniel Barenboim insists on playing Wagner in Israel.)

But there is a more sophisticated objection to Wagner's music: that it is aesthetically, rather than politically, totalitarian. The Marxist Theodor Adorno found in Wagner a lure of theatrical unity that drew upon myth in order to ban rationality and induce unquestioning intoxication – 'a fear of sobriety', he called it – a 'synthesis of idealism and lust' which leads to 'mental flight'. In Wagner, he wrote, 'ecstasy is an inescapable principle of style'. Adorno addresses the idea of the total work of art, and its synthesis of music with words. 'The basic idea', he writes, 'is that of totality. The *Ring* attempts, without much ado, nothing less than the encapsulation of the world process as a whole' rather than expressing a real world wrought with difference, diversity and division.[12] Most pernicious, Adorno argues, is the idea that having posed questions about our existence and our past – his music opening us up and exposing our raw wounds – Wagner offers his art as the answer. 'The wound is healed only by the spear that caused it': it is as though these lines from *Parsifal* were a motto for the whole enterprise. The problem is not proto-fascism, it is that Wagner's music is artistically totalitarian.

Adorno's view of ruptures in a class society objects to the 'wholeness' of Wagner's universe, and his views on 'progress' must be at odds with the collapse of society in the *Ring* bringing a return to Mother Nature. We end where we began, in the un-sullied natural state of the Rhine riverbed: it is to Erda the Earth goddess – the Nordic Gaia – that Wotan runs when all falls around him. Change and revolution in the *Ring* are not linear in a Marxian way, but mystically cyclical: the end of *Götterdämmerung* recalls the opening Rhine music, stolen gold restored to innocent

Rhinemaidens for whom it has no value other than its beauty; nature triumphant over the ashes of Valhalla and power.

This is overwhelming stuff: and even more alarming is this sneaking suspicion, listening for hours on end, that Wagner is a form of upscale titillation; it is important while immersed in the *Ring* to mentally exit every so often, and afford like King Marke a moment of rational doubt, a reality check. Yet for all its exhausting, dangerous beauty, the *Ring* is also about what Thomas Mann called 'the purely human' when confronted with power, the 'poetic soul' of ahistorical humanity. When Wotan condemns Brünnhilde for her rebellion, he tells her that she is now 'merely yourself'. He, the Führer-god, thinks it is a punishment. She is no longer a *Walküre*, a spiritual life-force, she is a woman: 'henceforth remain what you choose to be'. She has arrived at this state through human feelings towards the lovers; all of this is selfless, she tries to explain to Wotan, but he is too proud to understand, and from this moment is doomed.

It is even stranger, then, that the Nazis should have elevated their own cult of Wagner – given the overt didactic messages of the *Ring* – over Bach, whose music is, after all, thematically neutral in a way that can 'belong' to no one. There were plenty of reasons for the Nazis to claim ownership of Wagner, but more that made their acquisition of such music outrageous. The subject of the *Ring* is that power corrupts, and that even at the end, though Siegfried is killed and Brünnhilde burns like the Jews at Birkenau, the 'purely human' remains intact, as it did beyond the transports from Terezín and the ashes of Auschwitz – along with the music.

9

Symphony under Siege

Shostakovich, Seventh Symphony, Leningrad Radio Orchestra, August 1942

Edith Katya Matus liked to dance, despite bandaged legs and her eighty-four years. She sat by the window of a small but neatly arranged sitting room overlooking the forlorn southern suburbs of St Petersburg. Her eyes were bright and mischievous, and music, she said, 'is my life'. She smoked strong Russian cigarettes with long cardboard filters and lived mainly on coffee, candy when she could get it, and her memories – one memory in particular.

When they placed Mrs Matus's ashes in a grave at the remote Bolsheokhtinsky Cemetery in May 2001, Russia lost one of the last survivors of the night she played oboe in the most extraordinary concert ever. That concert was given at the height of a furious siege, on 9 August 1942, by the Leningrad Radio Orchestra performing Shostakovich's Seventh Symphony – a mighty work dedicated to the composer's 'native city'. It followed the snows of a devastating winter that had thawed to reveal a million dead from starvation. It marked the pinnacle of the blockaded city's defiance, when death stalked every corner and all seemed lost. Those who played like to think it might even have turned the tide of the war, marked the beginning of the Red Army's rolling back the panzer divisions that had occupied the western USSR for two years. By a twist of fate, 9 August was also the date the Nazis had printed on invitations to a reception at the Astoria Hotel, opposite St Isaac's Basilica in the heart of Leningrad's imperial centre, to celebrate the capture of the city. 'They never had their party,' said Mrs Matus with a grim smile. 'Instead, we played our symphony that night, and Leningrad was saved.'

Although it was high summer, 'it was too cold to play without gloves,' she remembered. 'We wore them like mittens with fingers cut off, and even then it was hard to move the keys on my instrument.' Cold in heat: a syndrome associated with starvation, described by Primo Levi in Auschwitz. 'But it was the greatest night of my life,' she said, her fingers shaking with age now, pulling on her cigarette and flashing the inimitable smile of a survivor. This was the last of the conversations we had had throughout the summer and winter of 2000. Of the four remaining survivors of the orchestra at the time, she said: 'I am the only one in the prime of life.'

After a reunion performance of the symphony in 1992, during which the then fourteen survivors had played from the same seats in the same hall as they had done half a century before, Mikhail Parfionov, the trombonist, greeted Mrs Matus. 'Dear Edith,' he said, 'when we first performed this together we were young and beautiful.' 'And now?' challenged Mrs Matus (I can imagine the glint of flirtatious defiance in her eyes). 'Now, dear Edith, you at least are more beautiful than ever,' replied the debonair Mr Parfionov.

Parfionov was the senior officer among a reinforcement of musicians drafted from the trenches to make up the numbers required to play Shostakovich's massive score, following a first rehearsal to which only fifteen emaciated players, including Mrs Matus, had turned up. Word had then gone out to the front lines that anyone who could play an instrument should report for musical duty. Parfionov led a military band touring the Front to perform operetta and songs to stir the spirit, with titles like 'Greetings, Russian Machine Gun!', and airs Shostakovich himself had written in praise of Commissar Stalin.

I last met Parfionov in June 2000, and he died six years later. He lived on the edges of the city near Pishev Station through which trains crash and rattle and to which a makeshift market clings – peasants from around selling small bundles of vegetables. 'Rehearsals in the morning,' he recalled, 'then straight to the Front or to factories for concerts, then our military duties. One day we went straight from a rehearsal to the Piskaryovskoye Cemetery to bury piles of corpses in mass graves. We were digging all afternoon' – Parfionov puts his hands to his head, and clutches at his white hair – 'and the commander of the unit said: "Now start carrying the bodies and put them in!" They stank, but we were back to rehearse the music next day.'

Viktor Koslov, one of Parfionov's men, played the clarinet. Koslov lived until 2009 on the twelfth floor of a Lego-brick apartment block among scores of identical blocks, a tram ride beyond the metro's reach in a dormitory quarter where heroin is ubiquitous among the young. He had a handsome, cheery face and, once retired from professional music, went into cameo movie acting. But that face darkens when he plays a documentary video about the siege, which he watches obsessively, 'hundreds of times'. The commentary barks over images of streets lined with Leningrad's victims, limbs skeletal, skin dry as parchment stretched over protruding jawbones, the inward stare of death in their hollow eyes.

Koslov watches his own history. 'Of course we saw all this!' he said almost indignantly. 'It's what we lived with every day! It's what we walked past on the way to rehearsals. Even now I cannot believe it was real. Ah, but the concert itself – it was our answer to the suffering. I have seen it in my sleep many times, and still hear the thunder of applause from the audience. That will be the last image before my eyes when I die.'

The White Nights of St Petersburg were marked in that summer of 2000, when I last saw some of these musicians, by throngs of young people sipping beer along the banks of the wide Neva, as the midnight sun set the gilt of the Winter Palace ablaze.

The scene six decades earlier had not been dissimilar. On Saturday 21 June 1941, the longest day of the year, Finland Station at which Lenin had arrived from Switzerland to detonate the Bolshevik revolution was teeming with Leningraders buying ice cream and heading for the coastal promenades. The director of the Radio Orchestra, Karl Eliasberg, a tall, thin, bespectacled man, had been rehearsing all day and returned home to read his newspaper. He spotted a notice for an exhibition next day at Catherine Palace to mark the centenary of the death of the poet Lermontov, and decided to attend. The highest political authority in Leningrad, the feared Andrei Zhdanov, was on vacation. And the city's most famous son, Dmitri Shostakovich – whom Zhdanov had deemed to be in need of some 'comradely advice' during the Great Terror not long before – also had plans for the morrow. The composer had bought tickets for a home fixture of the soccer team he passionately supported, Zenith Leningrad.

But there was no match. Through that shortest night, while stars twinkled in a luminous sky that never darkened, Adolf Hitler unleashed the Luftwaffe against Minsk, Smolensk and other industrial cities to the south. Commissar Stalin had for weeks defied all warning of the upcoming onslaught, insisting that the Führer would uphold the Nazi–Soviet pact he had signed two years previously. Stalin finally issued orders for mobilization before dawn on 22 June, but by the time they reached Leningrad the sun was high in a deep blue sky, and by midday the USSR was at war with Germany.

Leningrad held a special fascination for Hitler; the capture and destruction of the city at whatever cost was central to his dream for the East, even when it made little strategic sense. Beyond the ancient Teutonic claims to the Baltic, Leningrad had been the one imperial capital as majestic as either Berlin or Vienna. Moreover, it was the city that had spawned what Hitler regarded as the 'Jewish' ideology of Bolshevism. The Führer said publicly and in leaflets dropped on the city that in order to avoid obliteration, Leningrad must surrender. Secretly, however, he ordered his commander in the East, Field Marshall Wilhelm von Leeb, to refuse Leningrad's capitulation and decimate both city and citizenry, whatever. In a directive headed 'The Future of the City of St. Petersburg' the Nazi general Walter Warlimont wrote: 'The Fuehrer has decided to raze the city of St. Petersburg from the face of the earth. After the defeat of Soviet Russia there will be not the slightest reason for the future existence of this large city.'

After Shostakovich's ordeals of the mid-1930s, the advance of the panzer divisions brought stark moral choices and clarity of sorts. Plus deliverance through distraction, the authorities' attentions drawn away from internal dissidents to the external enemy. Concessions were made to freedom of expression, as artists in return rallied behind the defence of city and mother country. Shostakovich volunteered for the Red Army but was turned away because of bad eyesight. By 30 June 1941 a call had gone out for People's Volunteer Army brigades, and he applied again: 'Until now I have known only peaceful work. Now I am ready to take up arms. Only by fighting can we save humanity from destruction.' This time he was accepted, assigned to trench-digging around the city's outskirts. Later he was moved to the fire brigade and *Time* magazine would feature a famous cover showing the composer in profile, wearing a firefighter's helmet.

He continued to write, mainly arrangements of popular operatic arias for performance to the troops and rousing songs for the military bands, among them 'The Fearless Guards Regiment Is on the Move!' and 'Oath to the People's Commissar', which ended with the line: 'The hour has come for Stalin to lead us into battle! Go bravely to war!' By the end of August, the last railway line into and out of the city was cut and the shelling began. The noose was tied, the siege of Leningrad under way.

Trams clatter beneath Viktor Koslov's apartment, and he turns up the volume on his video, better to hear a passionate voice rasping over a crackle on the airwaves, the voice of Dmitri Shostakovich. The genial clarinettist is listening, like a man possessed, to the composer's radio announcement of 1 September 1941. 'Just an hour ago,' says the voice, 'I completed the score of the second part of my new, large symphonic work. Notwithstanding wartime conditions and the dangers threatening Leningrad, I have been able to work quickly . . . Dear colleagues and friends, remember that our art is threatened by great danger. We will defend our music. We will work with honesty and self-sacrifice, that no one will destroy it.' Koslov presses the Pause button. 'I heard that broadcast at the time,' he says, 'and must have played it a thousand times since.' The caption frozen on Koslov's screen reads: 'No one, ever, in any way, will explain the meaning of the siege. Not by word, nor by sound, nor by song.'

But by the time of his broadcast Shostakovich was trying just that, the ink on his score for those first two movements of the Seventh Symphony only just dry as he made for the studio. The opening movement contains a terrifying musical invocation of the Nazi advance, a kettledrum driving the march to a mighty crescendo, followed by what the composer later called 'a requiem for the victims of war . . . Maybe what is here are a mother's tears, or even that feeling when grief is so great that there are no tears left.'

On 19 September, Luftwaffe bombs hit the Gostiny shopping area, killing and wounding hundreds of civilians. That night, Shostakovich had invited a group of friends to hear him play the piano score of the music he had written. His guests arrived to find manuscript sheets scattered across the floor of his fifth-storey apartment and the composer at his instrument in a state of exuberant anxiety. Just as he began to play, the sirens wailed, and at the end of the long first movement Shostakovich finally dispatched his wife and two small children to the shelter, but implored his visitors to stay for the second. The bombers roared above and their payloads exploded in the buildings and streets around, but the recital continued, guests waiting until the all-clear before making their departure.

During the week that followed, gaunt and working by candle-light, Shostakovich moved on to the Adagio, perhaps the most passionate piece of music he ever composed on warfare, opening with a haunted, almost sacral evocation of war, the meaning and pity of war. He called the passage 'the dramatic centre of the work'. It opens with a mighty fanfare: as though the orchestra has filled some capacious lung and now exhales to announce through the mouthpiece of its massed wind section the forth-coming drama – the opening bars are ominous, but resolved. They cue a devastating, withering tune, a reply on the strings that begins on a high strain and proceeds – slow, pronounced, clear and vast in both its vision and its setting the scene for what is to come. We are not yet in the nightmarish world of the Eighth Symphony, to follow: this passage confronts warfare head on, through tear-filled eyes, or – as Shostakovich himself said, empty of tears, for there were none left to shed.

During August, before the blockade was sealed around

Leningrad, the city's cultural elite had for the most part been evacuated, including the Philharmonic Orchestra and its principal conductor, Shostakovich's friend Evgeny Mravinsky. And throughout his work on the Adagio, the authorities pleaded with Shostakovich to follow suit and join the select few spirited out at night. But he refused. So too did the poet Anna Akhmatova, whose radio broadcasts and poetry readings rallied the city's pride, until even she agreed to go, on 28 September. The following night, his Adagio complete, Shostakovich took a call from Communist Party headquarters commanding him to leave. He grudgingly agreed and, with his wife and children, did so on 1 October. He grabbed the music so far written for the Seventh, that of *Lady Macbeth* and Stravinsky's *Symphony of Psalms*, and stuffed them into a suitcase. But he left behind the score, which he had pledged to bring, of an unfinished opera by his friend Veniamin Fleishman, *Rothschild's Violin* – an omission that tortured him all the way aboard a military transport plane to Moscow, and for a long while afterwards.

Edith Katya Matus, who had learned music in a church choir, was meanwhile a student at the Conservatoire. 'But as the enemy drew closer,' she recalled, 'we were sent to dig trenches, carrying gas masks. The order would come for us to collect shovels at two o'clock. I can remember the first bombing raid on 9 September – we went onto the Conservatory roof to watch the planes come over and the bombs fall. We saw dark clouds rise from the ground to heaven; they had hit the store where bread and sugar for the whole city were kept. We didn't think about ourselves at that moment, we never thought the bombs could fall on our heads. Music lessons were stopped, and it's hard to remember the days after that. And now we ask: "Where were the best years of our youth?" We have only one life to live, and they had to go to defending our country.'

Mrs Matus 'cannot remember' the year of her birth – '1916, I think,' she said, the year before revolution and protracted civil war, eight years before the ascent of Stalin. 'It's hard to remember what happened during the years I grew up, surrounded by trouble, I kept out of its way. The problem came when they said we should not have professional musicians in church, so my mother's choir lost its orchestra. We were left with only a drum and a piano.'

Although the Philharmonic had left Leningrad, the second, reserve, orchestra – affiliated to the radio station – was ordered to stay. The Leningrad Radio Committee Orchestra had become an understudy to the famous Philharmonic in 1931 and put under the direction of Karl Eliasberg, respected deputy to Mravinsky. The Radio Orchestra played throughout the besieged autumn of 1941, including a performance of Tchaikovsky's Fifth Symphony, broadcast to Britain on 28 September. The programme of the last concert before the season was abandoned, given on 14 December, included the rousing '1812 Overture' depicting the defeat of Napoleon's invading army by that of the tsar. Thereafter, the orchestra's log carries a valedictory note: 'Rehearsal did not take place. Srabian is dead. Petrov is sick. Borishev is dead. Orchestra not working.' There followed, Eliasberg recounted later, 'the worst period of the orchestra's history, during which many musicians were killed and some of those closest to me died of starvation'.

The winter of 1941–2 was without mercy. Corpses scattered the streets – covered by snowfall daily added to afresh – and children's sleds were used to haul them to the mass graves. The city was saved by the 'Road of Life', a miracle of engineering and courage cut across the ice of Lake Ladoga, which enabled an initial ration of 125 grams of bread per working adult to be distributed from Christmas Day onwards. Yet every imaginable hardship was endured and every imaginable barbarity committed in the pursuit of food, as even that small ration was cut and cut again. Still the bombs fell: Leningrad burned as it froze, and death itself, not the Third Reich, almost claimed the city of ice.

'All I can remember about the winter,' Mrs Matus continued, 'is starvation, bombs and cold. When I walked the streets, the dead were lying everywhere; no one to clear the bodies.' 'There was not a trace of joy in a single face,' said Mikhail Parfionov, 'Everyone pale, thin, exhausted . . . I was on Troitsky Bridge one day when a man collapsed in front of me. He looked into my eyes and pleaded for help; I told him there was nothing I could do for him, and walked on. The only thing anyone thought about was the next meal; to get to the end of the day alive. Even in the military canteen, soldiers crawled around the floor to see if anyone had allowed crumbs to drop before going out to sit in the trenches in the cold.' Temperatures dropped to thirty degrees below zero.

The horror of cannibalism during the siege has been examined by some Western historians but is taboo in Russia: a self-imposed blackout in Soviet and post-Soviet memory. The American historian Harrison Salisbury cites such details as the arrest of one woman on her way back from a graveyard with the bodies of five children in a sack, but notes: 'the memory of trauma – of minds and bodies frozen by fear and by the horror that everyone was forced to see – has been almost entirely lost'.[1] Mrs Matus turned the stone of taboo a fraction: 'I remember a neighbour, a woman, used to come knocking at the door of our apartment shouting at Mother, "Let me in!", and she would run through the door to hide because, she said, her husband was trying to kill her to eat her.'

Viktor Koslov is – heretically – bolder. Born in Bryansk near Moscow, he had become a clarinettist like his father and in 1935 joined the illustrious Kirov Ballet in Leningrad. He has a vivacious, easy-going face, but when he conjures up that winter his eyes narrow, his muscles tighten. The images on his video screen are appalling enough, but the memories they stir are even worse: 'People were going out onto the Neva to cut into the ice for water, filthy water, to drink, with bodies lying around the ice holes. And those were the ones who lived near the Neva – what about the others? Some were dead, others half dead, sometimes from injuries they had done to themselves. People were cutting off and eating their own buttocks to live. We only really saw what that winter did when the snow began to melt. We thought: Look, here comes spring! But what did it bring? Decomposing, dismembered corpses in the streets, severed legs with the meat chopped off them. Bits of bodies in the garbage cans . . . women's bodies with breasts cut off, which people had taken to eat. They had been buried all winter, but then there they were for the city to see how it had remained alive.'

During this nightmare of life-in-death, Shostakovich was torn between distress for his native city, anxiety over his mother and sister who had remained there, brooding melancholy, and the struggle to finish his symphony. He had been evacuated to territory out of the invaders' range, to Kuibyshev near Moscow, along with a number of artists.

His letters to his friend Isaak Glikman, mostly from Kuibyshev, are moving and illuminating. They express absolute commitment to staying in the USSR, even while war ravaged the occupied territory and wrought fear and hardship throughout the rest. He writes in November 1941: 'They want me to stay here because of the possibility of my visiting the USA. If they leave it up to me to decide I shall decline, because I have no inclination whatever for the trip. I would rather finish my symphony and stay in my homeland.' After appearing on the cover of *Time* magazine, Shostakovich was by now as much a celebrity in America as he is now. The opportunity, if it existed, offered him safety, adulation and the ability to work in peace and probably luxury – but he was utterly uninterested. The same letter contains a longer, compelling passage on Dynamo Leningrad footballers joining the wartime police divisions, fighting as boldly as they played.

Along with this committed loyalty, however, come tributes to communism and Stalin that are scathing in their playfully over-blown humour. On 6 November 1942, he would write to Glikman: 'My warmest congratulations and best wishes to you on the twenty-fifth anniversary of the Great October Socialist Revolution. I have just listened to the radio broadcast of the speech by Comrade Stalin. My dear friend! How sad it is that circumstances have forced us to hear this speech so far apart from one another.' But in January the following year: 'Sometimes at night I don't sleep, and I weep. Tears flow thick and fast and bitter. Nina and the children sleep in the other room, so there is nothing to prevent me from giving way to my tears. Then I calm myself. My nerves are really playing up.' Not until May 1943 was he able to write: 'Although I haven't yet managed to sort out a proper way of life, I am feeling quite buoyant.'

For now, though, as the planned premiere of the Seventh Symphony came into view, work on its last movement, intended to envisage 'a beautiful future time when the enemy will have been defeated', had eluded him. He reports to Glikman in the same letter that another friend, Soso Begiashvili, 'thinks it not optimistic enough . . . It has quite enough optimism as it is' – which it does. Before a Christmas party at the family's billet in Kuibyshev on 27 December – at which guests found him in sudden and unusually fine spirits, drinking vodka and singing – Shostakovich whispered to a friend that he had completed the work. A few days later, he performed a piano version to a group of friends and neighbours, one of whom, Flora Litvinova, remarked: 'When Dmitri Dimitriyevich finished playing everyone rushed up to him. He was tired and agitated.'[2]

The Philharmonic and Mravinsky – whom Shostakovich

wanted to premiere his symphony – were billeted at Novosibirsk in the heart of Siberia, so it was impractical for his wish to be granted. But the Bolshoi Theatre Orchestra was based at Kuibyshev with its conductor Samuil Samosud, which made for a feasible first night. Rehearsals began in February and the work was duly premiered on 5 March 1942 to a thunderous reception. Next, the score moved to the capital, where a performance under the baton of Grigory Stolyarov was broadcast from Moscow around the world. And as if the event and the music themselves were not dramatic enough, the Luftwaffe provided a backdrop, so the global audience also heard a distant thudding of bombs. With the world's attention captivated, a microfiche score was smuggled to the West via Tehran for performance in London, Stockholm and across the USA, where Arturo Toscanini gave a premiere in July. At the same time, virtually every unoccupied Soviet city that could muster the number of musicians required to play the vast symphony duly heard it. Mravinsky finally got to conduct his friend's work during the same month as Toscanini.

Shostakovich's face adorned newspapers across the planet. His dedication had been: 'To the historic confrontation now taking place between reason and obscurantism, culture and barbarity, light and darkness. I dedicate my Seventh Symphony to our struggle against fascism, to our coming victory and to my native city of Leningrad.' And yet the city to which the symphony was dedicated had yet to hear it. 'People heard about all the concerts,' remembered Viktor Koslov, 'and all saying: "Why isn't it performed here?"' And when Leningrad did finally hear the work, the epic moment went almost unnoticed in the outside world, quickly forgotten even in the USSR.

On 2 April 1942, for all the deprivations of winter – and because of them – the Leningrad edition of *Pravda* announced that the city arts department was preparing a season of symphonic and other concerts. Plans had been incubating for some time and the authorities knew there was only one way to effectively climax the run, however fantastical the notion might be: a performance of Shostakovich's 'Leningrad' Symphony. Ostensibly, this was the decision of the head of the arts department, Boris Zagorsky, and the radio committee director Yasha Babushkin – according to the official history, as recorded in the only (tiny) booklet (by Andrei Krukov) published on the concert by the year 2000, and then long since out of print. Krukov, a schoolboy studying music in 1942, has his own memories of the siege: his school was closed because of bombing, but his teacher 'used to go from house to house, to visit his pupils to carry on [with their lessons], until he died of cold and ill health in February. At that time, we were exchanging anything for bread. In our block lived a director at one of the factories. My mother invited him into our apartment and he took all the beautiful things in return for bread, wood and glue – we ate carpenter's glue in those days, just one of the industrial products we used to eat.'

Professor Krukov is a small sage – mischievous and with a cool smile – who loves to discuss his obsession with the night of the concert. But in conversation, curiously, he subverts many of the salient details in the official Soviet history of it, written by himself, with a resigned shrug of each shoulder, a gesture to history's seasonality. He coyly confides the true origin (and central political purpose) of the idea to stage the concert in the first place: 'They say that Zhdanov paid very close attention to the radio schedules. He said there were too many political problems on radio, and "too much silence". Zhdanov's order was not to broadcast sad or serious things, but music. And that the city's morale must be raised to avoid defeat. That was the impetus for the performance of Shostakovich's symphony – Zhdanov's word. And given the importance of Zhdanov, his word tended to be taken as an order: quite enough to ensure it would happen. That is how the orchestra was guaranteed all it would need in its dealings with the leadership.'

Zhdanov, the man who had goaded Shostakovich during the mid-1930s (and who would do so again), was still Leningrad's political commissar, and unlike any other Soviet leader – such as Supreme Commander Marshal Andrei Zhukov, who briefly took over the defence of Leningrad, but left – his own political future was inseparable from the outcome of the blockade. In the Radio Orchestra archive there is a fragment of an order from Party high command instructing its committee: 'By any means, get a score of the Seventh Symphony from Moscow. Transport it to Leningrad as soon as possible.' But how? There were night flights still operating over Nazi lines but they were more and more frequently shot down.

However, sometime during March 1942, a score for the completed symphony had finally reached Leningrad aboard a light plane otherwise loaded with emergency first aid. 'When I saw it,' Eliasberg told Professor Krukov, 'I thought: We'll never play this. It was four thick volumes of music.' The Seventh is indeed a colossal work, scored for more musicians than almost any symphonies other than Mahler's. It demands battalions of strings, but what worried Eliasberg most were the voluminous arrangements for woodwind and brass, including eight trumpet parts, six tubas and six trombones – in a city horribly short of breath and strength to blow. Eliasberg, quartered in what is now again the Astoria Hotel – then intended to host the Nazi celebrations, later converted into a wartime hospital – procured a list of musicians, of whom twenty-five were already inked out, dead. Those known to be alive, circled in red, were ordered to report for duty.

'I knew that Shostakovich had finished his symphony,' recalled Mrs Matus, 'and in April I heard an announcement that all members of the orchestra who had stayed in the city should come to the radio station and register.' Mrs Matus was not actually a member of the orchestra, but answered the call because she knew most of its players. How? 'Because they were my lovers,' she replied, only partly in jest. Preparing her oboe, however, was more of a challenge. 'It was in poor order because of the general conditions. What was needed was a master restorer, but there was none. I went to a man I knew could do it. The door was open and the man covered in blankets, more dead than alive. The room was unheated, there was nothing to eat, but maybe he was happy to have a reason to help because I said it had to be done because of the Shostakovich concert, and I saw him smile. He asked "When do you need it?" and I said next day. And he said "Please return tomorrow."

'When I came back, my oboe was fully repaired. I asked if there was anything I could give him. I had noticed when I went before there was what I thought was a fur hat on his sofa, but didn't pay attention to what it really was – a dead cat. I again asked the price and he asked me to get him a cat or dog, since he had nothing to live on. He said there were hardly any cats or dogs left in the city to eat, but the meat was tasty enough. I paid some money, thanked him, and that is all.'

It was time to go to the first rehearsal. 'The studio was on the first floor of the radio station,' Mrs Matus continued. 'When I got there, I nearly fell over with shock. Of the orchestra of about a hundred people, there were only fifteen left. I didn't recognize any of the musicians I knew from before, they were like skeletons. I don't think Eliasberg really called the first rehearsal to look for musicians. It was evident that we couldn't play anything, we could hardly stand on our feet! Nevertheless, he said: "Dear friends, we must start our work . . . we have a great responsibility. We are weak, but we must force ourselves to perform this symphony," and he raised his arms to begin. He lifted his stick, but there was no reaction. The musicians were trembling. Even those who could play were unable to keep time; when Eliasberg got to the fourth bar, they were still on the second! But those who were able to play helped the weaker musicians, and thus our small group began the opening bars.

'I remember the trumpeter – he didn't have the breath to play his solo and there was silence when his turn came around. He was on his knees, poor man. Eliasberg was waiting; he said: "It's your solo. You're the first trumpet, why don't you play?" But the trumpeter replied: "I'm sorry sir, I haven't the strength in my lungs." There was a terrible pause. Everyone asked him to try. Eliasberg said: "I think you do have the strength," and then the trumpeter took up his trumpet and tried again, and played a little. And so the rehearsal continued, but broke up after fifteen minutes. It had been scheduled to last three hours. Quite often there would be a situation like that, when someone just couldn't play, either because they didn't have the strength or their instrument wasn't in working order. Everybody knew at the beginning the musicians were starving, everyone did their best, but we played badly, it was hopeless.'

Eliasberg walked the length of Nevsky Prospekt, over the canals, from the Astoria to military headquarters at Smolny Palace, with a simple request: he needed men and women from the Front, anyone who could play an instrument. The order went out almost immediately from the commander-in-chief, General Leonid Govorov himself: military bands, orchestras and anyone else capable should report for duty at the studio. Captain Parfionov was a senior officer in the orchestra of the army's 45th Division. 'We were good,' he said, 'but all we ever got to play were short concerts during pauses between fighting.' The songs they performed, such as 'Oath to Leningrad' and 'Forward Against the Fascist Enemy', were published in special booklets with Constructivist poster graphics on the cover. 'Then,' recalled Parfionov, 'we received an order to report to the radio on a very important matter.' His band along with others was to be signed up.

Parfionov was raised in an orphanage from the age of four, studied music as a child, and graduated from the Mussorgsky Academy in 1933. He harbours little nostalgia for pre-war Leningrad: 'Even then music was a substitute for food – you got a specific amount to eat, but it wasn't enough to live on. It was a system made by rats for rats to live in.' He joined the army in 1936. 'I never thought in terms of long military service,' he reflected now, 'but I stayed thirty-nine years' in the Red Army.

Serving during the siege was, he said, 'a nightmare. The commander used me as a dispatch rider taking papers to head-quarters. Shells would fall suddenly; people blown to pieces, blood everywhere. Some of the heaviest shelling fell just over the river from the Philharmonic – screaming, sirens, people who had been walking along the street suddenly just a mound of meat.' At rehearsals 'there was no time for fun or to ask anyone who they were. We came, did our job and left to come back the following day. People were in a terrible condition. Often Eliasberg would have to repeat instructions two or three times before people could understand, the reaction was so slow. We had to go over the same passage of music over and over, not for lack of emotion or ability, but simply to get it strong or loud enough . . . when we were rehearsing, no one was very enthusiastic.'

'We would start rehearsing,' recalled Viktor Koslov, one of Parfionov's men, 'and get dizzy in our heads; they'd start spinning when you blew with your lungs. The symphony was too large and complicated . . . we might talk to the person sitting next to us, but the only subjects were hunger and food, not music. Commander Parfionov used to line us up, march us in and march us back to our duties again.

The next task was for each player to produce his or her part. They were ordered to copy out their own by hand – the pianist, Nina Bronnikova, helped with more than her fair share (after the concert, she married Maestro Eliasberg). They were given special

ID cards allowing them to pass through checkpoints with 'Eliasberg's Orchestra' printed on them. Some were working in anti-aircraft units and had to leave rehearsals when the sirens sounded. Others, similarly, were called away for emergency firefighting duty. One trombone player was arrested under a new law covering 'food crimes' – for stealing corn, said Parfionov: 'He was put on trial at the military tribunal and sent to special detention.' 'And not everyone who planned to play in our concert did so,' he added. 'Some of our orchestra died. Three, as I recall, including a flautist called Karelsky. People were dying like flies, so why not members of the orchestra? Hunger and cold every-where. When you are hungry, you are cold however warm it is. Sometimes, people just fell over onto the floor while they were playing, from cold-hunger.'

'We rehearsed every day except Sunday,' remembered Mrs Matus, 'sometimes twice a day. They gave us a little extra food in the canteen of the Pushkin Theatre. Not really soup, more water with a few beans in it, and a little spoon of wheatgerm.' There is disagreement over this enticement of 'extra food' for the musicians. Professor Krukov said the original call for players promised as much, and that 'some came just for the additional food'. But Parfionov disputes this: 'Only Eliasberg,' he said, 'was given extra food. We in the military had 250 grams of bread a day, and civilians 125 grams. That was all.'

Eliasberg would remain in the radio building – and later, in the Philharmonic Hall – long into the night, after his musicians had left. 'He was very strict,' said Mrs Matus. 'He would allow for no mistakes, or delays. If a musician played badly or was late, they would lose their 125 grams of bread. If someone was late because of a bombing raid, he would accept the excuse only if there had been no warnings from the siren. One day, a man came late and explained it was because he had had to watch them bury people, one of whom was his wife, that morning. She died of starvation. But Eliasberg said that was no excuse, and the man would lose his extra ration – that was the rule.'

Koslov remembered the episode of the widower. 'He said to us all: "This must not happen again. Even if your wife or husband dies, you must be at the rehearsal!" He demanded absolute commitment and attention. When people said, "It's no good, I can't play it" or "I can't move," Eliasberg would reply, "Go on! No complaining!"' Parfionov also recalled the bereaved man. 'It sounds harsh, but he was right. He had a concert to prepare. It worked both ways: on another occasion I met Eliasberg walking by the military canteen . . . He asked if I had a spare ticket to get bread, he was so hungry. I said I didn't have one and anyway, in the studio we were under his rules, but here under military orders, and it was against *our* regulations for him to come in. I respected him as a thorough professional, but he was a strange man . . . it was impossible to get to know him. He was not interested in personal contact.'

'Summer came,' recalled Professor Krukov. 'Finally, some hope after counting the dead. At last, leaves, blades of grass, and the will to live. The people were different, of course, but not broken. Their stomachs were empty, but the streets were full.' Even Koslov, with his terrifying memory of what the melting ice had revealed, remembered 'the running of the first tram along its route. That was joy, real joy.'

When the orchestra moved from the radio building to the Philharmonic Hall, said Koslov, 'it was still freezing. The windows were broken by blast, the reed of my clarinet frozen and my lips were cracking so it was hard to grip the mouthpiece.' But as June paled the white nights' sky, so the rehearsals grew longer. 'We had begun playing small sections of the symphony,' said Mrs Matus, 'and slowly added more and more. But we never played the whole thing, until finally there was a dress rehearsal, three days before the concert. Only once – the first and only time we had the strength to perform the whole piece from beginning to end.'

August 9th arrived. 'I remember waking up that morning,' said Koslov, 'and feeling a different man.' 'It was a holiday,' reminisced Mrs Matus, 'the first we had had since the blockade began.' A programme had been printed, quoting on the cover from Shostakovich's radio address; and inside, the writer Alexei Tolstoy saying: 'The Seventh Symphony arose from Russia's fight against dark forces. Written in Leningrad, it has become a work for the world, understood on all parallels and meridians, because it is about human beings at a time of trial and struggle.' Shortly before six o'clock, Eliasberg, prerecorded, went on air:

> *Comrades: a great occurrence in the cultural history of our city is about to take place. In a few minutes, you will hear for the first time the Seventh Symphony of Dmitri Shostakovich, our outstanding fellow citizen. He wrote this great composition in the city during the days when the enemy was, insanely, trying to enter Leningrad; when the fascist swine were bombing and shelling all Europe, and Europe believed the days of Leningrad were over. But this performance is witness to our spirit, courage and readiness to fight. Listen, Comrades!*

Parfionov recaptured the moment: 'It had been an everyday job until now. But we were stunned by the number of people, that there could be so many people starving for food but also starving for music. Some had come in holiday clothes, some in uniform from the Front. Most were pale, thin and dystrophic. Some were friends I recognized from fishing before the war. That was the moment we decided to play as best we could.' Parfionov was a composed, even rigid, military man, but his hands shook at the memory.

'At first,' said Mrs Matus, 'I was nervous when I saw the hall so full. All the elite was there; Zhdanov, the party leaders and generals.' (Krukov, however, points out that 'not all the highest authorities were lovers of music, and many did not attend'.) 'There were loudspeakers everywhere,' continued Mrs Matus. 'The concert would be broadcast all over the city! The musicians were afraid we just wouldn't be able to do it.' Despite the summer day, 'we were dressed like cabbages, with layers of clothes on. The soldiers had army uniforms, and the civilian men wore white shirts and smoking-jackets with tails. I was wearing thick trousers, stockings and my gloves with cut-off fingers.' 'I'll never forget the lights [above the stage] going on,' remembered Koslov, 'they'd never been on before; I'd forgotten what electric light was like. It was more like a ceremony than a concert.' Mrs Matus: 'For the first time in months, there was silence. Eliasberg lifted his baton, and we began.'

Eliasberg, talking later to Krukov, recalled 'a strange, deep silence falling on the hall as I turned to the orchestra. It was also quiet outside because the German artillery had stopped firing . . . Far and wide they heard the opening of the symphony, as we plunged deep inside the music.' The first movement and the march reached their terrifying crescendo. 'There was an outburst of anger,' wrote one of those present, in a diary, 'like shelling, in the hall.' Meanwhile, in apartments rising from the empty streets and along front-line trenches dug cheek by jowl with the Führer's invading army, citizens and soldiers listened. An artilleryman called Savkov wrote in his journal: 'On the night of 9 August 1942, my artillery squadron and the people of the great front-line city were listening to the Shostakovich symphony with closed eyes. It seemed that the cloudless sky had suddenly become a storm bursting with music as the city listened to the symphony of heroes and forgot about the war, but not the meaning of war.'

Shostakovich's symphony surges towards the conclusion over which he agonized in Kuibyshev – like a torrent of defiance and desperate hope, rather than the crass 'optimism' required of him; a promise of liberation that was still a reckless, distant dream in the summer of 1942. And the finale is remarkable for that alone – 'so loud and mighty I thought we'd reached a limit and the whole thing would collapse and fall apart,' said Parfionov. 'Playing that, only at this point, did I realize what we were doing, and hear the grand beauty of the symphony.' 'When the piece ended,' said Mrs Matus, 'there was not a sound in the hall. Then someone clapped at the back, and then there was thunder, a storm of applause. It was improper to embrace each other, but we wanted to.' Eliasberg was called back to the podium countless times, and a bouquet presented by a girl called Jakova Luboká.

'People stood and cried,' said Eliasberg later, 'They knew this was not a passing episode but the beginning of something. The hall, the homes, the Front, the whole city was one human being seizing this victory over the soulless machine. And we had it, in the music. When we had finished, everyone was satisfied. Me, I was only shattered.'

'Afterwards,' recalled Mrs Matus, 'we held each other, kissed and were happy. We were invited to the Pushkin canteen for a reception by Zhdanov himself, who said he was proud of us. He greeted us personally and on the table there was beefsteak and – oh, everything delicious! We ate and ate; it was the first we had eaten since the beginning of the siege. But the meal made our stomachs too big, so we had to go and throw it up.'

General Gorlov took Eliasberg aside, saying: 'We played our part in the symphony too,' and Eliasberg would write later that 'at the time I did not understand what he meant'. It was an explanation for the silence outside that had baffled the conductor: Gorlov's artillery had the previous night unleashed a barrage against the Nazi lines – using ammunition beyond what was militarily prudent – so ferocious that it would guarantee a degree of quiet from the stunned German gunners for at least sufficient time to allow the audience to arrive, listen and depart safely, and for the symphony to be played uninterrupted. And, crucially, to be heard by the Germans themselves – for special speakers had been arranged by the authorities, pointing outwards from the defences towards the invader, and ensuring a lusty volume.

'I think it gave everyone a shock,' said Koslov, 'Russians *and* Germans, to hear this music in what they thought was a dead city. That's what people were saying out at the Front, when we returned that day – "How did you do it?"' Professor Krukov, however, has a typically mischievous view of the concert's aftermath: 'Outside Leningrad, the symphony was received like the explosion of a bomb. But here, people didn't receive it that way. Most of the intelligentsia had evacuated itself and there were not many passionate lovers of serious symphonic music left. The most popular music in Leningrad was musical comedy. The city's favourite was not the Seventh Symphony – it was a terrible tune called "The Blue, Blue Sea", which was played a thousand times.'

Not everyone was invited to eat Zhdanov's beefsteak. Koslov was 'sent out immediately after the concert, on patrol to look for spies' – the fifth column of 'rocket-launchers' who were said to send up flares from target roofs to guide the Luftwaffe's bombers. Parfionov was sent straight round the corner from the Philharmonic Hall onto Nevsky Prospekt to check passes. Indeed, after the applause had died, so did any official acknowledgement that the concert had taken place at all, until after the war. 'There was no feedback, nothing, until 1945,' Koslov said. The end would be a long time coming. Leningrad endured eighteen more months of siege before the Red Army rolled back the *Wehrmacht* and the first train rolled into Finland Station carrying bread, meat, milk, medical supplies, vodka and other fuel. The city liberated and fed, each musician was given a special medal, but it was twenty years before Leningrad staged a commemorative reunion concert.

Behind the Philharmonic Hall in what is now St Petersburg again lies one of the hidden treasures of music and its history: the orchestra's archive, which back in 2000 was in the care of Galina Retrovskaya, its curator. The story of the Philharmonic and of everyone who ever played with or conducted the orchestra was crammed into this small space, on shelves full of manuscripts, books, posters and programmes, with details of every concert performed handwritten on thousands of index cards filed in towering wooden cabinets with brass handles. The manuscripts include first editions of many Russian masterpieces, such as *Eugene Onegin*, autographed and dedicated by Tchaikovsky to the tsar. Everywhere is paper, yellowed like the stone of an old church, and the musky scent of dust and time.

Mrs Retrovskaya is a human dynamo (or metronome), in a smart two-piece suit and brooch, here since 1956 and always with too much to see to. 'It hasn't changed much,' she said, making a self-evident point. 'However, we were told six years ago we would get a computer.' She pulls on an electric cord in a terminal on the wall, but impotent, unattached to any machine. But Mrs Retrovskaya does not need one: the history she curates is contained in those cross-referenced index cards. Her records are not only those of the orchestra, she insists, but of all music at what she calls 'the zenith of cultural life in this city'. It was in this room that Eliasberg and the surviving musicians of 1942 gathered for a party she organized in 1964, before a commemorative performance in Shostakovich's presence. 'There were sixteen of them and we had to take the desks out. It was the first time they had been together in twenty-two years, and they were almost in tears; it was pure, raw emotion.'

Mrs Retrovskaya was the thread that bound these people together. She is the only person who remembered people like Arseny Petrov, the crucial player of the first movement's kettledrum, who had performed in the tsar's orchestra – and had single-handedly, once the bombardment was under way, removed the chandeliers and decorative light bulbs from the Philharmonic Hall for safe-keeping in a basement. He was rewarded after the war with a job as caretaker of the building.

Or the trombonist Mikhail Smolyak, who told her about how, when meal breaks came around, even if bombs were falling, musicians would still make a dash for the canteen. 'They didn't give a damn,' she said, 'they were young and wanted to eat.' Or the first trumpet Dmitri Chudyenko, who developed tuberculosis, except that Mrs Retrovskaya never knew this until he arrived to visit her with fresh blood on his shirt cuffs one winter's morning. 'He said it was because he had had to cut the ice to go swimming in the Neva, which was the only way to help the pain.' Edith Katya Matus became Mrs Retrovskaya's best friend. 'I used to visit her nearly every day; it wasn't like we would remember everything; we would sit down and drink tea and sometimes memories of those times would arise. She was the only one who never used the formal way of saying "you" in our language,' she recalled – 'not to anyone, even Maestro Eliasberg.'

Mrs Retrovskaya hurries over to one of the cabinets and pulls out an index card: 'January 27th 1964. Shostakovich Seventh Symphony. Conductor, Karl Eliasberg' – the night of the party. The sixteen survivors played in their same seats, and Eliasberg said the concert was dedicated to those who had performed then but had died since. He revelled in the fact that the audience once again stood, applauding, but he added a melancholy after-thought: 'Those moments do not come often. I cannot explain the feeling I had. The glory of fame and the grief of loss, and the thought that maybe the brightest moments of your life are gone. The city now lives a peaceful life, but no one has the right to forget the past.'

The present, however, had forgotten Karl Eliasberg and the brightest moments of his life were indeed in the past. There is a detail in the top left-hand corner of Mrs Retrovskaya's index card: even this epic concert was played by the Philharmonic's second orchestra. That may have been appropriate, since it had given the performance in 1942. But Eliasberg's name appears on only one other Leningrad Philharmonic card between 1945 and 1964, dated 28 December 1961, when he conducted just the first movement of the Seventh Symphony, also with the reserve orchestra. He conducted in the city only once more, on 9 May 1975 – again Shostakovich's Seventh, and again the second orchestra. The reason: no sooner had the war ended and the *nomenklatura* returned from exile, than Eliasberg suddenly found himself out in a different kind of cold from that of the winter of 1941.

People in St Petersburg are coy as to how the hero of the city's iconic cultural moment could have been so quickly exiled into obscurity; the discourse treads on splinters. The fate of Karl Eliasberg turns into one of those conversations that hallmark societies where truths are like a set of Russian dolls, one concealed within the next. 'I don't know what happened and I don't want to know,' declined the usually four-square Mrs Matus. 'You know how things are in Russia. Let a man do a great deed, and he has far to fall. When the powerful people came back at the end of the war, Eliasberg found he had enemies, envious of his glory, among musicians and politicians.' Little credence is given to the notion, which immediately occurs, that Eliasberg's origins – German and Jewish – militated against him, though it may very well have accounted for his being ordered to stay behind in autumn 1941, deemed more 'dispensable' than the revered Evgeny Mravinsky, descended from Russian nobility. Professor Krukov said simply: 'After the return of all the musicians who had been evacuated, the rest were put aside. Eliasberg found he was no longer the foremost, and there was not space for two at the top of the Philharmonic.'

The genius had returned to claim his rightful, exclusive place. To speak ill of Mravinsky in St Petersburg is akin to spitting on an icon in St Isaac's Basilica. But everyone knows that his mastery, his friendship with Shostakovich and his uniquely deep insight into the composer's music were accompanied by authoritarianism and an intolerance of competition. 'Once the concert was over,' said Koslov, 'the honoured one was Mravinsky, and Mravinsky was never going to lead Eliasberg onto the Philharmonic's stage and allow him to demonstrate his strength and colour. There was great pressure on Eliasberg; a sad destiny for a man so famous after that concert, but not as famous or as good as Mravinsky.'

Mrs Matus kept in close touch with Eliasberg: 'He stayed mostly at home waiting beside the telephone for a call inviting him to conduct. But it never came. When he went out to buy newspapers, he would tell his wife to wait beside the phone for him, then ask her when he returned: "Did they call?", and she would tell him "No". I got to know her quite well, she said it was breaking her heart. Sometimes he went to the country to work; that was the only work he could get.'

'Instead of Leningrad, he gave concerts all over Russia,' said Koslov. 'He would pretend they were important, but they were not. I ran into him once or twice on Nevsky Prospekt. We hugged and greeted each other, which was not what I expected from the man I remembered from the war. I asked him: "How are you these days? I hear you're touring all over the Soviet Union!" He replied: "Yes, I'm only here for a day, then back out tomorrow." He didn't say much and I don't think he wanted to.'

Galina Retrovskaya, who kept in contact with the conductor, said she 'used to lend him scores he needed from the archive. I gave him whatever he needed, even the rarest manuscripts that were never to be removed.' In 1978 'he died poor and alone, apart from his wife.' His ashes were buried in a small plot at the back of the Piskaryovskoye Cemetery, assigned, as Mrs Matus

put it, for 'the common citizenry'. 'His grave,' adds Koslov, 'was
not well tended.' But Mrs Retrovskaya and the orchestra's
principal conductor after the fall of communism, Yuri Temirkanov,
led a resurrection of Eliasberg's name and reputation. In 1992,
they recruited a powerful ally in the city's new mayor, Anatoly
Sobchak, leader of the reform movement during glasnost (and
mentor of an ambitious young KGB lieutenant, one Vladimir
Putin). Sobchak was also 'a connoisseur of music, who came to
see us here during his first month in office,' said Retrovskaya,
and with his help the conductor's ashes were disinterred and
transferred from the 'common citizens" graveyard to the Alexander Nevsky Cemetery. 'The city's oldest,' said Mrs Matus,
'and the best of cemeteries, where the great cultural figures rest.'

Edith Katya Matus continued to play for her own pleasure and
Commander Parfionov remained in the military. Koslov returned
to the Kirov and stayed there, even though his first wife left for
the USA with their son: 'I said "Go! Why would I want to leave?
It would be death to leave the Kirov!"' But after retirement from
the Ballet orchestra and marriage to the manager of a local telephone exchange, Koslov launched a second career. For fifteen
years from 1982, he played cameo parts in Russian B movies,
which comes as no surprise given his debonair manner, good
looks, fondness for mimicry and his contacts in the musical elite.
He has quite a collection of promo snaps, including Koslov in
powdered bouffant wigs, Koslov in rugged peasant gear. He had
a bigger role in a movie called *Young Catherine*, about Catherine
the Great.

Koslov was an obvious choice for a film version of Tchaikovsky's
opera *The Queen of Spades*, and featured in romances with titles
such as *First and Last Meeting*. But most surprising is the role he
introduces with the throwaway line: 'I was in Hollywood once.'
Actually, Hollywood came to him: shaggy-haired, wearing
spectacles and a Russian mystic's long beard, he played one of

the escorts to Rasputin in the movie of that name made by Paramount Pictures in 1996. It starred Alan Rickman, Greta Scacchi and Ian McKellen – 'they all came here to film it; we used to eat together and sometimes talk together. Oh yes, it was terrific fun.' But he seems almost bored by the idea. 'Actually I've forgotten whether Greta Scacchi was here. I suppose she must have been. I've lost count of the number of films I was in – it was just one of them, the American one.'

In summer 2000, I went to the Philharmonic Hall to hear the 'Leningrad' Symphony played by the Philharmonic conducted by Mravinsky's and Eliasberg's successor, Temirkanov. The hall was packed, the audience mostly young, and we stood three deep in the gallery – even Mrs Retrovskaya was unable to procure seats. She brought with her a friend called Valeria, who remembered the siege well, and both ladies listened to the work with barely the flicker of an eyelash – Valeria, especially, wearing an expression of indescribable introspective reflection. Sitting on a velvet-covered stool backstage afterwards, Temirkanov looked shattered, wiping his brow with a silk handkerchief. 'I know what that music means,' he said, 'and the responsibility of conducting it from the podium on which Eliasberg stood sixty years ago.'

On the upper floor of a middle school on the outskirts of St Petersburg is a little museum organized by a teacher, Olga Prutt, dedicated to Leningrad's performing arts scene during the siege. On show are a score of the Seventh Symphony ripped by shrapnel, a printed ticket for Seat 13, Row 12 on 9 August 1942, Karl Eliasberg's pocket watch and a dummy dressed in the absurdly oversized tailed suit, white shirt and bow-tie he wore that night – and an oboe in a glass case, the one played by Edith Katya.

Our last conversation, and Mrs Matus lights one of her Sobranies. 'Cigarettes?' – she pulls a puff and grins like a schoolgirl sneaking one in during break. 'Oh, all the girls began smoking during the blockade if they could get cigarettes. Before that I never smoked. Then, everyone smoked if they could; my lovers in the orchestra used to get me cigarettes.' She pauses. 'So many years have passed since that day and memory is a funny thing, like drying paint – it changes colour as it dries. But not that symphony, which has stayed with me the way it was that night. Afterwards, it was still a city under siege but I knew it would live. Music is life, after all,' she says. 'What is life without music? This was the music that proved our city had come back to life after death.'

10

Radio Wall: Rock Under Siege

Ilijaz Delić, National Theatre, Mostar, October 1993
Amira Medunjanin, St George's Hall, Liverpool, 2012

The voice of Ilijaz Delić cuts through the thick air and the stench of sweat and fatigue. He sings gypsy-music timbres, rising and falling in quarter-tones, eighths even, as required by what is known across the Balkans as sevdah, *which means 'black gall' in Arabic (though it is also said to denote 'love, desire and ecstasy'). Ilijaz used to play with the masters of the genre, Mostar Sevdah Reunion, but now the group has been disbanded by war and Delić performs alone. In Mostar's theatre his audience has no tickets, nor did they come to hear him – he came to them, because they live here. They are not really an audience at all, but refugees with nowhere else to go.*

Outside, Mostar's ancient east bank had been levelled into the dust of its own stone. The famous arched Ottoman bridge that once spanned the river Neretva is now reduced to two stumps on either side; the rest collapsed into the current of turquoise waters after relentless bombard-ment, out of sheer philistine malice, by Croatian gunners on the west bank. The population of the besieged Muslim east side, entirely cut off, had increased from some ten to forty thousand – mostly women and children herded here from incinerated villages, their menfolk taken to concentration camps. People lived cowering in cellars, and when they went out they used passages made by the cuttings between the houses. Even so, some nine hundred died over seven months, trying to run across the little streets adjacent to the river, or fetching bucketsful of water from it.

When the cellars became full the deportees crammed into the theatre, and a theatre it remains, for now Ilijaz Delić sings. One song is about singing itself: 'Zapjevala Sojka Ptica' (Sing, Jay Bird). Delić hums the opening, played usually by his band on clarinet and drums, which indicates the bird's flapping wings, and he flutters his hands to imitate them. Even across the hollow faces, smiles break, irresistibly – and Delić smiles too, then giggles so that his introduction to the song breaks into laughter too – laughter, perhaps, at the absurdity of laughing in such a place.

But that's how it is in war, especially music in war. Delić resumes the song, imploring the jay to sing. His voice slides like the bird through the air, and his yearning in this nightmare is for the beauty of birdsong. In the mind's ear, people could also hear the familiar accordion, the flow of notes across the clarinet's registers. They'll remember this music from birthday parties or Bajram – as the last three nights of Ramadan are known in Bosnia – when those who refrain from alcohol make up, with a vengeance, for the period of temporary abstinence.

There's a song called 'Hanka', tribute to the diva of 'pop sevdah', Hanka Paldum, whom many a man pledges to wed in his next life. In the original, the lyrics are declaimed slowly while the music races like a lovesick beating heart. Here in the theatre there is of course no band to play the heartbeat – only Delić's cry, into the heavy silence, of love for a singer somewhere out there beyond the guns, a splash of glamour in a lost life. There's another: 'Mostarski Dućani' (Mostar's Bazaars), which captures the bustle of the bazaars that once lined this street, with its colours and bric-a-brac, flotsam and jetsam, and through which crowds would heave, along the old flagstones by the bridge. And Delić claps as he sings, to invoke the busy thoroughfare.

Some of the refugees manage to clap along – quietly, as if not to tempt *themselves with too much happiness, lest the contrast with the here-and-now become unbearable. Out there now, the night is bereft of human beings – alive only with the crack-crack of sniper fire, and the intermittent deep pounding of shells and mortars as the song comes to an end, and a few dare to applaud, as they would have done were they back within the world it conjures.*

Years later, sitting in peacetime with Delić beside the Neretva, over which an imitation of the bridge has been built, he remembers: 'I've played hundreds of concerts all over the Balkans, but none like those to the people in that theatre. Although my musicians were not with me, I had to sing, to remind the people who they were, that they did not belong in this misery – it had been forced on them. I had to sing about what their lives are really made of, not that war and fear. I wanted them to remember why that theatre was originally built, and . . .' Delić stops, picks a cigarette from the pack, licks the side to make it last longer, lights it and adds: 'I looked into their eyes. Part of me felt bad, because although the songs are beautiful, I think they were painful to hear. The songs made it too clear what had been lost. But they listened, they knew they had to, because we *are* those songs, and the songs are us – in the war more than ever.'

It was by accident that I became immersed in the worst carnage to blight Europe since the Third Reich – in Bosnia-Herzegovina during the early 1990s. I had at last achieved my lifelong dream, to live and work in Italy: as the *Guardian*'s Rome correspondent, occupying the highest apartment in the Trastevere quarter, with a roof terrace affording views across Michelangelo's, Borromini's and Bernini's domes and the greatest urban skyline in the world; briefed to cover southern Europe and 'keep an eye on Yugoslavia'. One glorious morning in 1991, though, a call came from the desk in London: 'There's something weird happening in Slovenia. You're next door, could you check it out?' I did, and spent the next four bloody years in former Yugoslavia, returning occasionally to Rome to keep an eye on the highest roof terrace in Trastevere.

Within weeks of the call I was in battered Vukovar, in Croatia – and amid the most relentless land siege of an urban community in Europe since 1945. I saw things entirely new: bloodied bodies drawn from the rubble, columns of refugees carrying what they could through the smoke and ash. I came to know new sounds: the whistle and whizz of bullets past my ears, the various depths of shell and mortar fire I came to know; 'incoming' from 'outgoing'. I was scrambling for a lexicon to describe these things for the *Guardian*, but had barely stopped to contemplate my private thoughts until one night, after cowering from shellfire in a town called Vinkovci, some colleagues and I took a short break behind the front lines, at Našice. There, at the modest Park Hotel, Robert Fox from the *Daily Telegraph* lent me a Walkman cassette player and a tape of Beethoven's Seventh Symphony. Robert, seasoned, knew warfare and counselled: 'When in doubt, Beethoven.' I repaired to my room to listen, and within a few bars, had burst into tears.

The following year, 1992, the Croatian war was descending towards an abyss in neighbouring Bosnia. It was my accursed honour, that summer, to uncover and reveal – with a crew from ITN – a gulag of concentration camps operated by the Bosnian Serbs. After interviewing the skeletal inmates in what emerged to be places of mass murder, torture and rape, it was hard to muster an apposite conversation to fill the eight-hour overnight drive to Belgrade. So we tried to remember, between us, the whole of the Beatles album *Sgt. Pepper's Lonely Hearts Club Band*: aloud, line by line, tune by tune, in order, from memory – and did pretty well. There was something about the Beatles' blend of psychedelic, poetic escape and unvarnished vernacular realism that made *Sgt. Pepper* the only fitting response to a day that was otherwise unrespondable to. This may seem inapposite, or even trite, but I soon learned in Bosnia that the many devastations wreaked by war do not switch off the music.

By the time I was back for the autumn I considered myself a proper 'war correspondent', whatever that meant, though unlike many of the others I hated war – that's why I wrote about it. I teamed up with a friend from Reuters called Andrej Gustinčić, a Yugoslav reared in New York, who quickly dismissed my Beatles collection: 'This is war, Ed, this needs Guns N' Roses.' And so we proceeded, listening to Axl Rose's wondering what on earth the term 'civil war' is supposed to mean – as did most other people. We would end each day with 'I'm still alive', from a song by Pearl Jam called 'Alive'.

After one particularly appalling day of killing in a town called Prozor, we got caught behind trucks carrying the soldiers who had perpetrated the violence and were now, singing Croatian fascist Ustaša songs along a mountain track back to the hotel where we – and they – were staying. When we pulled up in the car park, all we could think of doing was to turn up the volume and broadcast to the alighting gunmen a funky little song by Little Milton urging the world's sisters and brothers to hold on to, and love, one another – and dance around. The drunken killers looked at us with loathing and pity. Another time, through one strange moonlit night along those mountain tracks, we treated ourselves to Beethoven's Third, Eighth and Ninth Symphonies, to which Gustinčić and I listened in total silence. But all this was on a car cassette player. The real music was live, in the besieged capital, Sarajevo.

Sarajevo was the multi-ethnic cultural heartbeat of former Yugoslavia, now subject to a three-year siege without relent from artillery atop the hills around it. Much has been written about those years, each moment of which could be the last for every one of Sarajevo's citizens (and their visitors), exposed to the sudden crack of sniper fire and in plain sight of heavier guns; every endeavour was a game of Russian roulette. But there was also theatre and music. There had to be.

The roll-call of stars who braved the guns to work and sing in Sarajevo counts three names: Joan Baez, Susan Sontag and Bruce Dickinson of Iron Maiden. First came Baez, in spring 1993, to play a concert that more than twice the city's National Theatre's capacity of three hundred turned up to hear (to my bitter and eternal regret, I missed her – at the time, that really would have joined the dots in my life). The performance was part of a festival that included a running production of *Hair* – Baez joined the cast for the show's thirty-sixth night (ten more were cancelled because of shelling). She visited wounded children in Koševo hospital, clambered over rubble and joined a group of musicians on television for an ode to the city, sung in Bosnian. On Easter Sunday, she sang for French soldiers after Mass.

Baez's message was the first of its kind from a star of her standing: 'We just don't know out there. Even if we're sympathetic, there's no way to imagine the devastation, the shattering devastation, of a city – or the fortitude of these people.' There was carping of course, there always is. Baez recalled in the *Washington Post*: 'When a newsman suggested I would be fiddling while Rome burns, I recalled a line from a millworker's song: "Hearts starve as well as bodies; give us bread, but give us roses." I would take my finest roses to Sarajevo.' One night, she later wrote, 'a Serbian star of *Hair* sang a Macedonian gypsy rumba, and suddenly our host, a law professor who had watched over us with meticulous care, was on a table, dancing, and reaching for my hand. I jumped up and as we danced, the table collapsed. We fell in a hilarious heap of bread and wine and ashtrays. Too happy to leave, I sang until my throat was raw. And, for a few hours, there was no war.'[1]

One afternoon, Baez encountered the Sarajevan cellist Vedran Smajlović playing Albinoni's Adagio in G Minor, on one of the twenty-two days he had pledged to do so in memory of twenty-two people killed on the same spot by a shell. Upon finding him Baez stopped, listened, and in return sang 'Amazing Grace'. Smajlović was quintessential to the besieged Sarajevo scene – his performances were installations of defiance and mourning. A former player in the Sarajevo Opera Orchestra, he would pitch up among the city's ruins to play – memorably at the National Library, which had been burned on the orders of Nikola Koljević, a deputy president of the Bosnian Serbs and professor of literature.

Smajlović wore formal concert dress for his performances; he talked about his 'protest against violence and statement of pacifism', saying 'music can make a statement against an aggressor that a gun cannot. A gun can fight him on his own terms, but a series of notes can humiliate him, and render his violence ridiculous.' In 1993 the politician Paddy Ashdown, the actress Juliet Stevenson and I secured him an exit from Sarajevo for a concert in Southwark Cathedral in London. There, he was able to explain: 'My father was a Muslim, my mother was a Muslim, but I describe myself as a citizen of Sarajevo, and a musician.'

The director of Sarajevo's National Theatre during the war and afterwards was Haris Pašović, who famously staged, with Susan Sontag – one of Bosnia's greatest international advocates and friends – Samuel Beckett's *Waiting for Godot*, under siege and with all the cogency of that in a place waiting for the deliverance of international intervention that never came. Sontag cut a magnificent, at once charismatic and endearing, figure: droll, articulate, modest about the project but confident in herself for doing it. We made friends in Sarajevo and remained so until her death in 2004. She wrote of this bold production: 'Culture, serious culture, is an expression of human dignity – which is what people in Sarajevo feel they have lost, even when they know themselves to be brave, or stoical or angry . . . People in Sarajevo live harrowing lives; this was a harrowing *Godot*.'

Pašović echoed the same sentiment many years later: 'Art is a primal need,' he told me, 'even under siege, especially under siege. My idols created their greatest work under siege – Orwell in Spain, Anna Akhmatova in Leningrad – but I never expected to be in that situation myself. We realized during the siege that art, theatre and music in Sarajevo were resistance at the deepest level.'

The play was presented as part of the Sarajevo Film and Theatre Festivals of 1993, and ran for a month. 'It meant more to me than almost anything I've ever done,' Susan said years later, after an outing to hear Prokofiev's *War and Peace* at the Metropolitan Opera. 'To learn from those people – in that place, amid the sounds of war and fear of war – a lesson one had never expected to learn. Not just about war, but about what artists do and why, how it feels to be part of something creative in that nightmare, but in a state of total humility.' When we spoke, Susan had recently published *Regarding the Pain of Others*, about precisely that. 'The book came in part from Bosnia, and doing *Godot* there. One couldn't be in Sarajevo and simply watch; one had to go there with a clear purpose, an idea for a contribution, which in my case was to try and say something about – and try and draw attention to – this outrage in our time from where it was happening, with drama, specifically Beckett.'

The night I saw the play, I joined soldiers, doctors from makeshift amputation wards, men and women in their best, bedraggled hippies and bemused Sarajevans attending their first drama – all packed in. The cast was drawn from the three main ethnic groups – Muslim, Serb and Croat – and the set designer was Jewish. This time the carping, mostly back in America, was repugnant, misogynist, and envious of Susan. 'I wish I could pretend I was more angry than hurt,' she said long afterwards. 'Why is there a theatre festival during a siege?' one American reporter had asked at her press conference with Pašović. 'Why is there a siege during my theatre festival?' replied Pašović. He recalled later: 'It's perfectly normal to have a festival or a production of *Godot*. What is not normal is to be killing the people who want to see the productions!' But the jeering was irrelevant; Sarajevo adored Susan for as long as she lived, and adores her memory still – the piazza on which the National Theatre stands has been renamed Susan Sontag Square.

Of all European countries outside the Anglo-American axis, pre-war Yugoslavia produced some of the best rock music, and it made sense for the veterans of the 1960s to establish a wartime radio station broadcasting music and discussion as a form of resistance. The prime mover was the law professor who fell off the collapsing table while dancing with Joan Baez – Zdravko Grebo. With the onset of war, he founded Sarajevo's Radio Zid (Radio Wall) and wrote the station's manifesto, the most creatively articulate document to emerge from the war: 'Zid in Sarajevo', it read, 'has started a media that is primarily a mission of spiritual and cultural renewal . . . The political attitude will be the attitude of common sense, of social sagacity based on the European idea of rationalism and the urban mentality. Last but not least, that spirit is trying to preserve a sense of humour.' Looking back, Grebo explains his project: 'When the necessary electricity was available, we used the perfect medium, radio, in a city under siege and in danger from all sides and in all ways – physically and mentally. The point was to get on air and resist militarism and militaristic music. We thought the situation called not for martial marching music but for Pink Floyd and Johnny Cash.' Radio Zid operated from a cellar amply stocked with LPs. It was once my honour to be granted an hour as DJ – I played Hendrix's 'Machine Gun', and 'Long Time Gone' by Crosby,

Stills and Nash: 'the darkest hour /Is always, always just before the dawn /And it appears to be a long time . . .'

Around Radio Zid the notion emerged of live music to counter the violence. Involved in this endeavour were two friends: Sarajevo's best-known alternative painter, Nebojša Šerić Šoba, and Bekim Medunjanin, a music teacher who believed in his task of redemptive resistance. Šoba joined the Bosnian Army and became a war artist by default; he also played bass guitar. Bekim applied his conviction by teaching music to children at an orphanage, near the front line, whose parents had fallen victim to the gunners. Šoba and Bekim would arrange what the former called, when we reminisced over more drinks, years later, 'the best parties of my life, during the siege. Every one of them happened in darkness, with bad home-made booze, lots of laughing and love. Every one of them was maybe the last. We didn't have anything to lose. Then basements and shelters were turned into rehearsal studios, more and more young people played music, sometimes just to make noise so the sounds of explosions wouldn't be so loud.'

Bekim procured equipment, his reasoning starkly simple: 'I was young, caught up in a siege. I ate little, but I wasn't hungry for food. I was hungrier for something to counter the shelling, the news every day that this or that friend was dead or wounded. I was hungry for music, artistic events, rock 'n' roll, things that would keep me going. When we started to organize the gigs, we never worried: Are people going to come through shelling and snipers, without a curfew pass? – we knew they would.' I went to a couple – by definition under ground, sometimes lit by candles and hurricane lamps, alcohol from either the precariously functioning brewery or people with small plum-brandy distilleries. The bands sometimes had names – I remember one called Sikter, and Šoba's was called Burek, after the Bosnian pie. They would play while the amplification lasted; there was dancing of a fairly desperate kind and, as Joan Baez put it so well, a temporary end to the war.

Was all this gallivanting inappropriate, while people were dying? Šoba has an answer of his own: 'Quite often we'd crawl back up the hill to the front lines, still drunk, trying not to get noticed by the officer ranks. By the time the hangover set in, you'd be in the trench, scared stiff again, maybe another friend dead, but listening to the music from last night in your head.'

Add to the mix a group of young Irish, Brits, French and New Zealanders who turned up to do their best for battered Bosnia. The organization Serious Road Trip comprised hippies and jazzers with an office in Camden Town, London; they first rolled into Sarajevo during June 1992, only – unlike most aid organizations – they did so as part of an international peace convoy aboard a customized London bus. These people felt immediately at home in the demi-monde of slaughter and cultural foment – not 'career' aid workers but ad hoc concerned citizens whose first foray in 1991 had been a tour of aid to orphanages in Romania and Poland. The Road Trip now gathered a fleet of trucks in the Croatian port of Split, but unlike the white trucks of official UN convoys, theirs were painted with cartoon characters – Dennis the Menace and Minnie the Minx making their wartime debut. Radio Zid's stock of vinyl and CDs expanded as the Road Trip widened its concept of what 'emergency aid' could mean. The official agencies were scathing, and again: Was all this inapposite, during carnage?

Bekim replies: 'Who do you think my generation were most looking forward to seeing? People bringing tape to stick on broken windows, or people bringing music? Music of course! – it was the most important first aid of all.'

One of the road-trippers was Simon Glinn, a music producer who used to run the Jazz World Stage at Glastonbury, and so the idea of the Rock Under Siege festival was conceived. 'If one was to paste a philosophy on to that madness, which was brave and lucky,' says Glinn, 'I'd say just that this was about solidarity, multiculturalism and, well, the fundamental principles of good rock 'n' roll. Sarajevo was full of bands that wanted to be Rage Against the Machine, because they *were* raging against the machine – there was a real fear and anger against the continual barrage of nationalism in ethnically 'dirty', multicultural Sarajevo. And they created this scene – the underground gigs and eventually what became our baby: a festival called Rock Under Siege. After a while we were living there, supporting the underground gigs, but that was not why we were there. What we were about were the *reasons* for doing music, the transformative reasons.'

Among the first people Glinn met was, unsurprisingly, Bekim Medunjanin. 'Bekim was the energy in all this, the inspiration, the trustworthy conscience – making things happen.' Glinn was introduced, recalls Bekim, 'in this yellow Land Rover we called the yellow submarine. I saw clearly that Simon *got it* – the value of working with these children who I was teaching music, who'd been stranded by war in the suburbs of Sarajevo, had no parents or didn't know whether their parents were alive.'

In December 1994, Rock Under Siege helped advance its most preposterous idea to date: an invitation to the superstar Bruce Dickinson of Iron Maiden to perform, above ground, at the House of Culture. Dickinson accepted; he would call it 'one of the most important gigs of my life'.

I interviewed him about this adventure in 2007, aboard a flight – surreally – from London to Bangalore, where Iron Maiden were headlining India's first major outdoor rock festival. Transport to Sarajevo for the concert was guaranteed by British troops from the United Nations Protection Force – UNPROFOR, operating (to little or no avail) in Bosnia. 'But it wasn't one of those "entertain the troops" things,' explains Dickinson, 'this was going to Sarajevo to do something for the people getting shot at.'

The band flew from Birmingham to Split, where they were met by a Colonel Green, who informed Dickinson that the situation had become 'hairy' both en route to and in Sarajevo. Safe passage could not be guaranteed; the band were offered a meal and a flight home. Good news to some, 'but not Bruce', recalled the guitarist Chris Dale in his diary. 'He wanted to know more, how bad was it? Was there another way through?' There was: the Serious Road Trip – 'doing such a saintly task', recalled Dale, 'but worryingly for me, they were all quite clearly insane'. 'We had dinner with the army,' Dickinson said, 'then out of town to the Road Trip HQ. Very cool bunch of people, gave us some beer and showed us a video of their trucks driving through bombed-out villages. One bit had the truck in front almost getting hit – I don't know why they showed us that. But we decided to go for it.'

Dickinson and his band were loaded onto a flatbed truck camouflaged by a cartoon of Disney's Road Runner – 'cold as fuck, and some snow,' he tells me – 'just sitting in the back of this truck, on a load of supplies and a crate of beer, over Mount Igman which had just been having a battle'. Finally, dawn at a place called Hrasnica, and the Bosnian Army. 'It was a beat-up place, some kind of hut, and I went in to sign a few autographs and drink some vodka, or maybe it was their home-made brandy.'

At this point the musicians did accept transport in British and Danish armoured personnel carriers, rather than facing the terrifying ride across the no man's land of Sarajevo Airport, heart in mouth, to which we were accustomed. Once arrived, first port of call was an interview with Radio Zid, then a sound check – with 'fairly professional equipment and lights'. The support act Allmana, made up of musician-soldiers given the night off by their commanders, 'played like their lives depended on it', recalls Dickinson. Then on he came: 'Scream for me, Sarajevo!' he shouted, and it did. 'We ended up doing a life-changing show – I say that, well, it certainly changed mine. It messed with my head, in a good way. Next night, we played a little impromptu gig at a fire station and visited [Bekim's] orphanage, kids whose parents had been killed in the war – I'll never forget their faces, their smiles, even though they hadn't the foggiest who I was. When we got back to England, people didn't understand fuck all. I'd say: "I just did a gig in Sarajevo." "Wow, man, cool." And I'd just crawl into my shell and say: "Er, actually it was a bit different than that."

'I gave up trying to explain the emotional roller-coaster, so God knows what it must have been like for the people who lived through that every day. In my mind,' he concludes, 'it showed that in all the craziness, this island of rock and roll, of normality, could happen. As a musician I couldn't offer any solutions, make a political or a military speech, but I could say: There's something better, beyond this killing. It was an act of defiance by us and by them – and only after the gig someone told us that two fucking shells had landed right at the entrance to the cultural centre that afternoon!'

In late 1993, the critical mass of violence in Bosnia shifted from Sarajevo to Mostar, and the Serious Road Trip followed. Among those working to stage the Sarajevo concerts and bring aid was a music professor from Glasgow, Nigel Osborne. 'I was doing my best to get around Bosnia to find out more about what we could do to help,' he says, 'and all we got, back in England, was the hatred of the politicians in Bosnia – not only echoed, but amplified. So I thought: Fuck them – and please quote that – we need to do something creative. Mostar was becoming a nightmare we could barely imagine, and where we needed to be.' Soldiers from the UN 'Protection Force' simply ran away. Surreally, a kind of UN base camp was established in the town that also hosts the Catholic shrine of Medjugorje: there, originating from the Serious Road

Trip, a charity called War Child began its operation as a bakery for hundreds of thousands of refugees, then moved into ravaged east Mostar on the day of a ceasefire declared in February 1994.

A Bosnian soldier, one Ermin Elezović – a broken man by the time of the ceasefire – remembers: 'Once War Child came, I spent every hour away from the front line baking bread. We'd been in deepest hell, but were now baking five thousand loaves a day, and had a chance to talk about music and normal stuff, instead of just death.' 'Ermin never slept,' his wife Alma tells me, 'but the bakery saved him. It saved our stomachs, of course, but it saved Ermin in another way too.'

One night during 1994 Ermin, Osborne and others were sitting in Ermin's flat when, recalls Osborne: 'We thought, OK, we're distributing bread and medicine. What next? Music of course!' He later explained his thinking: 'In a world such as then – and now for that matter – when established politics is dead and trivial, and politicians are demonstrably part of the problem not the solution, culture becomes the only democratizing agent.' Osborne insists: 'Rock 'n' roll is inherently democratic, whatever else is done in its name. So against third-rate politics in Bosnia and across Europe we pitched first-rate music. If the politicians were going to have their sick speaker systems, then we were going to have our speaker system too.'

War Child established a music centre in Mostar, Brian Eno gave workshops and Luciano Pavarotti gave it his name. Ermin's son Jasmin Elezović, who remembers playing drums with Eno, would become an iconic figure on its promotional material, wearing a 'War Child' T-shirt. An album entitled *Help* became the most successful, the most quickly assembled charity record ever, produced in a week and for which stars including Paul McCartney, Sinéad O'Connor, Paul Weller, the Stone Roses, Oasis and others contributed a song each. At a time of failure by politics, it was probably rock and roll's finest hour.

Another important development from War Child's project in Mostar was a revival in *sevdah* around Ilijaz Delić and the arrival of a young singer from Sarajevo: Amira Medunjanin. With Mostar still bitterly divided, Delić re-formed his Mostar Sevdah Reunion, and found a protégée in this young talent who had survived the three-year siege and would in time make walls across the Balkans echo and crumble not with gunfire but with a new *sevdah* music, which she sings like no other: music from all the countries that had torn one another apart, now played again by musicians from all of them.

In 2002, twenty-eight-year-old Amira, who had recorded only a few demos, asked for an accompaniment to a *sevdalinka* (*sevdah* song) from Delić's band. Warily, they loaned their accordionist, and were amazed by what they heard. 'Where have you been all this time?' asked Delić. Amira had been among the regulars at Bekim and Glinn's wartime rock concerts, where, she says, 'we could pretend for just a few hours that we had a life as young people, that we could do something else, against that madness'. Otherwise, she had 'spent the war looking after my family, sleeping on a pile of coal in a cellar' – and singing *sevdah* music to herself and her family.

'I had listened to all kinds of music – jazz, Nick Cave – but *sevdah* was what I needed to inhale during the war, to keep me sane, while my family was on the front line and coal my bed. That's when I started to sing this music. We had lost our country of Yugoslavia, across which this music belongs whether you are Bosnian, Serb, Macedonian, Croat, whatever. To sing this music is to claim our identity again.' Amira met Osborne after the war, and 'while we were working on a music project of his for kids with special needs, I took part in a film made there. And I'll never forget that day with those kids – and their response to the sound of me singing our *sevdah* music to them; they knew it was their own.'

At that time Amira was supporting herself by interpreting for the European Commission, and one day in 1997 a man came into her office to be interviewed. 'I didn't know who it was, I'd never run into him,' she says. 'He got the job, we went out to lunch and I realized I'd been at all the concerts he'd organized during the war, and the Rock Under Siege festival.' The interviewee was Bekim. 'He told me about his work with children in the orphanages during the war, and that's when I fell in love with him. I'd never thought of becoming a singer, but he said: "You've been given this voice – it can't belong only to you, you have to share it." Suddenly all my inhibitions disappeared, Bekim opened my eyes. Two weeks later, he asked me to marry him. I knew I would in the end, but I told him to wait two years.'

Five years after their meeting, Amira asked Ilijaz Delić of Mostar Sevdah Reunion for an audition. The result was her first album, *Rosa*. 'It means "dew", not "rose",' she says. The album is traditional *sevdah*, simple yet passionate, of a kind Amira would later stretch in all directions. A sound of raw beauty, some of it recorded in complete darkness, writes Bekim in the cover notes, so that 'Amira could not hide her emotion'.

Liverpool, 2012

On the twentieth anniversary of the onset of the siege in Sarajevo, Amira has become the artist who blazes the trail from war to precarious peace in the Balkans. Now, amid the Corinthian columns of St George's Hall in Liverpool, she asks her (Serbian) backing musicians to unplug their instruments, and the mixing desk to switch off everything. She proceeds to sing – and the musicians to play – unamplified into the significant space, with emotional depth but not a hint of sentimentality. In the audience there's a lady called Medisa, whose eyes fill: partly from the beauty of the song and partly for its evocation of home, where concentration camps took the lives of her father, uncle, neighbours and closest friends. Other faces were similarly transfixed, for similar reasons.

'This is sevdah, this is what we know,' Amira tells her audience, about a fifth of whom are Bosnian, the rest concerned or curious Merseysiders – one of whom says of the songs: 'I don't understand a word but they give me goosebumps.' From the duffel coat in which she has been touring Liverpool all day, Amira has changed into a ball gown that would grace a diva singing Verdi. There is power and stillness in the music, a drawing-in of the audience, so that the great hall shrinks to hearth size. The unamplified song is from Rosa: 'Bogata Sam, Imam Svega' (I Have Riches, I Have Nothing), in which the wealthy heroine misses the man she loves: 'Oh beloved, grant me a kiss, grant me your lips.'

For someone else, sitting at the back of the hall, the music evoked a different memory of the war from those of its victims among the audience: listening carefully, sitting alone, was the evening's promoter Simon Glinn, in 2012 the Director of the Liverpool Philharmonic Hall, for whom the occasion made no commercial sense but was a heartfelt ambition achieved – to bring his Sarajevo back home to his native Liverpool, to tie all kinds of threads and memories together. And for me too: the memory of listening to Delić during the fury of war; and now his music sung by his protégée as a cry for peace, in my mother's hometown.

The following morning, Amira and I were up early so that the Philharmonic's kind driver could take us to the place at which she had to pay homage: Strawberry Fields – quite a moment, and visibly so. 'When the war ended,' she reflected afterwards, 'our national *sevdah* music had to reinvent itself. It comes from all across a region that had torn itself apart, out of narrow, inward-looking tribalism. So I wanted to sing *sevdah* music that would re-establish itself across the ethnic divisions that destroyed our country, and open itself to the world.'

Amira's second album was shaped in part by the jazz pianist Kim Burton, who had been around Sarajevo during the war – 'to see what the colours of Kim's playing would bring to our national music'. Jazz, Amira finds, 'is music you can do anything with, and it can do anything with you'. So already the fusion had begun, 'by coincidence, really. Though what happened next was not at all coincidence.' There remained something unsaid, arising from the pain of war in a city proud but still deeply wounded. And so followed *Zumra*, the musical record of Bosnia's war, expressed through the apparently traditional form of voice accompanied by accordion – though 'I hated the accordion . . . and never liked its influence on Bosnian music,' says Amira. 'But I met the accordionist Merima Ključo and knew we had to make this album the way we did.' Voice and instrument veer from *sevdah* to psychedelia, and from there to stark darkness; thrilling and terrifying, *sevdah* as though mixed through Jimi Hendrix's guitar on 'Machine Gun'.

'Sometimes I think people are almost comfortable in hating one another in this part of the world,' she says. 'But this music is the very opposite of that tribalism. So when I, from Sarajevo, sing, and my Serbian and Croatian musicians play songs from all our cultures, songs their ancestors sang, are we Muslims or Serbs? Macedonians or Croats? – No, sir, we are musicians; and while these songs are sung, the hatred is just ridiculous.'

'We lost heroically,' says Zdravko Grebo – Joan Baez's momentary dancing partner – of his now bitterly divided country. 'A peace agreement carved up and condemned Bosnia, and the Bosnian people went along with it. The nationalist parties took power and people continue to vote for them. I have stood against them' – he spits in disgust – 'in some attempt to create a normal political language, and for this I happened to not be elected, such is the hatred. I don't complain, I just say that if there is any hope left for this country, it is where it always was – not with the rascals and idiots in politics, but in the public spaces of culture – and, of course, above all, music. That was what these good people realized after one look at Sarajevo. It was our only chance then, and it still is.'

7" Single: La Louisiane

The rain is lashing the bayou outside like it'll never stop, but what the hell. Here at Randol's Salle de Danse on the edge of Lafayette, Jean-Pierre Blanchard has picked up his accordion and struck up a song called "Tite Nana' (Little Nana). Even Grandpa is on his feet, the kids too. It's good to dance in Louisiana with an earful of guttural, reedy French and a throatful of fiery spice.

Cajun music – vibrant but wistful – is the white blues, a heady mix of love and celebration in the face of poverty and a historical memory of calamity. I chanced upon Cajun and its black cousin Zydeco by accident: in New Orleans one night, pitched up at a bar called Patout. Here the band of the evening was tuning up, fronted by a tall, long-haired man called Steve LaFleur – the band called Mamou, after his native village.

This was not traditional Cajun – it was electric and it rocked – but I was enthralled. The music was insane at first, and infectious – it wasn't French, it wasn't blues, it wasn't bluegrass or country; it contained but transgressed all of the above. Yet this was no potpourri either: it had distinctive texture, a forward drive all of its own, it *came* from somewhere. And from one of the strangest stories – the 'ethnic cleansing', by the British, of tens of thousands of French-speaking *Acadiens* from what is now Nova Scotia in Canada during the decades after 1700. Many of those who survived the violence resettled in Louisiana, where they became known by their Anglicized name 'Cajuns'.

The French peasants who colonized the Atlantic seaboard during the seventeenth century loved where they settled in eastern Canada so much they called it Arcadia; after a while they dropped the 'r', hence *Acadie*. They were a rough and resourceful lot, fiercely egalitarian, innovative and good with land. After the arrival of the British in 1703 they swung between French authority and that of the newcomers, who were jealous of Acadie's abundance and wary of the Acadians' hearty relations with the native Micmac people. So that in 1755 Governor Charles Lawrence conceived a plan to forcibly deport the 'perfidious' French: some eighteen thousand Acadians were rounded up and put onto waiting ships, families torn asunder, homes and farms ransacked, many slaughtered there and then.

The first wave of survivors were interned in labour camps along the mid-Atlantic seaboard, where hundreds died of starvation and disease while the living were set to work alongside black slaves on the tobacco plantations. In 1758 the governor began a final hunting-down of the remaining Acadians; and those who escaped, hearing of empty marshlands in Louisiana (then Spanish, soon to become French), resettled there, joined in trickles by escapees from camps in Maryland. The Acadians were the only people hardy and capable enough to cultivate the swamps and bayous that flowed so slowly they could do so in either direction. A few climbed the ladder into the Creole plantation class and took slaves – but most remained *petits habitants*, self-sufficient and self-contained.

In 1803 came the purchase of Louisiana from the French by the USA, then civil war, the Cajuns caught between Confederate conscription and Yankee advance, their lands plundered by all sides. They sank into economic hardship, from which they've barely recovered today; only in 1980, after 225 years of subjugation, did a US court classify Louisiana's five hundred thousand Cajuns as a national minority – after a labour-relations dispute in which the judge ruled that a Texan acted improperly by firing a Cajun who objected to being called a 'coon-ass'.

The Cajuns still have their ballads of bygone days with roots in France, adapted through cohabitation with slaves – two-steps and waltzes mostly, infused with blues, Creole and country. Raucous *bals de maison* used to be held – Acadian house dances that would last until dawn after 'gumbo at midnight'; their organizers would convene these shindigs by going around the villages firing guns into the air to announce: '*Bal ce soir, chez . . . !*' – whoever. Cajun music was also known as '*Fais dodo*' – do it with two backs – because children were included and babies held piggy-back, as they still are; it also means 'Go to sleep' in French babytalk (babies sleeping on their mothers' backs while the adults dance).

But there was that other ingredient in the muggy air of bayou country: Zydeco, or Zarico – so called, they say, after the Creole dialect for the saying, 'The beans aren't salty' (*Les haricots ne sont pas salés*), meaning that one has no salacious news to impart. Some musicologists source both the music and its name to marital unions between Atakapa natives and West African slaves. Zydeco is adrenalin-charged dance music based on button accordion and washboard, from the deep and complex history of Creole Americans and their ambivalent relationship with slaves, with whom white arrivals in Louisiana, after the purchase, grouped them. After the Civil War too, white America categorized Creoles and freedmen together, and together they came – in

Zydeco, which, alongside its cousin Cajun, with which it inter-married, is pure transgression.

LaFleur grew up in Mamou, the village out on the bayou that considers itself the epicentre of this culture and music. His father loved traditional Cajun music, which the teen rebel Steve thereby felt obliged to loathe. 'I needed something else, the Ramones and the Sex Pistols.' But when Steve started on guitar himself, 'I realized the limitations of what I was listening to, understood the subtleties in Pa's music and where it came from. But I was still a punk, needed to give it some – you know.'

The result is that his band Mamou are the Cajun Pogues – roots music plugged in, as with Shane MacGowan's – Howlin' Wolf's too, for that matter. This is full-blooded Cajun rock, hot as bayou Tabasco. Until, that is, a number that casts a sudden spell over the evening: 'La Louisiane', the girl from Louisiana, a ballad exchanged between voice and violin, so beautiful that even shrieking jocks at the bar shut up to listen – a love song to '*La Louisiane*', for whom the singer would '*mets ma vie*' – 'lay down my life' – and during pauses for breath between fiddle and lyrics you can hear the ripple and patter of the rain.

I returned often to hear Steve, who, once his set was done, would take me round the New Orleans night to hear his own favourite bands, including the Zydeco Twisters at a bowling alley; after which his musician friends, mostly Irish, would repair to a dingy quarter of town and drink at home. Steve would talk, about how 'The *Acadiens* were the white niggers, and Cajun music is our blues – when you're so far down the bottom of the pile, you pick up an accordion, or a guitar or fiddle, and – fuck it – I never thought it'd be hip to have a Cajun accent.'

I've called in at Patout since those days, trying to find Mamou, without success. Steve had blown out of a number of sets; missing, presumed drunk. The rest of the band got embarrassed and the manager got exasperated. I never saw Steve LaFleur again.

12" Extended Version: 'I Think You'd Better Wake Up, the World Trade Center's on Fire!'

In late August 2001, the British band Radiohead played a concert in Liberty State Park – where I was now living – across the water from the World Trade Center's twin towers. A friend and I were in the audience and at one point we turned to look up at the two columns of clean silver steel and twinkling light, towering over the crowds: omnipotent pillars of capitalism, more elegant than the system they represented. Thom Yorke was singing what felt like a serenade to the towers' arrogant beauty: 'Everything In Its Right Place'. It wasn't.

'I think you'd better wake up,' said a voice in my left ear some mornings later, 'the World Trade Center's on fire.' It was very decent of my partner Caroline to stir me. I had stayed out late after a New York Yankees game had been rained off, and slept on the sofa, clothed. Within thirty seconds we were down on the corner of my block where West 11th Street crosses 6th Avenue, to behold smoke billowing from the North Tower. Caroline had arrived in America from her native Sweden a week earlier, and just now had almost seen the first plane crash in while taking her daughter to school across the avenue. Now people were staring down 6th with no idea what to do; coffee shops and Nikko's newsagent remained open, serving, though traffic must have stopped because we walked instinctively and briskly, albeit inexplicably, down the middle of the road towards the now burning towers.

Just as we crossed Grand Street, the unthinkable happened: in slow motion, and in what seemed to be a murderous silence (though that cannot have been), the top of the North Tower peeled away into itself, belching a cloud of black dust, crumbling and tumbling into its own footprint. Again inexplicably, we continued towards the now single, standing, burning tower. Somewhere south of Chambers Street a police cordon blocked the way, while crowds streamed northwards away from the pale grey dust that burned one's face. Looking up, we saw what seemed to be flies hurtling into mid-air from the upper floors of the tower – not knowing, or thinking to know, what they were.

I pleaded with a police officer to let me through, brandishing my press card. With a stubbornness for which I'm eternally grateful he refused me passage, and I had just spotted a means of getting past him when an awful sound, like a train rattling into hell, filled the heavens, and the tower above us followed its neighbour, crumbling into the dust of its own once mighty prowess. Now we all fled, and a few blocks north turned to look at . . . at nothing but smoke and dust into which the towers had been felled by a force America had hitherto never encountered on its own soil.

I had for years seen the towers from my block, every time I crossed the avenue. They were a way to tell the time, by the strength of the sunlight on their vertical steel girders: deep gold at the eastern edge in early morning, paler towards midday, deepening again against the west at dusk. At twilight, the towers shimmered, and if low cloud wrapped New York they pierced it from below, like on the cover of Don DeLillo's *Underworld*. Now they were gone, and I called – from a public phone some four blocks from the wreckage which, unlike cellphones, was working – the *Observer* and the mother of my children (in that order, I confess). Everywhere, people were running while others simply gawped, or wiped the dust from their faces.

A woman hurled herself at the police line: 'My baby's in there! My baby's in there!' By nightfall, tireless paramedics at St Vincent's Hospital, a block away from my apartment and next door to my fantastic local bar – Johnny's, where ancillary workers and nurses used to drink post-shift – were unloading dead and wounded firefighters (and, we thought, survivors of the towers) from ambulances. The Revd Lloyd Prator, a neighbour of mine and rector of St John's Church, answered ministerial calls to St Vincent's and Ground Zero. He said he felt 'sad and anxious . . . wishing I could do more, wishing I had worked harder'. During mid-afternoon the first flyer appeared, attached to a post on my corner, by Ray's Pizza: 'Missing: Giovanna "Gennie" Gambale'. She wore a smile and there was a number to call.

By the morning of the 13th, a form of unwonted life had taken root; with unwelcome haste the inexplicable had become almost routine, the monstrosity a natural condition, canons established. The wall between Ray's and Johnny's Bar was covered, by midday, with notices headed 'Missing' and photocopied portraits staring at us, phone numbers screaming for information. An inquiry centre was established across the road from my front steps, in the New School where I attended Russian classes, to connect people to the missing. We kept using the term 'rescue workers', but the last survivor hauled out of the wreckage was found that morning, so in reality the New School became a place connecting relatives with howling silence. A lady called Sara Midgley tried to help Luís Morales with news of his missing wife; she told him there was none and made him coffee, which he sipped, sitting in a chair with a little fixed table for students to take notes on, in tears of disbelief. Carpets of tributes, candles and flowers had begun to form, strewn all over; at makeshift shrines, gifts people had wanted to leave for the dead – primal offerings of favourite cigarette lighters, teddy bears, watches, pens.

Exhausted firefighters were endlessly urged to leave the scene when their shifts were done, and endlessly they refused. 'If any of you have completed your extended eighteen-hour shift, please go,' came a deputy chief's plea down a loudhailer in Battery Park. No one moved. Teams of 'moles', experts in subterranean work – including a man I knew who looked after the piping system beneath Grand Central Station – joined the firefighters to search out viable routes through the catacombs beneath Ground Zero. 'There's always pockets, like caves,' insisted a fireman from Ladder Company 18 round the corner from my apartment. On 15 September he got me in there – to smell the drifts of burnt dust and mountains of mangled metal, to hear the quiet, to see the determined work – and that shard of the building itself, still standing.

The ground was so hot that the rubber on our soles melted – a sensation I recalled from an eruption of Mount Etna in 1991. I met a man called Joe, built like a prizefighter with curses to match, from the New York City Fire Department, who over two days had lost three of his workmates, but when Joe heard that one of his missing colleagues was safe after all, it was too much. He ripped off his helmet and mask, collapsed on the kerb, took a deep breath, choked and quietly wept. He took me to meet drivers of what felt like a funeral procession through the Brooklyn–Battery Tunnel and over the Verrazano–Narrows Bridge, hauling debris ten miles and through ten checkpoints to a landfill site called – they couldn't have made it up – Fresh Kills.

There was much in the air about how New York would become

a humbler city from now on, the vanities not so much bonfired, but moderated. But I noticed one thing at lunchtime on 13 September that I pretended to ignore. The corner of 6th Avenue and Houston Street was on the outer barrier around Ground Zero, the furthest south the public could go, where paramedics arrived to load vehicles with body bags. The fire services used this junction for logistics work that did not need to be done at the kernel of the catastrophe. Also at this intersection was the Da Silvano restaurant, preferred haunt of the beautiful people – but why should this calamity necessitate the cancellation of a lunch date? There they were around the outdoor tables, Brooks Brothers blazers, expensive shirts, elegant legs crossed and stiletto heels flicked by perfect ankles as laughter and chatter flew across the tabletops. Heavy beads of grimy sweat meandered down crevices in the firemen's faces; delicate drops of condensation glided down the glasses of Chablis. Everyone was saying that Al-Qaeda would not cow New York – and they were right.

The question soon arose: what would happen to the site, the mass grave, itself? There were some simple but good ideas, one of which was to keep two columns of light projected into the sky like ghosts where the towers had risen; another, to preserve the glaringly obvious monument: the still-standing shard of the South Tower, which could so easily have been secured in a park upon the site. But the lights were switched off and the shard removed to make way for the hideous 'Freedom Tower', another cash cow.

Money means more than does memory in New York, and within a few years the city experienced a different kind of collapse – that of Lehman Brothers and other titans of international finance. Lehman had given an early clue: in the immediate aftermath of 11 September, it negotiated a friendly takeover of the Sheraton Manhattan Hotel on 7th Avenue north of 51st Street, and within a week of the attacks was refurbishing 665 rooms so that fifteen hundred bankers could get back to work, selling stocks, bonds and, as it turned out, toxic debt. And it was around the time of the Lehman crash that St Vincent's, the 'hero hospital' of 9/11 (with whose staff I'd drink most nights at Johnny's Bar, next door), was closed for conversion to luxury housing – those same wards that had treated the survivors. This was how New York paid its debt of gratitude.

Johnny's had reopened a couple of weeks after the attacks, not least to cater for the soon-to-be-unemployed 'hero' ancillaries and nurses, and something suddenly struck me: music had vanished from New York. But not for long – the most played band on Johnny's jukebox had been, by coincidence, Radiohead, and we began tentatively to accompany the early-morning hours with 'How To Disappear Completely', a Radiohead song that denies one is here at all, or that any of this is happening. One night two women came by, working with a touring band. 'Anyone I've heard of?' I asked. 'Probably. U2,' replied one of them, and gave me a ticket and a backstage pass for a concert at Madison Square Garden which the Irish group turned into a tribute.

But the music did not vanish just because it fell mute: after the attacks, 160 songs were banned on radio because they were deemed 'lyrically inappropriate'. Some were not without a macabre logic: 'What A Wonderful World' by Louis Armstrong, 'War Pigs' by Black Sabbath, 'Knockin' On Heaven's Door' by Bob Dylan, 'It's The End Of The World As We Know It' by R.E.M., 'When You're Falling' sung by Peter Gabriel, 'She's Not There' by the Zombies, 'When Will I See You Again' by the Three Degrees, 'I'm On Fire' by Bruce Springsteen, 'Benny And The Jets' by Elton John. Also, morbidly, 'Bits And Pieces' by the Dave Clark Five. Others were downright weird, including 'Ticket To Ride' and 'Ob-la-di, Ob-la-da' by the Beatles.

More ominously, radio stations were told that the entire oeuvre of the radical band Rage Against the Machine was considered 'questionable' – a diktat so outrageous that guitarist Tom Morello was obliged to put out a statement saying that the band was 'diametrically opposed to the kind of horrible violence committed against innocent people ... If our songs are "questionable" in any way, it is that they encourage people to question the kind of ignorance that breeds intolerance – intolerance which leads to censorship and the extinguishing of our civil liberties, or at its extremes can lead to the kind of violence we witnessed last week.' Johnny's kept playing Morello's music, and at home we made a point of playing it at high volume, windows wide open, especially a song called 'War Within a Breath' – and how bitterly ironic, because in the end that's exactly what happened.

The musical backdrop to my years in New York was jazz at the Sweet Basil, Lenox Lounge and Village Vanguard clubs – some of the happiest and most instructive evenings of my life. I was there for the last night – all night – of Sweet Basil's long history, for which a galaxy of its veteran guests gathered to play (now the Lenox has closed too). But the soundtrack to the upheavals that followed 9/11 was played not so much by the John Hicks Trio, Houston Person or Gonzalo Rubalcaba, as by Patti Smith. Patti had developed a tradition of giving two intimate concerts at the Bowery Ballroom in New York on her birthday, 30 December, and another on New Year's Eve. Smith's concerts are always surprises in the moment, but the one she gave as 2001 came to a close, ten weeks after the attacks, had a singularity of its own. There was a beautiful version of 'Frederick', for her late husband, but it felt as if it was for everyone's lost love; 'Ask The Angels' spoke for itself. Uncannily, she played Led Zeppelin's 'Kashmir' – a doff to the East, and eerily prescient of where all this would take me, as we shall see. A propos of which, the concert on the cusp of 2002–3 could not have been more different. By then, mourning for 9/11 had morphed through war in Afghanistan to the eve of the invasion of Iraq. My own life, like America's, was on tenterhooks.

Patti Smith's Bowery concerts feel like private parties, almost. Many people there do know Patti personally, and those who don't feel as though they do. Patti's 2002–3 concert opened with my favourite song in her repertoire, 'Waiting Underground', which described how we felt on the eve of the catastrophe to come, followed by 'When Doves Cry', with all its poignancy. On the dot of midnight, to ring in a tumultuous New Year, she drove into 'People Have The Power' and then, when I heard guitarists Lenny Kaye and Oliver Ray crash the chords to the next song, my heart missed a beat: there it was, a reminder of what America had been through in Vietnam, and of what it now feared was to come: Jimi Hendrix's 'Machine Gun'. Within a few weeks, I'd be in Iraq.

There was a third Patti Smith performance in what I think of as this 9/11 trilogy of concerts: in August 2003, by which time I had returned from two assignments into the Iraq nightmare. It was my elder daughter Elsa's ninth birthday outing, her first ever rock concert. Patti – hair tied back, black T-shirt – began reading the Declaration of Independence, which she morphed into an indictment of 'President George Bush!' – applause – 'for abuses and usurpations ... absolute despotism' against the American people. 'It is their duty,' she thundered, 'to throw off such government' for its 'history of injuries and usurpations.' Then, fist clenched: 'Truth is just, and truth is here, we indict him, we indict George Bush just as the revolutionaries indicted King George' – the audience clapped time, Patti raised her voice – 'for killing innocent Iraqi citizens ... Rise! Rise!' I took Elsa backstage afterwards; Patti took the black ribbon from her hair and gave it to her. 'Happy birthday, and welcome to rock and roll,' she said.

I spent a couple of evenings at Patti's house in Greenwich

Village – sitting room full of guitars, a cat prowling about nervously and as gracefully feline as Patti herself. 'I don't interact with a lot of people,' she explained, 'I don't know a lot of famous people. I work very simply. I spend my time with my children and my work. I stay home and listen to opera.' We sat on the deck at the back until late, and chatted about Iraq. 'The Iraqi people . . . were living under a terrible regime, but were completely capable of figuring out a way to overthrow it. They didn't ask us there. And we . . . had no plan, beyond the knowledge that there was oil beneath the place where civilization began. Dollars beneath the garden, the original Mesopotamian Garden of Eden . . . The bloodthirsty arrogance of it. Right in there, on the basis of a bullshit pretence story. "Shock and awe", with no thought about who may be beneath those bombs, what their lives were like, what they were hoping or dreaming or planning to do tomorrow.'

Patti signed for me a photograph she had taken of the opening line of the Declaration of Independence, a copy of her album *Radio Ethiopia* and a book of poems. 'I've never lived,' she said, 'in such an atmosphere of fear, paranoia and division among our own people. We are so polarized – I feel like we're back in the Civil War.' She was scathing about how few artists had come forward to be counted, on Iraq. 'Where is everybody? Just think back to the time of Vietnam, which was no worse or better a crime. You had pretty much every serious artist making a point. Now – well, there's—' 'Neil Young,' pitched in a friend. 'Yes, Neil Young, Graham Nash . . . it's not a long list.'

The other music blasting from the rooftops over the invasion of Iraq was indeed Crosby, Stills, Nash and Young's performance, on tour, of the latter's enraged album *Living with War*. Young explained that 'if no one else is going to do this, we'll have to', and a DVD of the tour shows its impact on audiences: in Atlanta, half the audience booed and hissed a song called 'Let's Impeach

The President', and many walked out, spitting fury at CSNY's 'political bullshit'.

In conversation Graham Nash ponders, looking back: 'This was the situation as I saw it: George Herbert Bush, the father, realized that if this world was going to be the way he wanted it, then he needed to install as vice president, next to his son, a man who understood what we want: war, with all the power and money it brings. That man's name was Dick Cheney. So Neil, Stephen, David and I set out to impart our view on that situation. And these people came to listen. Now, why would you buy a ticket to see us four, playing from an album called *Living with War*, and be upset? *Because* we are talking about the situation? What did they expect? They were the people voting for Bush then, and for Trump now, and I don't understand why they like our music!'

The year after the invasion of Iraq, in 2004, Patti Smith would release the epistle coursing through her head throughout this period, 'Radio Baghdad' – about the city at the cradle of the ancient world, reduced now to ashes. The song lists the long litany of lore, legend and knowledge nurtured between the Tigris and Euphrates rivers, which she likens to a garden to which the Anglo-American coalition sent their bombers, 'shock and awe'. It's a frightening song, written, incredibly, by a poet who had never been to Baghdad (to my knowledge, never to war). But she understood it all right, not least in a sudden poetic switch from the assurance to a child – 'Sleep, Sleep' – to an urgent 'Run, Run!', as an electronic air raid rips across the song.

'We do what we can,' she told me when we met sometime later in London. 'Some give a song, some give a life. On my album *Trampin'* we developed all these ideas, and that idea of "Radio Baghdad" – the notion of a mother trying to sing her children to sleep while the Americans are bombing overhead.' The song has a genesis typical of Patti: 'Oliver [Ray] wrote a riff, and the shift from the riff into a reggae feel. And the band was just jamming on it, and then I came into the practice room and heard the music. We had just hit Iraq, the first bombs. And I just decided that I was going to use this music as my field for expressing my feelings about the war. I didn't have any lyrics when I went into the studio. All the lines in the song were improvised.'

After my attempt to live *la dolce vita* in Rome had crashed into Bosnia, I'd moved to New York in part to try again. Now, life on 6th Avenue had veered not only to Ground Zero, but was about to send me into another war. When Patti Smith had sung 'Kashmir' on New Year's Eve 2002 we were not even sure whether the madness aimed at Iraq would go ahead, though we all had a pretty clear indication of it. And I had no idea that by the time we'd reach that concert the following August I'd have spent much of the time in between right there, 'on the banks of the Tigris and the Euphrates', in Baghdad – and worse, listening to that very song.

I I

Al-Malwiya – the Spiral

Led Zeppelin, 'Kashmir', O2, London, December 2007

Led Zeppelin break into the unmistakable, rising, pre-explosive opening chords of 'Kashmir' – the band's symphonic-rock piece for which Robert Plant injected its hallmark heavy blues with the half-tones and chromatics of Arabic music. This is not Led Zep's heyday of yore, but even more special in its way: a one-off reunion in London – the place of deceased drummer John Bonham taken by his son Jason. Everyone in the band apart from vocalist Plant wanted this to be the start of a world tour, as did Richard Branson, reportedly offering \$800 million to promote it. But Plant said no: tonight had to be apocalyptic, and you cannot have serial apocalypse.

Twenty million people had applied for tickets; some paid up to £80,000 to be here. In line for T-shirts were businessmen from Colorado and a lawyer who'd flown in from Australia. But I was here gratis, due to a freak convergence of circumstances with origins in this song, 'Kashmir'.

It coursed at a slow tempo tonight, intensifying its symphonic scale; spattered with vocal echoes and eeriness, underpinned by growls in Jimmy Page's guitar to make the texture part oriental, part primal cry

– the rising eighths, like part-steps breaking through not just the diatonic scale, but what felt like distances towards a desert sky – then held there by immense major chords. 'Kashmir' was a deluge of senses, an immeasurable sound. But I doubt anyone else in the audience shared my reason for this song being the highlight, let alone my route here: bizarrely, as a guest of Plant himself. As 'Kashmir' played, I closed my eyes and drifted back – uncomfortably – to the explanation for this, to spring 2003.

I had spent three months driving around the battered country that had been Iraq – by now in a limbo between war and worse. I was entirely 'un-embedded' with any Western army, as most reporters were; or rather, I had been embedded in a rusty old GMC with a map, a photographer friend called Steve Connors, a translator called Magdi – and only one CD: No Quarter by Plant and Page. This was April 2003, and our aim was simple: to record the civilian cost of the supposed 'liberation' of Iraq and gauge what might happen next. Execution of the plan was less straightforward: Iraq was a dangerous place, on a hinge between invasion and insurgency. But we met the demand we set ourselves: going to places that were about to become no-go areas for any Westerner – Fallujah, Ramadi – uncovering violence and war crimes by the 'coalition' forces. And we did all this to a soundtrack: this song 'Kashmir', on the album to which I was now listening, live.

It being the only music we had with us, we must have played the album – over weeks on end – a hundred times; 'Kashmir' itself, several hundred. Here, in the O2, on this monstrously huge occasion, I transported myself back to people we'd spoken to during those days of fear, death and desert dust that always ended with 'Kashmir'. Leaving behind stories of loss and massacred families in towns too dangerous after dusk – and which would become insurgent fortresses later held by 'Islamic State' – but always slotting 'Kashmir' into the CD player at the end of, and during, each day, so that we knew every note and interval better than we knew ourselves.

A year passed, and I found myself back home in England, covering the funeral of the radio DJ John Peel with a raconteur of things rock and roll, Mark Ellen. He took a call on his mobile phone: 'It's Robert Plant,' he said, 'in the Queen's Head with a cup of tea.'

Mark introduced me to Plant with the story of 'Kashmir' in Iraq. Plant – who has a keen interest in the Middle East – was gracious, even rather intrigued. Years afterwards, I received a call from his office: would I like to write liner notes for his boxed set? You bet I would, and I did – spending time with Plant in England and later Canada, hearing his own extraordinary musical odyssey, about the deaths of his super-group, his son and his drummer – and redemption, back on the road with a touring band. He said of Led Zep: 'We were great when we were great. I was part of something magnificent which broke The Guinness Book of Records, but in the end, what and who are you doing it for? You have to ask these questions: what is valuable in this life? So I returned my winter fuel allowance' – and said no to the reunion tour that never happened, thus making this night at the O2 irreplaceable.

When Led Zep announced the reunion, I wrote an email: Would there be perhaps the slightest chance . . . ? To my amazement there was an immediate and gracious reply from Plant's manager, Nicola Powell: two VIP seats (the other for the girl most deserving of the honour), access to all areas, after-party, the works. At one point during this one-off wonder Elsa and I had to go to the lavatory. It need only have been a few moments, but Elsa took much longer although there was no sign of a queue for the Ladies', while the music played on. Of course, I had to wait, and I confess to having been slightly (privately, very unduly) irritated. Elsa returned after a while: 'Sorry Dad,' she chirped, 'I've just been talking to this nice lady.' She introduced me. 'This is Jimmy Page's mum.'

The spiral minaret of the Great Mosque in Samarra, north of Baghdad, is one of the wonders of the world. It is just that: a spiral, in Arabic *al-Malwiya*, around the outside of which runs a ramp, taking worshippers or visitors skywards. The spiral, as its architects must have known, is a mystical design: basis of the 'golden section' in art and geometry. Perhaps they also knew that it is the shape of the shells of some of the first living things. They may or may not have known that it is also the shape of the Milky Way (the painter of a fresco in the Church of Christ in Chora in Istanbul did, depicting the universe as a translucent snail full of stars!). But probably not that the human genome is shaped like a double helix.

When you ascend *al-Malwiya* and reach its summit, you feel something like a cosmic drill running through you towards the heavens, as is no doubt intended. When I first visited the structure with Steve Connors, as I babbled on about spirals, he said: 'You sound like Umberto fucking Eco.' When I returned a few months later, *al-Malwiya* was closed to the public, surrounded by American Humvees and barbed wire; smoke rising from a nearby Sunni bomb, aimed at them and a Shia shrine. 'Get outta here!' urged an American soldier. Iraq was in a Dantean spiral of its own, traversing the circles of hell.

Steve and I had begun our project – to put names and faces to 'collateral damage' – in Nasiriyah. The southern Iraqi town had become enshrined in Hollywood lore because this was where US Special Forces 'rescued' Jessica Lynch of the 507th Ordnance Maintenance Company, who had gone astray and been captured by the Iraqis. And most famous of all is the first floor of Nasiriyah General Hospital, where Private Lynch was being treated when snatched in what cinema screens narrated as a raid of daring heroism. Doctors and ancillary staff here, though, recall the episode differently. The Americans were welcomed and shown to Private Lynch's ward. Every major American television network dutifully traipsed through this corridor, but none of them bothered to visit Ward 114, a few doors down from Jessica's. There, separated by a curtain, lay Daham Kassim, aged forty-six, and his thirty-seven-year-old wife Gufran Ibed. Daham had his arms bound and a stump where his right leg used to be; Gufran could not move her arms, wounded by gunshots, and probably never will. But the pain was not in their bodies, it was in their faces.

Kassim spoke in English; an educated man – until a few months before, director of the southeastern electricity board. His story began on the evening of 24 March 2003 when, after the American bombing of Mutanaza, his home district in Nasiriyah, Kassim told his family to prepare to depart for the safe haven of his parents' farm. 'We packed anything valuable, and the children were allowed to take a few toys each.' The family set off and reached the American checkpoint at the north gate to the city. 'I could see two tanks,' recalls Kassim. 'I was afraid and stopped my car. I saw no one, it was silent.' The American tanks kept their hatches down. The Marines inside would have been looking through their tinted rectangular window at a civilian car carrying a couple and four children.

'I was frozen with fear,' continues Kassim. 'I could see their guns moving down. Then there was a terrible noise, and my car was buried in shooting.' Kassim's voice begins to crack. 'I saw my eldest daughter, Mawra, die. She was nine; she took the first shot, opened her eyes, and closed them again.' Gufran, his second daughter, was also killed immediately. 'But my son Mohammed, aged six, was still breathing. And my Zainab, she is five, was also still alive, although she had been shot in the head, my wife and I shot too.' Two Americans approached the car. 'They said their names were Chris and Joe. They took out my two dead children, then tried to give my son oxygen, but it was no use, he died there. I asked for a helicopter to take us to hospital. They refused, but Joe gave us some morphine in exchange for my watch. They tied my shot leg to the other, then took us to their base.'

For two nights, the remains of the family – father, mother and Zainab – slept in a bed. But on the third night, 27 March, 'there were some Americans wounded in the fighting, they needed the beds so they told us we had to go outside. They carried us like dogs into the cold, without shelter or a blanket. It was the days of the sandstorms and freezing at night. And I heard Zainab crying: "Papa, I am cold, I am cold." Then she went silent. Completely silent.' Kassim breaks off in anguish. His wife continues the story: 'What could we do? She kept saying she was cold. My arms were broken, I could not lift or hold her. If they had given us even a blanket, we might have put it over her. We had to sit there, and listen to her die.'

'We'd had trouble having children' – Kassim re-entering the conversation. 'We'd been trying for six years without success and given up hope. But then God blessed us, and everything went right. Four little flowers – and now four little flowers cut down. What for? For oil and a strategic place for America? Why did they put my Zainab into the cold? I tell you, Mister, she died of cold, she died of cold.'

Kassim has not concluded, however – indeed, he is reaching his purpose in talking. The three Kassim children put to death at the checkpoint had been buried at the site of their shooting, then taken by neighbours to the holy city of Najaf for entombment, as is mandatory custom. Zainab, however, had been interred inside the US base; 'And the question now,' pleads Kassim, revived by the urgency of what he has to say, 'is that we must get her to Najaf, where there is a space for her with her brother and sisters. Please, Mister, I cannot move; you must go and ask how we can take my Zainab to Najaf.' We got back into the GMC, and after a long silence played 'Kashmir' several times.

The US encampment and airstrip are under speedy construction on a site chosen alongside one of the world's most ancient manmade creations, the Sumerian ziggurat at Ur. 'There is no one buried at this site,' assures US Marine Sergeant Jarrell, offering nevertheless to put us through to the authority able to deal with Kassim's request, the Civil Affairs Department. The voice of Civil Affairs accordingly comes down his radio: 'Tell them this is a waste of Civil Affairs time.' 'Kashmir' again, and we try again the next day, with a kindly woman, Private Hurst from the Medical Corps. 'Oh yes,' she says rather nervously, 'I think I know who you're talking about.' But nothing doing. Steve and I drove to Mr Kassim's neighbours, and I put 'Kashmir' into the CD player.

An examination of Kassim's car showed the attack to have been a fusillade of heavy-calibre chain-gun tank fire, some rounds twisting into the metalwork but most fired straight through the windows. Beyond a dilapidated fairground nearby are homes hit by the bombing, including the one Kadem Hashem had lived in since returning to his native Iraq. Hashem was a computer consultant, and well travelled. But in 1996 he elected to join his parents and two brothers back in Nasiriyah, bringing with him his wife Salima and six children. They lived in what Hashem remembers as 'a nice house, with a TV'. He was, however, 'distrusted by the government of Saddam for being away for so long'. Of the fourteen members of Hashem's family that shared or were visiting the house on 23 March, only he and his youngest daughter survive.

Now Hashem surveys the wreckage of his 'nice house', its walls imploded, its roof collapsed by the bombs of 'liberation'. The missile that destroyed Hashem's family struck at 1.15 p.m. 'I was outside and heard something like the wind, then something thrown at the house. I went flat on the floor, and felt the heat on my body. When I looked up, the house was falling in, on fire. My eldest daughter Bashar was buried beneath it, dead. My father and mother, Ali Kadem and Reni, died, but I did manage to wrap my wife in a blanket and get her to the hospital, where she died that night.' He finds a photograph in the cinders. 'This was my middle daughter, Hamadi. I found her burnt to death by that doorway, she had shrunk to a metre tall.' And another picture, this one from inside his robe: 'This was my sister when she was little. She died over there, by the gate. For three days afterwards, I sat by that gate. I didn't sleep or go anywhere, I didn't know who or where I was.'

It is now twilight, a purple hue in the sky; we agree to leave, play 'Kashmir', and return to the neighbourhood in the morning to visit Hashem's one surviving daughter, Bedour. 'Bedour is eighteen years old, but doesn't look it,' we are warned in advance, as a cockerel heralds in another day of Hashem's laden life. 'In fact, she doesn't look like herself at all. She cannot walk, talk or sleep, and has something wrong in her head.' What remains of a beautiful girl lies on a piece of floor at a relative's house, having been discharged by the American military hospital; no room for her at the local one. She is shrivelled and petrified, her skin is like scorched parchment folded over her bones. Unable to move, she appears as if in some troubled coma, but opens her eyes, with difficulty, to issue an unintelligible cry like a wounded animal. Hashem understands it: 'We should leave her.'

Hashem has dug his own mass grave in the holy city: 'I collected them all and put them in a single grave at Najaf; my money was burnt too, and I couldn't afford to bury them separately. Now the holy men are blaming me for doing something not in accordance with the religion.' Steve and I left. We said nothing to one another, though Magdi, our interpreter, a tough guy, cried. We just played 'Kashmir' several times, I don't know why, over several desert miles, listening without a word spoken.

Few serious war correspondents do and endure whatever it is we do without a soundtrack. Just as Šoba in Sarajevo needed music in his head when he crawled back to the trenches, so we needed it to try to both absorb and escape the day. But I've never had so repetitive an accompaniment as 'Kashmir' in Iraq – to the extent that, perhaps absurdly, I cannot recall one without the other. It's with the music in my head that I have to tell the stories.

Back on the outskirts of Baghdad, it had been Rahad's turn to hide. The nine-year-old found a good place to conceal herself from her playmates, the game of hide-and-seek having lasted some two hours along a quiet street in Fallujah, on the banks of the Euphrates. But while Rahad crouched behind the wall of a neighbour's house, someone else – not playing her game – had spotted her and her friends: someone above. The pilot of an American A-10 Tank Buster aircraft, hovering in a figure of eight. He was flying an airborne weapon equipped with some of the most advanced and accurate gear for 'precision target recognition'. And at 5.30 p.m. on 29 March 2003 he launched his weapon at the street scene below. The 'daisy-cutter' bomb bounced, then exploded a few feet above ground, blasting red-hot shrapnel into the walls not of a tank but of houses. Rahad Septi and ten other children died; another twelve were injured.

Juma Septi, father to Rahad, holds a photograph of his daughter in the palm of his hand as he recalls the afternoon he lost his 'little flower'. A carpenter, Septi had been a lifelong opponent of Saddam Hussein, for which he had been imprisoned, then exiled to Jordan in 1995. In October 2002 he had returned under an armistice, reunited with his family. 'I don't really know what to think now,' he says. 'We have lost Saddam Hussein, but I have lost my daughter. They came to kill him, but killed her and the other children. What am I supposed to make of that?'

Jamal Abbas joins the conversation. 'I was driving my taxi and heard a noise like thunder, when someone told me, "Jamal, they've bombed your street!" When I got back here, the smoke was so thick it was like night – children lying wounded, women screaming.' Abbas learned that his niece – eleven-year-old Arij Haki, had been killed immediately. 'She was playing a guessing game with her cousins,' says his brother Abdullah Mohammed, the child's father, 'when the top half of her head was blown off.' 'But there was no sign of *my* daughter,' says Jamal, 'so I went outside to search in that madness; it was half an hour before I found her, right there, on the ground' – Miad Jamal Abbas, aged eleven, her body bloody and ripped, was taken to the same hospital ward as Rahad Septi. The two fathers sat in vigil together, as their daughters 'died together, just as they had played together', says Abbas.

At the cemetery on the edge of the town where Fallujah dissipates into desert, eleven small mounds of earth have been dug, the children having been buried together rather than in family plots. Saad Ibrahim, whose father Hussein was killed in the corner shop he kept, has a few questions for the daisy-cutter's pilot: 'I want to ask him: What exactly did you see that day that you killed my father and those kids? Do you have good eyesight? Is your computer working well? If not ... well, that's your business. But there was no military activity in this area. There was no shooting. This is not a military camp, these are houses, with children playing in the street.'

This is how it is to try and write about war: you have to have something to hold on to, if you can – and all we had in Iraq was this damned CD. Steve climbed back into the GMC and started the engine; not for the first time in such circumstances, neither of us said a word. I put 'Kashmir' into the stereo; when it finished, I played it again. And again, as the red sun set through the layer of black smoke wrapping the city: yet another story for us to do – a boy losing three of his limbs after an explosion. Then 'Kashmir', and back to the hotel. This was April–May 2003, when after President George Bush had announced: 'Mission accomplished'. I wrote a story about it for the paper that concluded: 'But wars, unlike football matches, do not end when the whistle blows.'

*

Four years later, Nicola is driving me to a studio tucked away in the Wiltshire countryside. The place looks more like a barn, and when the door opens, music escapes like a gust of wind: familiar, esoteric, primordial. And that voice: instantly recognizable yet unpredictable. Plant is rehearsing his band, Strange Sensation, as though he can hear in his head the final sound he's after. But then it's all cut loose, pure improvisation – then back together again like a flock of birds, expanding and contracting. The music derives from an exhaustive range of sources and from Plant's voracious curiosity, down history and across the planet: a Pandora's box comprising West Africa; Clarksdale, Mississippi; the Celtic Atlantic edge. As Plant says when we start talking: 'Subliminal flutters, passing Beefheart, Son House and the call to prayer from the minaret of the Koutoubia [Mosque] in Marrakesh ... Every sixteen bars, we visit another country.' And that voice: soft, angry, seductive, ecstatic, tortured, joyous, reflective, orgasmic.

Why did you write that song, 'Kashmir'? I asked him. He had 'the sound of Niger and Mali squeezed through a two-hundred-year-old grinder' in his head, he told me, when 'someone recommended me to go to Morocco in the 1970s. It all started off in Tangier, where literature and bohemian cultures lured, then later I heard music by Umm Kulthum and a famous piece called 'Leylet Hob'. I was transfixed. It changed everything, but looking back at it now, I suppose I was always going to get something I never bargained for.' He talked about Led Zeppelin breaking up after drummer John Bonham died, and he himself losing his son in a car crash: 'The end of a beautiful, creative whirlwind, the rudderless finale of the Mothership. There was a deep sense of frustration, and waste. I had met Jimmy Page when I was nineteen, now I was thirty-two, with everything but nothing, staring into the sharp, real fresh air and sunlight of a new world. I could have walked away from music altogether.'

But in 2003, while I was listening to 'Kashmir' in Iraq, Plant played at a remote festival in the southeast Sahara, fifty miles from Timbuktu, reachable only by camel and four-wheel-drive. He described the event to the *Los Angeles Times* as 'one of the few honest things I have been part of for a long, long time'. And this was the spirit that propelled him past the series of solo albums for which I wrote liner notes in 2007. Four further years on, in 2012, Plant prowls on stage in Toronto wearing outrageous winkle-pickers but a fisherman's sweater, for the temperature outside has plunged past minus 20°C. 'Ladies and gentlemen, boys and girls,' he greets the crowd, now more ringmaster opening his circus act than rock star. 'Welcome to another amazing evening with the scintillating, transcendental Band of Joy!' This is the man who wrote 'Kashmir'? What's going on?

'Well,' says Plant the following day, when the sky is blue but the air even colder, 'this was the name – Band of Joy – of the first group I played in all that time ago, so the plan is to go back to the place where much of the music we were playing in the sixties originated, and play it with these people.' 'These people' are some of the most accomplished musicians ever to come out of Nashville: Buddy Miller – variously guitarist to Emmylou Harris, Steve Earle and Lucinda Williams – and Patty Griffin, diva of Americana country. 'I would say it was restlessness if it was not something else,' says Plant, 'which is . . . curiosity and the need to challenge myself. Being a singer, you can get lost in your own tedium and repetition.'

There is close harmony in this sound, there is silk and there is American dirt-road grit. It achieves emotional effect with restraint and note-perfect economy, the nemesis of Led Zep. 'I think this course of events and the music I'm making are appropriate for my time of life,' says Plant. But this is also Plant's band, and something else is happening: he cannot escape the Atlas Mountains whence came 'Kashmir'. 'When you hear north

African or Indo-jazz fusion in the Band of Joy mix,' he says, 'that's mine. If I take credit for anything in this band, that's it, that's something I've brought to Nashville, and I'm proud of that.'

I still don't know why it was always 'Kashmir' in Iraq; beyond that it was all we had, there was something in the rise and fall of the notes that was also in the sand – I'll never know. But then nor, it seems, will the man who wrote it. Sometimes in journalism, a stupid question can get a good answer.

Plant is late for his tour bus; it's an overnight run to Pittsburgh and he must leave soon. 'But you don't have to do this,' I blurt. 'Yes, I *do* have to do this!' he retorts. 'It's exactly what I have to do. If you're a singer, the job is never done, you cannot sit on it. I have to try and change the landscape, whatever it is. I have to find a new place to ply my trade, to get lost in another place, and locate myself again. I'm an older man now, so it's even more important.' And, he beams, 'it's all by bus, a great way to see America. I've got the big name, but I've always wanted to just be in a touring band. And I don't want to arrive to join that band in a limo. A touring band with another gig in another town tomorrow night by bus – it's something I've hardly ever done.'

Then he asks me, as the crew prepares to frogmarch him away: 'But hell, Ed, all that time in Iraq – why "Kashmir"?' I flounder. *I'm* supposed to be asking the questions. 'I've no idea, it's just . . . Listen to it . . .' I mumble, but he's gone.

7" Single: Singing Like a Saxophone

The French group Magma composes songs with lyrics that mean nothing to us at all; deeply rooted in onomatopoeia, they are sung in an imaginary language. The band's founder and drummer Christian Vander decided its lyrics should be sung in the tongue of an imaginary planet of greater intelligence than ours called Kobaïan, a tongue that he accordingly invented. And it was fascinating to hear them play and sing in it – all texture, language reduced to primal musical expression, and that alone.

I saw Magma at Oxford Polytechnic in 1975 when the group first toured the UK, sounding like nothing anyone in the audience had ever heard: classical, jazz, symphonic, rock – all and none of the above, and language stripped, with no meaning so far as its audience was concerned.

The concert began in total darkness, with a percussive barrage overlaid with onomatopoeia – a mix of gritty *Sprechstimme* and operatic melody from a row of vocalists led by Vander's wife Stella. The vocal lines were, effectively, instruments, which was as unsettling as it was inspiring. It derives from what Richard Strauss did in *Salome*, Shostakovich in *The Nose*, Schoenberg in *Moses und Aron*: making the human voice into a sound-instrument. It comes too from concrete verse, that of Apollinaire and Stéphane Mallarmé, who insisted that poetry was about words themselves, not their meaning. Magma's sound was like a musical concrete poem.

The second performance was an odd one: courtesy of the snooker champion Steve 'Interesting' Davis, who spent the money he had made pocketing balls on achieving his dream – to bring Magma out of relative obscurity, in 1988, for three nights at the Bloomsbury Theatre in London. The band's mark is a mystical symbol 'illustrating the integration of the positive and the negative,' said the severe, deep-eyed Vander when we sat to talk. For him, Magma is a project in deadly earnest, aiming to 'strip down all personal experience, plumb the depths of feeling, to confront violent emotions and dissolve them through a new consciousness whereby we understand exactly where we are, what things are around us'. This 'peace,' he says, 'can only be achieved when we heed outer voices from afar, and it is the sound of these that our music and its language seek to emulate. But this is a parable. The outer voices are from afar, but they are also our own inner voices, from afar but deep inside, things we have forgotten.' And so we have a song like 'Joia – Song of the Sorcerer', a driving rhythmic undercurrent as Vander assails his drum kit, overlaid with 'Kobaïan' onomatopoeia and mysterious soaring soprano from backstage.

I saw Magma a third time in Paris in 2017, playing a first set by themselves, then a second with full orchestra. 'I spent my youth listening to John Coltrane,' said Vander after that occasion. 'He was the man who spoke with the saxophone, its sound was his language. So I grew up wanting to become a man who could play the saxophone in order to speak, but I end up as a man who sings words which I invent, to sound as close as possible to the sound of a saxophone.'

12

Please Step into the Next Hall, Comrades!

Shostakovich: Moscow, Cheryomushki, *Mariinsky Opera, Gergiev, London, 2006*

'Please step into the next hall, comrades!' *sings the property agent showing prospective tenants around a new housing development in Moscow. There ensues a slapstick aria praising the properties on show, as this blend of irony, comedy, banter and farce proceeds through a racy musical score. This is* Moscow, Cheryomushki, *a comic operetta by Dmitri Shostakovich written not long before his devastating Eighth String Quartet, the piece he called an expression of his 'moral suicide'.*

So, two faces of the same man and composer: the difference being that while the Eighth Quartet is rightly played ubiquitously across the West, Moscow, Cheryomushki *is hardly ever performed. It did, however, form part of* Shostakovich on Stage, *an unforgettable ten-night series of lesser-known works from the 1920s and '50s, at the London Coliseum in 2006. The pieces were brought here by the Russian maestro Valery Gergiev and his Mariinsky Opera and Ballet company of St Petersburg, as part of the centennial marking Shostakovich's birth.*

Moscow, Cheryomushki *belongs to the tradition of Mozart's* Marriage of Figaro: *vernacular – about Russia's housing shortage and a group of people vying for space in a new development – but also*

*charged with some of the composer's most profound and enigmatic state-
ments about any society. Two young newly-weds cannot live together
since they are homeless; in their quest for a berth in the new estate, they
encounter all kinds of rogues, including an explosives expert, the property
speculator and his agent Barabushkin. All is resolved by resort to a
theme rooted in Russian folklore: a magic garden.*

*Gergiev's production was sparse, with pictorial boards and period
casual costume. The arias, ditties and angular exchanges raced along –
pungent, salty, slapstick – yet this is social commentary in deadly earnest.
One of wretched Barabushkin's arias is daft but crucial: he preaches that
two plus two need not necessarily equal four, but any number, according
to circumstances and 'the connections' involved. It's a bitterly comic
description of the truth during any dictatorship, but also in our own
society – a manifesto for the absurd, cocking a snook at power, all
couched in a dotty ditty saying everything and nothing.*

Moscow, Cheryomushki *(Moscow, Bird-Cherry Trees), named
after an existing housing estate, was premiered in 1959. The libretto was
by Vladimir Mass and Mikhail Chervinsky, two leading craftsmen of a
Soviet humour that failed to reach the West during the Cold War. It is
one of Shostakovich's longest works, a dense score rich in romance and
idiom, sung and played by this company and orchestra from St Petersburg – Shostakovich's Leningrad – as though it belongs to them, which it
does, for not many others perform it.* Moscow, Cheryomushki *and
other pieces in the Coliseum run are hardly ever put on in the West,
partly because they undermine the stereotype of Shostakovich upon which
the West appears dependent, and partly because few conductors other
than Gergiev understand the composer in such a way as to commit to a
comic operetta with equal devotion as to the symphonies.*

*The piece draws on Soviet pop songs, parodies Russian ballet (even
Sleeping Beauty) and pastiches nationalist songs. The cast and its
libretto are as zany as the score, replete with cranks, quips and hilarity.
This is Shostakovich the wag-wit but serio-comic – saying something
about the severity of absurdity, and vice versa. As such, it falls within a*

rich tradition from Molière and Beaumarchais to Gogol, Ionesco to Beckett. Gergiev's series demonstrates Shostakovich's bittersweet, comically dark nature; starting in the 1920s at the height of his inventive powers, but continuing towards Moscow, Cheryomushki, written late in his life but echoing his work back in the avant-garde heyday.

From that earlier time we heard Shostakovich's surreal masterpiece The Nose, of 1928; from 1929, a ballet setting of Vladimir Mayakovsky's farce The Bedbug, which brought Shostakovich into an all-star collaboration: with the poet Mayakovsky himself, the avant-garde director Vsevolod Meyerhold and the Constructivist artist Alexander Rodchenko. But also, from as late as 1962, The Lady and the Hooligan, based on a film of that name from 1918, about a street yob who falls in love with a teacher and is murdered for his loyalty to her in class.

Last, a one-off chance to see The Golden Age, Shostakovich's ballet about football, and the Soviet team caught in a web of dastardly match-fixing during a tournament in the capitalist West. At one point our heroes are jailed, but then released by an uprising, so that the ballet ends with a joint celebration between workers and footballers. Shostakovich is said to have coined the phrase 'Football is the ballet of the masses.' The staging was mock-heroic, droll and biting, and the rich score full of frolic and antic wit. The ballet reflects, of course, Shostakovich's passion for football, for his team Zenith Leningrad – barely acknowledged in Western accounts of either man or music; again, it spoils the West's Shostakovich story. In fact he kept nerdy books of results and scorers; he once wrote a match report when a correspondent covering the game for the Sportski List paper had gone missing, presumed drunk, after a Zenith game. Anecdotes abound about Shostakovich's antics at and around matches, not least the evening when he invited the entire Zenith squad to dinner. The few photographs of Shostakovich laughing out loud and clowning around were taken at matches.

Shostakovich's wartime letters make poignant reading – but invariably revert to a discussion of football. A letter of 4 November 1942 *contains two paragraphs: the first expresses his concern for his sister Zoya, whose husband has tropical fever, and sorrow over the deaths of two friends. 'I am overwhelmed by feelings of sadness', he writes.*

The second paragraph, without any bridging from the first, continues: 'Krasny Sport [Red Sport magazine] of 27 October carried a report of our Leningrad football clubs' successes in Alma-Ata: Zenith won 2–0 against Alma-Ata Dynamo, and Leningrad Dynamo won 7–2 ... P. Dementiev and [Boris] Levin-Kogan were outstanding for our Zenith, and for the Dynamo team, [Evgeny] Arkhangelsky, A. Fyodorov, Alov and some others had a brilliant game. I am so happy for them. I saw Dynamo play in Moscow, and thought back to our times together in the Lenin Stadium. Happy Days.'

Valery Gergiev leaps onto the podium, shakes the hand of the orchestra's leader and bows to the musicians, hand on heart. One would now expect the lights to dim, but this is not a concert – Gergiev is greeting the orchestra with a pastiche of what will follow tonight. It's 2006, a rehearsal at the London Barbican of a programme of Russian music with the London Symphony Orchestra. Gergiev flicks a forelock from his brow. 'Good morning,' he grins.

Before we get to the importance of those Shostakovich stage comedies, and Gergiev's tearing through the musical Iron Curtain to bring that series West, we must spend time with this man, which will amount to a masterclass in how music is made. Gergiev has a spell-binding effect on audiences, which has culminated in a reputation not unlike that of a rock star with a frenzied schedule. But there are reservations in the West over his proximity to Vladimir Putin; over his performance of Shostakovich's 'Leningrad' Symphony to Russian soldiers amid the ruins of his homeland Tskhinvali in South Ossetia, Georgia; and over a concert in Palmyra, Syria, after it had been 'liberated' by Russian troops from 'Islamic State' on behalf of the dictator

Bashar al-Assad. So here's another ownership problem: Gergiev is the darling of the Metropolitan Opera in New York and the West loves him for bringing the Mariinsky to us – but wishes he was someone else.

In 2007 Gergiev became principal conductor of the LSO, a position he held until Simon Rattle took over in 2017. His performances were exhilarating and exhausting for audiences and musicians alike, for their impetuous intensity – the musical equivalent of rounding a hairpin bend holding the road.

Born in 1953, Gergiev went to his adoptive home, Leningrad, in 1972 to study at the Conservatoire. His musical education was steeped in the work of the conductors he cites when he explains his own music-making. Asked: What is going on at these concerts?, he replies: 'It's easier for me to explain what I felt when I was a student, able to listen to great recordings of the past. Especially Furtwängler who, because of the outcome of the Second World War, was like a trophy for Soviet Radio. We young musicians had this incredible opportunity to hear recordings that the Red Army had found among the archives in Berlin, of Furtwängler conducting Beethoven, Brahms, even our Tchaikovsky.'

He gives an example: 'In Furtwängler's Brahms Fourth Symphony, at the end of the first movement, there is this incredible surge forward, all the forces of the Berlin Philharmonic in this crazy, uncalculated *crescendo* or *accelerando* or *stringendo* or whatever you choose to call it, it doesn't matter. And this is Furtwängler, his mysterious power. That's what made me realize that conducting is not beating time, or showing the entrances. Because Brahms is not about who is entering and when – it is about something else, something intangible, which conductors must reach, which Furtwängler reached.' The fact that Furtwängler served the Reich that besieged, starved and laid waste to Gergiev's adoptive city is 'irrelevant', he says. 'What matters is the music he made.' This 'mysterious power' – which Gergiev echoes – is not serendipitous. There is calculation in the savagery, and if there is a key to the mystery of these concerts and stage productions it is in the way he rehearses, and how he sees the relationship between rehearsal and live performance – which is, he says, 'exactly that: live, of the moment, never to be repeated'.

At the Barbican the rehearsal is of Rachmaninoff's *Symphonic Dances*, the composer's last piece, written in America in 1940 and reflective of the country from which he was estranged. The delivery of the work's emotions is personally important to Gergiev. His rehearsal technique is to take the orchestra over and over again through a short passage, as if it were a detail of a painting, until he and they have achieved the exact sonority he is after, then unleash his musicians across the rest of the canvas during the performance itself. 'He will go through a short passage over and over until the palette is right,' says double-bass player Matthew Gibson, 'then improvise the whole picture on the night.'

'The thing about a rehearsal,' says Gergiev as we take a break, 'is that it is not something once and forever made of stone. I respect and admire certain moments during the rehearsals, when wonderful solos are played and I want to stop and say "This is beautiful, just keep it this way" – but during the concert, it has to be done as a totally new and, in many ways, improvised inter-pretation.' In conversation Gergiev constantly cites and invokes his heroes, Mravinsky and Furtwängler, both notoriously tyran-nical. Gergiev's menace is different: he intimidates his musicians with the ultimate compliment: trusting them to 'wing it', says Rachel Gough, principal bassoonist. 'The most frightening thing of all is to be trusted to get it right. He throws us in and expects us to rise to the challenge.'

The slice of Rachmaninoff for rehearsal is evocative of a pastoral landscape, with demanding passages in woodwind and lower strings. Gergiev communicates in a way that is not humble, for sure, but collegial – affection and respect in equal doses to insistence and authority. 'We are equals – but I am at the centre,' he says later. And from the podium: 'Because you're musicians, you won't mind me saying this: when you see the word "*crescendo*", it does not mean what it says, exactly, it means something towards the heights. It is not about volume, loud or quiet, it is about coloration, sublimation of what is written on the page.' This we expect from Gergiev; what we hear less about is his fascination with '*pianissimo*'. 'Don't run away from this!' he pleads above the faintest trace of sound from the violins, eyes tight shut. Cellist Noel Bradshaw observes: 'It's often said Gergiev focuses on that Russian tradition of playing everything louder. But he can also stretch "*pianissimo*" to the limits of inaudibility.'

My father used to enjoy watching orchestral music on television with the sound muted, and once wrote an essay called 'The Physicality of Music'. Which does not come much more physical than when Gergiev is conducting. So many batons have flown from his hand that he tends now to use a toothpick instead. His fingers flutter, he appears to drift away, then suddenly pounce, catching a musician's eye. Gareth Davies, principal flute, is in the firing line, 'because of where I sit in the orchestra, right in his line of sight when he looks straight ahead'. He talks about how the conductor 'brings out the coloration in a piece so you find yourself playing, hearing and feeling the notes completely differently. Suddenly, there's totally different coloration or tempi – and a lot of this is done with eye contact. I'll suddenly find him staring right at me, which can be pretty terrifying – and it's entirely intuitive how one responds. It adds a frisson of excitement, I can't explain it, but it works. I remember doing Tchaikovsky's "Pathétique" Symphony in Dublin, which we must have played a hundred times. And I went into some kind of trance. Next thing I knew, the symphony was over, and we had played it like we had never played "Tchaik Six" before.'

I remember a similarly bewitching 'Pathétique' at the Proms, after which cellist Bradshaw said over a drink: 'I thought: We know this so well – but instead, Gergiev led us through some visceral, wild world. I couldn't believe what we were creating . . . [I was] bowled over by the sound he was getting from us. It was one of the most emotionally intense concerts we've ever played. I just sat there, playing, listening, and thinking: Is it really *us* doing this?'

The rehearsal at the Barbican over, Gergiev explains: 'We all like safety, it helps, to know a piece. But by far the most important thing is what we did today with the *Symphonic Dances*, reaching into the character of the piece by rehearsing a short section. The most criminal thing a conductor can do to an audience or a composer is to deliver a faceless performance that makes for a faceless piece, and you do not feel excited. If the piece is still played after a hundred years, there's something important about it – the conductor has to find out why, then convey that "why" . . . it's about the sonority,' he emphasizes, 'and to find it, a conductor must take risks.'

The Rachmaninoff dances are played that night with sumptuous sonority – lyrical, wistful; one can feel the composer looking back on his life in a country he will never see again. But, as Gergiev has promised, there is no 'definitive' performance, and next day he and his orchestra resume for another rehearsal of the same music. Just as we reach an apparently sublime moment, he interrupts: 'No! It's played very well, but a little sugary. Rachmaninoff is looking back, nostalgic, but restless, never sentimental.' At the end of the morning he wanders over for a conversation with Bradshaw, who's putting away his instrument. 'Rachmaninoff was never sugary. Nostalgic, but there's a bitterness,' says Gergiev. 'The second movement has a decadent sensuality,' Bradshaw replies, 'almost like a tango.' 'Exactly,' concurs the maestro, 'tonight, we give a bitterly nostalgic Rachmaninoff, like a tango.' And it is: introverted, unquiet and delicate.

Next day, Gergiev and the orchestra depart for a tour of Eastern Europe, starting at a communist-era hall in Vilnius, Lithuania. Gergiev is worried about the acoustics, which threaten to swallow sound and blunt edges; he rearranges the musicians' seating accordingly – 'Everyone forward two paces, please' – so as to project more forcefully. 'In here,' he says, 'we'll need more emphasis, greater richness.' Tonight's audience arrives like a 1960s fashion parade, drinking brightly coloured fruit cocktails. In Vilnius, there's no fussing about those who have not found a seat sitting in the aisles or standing at the back. Gergiev turns up the volume to maximum, so that tonight's Rachmaninoff is amplified to Wagnerian levels – he and his orchestra hurling the music into every cranny of the stolid Stalinist oak. The account is almost disturbing, but the audience stamps its approval. Gergiev – even more than usually unshaven, tails even more crinkled than usual – looks at once exhausted and possessed, but afterwards he relaxes, nearly home, chatting in Russian over a spread of cakes and cocktails.

'There are orchestras in Berlin and Vienna who will rehearse and rehearse their own beautifully honed, glowing sound,' says double-bass player Gibson on the plane to Stansted at the end of the tour. 'What they do, no one can do better. But what you heard last night was another level of engagement, voltage, risk and spontaneity. We can be on the edge of calamity, and it turns to gold.'

Six years before our Baltic tour, in 2006, Gergiev had prepared for his term at the LSO with a cycle of Shostakovich symphonies at the Barbican for the centennial. The series – also played in Russia, Japan and the USA – seemed to stake Gergiev's claim to the composer's mantle, after the death of Shostakovich's friend Mstislav 'Slava' Rostropovich in 2007. Five years before his death, Rostropovich had played what felt like not only his own farewell to Shostakovich, but ours to a generation – with the LSO in New York playing the composer's seventh, eighth and eleventh 'War' symphonies. They were shattering performances, after which Slava held the score aloft in acknowledgement of the applause, so that his friend rather than he might be its recipient. Now, it was Gergiev's turn.

The centennial year 2006 also saw that run of lesser-known opera and ballet at the London Coliseum, and a chance to talk to Gergiev about these works that brought Shostakovich the man back to life, after the appropriation of his legacy by the reductions of Solomon Volkov and his followers. Gergiev began: 'I welcome your chance to listen to this music, rather than listening to Stalin or Zhdanov, Volkov or whoever. Listen to the music of a great man, and an interesting man . . . I will not conduct any piece of Shostakovich according to anybody else's "testimony". I try to open my ear totally to this great music. When I am rehearsing with the orchestra or looking at the score, when I am going to conduct finally the public performance, I try to be inspired by the music itself, and only the music. Not by the fact that someone heard Shostakovich say this or that, or what he might have said, or what Stalin said he said. Or what Volkov said Shostakovich said.

'Shostakovich was not often openly articulate about content. He was interested in the power of music expressing everything – not just the political situation – including the beautiful, in- cluding what he found funny, or that which is strange. Shosta- kovich,' continued Gergiev, 'had his own world of dreams beyond the politics of the Soviet Union, though you would not think that if you read what people write about him. What people don't realize is that he was an extremely sensitive man, and if he goes into the depth of his own soul and opens it honestly to the public, it is through the music alone. He does not communicate like every musicologist who talks about him. He would say: "I don't know what to tell you, *just listen*."'

We are back with what we can now call our 'Shostakovich–Ančerl problem', and saying something apparently at odds with my point about Karel Ančerl's conducting and the music written in Terezín. There, the setting of the music becomes inevitably cogent to our understanding of it. Here, Gergiev pleads for an independence of the music from context. Again, we're on that path without a map: how free is music from its time and circumstances? One writer, Esti Sheinberg, charts with academic rigour the deployment of 'musical ambiguities' – irony, satire and parody – in Shostakovich. She laments the fact that scholarship on the composer has become 'so loaded with political and ideological considerations that even works which sincerely aspired to be purely analytical could not entirely avoid ideological preconceptions'. Sheinberg posits, with a bedazzling display of diagrams and examples from the scores, that these things present particular problems because they are themselves about incongruity and contradiction. These 'satirizing techniques', 'the satirical grotesque' and the 'improbable juxtapositions' in themselves demand detachment from circumstance, because this is their essence in a sense that is almost as literary as it is musical (she cites the critic Mikhail Bakhtin and his notion of 'polyphony' in a text).[1]

With Shostakovich, it is not just the extreme case of his music having been entrapped within its time, it is also a case of ironic nuance: Gergiev explains that something he says is 'difficult to translate into English. When Shostakovich spoke, his words in Russian were very fragmented. He would break a sentence into five or six pieces you cannot follow, because he didn't want to get caught. He would *not* say: "OK: the beginning demonstrates the revolution, then you see Stalin, this or that, then Hitler, then a forest, then the Kremlin." Absolutely not. This is the mistake these people make. But this is what, for half a century, people have been told to find in this music. So far as I'm concerned, we, the interpreters ... – orchestras, conductors, singers, quartets, directors, choreographers – must hear his voice in the *music*, not in any other narrative, and this is what I'm trying to do.' Gergiev began this liberation of his music by bringing into the mainstream repertoire, together with the conductor Gennady Rozhdestvensky, works of the kind he brought to the Coliseum in 2006 – a whole canon of which fitted neither Soviet nor Western claims on the composer: the work of a real, living, breathing Shostakovich.

After the Vilnius concert I got to sit next to Gergiev on the plane to Tallinn, where that night he did just the opposite to fill a sound-hungry Lithuanian hall: in the Estonian capital, with the same music, he blew the roof off a tiny, elegant baroque space. During the flight, Gergiev comes alive even by his standards when he addresses Shostakovich's overlooked characteristics that he himself recognizes only too easily. 'Shostakovich was full of energy – sharp and extremely funny. He was known among friends as someone who comes to the party and right away, after entering the room full of some of the most important people, carrying a glass full of vodka' – Gergiev gestures, to demonstrate its size – 'like we drink a *grande* cappuccino, 250 centilitres! And he'd down it in one gulp! Just once, over the entire evening, but he would empty it in one second – *pah*! This is not a huge man, but he was able to do it. Only one in a thousand can do that, and Shostakovich was one of them. That was his way of living: if you do it, do it to the maximum.'

The conversation progresses to Shostakovich and football. 'Football drove Shostakovich crazy,' says Gergiev, fondly. 'In Leningrad, he would go mad because the Moscow–Leningrad rivalry was so huge, like Manchester–Liverpool – maybe even more furious. Shostakovich was completely insane about football, and we are not talking about the kind of people who compose pessimistic symphonies all their lives and then suddenly go to the stadium to laugh and scream or jump about like idiots. He really loved and knew about his favourite teams and players; he took it all extremely seriously, but loved the funny side too.'

Shostakovich 'would buy a season ticket and turn up at the game in all weather', wrote Dmitri and Ludmilla Sollertinsky in their book *Pages from the Life of Dmitri Shostakovich*, 'and enter results and match details in scorebooks he kept all his life'. Even without which 'he retained in his memory all the complex figures connected with the soccer championships. His friends would test him – did he remember, they would ask, how many Zenith had won by against Moscow's Spartak in the first round for such-and-such a year? He would promptly name not only the score but who scored and in what minute of the game.' Shostakovich did, after all. invite the entire Leningrad Dynamo team to his home for dinner, and had been taken on as a trainee referee.

It takes one to know one. 'Me?' says Gergiev. 'Oh, yes, I still scream if there's a great goal. I'm not fanatical about any particular club like Shostakovich was, but the last great game I saw live was everything I could wish for: Manchester United versus Chelsea, high tension, drama, fantastic playing from Cristiano Ronaldo.' There's a story about how Gergiev and Placido Domingo kept an entire opera company waiting so they could watch a World Cup match together. 'I respect artists,' Gergiev continues, 'I don't like to see machines play music, and it's the same with football. My generation is spoiled from the times we saw Pelé, Maradona, Michel Platini, Johan Cruyff – they were artists, they were different. This is genius, when something happens on the field and you think: God, how can a human being do that? It's like having Mozart on the soccer field, a genius impressing the crowd and millions watching on TV. This is what makes soccer one of the most powerful things in our lives, and Shostakovich knew that long before Maradona was born.'

One way to account for Shostakovich's Janus faces of 'comic' and 'severe' is to say that the springtime of his avant-garde urge during this period was blighted by the persecution that began after *Lady Macbeth*. But *Moscow, Cheryomushki* is among many works that give the lie to this, premiered ten years after some of Shostakovich's deepest humiliations in the late 1940s – premiered along with, on another continent, 'A Fool Such As I' by Elvis Presley and 'Broken-Hearted Melody' by Sarah Vaughan. Shostakovich the wise fool had another sixteen years to live, pin-up Presley eighteen. *Moscow, Cheryomushki* is Shostakovich in the tradition of Rabelais' carnival of fools, his equivalent to that painting by the surreal Symbolist James Ensor, *Christ's Entry into Brussels*; Shostakovich taking a leaf from Lear's timeless Fool. '*Moscow, Cheryomushki*,' says Gergiev, 'is such a brilliant opera precisely because it is about real, everyday life, and at the same time, the significance and absurdity of what ordinary people face every day. It is set in Russia of course, but it could be anywhere, at any time, in the world.'

Here lies the liberation of Shostakovich from the Western stereotype, the challenge to those who would appropriate him and impose narrative. But more than that: this is a cautionary and fundamental lesson about all music, the dangers of appropriation, of trying to pin music down. The lesson lies not just in the fact that Shostakovich wrote absurd serio-comedies, but that he wrote them alongside the great symphonies and confessional quartets, during periods of both persecution and favour. He was – like any artist, and more than most – influenced and impacted by the world in which he found himself; in no society more than the USSR were the arts considered part of public life, and artists therefore under the stress of its demands. One of those who contest Solomon Volkov, the musicologist Richard Taruskin, writes: 'Shostakovich was willy-nilly the most important artist in the country where the arts were most important – and the most watchdogged, precisely because this was the medium with the most potential slippage between its manifest and its latent content. Because of this, Shostakovich was the one and only Soviet artist to be claimed by the official culture and the dissident culture.'[2]

But Shostakovich belonged to neither the 'official' nor the 'dissident' school. That no music really can 'belong' to anyone is a foundation stone of this book; that is its mystery, magic and incertitude. A friend of his, the mathematician Lev Mazel, likened Shostakovich's work to algebra in which the same formulae can reach various solutions so long as they contain an unknown. His music contains too many unknowns, he argued, to accommodate any reductive solution. Mazel had good reason to know what he was talking about. He was privileged to hear a first-hand account of Shostakovich's composition of the 'Leningrad' Symphony, which Volkov and his followers claim to demonstrate has nothing to do with fascism, but is a musical polemic against Stalin. It may have been that too, but Mazel came to know that friend of Shostakovich's while he completed the work in Soviet-held territory, Flora Yasinovskaya, who recalled the composer explaining to her that his symphony concerned 'Fascism, yes. But music, real music, is never tied literally to any theme. Fascism is not simply national socialism, and this is music about terror, slavery, spiritual exhaustion.'[3]

The surface of Shostakovich's oeuvre, from the comedies to the symphonies and in between, is fraught with overt and covert significance, extrovert and introvert, meaning and non-meaning, slapstick and tragedy, layers of latency, feeling and mood. The musicologist David Fanning uses the compelling image of reflection in an essay on Shostakovich's Eighth String Quartet, describing the surface of his music as 'overlaid with mirrors', and adding that 'we can never be sure precisely where and at what angle they are placed'.[4] Shostakovich's music cannot, writes

Fanning, 'be merely – or even principally – a translation of ideology into sound'.[5]

Anyone acquainted with Russia or the ex-communist countries knows that fearful, canny doubleness with which people were obliged to live, those watched people who were – and in Russia still are – required to play out their lives on different levels. And the Shostakovich we glean from the evidence lived in a state of doubleness from which he wrote both music like the Fifth Symphony and comedies and film scores – this is the mosaic of his music and the purgatorial genius of his work.

'Shostakovich was too great a musician to be miserable,' insists Bernard Haitink, before a performance of the Fourth and Fifteenth Symphonies in 2014. 'Sometimes his music depresses you, yes; and he embraces you in this sadness – this is Shostakovich. But he is also sarcastic, quirky, humorous. And what Shostakovich does to hide himself is quite another thing.' Haitink recalls the Shostakovich he met in 1975; and what a meeting – the last great composer of that generation and the last still at work at the time of writing from a golden age of conducting: 'That special character Shostakovich exuded, but haunted all the same. How do we know that he was like that because he was the victim of the political pressures? Maybe that is who he was, the man himself, and he'd have been that same Shostakovich wherever he had lived. I wonder. What matters is the music he wrote and what we will play.'

7" Single: La Discothèque

Many testimonies exist to the horror of the coup and dictatorship of the Chilean general Augusto Pinochet, who – two years before Shostakovich's death – overthrew the democratically elected government of Salvador Allende in 1973. But few capture the ethos of the period's suffering with the cogency of a still-expanding collection of music made, performed, heard and sung by prisoners – even used by their captors – in the network of camps and detention centres operated by Pinochet's regime. I came across *Cantos Cautivos* (Captive Songs) in 2016, like an echo of Terezín in my lifetime.

Cantos Cautivos is a digital archive compiled by Katia Chornik, daughter of two opponents of the dictatorship who were detained in – and survived – an infamous detention centre named La Discothèque by agents of the DINA (Dirección de Inteligencia Nacional, secret police): so called – relevant to Joe Boyd's point – because guards deployed loud music to torture their quarry, or as soundtrack to abuse. Chornik spent her childhood in exile, between Venezuela and France, returning to

Chile with her parents at the end of the dictatorship. She trained in violin and musicology in Chile and the UK.

There is no overstating the horror in Pinochet's jails and camps. Serial human rights groups, international and Chilean, have documented the litany of maltreatment and torture – starvation, beating, sexual abuse – of some forty thousand people, plus 2,250 more murdered and thirteen hundred 'disappeared'. Among the most famous victims was the folk singer Víctor Jara, and Chornik seeks to record the strange story of how those subjected to this brutality responded by singing and playing, or listening to, music. 'It was emotional, cultural, but also social,' she says; 'there are many accounts of people singing between sections: men to women, women to men – they'd sing to one another, like a dialogue. And singing as a way of establishing presence to people outside the prison walls.' One witness, Beatriz Bataszew Contreras, says that after she had been interned in the Tres Álamos prison camp, 'I met someone who lived a block away from Tres Álamos and said that she could hear us.'

About a third of the songs were partly or fully written in captivity – 'Some people became musicians or songwriters while detained,' says Chornik, 'and the originality of these songs is one of the valuable things about the archive.' Some were written or sung in the camp, then recorded recently – in some cases by groups of survivors specially convened to do so. But Chornik also collected recordings never heard before, made in captivity and either smuggled out or hidden.

One such song was by the famous Chilean songwriter Ángel Parra, who survived the Chacabuco concentration camp; it was called 'Oratorio de Navidad segùn San Lucas' (Christmas Oratorio according to St Luke). One of the singers in Parra's band in the camp was Marcelo Concha Bascuñán, who disappeared in 1976 and was never seen again, but Chornik collected a recording of his voice while he was imprisoned in Chacabuco.

'After I collected the tape,' she says, 'and his family heard it, they said it was the closest they've ever felt to having Marcelo alive.' His now heartbreaking words thank Parra and explain: 'These songs are ... a reflection of love towards the people who are waiting for us ... Therefore, a manifestation of hope, of trust, of faith, in sum: of love for life – which is love for freedom.'

There's a song by the composer Sergio Vesely, sung at shows laid on by prisoners to entertain their children on family visiting days at Melinka prison camp; the camp commander and his guards would sit in. It's a light-hearted song, about a King Ñaca-Ñaca, but pokes fun at the commander and indirectly at Pinochet himself: 'At the end Ñaca-Ñaca loses his voice – that is, his power – and he loses his mind,' says Vesely. 'Thus the captives become free. The show's language was so poetic that the commander, seated as always in the front row, did not get it. If he had understood, we surely would have been punished.' Exactly the same trick was played in Terezín, with Ullmann's *Kaiser of Atlantis*.

'Both sides recognized the power of music,' says Chornik, and sometimes it was 'imposed on the prisoners'. Inmates were in some places subjected to 'loud music as an accompaniment to interrogation and as a loud intimidatory sound'. At La Discothèque, also known as Venda Sexy, at no. 3037 Calle Irán in Santiago de Chile, scores of leftists and others were kept and tortured. There are no testimonies yet of music having been sung there, but Beatriz Bataszew Contreras – who was detained there as well as at Tres Álamos – recalls incessant music played 'very loud' to 'pressure you to collaborate'. Bataszew Contreras describes one way of surviving: 'I manufacture the silence: I close the door, I shut myself in ... the noise was loud but I was doing my own thing.'

According to an ex-member of the DINA interviewed by Chornik, the name Venda Sexy too was coined by the agents: *venda*, from the blindfold that prisoners had to wear at all times;

'sexy', from the level of sexual violence perpetrated by the agents, especially against women – they even had a dog called Volodia (after Volodia Teitelboim, General Secretary of the Chilean Communist Party) that had been specially trained to rape women. But to Chornik, the additional significance of La Discothèque is that her parents were there. 'I experienced Chile in a fragmented way,' she says of her homeland. 'My parents were exiled and moved back at the end of the dictatorship [in 1988]. I was a child when I learned that my parents had been in La Discothèque, and have quite vivid memories of them meeting together with other ex-prisoners who had been there, and going to find the house after the dictatorship ended. But I was well protected; my parents told me a little, but not the details.'

By the early 2000s Chornik was studying at the Royal Academy of Music in London, and a number of circumstances converged: 'All my paternal antecedents were refugees, Jewish from the 1906 pogroms, and my paternal grandmother was a violinist in an all-women's orchestra in Chile, the Orquesta de Señoritas.' Thus inspired, Chornik began to study Alma Rosé, niece of Gustav Mahler who, from the violin, had directed an orchestra in Auschwitz so as to stay alive (though she was to perish from disease). 'Then,' says Chornik, 'I switched my idea to a comparative study between music in the Nazi camps and in the Chilean camps. So it was a revelation. The penny dropped. Against my parents' wishes, I went with them to La Discothèque for the first time. And because I am a musician, I was touching some sensitive fibres: the idea that this place was called "the Discotheque" opened a rainbow of questions I had put aside for many years . . . I was aware that I was working out my parents' life, except through the experiences of people who went through similar. It was a way to learn about them sideways.'

Music comes too from within a concealed internment compound called Cuatro Álamos, and from there, testimony by Luis

Alfredo Muñoz González: 'One night,' he says, 'between the guards' shouts and bustling, all the prisoners were taken away . . . Very early the next morning, I was awakened by the voice of a woman calling my name . . . The voice cautiously persisted . . . from the right of my cell. Naked, I went to the window (I showered dressed so as to wash the blood from my clothing, which I then hung to dry from the bars of the window). "Who are you?" I asked. "They've taken everyone away. They told me they were going to kill those of us still here," she said. "Who are you?" I asked. "They call me *la jovencita* [the young girl]. I am from Argentina and they nabbed me in Valparaíso. Do you think they will kill me?" "No, they won't kill you," I told her. "That will be me, not you . . ."

'After a long silence, *la jovencita* said: "I feel very sad and very alone. Would you sing to me? . . . that song you sang the other night, the one about the doves?" My voice rose,' remembers Muñoz González, 'as if it had a will of its own.'

13

Strauss Is Cooler Than Salsa

The 'Alpine' Symphony, Simón Bolívar Youth Orchestra,
Caracas, 2007, El Sistema

The massed musicians surge towards the climax of Richard Strauss's 'Alpine' Symphony – a vast contemplation of nature by the composer whose work constituted a bridge between fin-de-siècle romanticism and twentieth-century modernism in Vienna. But the scene outside the concert hall could hardly be in starker contrast to Alpine peaks or the final throes of the Habsburg Empire. While the young musicians and their audience have been mingling on a balcony, the landscape below has turned to a tropical tangerine twilight: the concrete jungle of Caracas, Venezuela – throbbing salsa, whizzing scooters and murals exalting the then president, Hugo Chávez. Down the hills tumble makeshift barrios where most of the city's five million people gouge out a living – and whence most of this orchestra come.

Strauss is rarely played to this standard; major figures in classical music concur that this Simón Bolívar Youth Orchestra of Venezuela is a phenomenon. Named after 'the Liberator' who led the uprisings against the Spanish colonial yoke in the 1820s, it's an orchestra with a difference: these young musicians come not from elite conservatoires but from some of the most desperate shanty-town slums in the world. Attention has been focused on the twenty-six-year-old prodigy conducting Strauss this evening, with his mop of curls and his passionate communication with the musicians from among whose ranks he came as a violinist: Gustavo Dudamel. Sir Simon Rattle has rated him 'the most astonishingly gifted conductor I have ever come across'.

But this is not the story of one prodigy from a poor family on the outskirts of Barquisimeto in the Venezuelan interior. This is about what Dudamel calls 'music as social saviour'. He and his orchestra are but the apex of something broader and deeply rooted, formally entitled the National System of Youth and Children's Orchestras of Venezuela but known simply as El Sistema, which has flourished on the basis of a simple dictum: that in the poorest slums, where the pitfalls of drug addiction, crime and despair are many, life can be changed and fulfilled if children are brought into an orchestra to play. This concert was a decade ago, but even as the country implodes at the time of writing, young barrio dwellers now spend their afternoons practising Beethoven while their peers learn to cut crack cocaine. They are teenagers like René Arias, playing Bizet's 'Carmen' Suite at a home for abandoned and abused children, who when asked what he would be doing if he had not taken up the French horn, replies straightforwardly: 'I'd be where I was, only further down the line – either dead or still living on the streets smoking crack, like I was when I was eight.'

Dudamel's rehearsals for the 'Alpine' Symphony approach their end. It is even more compelling to watch him in rehearsal than in performance – his combination of intensity and charm, severity and exuberance – coaching the young orchestra that has been his life and is now his springboard as he leaves to take over the Los Angeles Philharmonic. Dudamel always uses the expression 'Let's do this', never 'Do this.' He talks the musicians through the piece's meaning as well as its structure: 'Let's consider each bar as part of the whole,' he coaxes, 'as I think Strauss wants us to feel part of the perfect union of the whole – a philosophical reflection by man confronted with nature.' He loves crescendos – 'Let's give it some push!' – but for the hushed finale he requires the musicians to rehearse in pitch black, whispering as the lights dim: 'Let's take it down – right down – slowly – turn it off'. . . until there is silence and darkness. 'Ah, si!' *sighs Dudamel, breaking the spell, and the orchestra applauds itself.*

The 'Alpine' Symphony is particularly demanding for the bassoon, which Edgar Monroy, twenty-two, his hair spiked with gel, is packing away. Edgar's journey home after the concert is via subway, then minibus up a steep, pitted road to the ramshackle barrio of San Andrés, into which one climbs, winding step by winding step, past breeze-block shacks with roofs of corrugated iron and zinc crammed together in the humid heat of the night. Edgar's house, shared with his parents, sister and baby niece, hides its poverty behind careful upkeep and pride at what Edgar has achieved. 'There are times when the rehearsals end late and I daren't come home – it's just too dangerous; I stay in town,' he says, with the puckish grin of any lad his age. He joined the local orchestra, 'and they gave me a bassoon because it was the only instrument for which there was a vacancy'. There were no private classes, just orchestral practice at Caracas racetrack, whether or not the horses were racing that day. 'It's hard to say what happened exactly,' says Edgar. 'I fell in love with the music, though it was strange to me. I motivated myself and started to dream this could be my future.

'Our experience is reflected in how we play,' he tells me. 'Most of us are from the barrio and that's our bond – to rise above what happens where we live. Bad things happen every day around here. I don't often keep my instrument at home because it's likely to get stolen.' Edgar still has 'a few friends I used to hang around with' who never joined – even sneered at – El Sistema. 'People I've known since I was a kid who've got problems with drugs and crime. But now most of my friends are musicians; we're a family as well as an orchestra.'

We go for a walk. Some houses don't have roofs at all, and outside one a young man of Edgar's age sits cross-legged in a plastic chair, his eyes glazed, skin pock-marked, motionless – the glue-sniffer's burning red rash around his mouth. I look at Edgar for some reaction, but he *hardly notices, chatting as he climbs the steps: 'I like Brahms best – so romantic – but my favourite is Shostakovich's Ninth, because of the long bassoon solo!'*

The more prominent orchestras that make up the network of El Sistema are known as *núclei*, and the *núcleo* in the barrio of Sarría operates after hours at José Martí School, an oasis of calm in a barrio through which one climbs up and up, while a single round fires off in mid-distance, echoing through the dusk. 'In school,' says the *núcleo*'s director Rafael Elster, 'you don't see the poverty outside. You watch these kids play, but sometimes their parents are the drug dealers and car thieves.' 'At first,' says Gladiani Herrara, violin teacher, 'they can reject you and the music. They're afraid of everything in their lives, they distrust the strangeness of classical music, and it takes time to break down the wall.' 'There was one girl,' recalls Rafael, 'whom I asked to shut her eyes to hear the music better. But she refused, terrified to close her eyes with anyone else in the room.' 'Physical abuse,' says Gladiani, 'is often the first thing to overcome.'

People like Rafael are the spine of El Sistema. He studied trumpet at the Juilliard School in New York, won numerous prizes and could have embarked on an orchestral – even solo – career. 'But I prefer this,' he says. 'I've never enjoyed myself more . . . some of them scare me at first. But most of them don't have a father; I become a sort of father, and they become my sort of children.' Rafael mounts the podium of the school theatre and takes the orchestra through Sibelius's icy *Finlandia* – here in the tropics. 'These are the young kids,' he cautions. 'There's a critical point around thirteen. If we can keep them past that, their lives will change, otherwise we lose them forever.' Genesis, eleven, packing away her violin, says her friends 'keep telling me to quit the orchestra. They think it's shit and prefer to kiss boys, but I think actually they're jealous.'

Aluisa Patino, also eleven, skips home through the concrete alleyways, her route lined by graffiti, discarded crack tubes and bags of burned glue. Aluisa says plainly that she learns the viola 'to get myself and my mother out of the barrio. It's got to the point around here,' she chirps, 'when it's much cooler to like Strauss than salsa.' She introduces her mother in the little room where they live, behind an iron grating, with an ascendant Virgin on the wall. 'It's hard to believe,' says María Ángela, Aluisa's mother, 'that she's hooked on something like this. I can't say I understand it, but it's changed everything in our house. It gives me something to aim for too – to keep her this happy, and different from other girls. Her father visited recently for the first time in eight years, out of curiosity, and left some money – something he'd never done before.'

Further out on the frayed edges of Caracas, Los Chorros residential shelter for runaway and abused children still exudes the aura of its former existence as a 'correctional facility' for juveniles – not least, bars on the windows of some buildings. But now, from the main hall drift lilting melodies of Bizet's 'Carmen' Suite.

Their conductor, Ángel Linárez, explains that he was himself a car thief before training through El Sistema, then worked as an organizer. He greets some of the youngsters he taught when they were waifs a decade ago, some of whom recall their former lives. Miguel Niño is a swarthy cellist with long hair, but aged six had 'fled my home in Barinas because of physical aggression by my father', and arrived in the capital to make a home on its streets. 'I was stealing – to live and feed my habit. The police caught me,' he says both simply and evasively, 'and brought me here. And here, the orchestra caught my attention, something different. Now I play; I want to be a professional musician, raise a family. If I hadn't found this? Obviously I'd have gone back to the streets, steal and do drugs, maybe sell myself.'

The leader of Los Chorros's orchestra, tipped for a professional future, is Patricia Gujavro. Her face while playing looks as though it knows more than her seventeen years should afford, but the severity vanishes when she speaks. Patricia lives in Palo Verde barrio with her two brothers. Her father has 'never been in the family' and her mother disappeared to Ecuador last year. 'I've thought a lot about what my life would have been like if I hadn't started the violin,' she says. 'I suppose I'd be like most seventeen-year-old girls in Palo Verde – hanging out with gangs and pregnant.' Her ambition, inevitably: 'to join the Simón Bolívar Orchestra', and if that doesn't work out, 'become an engineer, music having given me discipline, respect for others and for myself'.

More than 380,000 children are engaged in music programmes like this, more than 80 per cent from low- or middle-income families. Of the two million graduates of the programme since its inception, many have gone on to become not just musicians, but lawyers, teachers, doctors and civil servants.

Sir Simon Rattle believes that the man who founded El Sistema in 1975, Maestro José Antonio Abreu, warrants the Nobel Peace Prize. It was a campaign Rattle and I tried to mount through the pages of the *Observer*, to no avail. 'I never met Nelson Mandela,' says Rattle, 'but I have met Abreu. There are certain people who have given so much to so many in the world . . . What he has done for peace and the higher good in this world is immeasurable. It is a prize for peace, of course, and people would say that Abreu is not ending a war. But I've been to those barrios and it is a war zone. There are parts of Caracas in which it's just too dangerous to walk . . . what Abreu and El Sistema have done there is to bring hope, through music, to hundreds of thousands of lives that would otherwise have been lost to drugs and violence . . . Abreu has saved those people physically in many cases and he has saved them in other ways too – he has given them life in all its depth. Abreu has built a system that provides nutrition for the soul.'

Abreu works from an office in an unremarkable shopping mall in central Caracas. He was born in 1939 in the city of Valera, became a concert pianist, then an economist and deputy in the Venezuelan National Assembly. He served as president of the Economic Planning Commission and as minister of culture, but disillusionment drove him from politics to 'devote myself entirely to music'.

Since then he has navigated his mission through political regimes of every colour and style, from hard right to hard left; whoever comes and goes, El Sistema survives – until perhaps now (of which more later). 'The idea came to me,' he says, 'because I saw that in Venezuela music education did not include orchestras for young people. But I could see, in the few existing music schools, that children participating in orchestras developed a more humane perception of their role within society. They had a completely different set of values. And I found insidious the situation whereby access to music had become a privilege of the elite. I had studied Beethoven the man as well as the composer, and imagined how outraged he would be by such a situation. So I set out to create a means whereby music could be a way of vindicating the rights of the masses.'

Meeting Maestro Abreu is like an encounter with a bishop who subscribes to liberation theology; his enlightened Catholic faith has propelled him as much as has his love of music.

The scheme was launched with eleven children in a garage. 'At our first rehearsal, I was certain,' he says, brown eyes glittering. 'I told those first eleven members of the orchestra that we were creating the beginning of a network that would turn Venezuela into a musical power by rescuing children.' El Sistema, despite the nickname, is not actually a 'system', Abreu insists, but 'a conception regarding the function of music within society'; it extends to all twenty-three provinces and touches an estimated three adults for every child engaged in the programme. 'For

Venezuelans,' he says, 'music education is now a constitutional and legal right' – in stark contrast to Britain or the USA. Simon Rattle has described it as 'nothing less than a miracle', but Abreu shakes his head. 'It's more hard work than miracle.' He indicates a poster on the wall emblazoned with the phrase 'TOCAR Y LUCHAR', the official motto of the programme since that afternoon in the garage. 'Play and Struggle': 'That came from our earliest experience when we had so many obstacles against undertaking the project. To play is a form of struggle, against the obstacles, on every level. So there was always this double meaning for the young people, to be both artists and social fighters.'

The slogan is more applicable today than ever, as Venezuela implodes at many levels. 'We are still facing the gravest social problems, and we have a challenge to incorporate as many excluded children as possible,' Abreu admitted even then, in 2007. He pointed out that 3 per cent of the population of thirty million is under fourteen. 'We know that the efforts we put into this are not enough, given the size of the challenge ahead,' he predicted, ominously. Abreu spells out his credo: 'The rich owe a burden of duty to the poor. And this is something they will never pay financially – that is why they are rich. But it can be done culturally. For the elites of society to deprive the poor of access to culture, to the rich traditions of music, is a terrible, unforgivable crime.'

His most illustrious pupil so far, Gustavo Dudamel, talks in a rehearsal room beneath Caracas's new Inter-American Center. His father played salsa trombone, 'and that was the sound of my childhood'. Gustavo joined the choir at the local *núcleo*, then took up the violin before conducting two years later. And just as painters prefer to talk about colour and light rather than philosophical abstractions, so we begin with his interpretation of the 'Alpine' Symphony: an unusually – very Latin American – human reaction to this masterpiece of European pantheism, humankind overwhelmed by nature.

'But how can a group of people like us encounter one of the great pieces about man and nature without feeling that they matter?' asks Dudamel. 'We've never played that piece before. We talked it through, tried to understand it together, and play as we felt. It's about the score, the dynamics, the tempo and the colours, of course – but also about feeling. We play it for the first time, as though it were the last, and for love.' Coming from a seasoned European conductor this might sound a bit trite, but this is Dudamel, and it doesn't. Because, as Henry Kissinger once said in a horribly different context, 'it has the additional advantage of being true'. 'These musicians are my blood, my best friends,' Gustavo says. 'I've played with eighty per cent of them; they don't really see me as their conductor, and I don't see myself that way either. There's collective pressure, but in a positive way. If a musician gets ahead of the group, the group must follow – that's how the social aspect of El Sistema feeds the music we make.'

Rehearsals for the 'Alpine' Symphony resume, focusing on a particularly difficult sequence for trumpets, engaging Dudamel with a young man called Wilfrido Galarraga who each morning rides his motorbike from the barrio of La Vega to Caracas's university (formally, the Central University of Venezuela), to work on his thesis about the methodology of music teaching. It explores, he says, 'how children can learn from the lives of composers like Verdi, with his political views, or Tchaikovsky's romanticism and homosexuality. These are interesting people, and this way we both educate children and break away from the idea that classical music is for the upper classes and the rich.'

La Vega is a barrio both as desperate and as defiant as the rest, whence 'most people with a job cross town to work. When I joined the children's orchestra,' he says, 'it changed not only my life but the lives of my family. My father was drinking too much, and my brothers had dropped out of school. When I got hooked on my instrument, my father stopped drinking, and one by one my brothers went back to school.'

We talk about Wilfrido's future, and that of the orchestra, drawing an analogy with the Brazilian national football team, hardly any of whom play in Brazil. So how many will be picked off, like the double-bassist Edicson Ruiz, who recently became the youngest musician ever to join the Berlin Philharmonic? 'I think many will stay,' says Wilfrido. 'Because we're a community. We're also very aware that for every one of us there are ten more younger people easily capable of taking our place.'

But whatever it may do for the people it touches, El Sistema demonstrates that it cannot, by definition, be shown to have changed society.

Venezuela, though it hosts and boasts the global role model in musical education for the poor, is at the time of writing in deep and dangerous crisis. And in 2017, El Sistema was plunged into exactly the kind of political limelight it has successfully avoided for decades. In May, after months of uprising and repression in his home country, Dudamel broke a silence many felt had lasted too long, with a plea from Los Angeles – where he is now Principal Conductor of the L.A. Philharmonic – after the fatal shooting by the National Guard of a demonstrator against the Venezuelan regime: Armando Cañizales, a seventeen-year-old former violinist in the orchestra.

'I raise my voice against violence,' said Dudamel, 'I raise my voice against any form of repression. Nothing justifies bloodshed. I urgently call on the president of the Republic and the national government to rectify and listen to the voice of the Venezuelan people. Enough is enough … Venezuelans are desperate for their inalienable right to well-being and the satisfaction of their basic needs.' The response of Nicolás Maduro's government was to cancel a tour of the United States by the Simón Bolívar Orchestra. After years of criticism from the left that El Sistema constitutes an elitist imposition of European music on Latin American children, it is now assailed from the right for taking subsidies from a decrepit Stalinist government. So it must be doing something right – but more as a dream, which occasionally, when one wakes from it, comes true. An assertion of idealism and of music – perhaps even redemption – in a world of poverty, but not an agent of political change.

During those months of protest, a young violinist from the orchestra, Wuilly Arteaga, became a regular figure on street demonstrations, playing his instrument amid the tear gas – a bold presence for art, peace and protest. In late July he was wounded, and on Twitter posted a picture of his injured face with the words: 'Neither rubber bullets nor pellets will stop us.' He was later filmed playing the violin from his hospital bed.[1]

So for the first time since it was founded, gold-standard El Sistema – though it placed Arteaga on the streets to play – may fall victim to the world that feeds it. El Sistema is, and represents, an idea, a philosophy, not a facet of Venezuelan government policy; not a plaything with which Maduro and his adversaries can blackmail one another, much as it suits them. It is as such that El Sistema has inspired projects around the world, including in Britain and the seaboard city that spawned the Beatles.

Through the rain of a leaden morning in one of the poorest neighbourhoods in Europe comes a flurry of music by Antonio Vivaldi, played by a group of children from Faith Primary School, sitting on little chairs in the Victorian space of what was the Church of St Mary of the Angels in West Everton on Merseyside. The church is deconsecrated and nowadays known as the Friary; I once lived in a block of flats up the slope of this urban valley, with a view of the church – one of three towers known as 'the Piggeries', now demolished.

One of the children playing in West Everton Children's

Orchestra is Christy, who 'started learning the violin when I was nine, and it was amazing,' she says in broad Scouse. 'I'd never even heard one before, and it wasn't like any feeling I knew – it made you want to play and dance at the same time, but you can't do that 'cause you have to concentrate. It's grand, really grand.' Only for a short time did her mates 'think it was weird to do this. Now it's dead cool to play a violin in West Everton.' The music that Christy, daughter of a taxi driver, has been practising is 'Autumn' from Vivaldi's *The Four Seasons*. 'It's beautiful,' she says. 'Like, at home I listen to Beyoncé, but this is better. Well, not better – just better in a different way.'

This project began after St Mary of the Angels closed and the Royal Liverpool Philharmonic Orchestra rescued the building from property speculators, turning it into a rehearsal, recording and education centre for their own use. Part of that brief was to team up with the school next door, and conjoin a project called In Harmony, established nationally by the cellist Julian Lloyd Webber and modelled on El Sistema. In April 2009, children from Faith Primary travelled to London to hear the Simón Bolívar Youth Orchestra; medals thrown to the audience by the Venezuelans now serve as prizes in their own orchestra. 'We'll try anything,' says Peter Garden, director of the project for the Liverpool Phil, and with reason: three months later, the children themselves played their own debut at the Philharmonic Hall. 'We've taken the values of El Sistema,' explains Garden, 'and adapted them locally. It had to be open to the whole school – that was important, no selection. The teachers play, so does the cook; the take-up is amazing – so are the results.'

While music disappears from curricula all over Britain, here it is integral to the school week, culminating in a Friday night music club at the Friary. A report by the schools assessment body Ofsted states that Faith Primary's 'achievement in playing musical instruments and performing in concerts as the West

Everton Children's Orchestra is astonishing'. But that's not all – Garden again: 'The percentage of children who improved their reading by at least two levels in 2008–9 before the project was 36 per cent. For 2009–10, it was 84 per cent.' The figure for numeracy increased from 35 to 75 per cent. The head teacher Sister Moira Meeghan, who plays double bass in the orchestra, confirms: 'For the children, it's about self-value, and a door into a different culture – no peer pressure either way because we're all doing it. For parents, it's about seeing children have an opportunity they never had themselves. For the community – well, people wondered about their church and all. But it couldn't have gone to better use, a little bit of God's work still here.'

For all the apparently relaxed joviality, this scritchy-scratchy Vivaldi cuts against almost every other influence upon these children, in a digital society steeped in celebrity culture and the pointless quest for quick-hit reward – as far from their quotidian lives as El Sistema is from the barrio. And there's an extra motive for practising, the possibility emerging that musicians from the Simón Bolívar Orchestra might be in Liverpool at the time of the Vivaldi concert, that they might come and listen, even play.

Two months later, the day of the concert has arrived and the children – scrawny, scally, mischievous – warm up with a square dance. 'Bravo!' – in a Spanish accent, cheers one of four older boys lounging by the aisle columns. This is the Simón Bolívar String Quartet from Caracas, cream of the orchestra's string section, on tour and dropping in on Everton – but not just to listen. For the next piece, the Venezuelans position themselves in the orchestra. 'Hola! What's your name?' the lead violinist Alejandro Carreño, bending to his level, asks a red-headed boy with freckles; then, the same to a little girl with the frame of a tiny flying insect. Later, he says: 'You play very good, but some of you sit like you are eighty-five or ninety years old! You must sit proud, so you can play proud,' he urges, 'play with attitude!'

Alejandro then gathers them round and tells the story of how 'a man called Abreu did something very important in my country . . .' – and the children hear about where all this came from. The quartet then plays them a private concert: the finale from Dvořák's 'American' Quartet, to which one boy dances as though to a pop song and another plays air violin. 'They're out of this world,' sighs Jack Mallon, the school-crossing lollipop man, who comes to all the children's rehearsals. 'Use your instruments,' counsels Alejandro at the end, 'to show people what you are feeling. Sit proud, play proud!'

He hears that this is one of the poorest corners of Europe, and responds: 'And look where the talent is – not only in the conservatoire. I can see myself in those children.'

Afternoon arrives and with it the big evening event: the public performance of 'Autumn', now coached and reinforced by the Bolívar Quartet. Christy is one of four children warming up. 'Can we do it *pizzicato*?' pipes a girl called Chloë McGreal during one passage. 'Why not?' replies Alejandro. 'For now, but not when your audience arrives. In chamber music, everyone's ideas are important!' There's another run-through 'because I don't think you feel quite confident yet,' he says. Now Christy is in tears, but not of sadness – 'It's just so exciting,' she whispers.

Then the audience arrives: parents, dignitaries – and the director of the Philharmonic Hall, Simon Glinn, formerly of the Serious Road Trip in Bosnia. The children and the Venezuelans play Vivaldi's 'Autumn', with thirteen Stations of the Cross as backdrop. Christy and Chloë give it all they have, faces fixed in concentration. 'It's like a dream come true,' says Christy's father Tony, 'a dream I never had, never imagined.' Christy's thirty-year-old sister Natalie says with an expression of both pride and sadness: 'It's something we just never had. She has a totally different attitude from the rest of us because of all this – she's talking about university, and off to the Tate Gallery tomorrow.'

Alejandro concludes the evening with a few words: 'This all began with a man called Maestro Abreu and a small group of musicians in a garage thirty-five years ago. Now we are in Liverpool, and all over the world – the youth of Venezuela is the youth of Liverpool and the youth of the world. Please, play with your heart, and fight.'

Next evening, the quartet continues its sold-out tour of Europe with a concert in St George's Hall. Scrubbed little faces from Everton line the front row of the balcony, leaning forward, eyes popping out with expectation. In London five nights before, the quartet performed in casual gear, but here they're in black tie – and I should damned well hope so, because Christy has changed into a polka-dot party frock and swapped her blue hairband for a lacy ribbon tied in a big bow. In London, better-off children fidgeted and whispered their way through Dvořák's quartet; here, they are enthralled, not a flicker of distraction, even during the vortex of Beethoven's *Grosse Fuge*.

The second half of the programme is Shostakovich's Eighth Quartet – agitated, difficult for a child. But as introspective anguish in the opening Largo twists into a turbulent, rushing Allegro Molto, Christy and Chloë turn their faces away from the stage and stare at each other, wide-eyed – 'Wow!' mouths Christy – then swivels back towards the music. At one point I fidget with my glasses to read the programme – Chloë swings round and throws me a stinging glance of reproach like a seasoned concert-goer scolding a child. The quartet wrestles its way to the end of Shostakovich's unquiet masterpiece, with its complex contrition and very adult fears.

The audience applauds seated, but the children shoot to their feet; from the stage, the Venezuelans wave to them, smiling, and the children wave back. 'Well, I'm hooked,' says Tony the taxi driver, exhaling with emotion. And Christy? 'It was wicked! I just wish they'd do it all again tomorrow.'

7" Single: Beethoven in Juárez

I came too late in my life to Latin America. I became jealous of friends and colleagues who had cut their teeth not in Bosnia but in Mexico, Central and South America; who became dissidents in the United States for having covered the 'dirty wars' of the 1980s, for whom the story continued across a vast and fascinating swathe of the Americas while Bosnia stagnated, and who now spoke fluent Spanish. Late in life I realized that the best way to understand capitalism was to investigate narco traffic, on the principle of a line by the anti-Mafia writer I came to know and work with, Roberto Saviano. The Colombian drug lord Pablo Escobar, said Saviano, was 'the Copernicus' of the narco traffic because he was 'the first to understand that it's not the world of cocaine that must orbit around the markets, but the markets that must rotate around cocaine'.[1]

It was a logical extension of my work in Italy and the USA to now follow the emerging carnage in Mexico wrought by narco traffic, and especially along Mexico's porous but harsh border with the United States, a territory I have called 'Amexica'. This work entailed spending much time in what was, between 2008 and 2013, the most dangerous city in the world with the highest homicide rate per capita: charismatic, terrifying Ciudad Juárez, a vast sprawl clinging to the frontier, opposite – and ten minutes' walk across the bridge from – El Paso, Texas.

The soundtrack to the narco war, and to every day's work and night out in Juárez, was music called *norteño*, or *ranchero* – throbbing, rollicking, libidinous dance music, usually two-step, the end of each line falling to an anchor note. Played on accordion, pounding bass and guitar, and sung with a yearning lilt, *norteño* filled the marketplace, the cafés at breakfast, lunch and dinner, and scary bars where my friend Julián Cardona – former assembly-plant worker, now photographer and chronicler of the city's violence – and I would sometimes venture by night. Bars like the Amsterdam, where the waitresses would wear very little and to which a narco hit squad arrived one night to kill two people (luckily, we weren't there).

There it was – always *norteño*, without relent or apology. And there was an offshoot from this music, called *narcocorrido*, narco ballads that told of heroic antics and struggles by the bandits and outlaws against a brutal state and its operatives. Cartels would hire and attach *narcocorrido* bands to laud their exploits, making them targets for rivals, a musical offshoot to the narco war, with many casualties of its own.

Narcocorrido claims a supergroup, Los Tigres del Norte, whose hits are now ubiquitous across not only Mexico but all Latin America. Even while I'm being driven eight hours in a truck by Marxist guerrillas from the *Fuerzas Armadas Revolucionarias de Colombia*, FARC, through deepest jungle in 2016, the music blaring is by Los Tigres. One of their better numbers is 'El Avión de la Muerte' (The Death Plane), which tells the story of a narco hero taken captive by the Mexican Army and boarded onto an aircraft. But he breaks free of his shackles, and in the ensuing scuffle aboard, realizes that the aircraft is about to crash disastrously into a school. He seizes the controls and plunges it instead into a hillside, killing himself and everyone else but saving the children. I saw Los Tigres play a concert at a casino in Tucson, Arizona, in 2009, to an interesting audience. On the lawns extended families, including grandparents, enjoying a picnic; loving couples in the covered seats. Then, lining up for a beer, one would feel it prudent to make way for a huge man with a Mohican, a long leather coat and a tattooed face with etched teardrops, some blank, but one filled in for each victim.

However, most nights working with Julián Cardona ended with unexpected conversations: about classical music in general, Beethoven in particular, and especially Beethoven conducted by Wilhelm Furtwängler and played by Claudio Arrau. Cardona was stuck in Juárez by choice, work, and a sense of belonging to the extent that he had built a house there; and he harboured a passion for Beethoven that he fed mostly by watching YouTube and listening to what he could order off the Internet for dispatch to his mailbox across the border in Texas. He invariably eschewed the big names, finding lesser-known archive recordings of his favourite music – a real specialist.

There was one night in particular. Cardona and I had been for dinner during an appalling period for Juárez, with a colleague of his, Sandra Rodríguez Nieto, who worked on the perilously busy crime beat for the local paper, *El Diario*. We repaired to Julián's house with a bottle of Chilean red to absorb the day, and for evening talk about murder, torture and the shifting plates that caused them. What to do? Julián put on a CD of his first-choice pianist, Arrau – from the same country as the wine – playing Beethoven's final piano sonata, No. 32 Op. 111 in C Minor. Towards the end, there's a moment when a passage of high trills comes to share the music with the deep, far end of the piano across its full four and a half octaves. It's an existential, Faustian moment, threatening to last an eternity, suspended. But Beethoven forges a way through the middle, to the denouement.

Julián, Sandra and I stood on the balcony of his house and listened without saying a word, sipping Julián's wine. No music seemed less suited to the warm Juárez night, though Arrau's fellow *chileno* Roberto Bolaño did bring his mysterious German writer character Archimboldi to what feels like this very street in his masterpiece, *2666*. Beethoven, it seems, can find his way anywhere.

Cardona and I had both been friends with the writer Charles Bowden, chronicler of the implosion of Juárez and of the suffocation of nature in the American southwest, who died in 2014. There'd been a book about migration across the parched deserts, with photographs by Julián, text by Bowden. Now in his reflections on Beethoven Julián recalls that 'in my last conversation with Charles before he died, we talked about how Beethoven's music takes you into a forest, opens up its rugged terrain of tall pines, streams and twittering birds and then leads you to the place where the whole journey disappears into itself. Beethoven's works are not just sound exercises. They represent the deepest individual and collective feelings to which human genius can aspire: willpower, happiness, reconciliation, brotherhood, freedom. In times of war – the abandoned houses, destroyed buildings, displaced populations – the Fifth Symphony, "Ode to Joy" in the Ninth Symphony and the piano sonatas have been my symbols of resistance.'

Arrau, for him, 'reveals this architectural richness of Beethoven's sonatas and concertos. These magnificent buildings stood in my consciousness amid the destruction wrought in Ciudad Juárez, initiating one of the darkest ages in Mexican history.'

14

Through the Wall

Music for al-Nakba, Sebastia, West Bank, 2008
Brahms: Fourth Symphony, West–Eastern Divan Orchestra,
Barenboim, BBC Proms, London, 2008

Villagers pick their way up a track to the ruins of a Roman amphitheatre,
and arrange themselves across its arc of stepped seats, their bright cloth-
ing luminous against the ancient stone and the silver-green leaves of the
surrounding olive groves. When they are settled, Montasser Jabriny,
aged sixteen, plays the first sensual but mournful notes of 'Al-Hammadi'
(The Beautiful Girl) on his clarinet. Resha Shalelda, of the same age,
follows on flute, and the evening's music is under way.

This is Sebastia, in the occupied Palestinian territories, where those
olive trees may tumble down the mountainsides but machine-gun posts
guard Israeli settlements atop them. The children playing are from the
city of Ramallah, in the Palestinian West Bank, and from Jenin, scene
of an atrocity by Israeli forces in 2002. Their orchestra, called al-
Kamandjati – the Violin – plays oriental music with heady melodies,
and this concert is part of a festival commemorating the sixtieth anni-
versary of what Palestinians call al-Nakba, *the Catastrophe, when*
in 1948 their land was given to Israel and tens of thousands were
evicted from it. A few kilometres away, Israelis are concurrently
celebrating the founding of their country out of the ashes of another

word loaded with terrible meaning: the Shoah, Holocaust.

There is a connection between this scene at Sebastia and the apex of classical music, a link to a unique figure and a project that, far from embodying the duality between the anniversaries, does the opposite – brings them together. Not the six decades of hatred, violence and sub-jugation, but a model for encounter towards peace – through music. That figure is Daniel Barenboim, probably the finest pianist of his generation and one of its great conductors, but also a visionary in the cause of music in defiance of war. He was also the first Israeli to take dual citizenship, holder too of a Palestinian passport.

The vision is an orchestra Barenboim founded with the late Palestin-ian writer Edward Said, which he brought to the London Proms soon after this concert in Sebastia: the West–Eastern Divan Orchestra, made up of young Israeli Jewish and Palestinian musicians. Barenboim and Said took the name from a collection of poems by Goethe, divan *meaning 'the other'. The link between the Divan Orchestra and the concert in the amphitheatre, built during the time of King Herod, is the man at the mixing desk, who turns towards his assistant, flashes a smile and gives the thumbs-up: Ramzi Aburedwan. The young musicians are pupils of a project he runs across the West Bank, and this concert is the climax to much hard work. 'For me, to see them play well is an even greater pleasure than to play myself,' he says. Ramzi, twenty-nine, also plays the viola in the orchestra, and his arrival among the musicians was propelled by a life shaped by those now seventy terrible years in this Holy Land since 1948.*

The last time I went from Arab East Jerusalem to Ramzi's hometown of Ramallah, twenty-five years earlier, it was a fifteen-minute breeze by car, albeit across Israeli-occupied territory. Not any more: it involves crossing the 'security barrier' – the Wall, violent in itself – which cuts not along the 1948 'Green Line' that separated Israel from the West Bank, but through the West Bank itself, like a scar, so that people live one side of the checkpoints with their workshops, fields and relatives on the other. On the Wall itself there's artwork by Banksy and someone has written, in hope: 'This Wall Will Fall' – in the spirit of the Divan Orchestra.

The Sebastia concert is held on International Refugee Day, and Ramzi emphasizes that he is one: born in 1979 at the concrete and corrugated-iron al-Amari refugee camp. 'I didn't understand what the occupation was,' he says, 'until my grandfather explained that he had another house in a village from which he had been expelled in 1948, with beautiful trees around it. There was only one tree in the camp.' Ramzi became a stone-throwing poster-boy, literally: a picture of him appeared in a magazine, rock in each hand, wearing an expression hovering between rage and fear. 'We used to go to a valley to play, to hear the echo of our voices. But then they built a settlement and a road for the settlers, so it was forbidden. So instead of play, we threw stones at the settlers' cars in the morning before school, and on the way home. I was shot three times, once while they had taken me and were beating me up' – and Ramzi shows a scar on his upper arm, the one that now holds the neck of his viola.

'Then came the change in my life: there was a music workshop, with instruments for twenty people. They gave me a viola. It made such a beautiful sound, I was happy, and that day my life turned 360 degrees. Well, actually, not immediately. The workshop was on a road with a line on it, which we could not cross. And I put my viola down for twenty minutes to throw stones and break some windows, then came back to the class. My teacher was shocked. He wanted me to understand that I can make the revolution with my instrument, not with stones, and only later did I come to see that music must make the revolution.'

For the concert at Sebastia, Ramzi wears a T-shirt reading 'Music Says No' in Arabic. It is dusk as the last notes sound, and he supervises the packing-up of the equipment and its loading onto a bus. The children from the al-Kamandjati orchestra climb in, and off we go back to Ramallah, winding past yet another olive-strewn slope, yet another settlement. The road is a long one, nearly two hours spent waiting at checkpoints; Ramzi is furious as the Israeli soldiers question his driver, himself, even the children, and sift through the instruments.

Next morning he returns to the al-Amari camp where he was born, and where his grandfather still lives. The orchestra plays at the children's centre where it was founded, among breeze blocks and graffiti, where a boy called Sefir, aged eight, watches them rehearse and joins in with a flurry on air clarinet, imitating Montasser Jabriny, whose notes opened the concert in the amphitheatre. Captivated, little Sefir says he wants to learn what Montasser can do, 'the magic sound he makes'.

'I firmly believe that it is impossible to speak about music,' Barenboim has written, '. . . But if I attempt to speak about music, it is because the impossible has always attracted me more than the difficult.' The West Bank is a good place to start.

The man who gave young Ramzi his instrument, one day in the late 1990s, was a viola player from Massachusetts, Peter Sulski, who arrived in Ramallah to play Mozart's G Minor Piano Quintet. 'I was amazed,' recalls Ramzi. 'It was not like our music, all the parts were different, I didn't know which to follow.' His playing was so auspicious, Sulski secured him a place at a summer school at the Apple Hill Center for Chamber Music in New Hampshire: 'Americans, French – musicians from all over the world – and I realized something. We were all reading different parts of the same piece, different aspects of the same organism. It was the idea of the sound of instruments playing together that won me.'

Ramzi is a detached but passionate man. In mid-conversation he'll say suddenly: 'I cannot concentrate, I must play.' The conversation on hold, he retreats to his bouzuk: to play, alone in a room off the sunlit courtyard, thereby saying more, in a way, than with words. But there is thus a chance to talk to Sulski, a droll Bostonian convinced that 'there are so many other Ramzis, and we need to find them'. The fact that the music is classical and from Europe – which annoys some – is irrelevant, he says: 'Beautiful music is beautiful music, and captivates those who see its beauty. I can play salsa pretty well, and people will say:

"It's not in your blood." So what? Mozart is not in Ramzi's blood, either, so what?'

After Apple Hill, Ramzi won a place to study at the conservatoire in Angers in France for seven years, during which time three things happened. One was an invitation to join the Divan Orchestra at its first meeting in Weimar, but his teacher François Hecht counselled: 'They have asked you not because you are good enough yet, but because you're Palestinian. You must know your limits, you are not ready.' The next was the detonation of the second Intifada in 2000. Ramallah was initially its epicentre, so that when another invitation came to join the Divan, Ramzi was 'too worried about my grandparents and family, needing to visit every summer and winter – I couldn't do any summer project. I couldn't concentrate, I was not playing well.'

The third, crucial development resulted from Ramzi's pressing desire to impart to the children of the camp in which he was born what he had learned about the power of music, especially its power to communicate. 'The children were pushing me to teach them, inviting me to bring my bouzuk and viola, wanting to hear the oriental and classical sound – all this during curfew. People called me a dreamer, they didn't realize music could help. They said "Why are you doing this? You have to fight, you have to eat." But I replied: "What they are doing here is killing people's lives. Bring music, you bring life. No one can live without music, only they don't know that." I noticed that the children who played became far more interested in their future, and that of their people.'

And so the al-Kamandjati music school was born, connected with a foundation Barenboim and Said had established in Ramallah. Ramzi found this lovely building in the old city, which was renovated by the Swedish government and now resounds with music made by children who scuttle across the courtyard to be taught by musicians from Europe and America. Mischievous little Ale Asfour, aged ten, spends all day there just listening, offering passers-by plums from a plate while a Bach cello suite drifts through a window into the morning sun, until it is time for her lesson.

'I was doing nothing, on the street as usual,' says the clarinettist Montasser in the amphitheatre, 'and Ramzi said: "Why don't you play?" "Me? You're joking," I replied, the idea seemed ridiculous. "Try it," said Ramzi, quite scarily. So I came to al-Kamandjati and tried the double bass but my fingers were too soft, and suddenly I heard the clarinet. It was the most beautiful sound I've ever heard, like a bird, and I asked if I could learn how to make it, and Ramzi said "Yes." And if it wasn't for this, I'd be on the streets, watching TV, wasting time and getting into trouble. Instead, music fills my life. Best of all, I like to play Mozart's Fortieth Symphony.'

'I'd be stuck at home washing dishes!' laughs Resha the flautist, tossing her hair as if to shake off the very idea. 'But instead, music is the air I breathe, and I couldn't live without it. Why? Because it makes me feel like I am flying, and proud of who I am.'

Ramzi finally joined the Divan in 2006, unprepared to find many – if any – kindred spirits among the Israelis. However, the first person he encountered, logically enough, was the leader of his viola section, Amichai Grosz, born in the mountain village of Bar Giora south of Jerusalem, and now violist in the celebrated Jerusalem String Quartet. Amichai, a committed young man, had also said an initial no to Barenboim, for different reasons: 'It was my first vacation with my girlfriend, and we were driving south from Madrid . . .' (The Divan Orchestra locates its summer camp near Seville, as guest of the Andalusian regional government, for historical reasons: during the Middle Ages, the area spawned a society famous for its enlightened cross-influences between Christianity, Judaism and Islam.) He continued: 'And a friend of

Barenboim said to me "Come and say Hi." I thought: Who wouldn't want to say Hi to Daniel Barenboim? But when the couple appeared, Barenboim asked: "Would you stay and play?" I thought, oh shit, I shouldn't have done this, we're on vacation. Months later, Barenboim joined Amichai's quartet for Dvořák's piano quintet in Jerusalem. 'And afterwards he said: "You have to join the Divan." One doesn't say no to Barenboim twice.'

The journey from Ramallah to Amichai's hamlet had been only twenty kilometres, but spanned many worlds. First the Wall, then through it on a 'Jewish Only' road, past the sprawl of settlements that Israel aims to extend as far as the Jordan Valley, cutting the Holy Land in half with what looks like a giant American mall with Walmart car parks. Signs saying 'Jericho', 'Bethlehem', 'Mount of Olives' and so on make the drive all the more surreal. Past Jerusalem's old city, holy to three confessions, one navigates the ugly spread of West Jerusalem and out to a verdant valley, past Palestinian houses burned out in 1948 but left standing, charred – as warnings to those who fled, one suspects, not reminders to those who came to replace them.

Amichai's background shares nothing with Ramzi's, but his family is also steeped in the violence of the twentieth century. His father Yehuda, a boisterous baker of good bread, tells how Amichai's paternal grandfather, a forester in Romania, avoided the transports to the death camps until 1944, when with fellow Jews he was herded onto a locomotive cattle truck bound for Auschwitz. With a friend, though, he jumped the train and made his way to France, where through business contacts he was able to connect with the French Resistance, the *maquis*. There he married an artist of Hungarian descent, most of whose family had, like Yehuda's, perished, and the couple emigrated to Israel.

Amichai first heard a recording of Isaac Stern playing the violin when he was four, but his enthralment was interrupted when, he says, 'my parents decided to take a break from working life and took me for a two-year trip round the world' – a kind of neo-hippie trail. When they returned 'I had rings on my fingers, long hair and a chain around my neck; people looked at me as though I'd come off a UFO.' He returned to the violin, only for an epiphany when at the age of twelve 'I heard a viola for the first time in my life, and immediately knew I wanted to switch – it was darker, deeper, more like the human voice'.

Amichai studied at the Jerusalem Academy of Music and Dance, set up the string quartet, and was then made the offer by Barenboim that he could not refuse. At first, 'it was a mixed feeling for me. There were rockets coming out of Gaza, and it shouldn't be like that. But then the way we treat the Arabs is not a solution either ... But to play music with Arabs – it was just natural. They were not Arabs, they were musicians, and music has no nation.

'Barenboim is always saying his project is not political. But this *is* a political statement, by both sides. It's more important not for people like myself, but for bigoted people, to see that it's possible to sit down with Arabs and play. The orchestra is a human laboratory that can express to the whole world how to cope with "the other [*divan*]",' says Amichai, even though 'there were a few rough times. After a bus bombing in Tel Aviv by a suicide bomber it was not easy, it was tense, but at the end of the day there was a concert. We had to share the music ... that's what we did. Everyone brings their dirty laundry; the idea is to learn from the other side.'

It is interesting to gauge official reaction to all this. Upon arrival in Jerusalem it's obligatory for journalists to register with the foreign press service, where an official delivers an off-the-peg lecture about terrorism. The Mexican photographer working with me, Antonio Zazueta Olmos, has heard it all before; they know him from serial projects on atrocities in Gaza and, warily courteous, they've got his number. But when I inform them that

I'm here to interview Barenboim's musicians there's a palpable icy frisson of disapproval. It's one thing to side with the Palestinians, quite another to work with an acclaimed Israeli genius who transgresses against the division and subjugation. The official did not use the word 'traitor', but his squint of hatred spoke it clearly.

This subversion inherent in Barenboim's project reached a zenith when the Divan played a concert in Ramallah during summer 2004. It is illegal for an Israeli citizen not on military duty to enter any area of the West Bank other than a settlement, but the Israeli musicians were taken from Jerusalem and through the Wall in a fleet of armoured cars carrying diplomatic papers issued by the Spanish government as host to the summer school. 'And there we were,' recalls Amichai, 'making music in the new concert hall at Ramallah for an Arab audience. I was proud of myself just being part of it, and just to see Barenboim so moved himself. For an Israeli, it was breaking all the rules of this horrible status quo that we live under.'

The time comes to leave and take Amichai's greetings with us to our next appointment, in Nazareth – part of Israel, but a Palestinian town with a large population of Arab Christians, as biblical history would suggest. Highway 6 to Jesus' family home is itself an ugly military installation, walled off from much of the view and skirting the Wall at times, as the occupied West Bank reaches its westernmost point at Qalqilya. Here, the fortified Green Line drawn in 1948 between Israel and Palestinian territories has divided neighbour from neighbour for seventy years, so that if a Palestinian from Qalqilya manages (against the odds) to fall in love with another Palestinian from an adjacent town on the other side, they are forbidden to marry. And this turns out to be a theme underpinning what the Divan Orchestra is doing in Nazareth: uniting not only Israelis with Palestinians, but Palestinians separated from one another. 'I can play with

Israeli musicians from Tel Aviv any time, I studied with them,' says Nabeel Abboud Ashkar, violinist. 'What I couldn't do was play with my own people on the other side of the Green Line.'

At the Barenboim–Said Conservatory in Nazareth, Nabeel, a front-deck violinist with the Divan, leads a group of children playing Corelli's Concerto Grosso Op. 6 No. 8. His tone is glorious, and that of the little boys to his left, Yamen Saadi, eleven, and Feras Machour, twelve, is pretty good too. Both Yamen and Feras admit that they want to be Nabeel when they grow up. 'When I went to see the Divan Orchestra in Ramallah,' says Feras, 'I started thinking that I could play for it one day, it made me aware of the future.' 'And it's good for people to see us do this,' adds Yamen, 'because we are Palestinians, and the outside world thinks that everything here is war.'

Only when he was twenty-five did Nabeel realize that music was his professional calling – he had played the violin alongside studying physics and engineering at Tel Aviv University. 'I was unsure about giving up science – then along came the Divan Orchestra.' His family were friends with Edward Said, and 'the orchestra needed a violinist. I joined, and the whole idea of how music could influence the lives of people became clear to me. The Divan opened my eyes to the role music could play in educating our young.' Meanwhile, Nabeel had connected with musicians in Ramallah, and 'I realized that classical music education was needed in Palestinian society.' With the children, Nabeel alternates between a benign elder-brother stance and the ruthlessness required to conduct even a children's orchestra with, he says, 'no compromise'; though in conversation, he is fascinating on the balance between passion and accuracy.

That same year, 2008, Barenboim performed all thirty-two Beethoven piano sonatas over eight nights in London, which I watched at breathtakingly close range, from the cheap seats right on the stage a few feet away from him. The cycle was hailed as among the most remarkable musical occasions in living memory, in large part because, for all his technical mastery, Barenboim emphasized the glow within the music, against a Zeitgeist of perfection at all costs. And this is what Barenboim also brings to the Divan. 'The playing of instruments has become a technical science,' says Nabeel. 'One has only to look at books on how to learn the violin, and compare them to those of the late nineteenth century. Similarly, I think audiences do not listen to music in the way they used to – always wanting perfection. Here, we are trying to do something more than technical science.'

It is true that when one hears the Divan, one is moved not only by the significance of who is playing, but also by an extra quality of passion and motive, of music meaning and *doing* something. The apex of this is Barenboim's own playing, but its roots are in what Nabeel does: 'In Nazareth, music is not just educating young people, but making them understand their identity. And that means a lot for a Palestinian living in Israel, where part of our personality is missing. Jewish people in Israel have a problem with me saying I'm a Palestinian – the official term is "Israeli Arab", but that is wrong – "Arab" is a culture, not a nationality. I was born into a Palestinian family that was here before the state of Israel; they don't want to face the fact that we were torn apart in 1948, and they don't like it that we play music together now. Music is connecting young people from here to young people in Ramallah, and opened doors to the rest of the world.'

The project had to involve European classical music, continues Nabeel, 'because in Arabic culture music is considered a hobby, it is a vocal music culture, and a folk music culture. The discipline of classical music is a cultural and intellectual challenge, and the children either find it too rigid, or they find it fascinating.' The Barenboim Foundation wanted 'a Palestinian orchestra in Ramallah', and 'because of the efforts we had made here, there were already young people playing classical instruments in

Nazareth'. All that was left was to break through the Wall, go to Ramallah and play, which, for all the difficulties, they did. 'Nazareth is a different place to Ramallah, the children grew up in different conditions. Maybe it would work, maybe not – and it was very pleasing to see that after half an hour, there was one homogenous group.'

With these children, says Nabeel, 'I never talk about politics, but only of being proud of what you are because of what you are capable of. And so it changes how they consider themselves, as individuals and as a minority people. We produce great doctors and lawyers here in Palestine, but the arts were always a shortfall, and the Israeli government has never made any effort to change that. Now, that is changing, and this change is making the young generation more complete in themselves as individuals and as a people.'

Critics sometimes write that the story behind the Divan is all sweetness and light. But it's not; it's more complicated and more human. 'Of course there is love going round,' says Nabeel, 'the Divan sex workshop! But it gets edgy, it gets difficult. People are coming from hostile backgrounds – after a concert, they tend to go off separately. But that's not important – actually, it makes the fact of playing music off the same page even more valuable.'

Daniel Barenboim enters his room backstage at La Scala in Milan wearing a pale suit and an expression that mixes wisdom and mischief. The purpose of the meeting is serious, but for a while it's more social catch-up: 'Ah, Ramzi, still playing that bouzuk too? Amichai, oh yes, I hear he's recording Schubert . . . Nabeel, one of the best.'

Barenboim studied under his father Enrique, and gave a first recital in his hometown of Buenos Aires at the age of seven in August 1950. Two years later the family moved to Israel and in 1954, aged eleven, he made his first recording. He has since been considered one of the foremost musicians of the age. But he wrote recently: 'I suffer from this situation in the Middle East, and everything I do has something to do with this suffering', including founding the West–Eastern Divan Orchestra. I ask about this propulsion of suffering. 'I suffer,' he replies, 'from the fact that on the one hand I went to Israel as a child, I went to school there, and I am obviously conscious of our history, being Jewish. And I suffer because I think that so much of what we do, and what has been done, is not worthy of that history.' Barenboim acknowledges the achievements of a country 'where people have been creative for sixty years'. But, he says, 'parallel to that, I see something which is so thoughtless and, frankly, stupid as to make the myth of Jewish intelligence totally ungraspable'. After the UN partition resolution in 1947, 'there was total Israeli victory. But there was no willingness or capacity to see the logic of the other side.'

The occupation of the Palestinian territories in 1967, he says, 'left Israel in an uncontested position, [that] of victors and in charge of a lot of land . . . Now, I have my questions about Jewish intelligence. We say we want a Jewish state. Why do we have to hold on to territories where there are no Jews? And then artificially settle them with people that come, most of them, solely to create a physical presence? Because of all of this, I suffer.' The conflict, he says, 'is not a political conflict, it is a human conflict, of two people who deeply believe they have a right to live on that same piece of land. And this is the symmetry,' he continues boldly: 'that there is a total ignorance of the other, on both sides, and a total lack of curiosity towards understanding the point of view of the other.'

Pitched against this comes what Barenboim calls 'the principle of intelligent orchestral playing in any context'. In his book *Everything Is Connected: The Power of Music* he considers how 'when one plays five legato notes . . . each note cannot be self-assertive, wanting to be louder than the notes preceding it; if it did, it would defy the nature of the phrase to which it belongs'. Drawing on the fundamentality of counterpoint in music, he describes how 'in the act of challenging each other, the two voices fit together' and how 'music is always contrapuntal, in the philosophical sense of the word' – indeed, 'joy and sorrow can exist simultaneously in music'. He further argues that 'acceptance of the freedom and individuality of "the other" is one of music's most important lessons'. And this is the philosophy that underpins the Divan orchestra, as he says in conversation at La Scala:

'You can't make peace with an orchestra, but you can create the conditions for understanding' and 'awaken the curiosity of each individual to listen to the narrative of the other . . . Divan is not a love story, and it is not a peace story,' he insists. 'It has very flatteringly been described as a project for peace. It isn't. It is not going to bring peace, whether you play well or not so well. The Divan was conceived as a project against ignorance . . . I'm not trying to convert the Arab members of the Divan to the Israeli point of view, and I'm not trying to convince the Israelis of the Arab point of view. But what I do want to do – and unfortunately I am alone in this now that Edward Said has died – is try to create a platform where the two sides can disagree without resorting to knives.'

But there is a further, fundamental point – about music, the Divan and Barenboim, which makes him and this project so unique. He says: 'Musicians very often have very little imagination about how to transplant what they do into the outside world, as if music was an ivory tower miles removed from the real world. Good music has its technical side, but that is only part of it. I am not interested in getting the orchestra to play the way I want it to play. What I am interested in is getting a hundred people to think and feel alike, to feel like one huge common lung; to breathe the music the same way. *That*'s what is interesting.'

He illustrates the point by singling out Brahms, whose Fourth Symphony the Divan is about to play at the Proms during the summer of these meetings, in 2008: 'Brahms had something to say that he considered very important, and he didn't write it in words but in sound. Therefore we cannot express in words the content of the music of Brahms; were I able to articulate the content of a symphony or piano concerto of Brahms, I wouldn't have to play it any more. But the fact that I cannot do that doesn't mean that it has no content. And that content must be a human content, which I would not reduce to a clash between emotion and correctness. The human content must be a human experience, in its totality.'

It was strange, and gratifying, to see them all aligned in the Royal Albert Hall, in their togs, having visited them at home: Ramzi, Amichai, Nabeel and others. The Brahms symphony was done in a way I had never heard it before: the opening swayed in currents of sound, sometimes apparently against itself, tide and rip tide in what felt like appositely dramatic contrast. *Pizzicato* parts in the slow second movement delicate as a flight of feathers, while the Scherzo that followed was confidently strident. The finale had a cumulative power – a statement, and a bold one, of something at once intangible but clear 'in its totality', as Barenboim had explained. Once the applause abated, he took the podium. In London he was usually asked to speak about what was wrong with the Middle East, he said. 'Here' – waving an arm towards his orchestra – 'is what is right about the Middle East.'

Nine years later, he found himself back on the same podium with the Staatskapelle Orchestra from Dresden, needing now to speak about ignorant bigotry not in the Middle East, but in Brexit Britain. 'When I look at the world with so many isolationist tendencies,' he said, 'I get very worried. And I know I'm not alone. I was married in this country and I lived here for many years . . . The main problem of today is that there is not enough education, there is not enough education for music ... there is not enough education about who we are, what is a human being, and how he is to relate with others of the same kind. This is why music is so important.' Half his audience applauded gratefully; the other half shuffled, uneasy and offended. The maestro continued: 'The new generations have to understand that Greece and Germany and France and Denmark all have something in common called European culture, and also in this cultural community called Europe.'

For his plea, Barenboim was assailed by British conservative politics and papers for 'poor conduct' and 'hijacking the Proms' for an 'anti-Brexit rant'. Critics joined the baying, like Norman Lebrecht: 'Barenboim should not have spoken.'

Bravissimo, Barenboim! While other celebrities and stars cower and watch their backs, it takes the world's most talented and respected musician to speak out.

7" Single: Postcard from Rome – L'Ange Voyageur

By the year 2014, hundreds of thousands of migrants and refugees from war, poverty and climate change were converging on Europe in an armada of ill-equipped boats; the Aegean and Mediterranean seas had become mass graves. Hungary erected a razor-wire fence along its border with Serbia – which was also the frontier of the European Union – to keep the huddled masses out. At Calais, an encampment called 'the Jungle' was ultimately closed by French police, and torched by those driven out. Incredibly, the whole scene had been staged in a new opera, some years before the crisis.

First, there was a battle across wasteland, migrants beating police and riot shields into retreat with a hail of stones. But later, the police return with dogs; the shacks that the migrants had built were razed, the migrants back where they began, the wind blowing them and their flotsam and jetsam out again along the road to wherever next. This was not a scene from alongside Hungary's defensive wire or the Jungle; it was enacted in 2008 at Rome's new performing arts Auditorium Parco della Musica in an operatic remake of one of Italy's best-loved films, *Miracolo a Milano*. The story of the film – uncannily prescient of what would happen in the real world over sixty years later – was set to music by Italy's foremost contemporary composer, Giorgio Battistelli, and staged by Daniele Abbado, son of the late maestro Claudio Abbado.

Miracolo a Milano is an icon in Italian cinema and popular culture, made in 1951 by director Vittorio De Sica and the writer Cesare Zavattini. Three years earlier, the pair had worked on the most famous Italian film of all, *Bicycle Thieves*. *Miracolo a Milano* is descended from a trope in art painted beautifully by Gustave Moreau in his series of depictions of *L'Ange Voyageur*, set amid the spires above Paris – leaving us unsure whether the angel is himself a wanderer, or protector of those who wander, or both. The Italian film concerned an influx of migrants arriving on the outskirts of Milan; oil is discovered beneath their campsite, whereupon they are forcibly evicted. But an angel watching from the heights of Milan Cathedral intercedes, transfiguring and transporting them skywards on broomsticks. The finale was taken by Steven Spielberg as inspiration for the famous last scene in *E.T.* Now the story was resurrected by Battistelli; that its theme would be so poignantly prescient, no one could have predicted.

The music critic Richard Morrison wrote that 'you never forget your first Giorgio Battistelli opera'; this was mine, and Morrison is right. Like the film, the opera is an entwinement of the celebrated *verismo* (realism) in Italian cinema during the postwar era and a last stand of Risorgimento liberal Catholicism associated with Verdi and the novelist for whom his *Requiem* was written, Alessandro Manzoni. The work opens with a cacophonic funeral march played by a marching band entering the theatre, while the scene depicted evokes the turbulent aftermath of war, the migrants literally blown on stage. They fight one another, build their ramshackle homes, are ripped off by a fortune-teller – and at one point stand in awe while one of them is obliged by a Brueghelesque peasant lottery game to eat a whole chicken. Once oil is found, they are doomed by an onslaught of sirens, dogs and batons.

Only at that denouement does Abbado allow a redeeming light to shine on and from the cathedral, as the migrants' clothes, now shed, ascend heavenwards. Most astonishingly, there are no words – only sounds, and music. The hidden choir (defying one's preconceptions about the ancient Chorus of Santa Cecilia) grunts and groans, giving this, like Magma's music, a primacy on the *sound* of a word, pure onomatopoeia, rather than on its meaning. The instrumentation is dense and jagged, intertwined with electronic loops and amplified recorded vernacular sounds of everyday life.

The presentation of this drama fitted into a context of didactic commissioning by the Rome Auditorium which the programmer of contemporary music, Oscar Pizzo, calls 'the staging of work towards a society that is more open', invoking 'the power of art to make people understand, but without rhetoric, without ideology'. Previous performances had included one by Ramzi Aburedwan's al-Kamandjati orchestra from Ramallah. After *Miracolo a Milano*, Battistelli turned his attention to a commission from La Scala to write an opera about climate change called CO_2, based on Al Gore's documentary film *An Inconvenient Truth* of 2006. He immediately points out, when we sit to talk, that the fact that the migrants in Zavattini's story and De Sica's film were evicted to make way for oil speculation is an important subliminal theme.

He has striven, says Battistelli, to create something in defiance of what he calls the 'technicalism prevalent in modern music – perfection at all costs. Music is not perfection – it should be an organism that breathes.' 'It's a cruel coincidence,' says Abbado, 'that this becomes an exhibition of a real-life drama.' But that is exactly as he would want it: 'This piece is not self-referential, any more than the film was, and in some scenes it is darker than the film. But it does not in any way refer to itself; it refers to the world outside the theatre. It is this self-referentiality in so much theatre nowadays that I find detestable.' One might expect such mischief from Battistelli and Abbado, but less so from the director of the Accademia Nazionale di Santa Cecilia, founded by Sixtus V in a papal bull of 1585, invoking the patron saint of music and counting Palestrina, Corelli and Scarlatti among its earlier collaborators.

The musicologist and critic Bruno Cagli, like a wise but courteous owl, appears part of that heritage; his shelves are lined with splendid books and scores, many of them published by the Academy (he is one of the world's leading authorities on Rossini). We talk about the liberal Catholic tradition of Zavattini's story and its roots in Verdi, before Cagli lets on: 'I knew Zavattini, we discussed this quite a bit.' Then he proceeds to align his friend's vision to our day: 'Zavattini was in many ways a great poet, applying himself to the time, and his story addresses the crisis in postwar Italy, and ruptures caused by crisis in a society of great need. But our society is also ruptured in some way, and what we have here with Battistelli is a work about society's crisis of well-being.'

Some among the crowds leaving Battistelli's premiere were touched and disturbed as he would have wished, others more disturbed that such aesthetic and political subversion could have been commissioned by the prestigious Academy and Auditorium. Very few of the audience – if any, things being what they are – were heading back to the migrant camps themselves, out towards Anagnina bus station, around which a makeshift marketplace has grown. It's a seamless journey from last night's performance to this place. Here, two groups are drinking coffee or beer at the Tex bar, neither communicating with the other. One comprises

Roman locals and drivers from the terminus to which coaches arrive from Timişoara as well as the Italian south; the others are from Romania and man the market stalls, across which drift the strains of gypsy music.

'You hear our music every weekend,' says Anghel from Sibiu, selling mobile phone covers. 'They call us *vu cumprà*' – a derogatory term for 'black migrants', playing on the way Africans might pronounce '*Vuoi comprare?*' (Do you want to buy?) – 'and it gets scary.'

The nearby encampment known as Casiglio 900 on the Via Casiglio near the *tangenziale*, the ringroad that circumnavigates Rome, was in 2008 one of the city's largest: a hotchpotch of breeze-block huts and caravans. The migrants – mainly gypsies from Macedonia, Bosnia, Romania and Morocco – had been here longer than most others. 'We're in a circular situation,' says Suleiman Batma, who came from Morocco in the 1980s. 'The worse things get, the more the young people turn to crime, and the more we are seen as outcasts. We are told that if we move, a permanent space will be eventually found, but if we do, we're nomads, and can be arrested. Now they are coming to fingerprint the children: how are they going to react to that?'

It was not Battistelli's intention to predict that this scenario would become ubiquitous across Italy, as now, but he nonetheless did. He is a cultural radical in an Italian tradition of intelligent *contestazione*, and as such wants 'these sounds, and these themes, to be posited against the code of the present. I hope that it might be some kind of incantation, giving people something to take home that is not necessarily decorative or consolatory, but human.' With all that means, in what had become punishing times.

7" Single: Postcard from the Recovery Ward, 2013

Coming round from serial anaesthetic is very weird. After my fourth operation in a week, I watched the orderlies putting labels on each trolley to indicate the ward to which the patient was to return, and I scolded the nurse: 'Here we are in the Underworld, and how cruel of you to be assigning these dead people back to life to fight for this or that Mexican cartel.' He looked at me sympathetically. 'Ah, I see!' I continued. 'This isn't Hades at all, it's a production of Gluck's *Orpheus and Eurydice*, one of those trendy stagings by Jonathan Miller, set in a hospital, and you're Charon the boatman cast as a doctor!' Basically, after more than twenty-six hours' surgery over four sessions in seven days, one is insane.

I told strangers I'd fallen, to avoid having to explain why I jumped off a wall five metres high after a partial blackout. I badly damaged myself, learned about levels of pain I never imagined, and about the tribulations of the disabled in a country largely hostile towards them. Also about the medical science of a Russian called Gavriil Ilizarov, whose barbaric-looking invention saved my leg. I'd returned in June 2013 from a too short week's holiday in Greece, my first real break in years. People had advised against this, saying that, strung out as I was, I should either take a month, or none at all, and keep going.

The morning after my return, while I was opening letters from utility companies and debt-collection agencies, my Tube train was again stranded at crammed Edgware Road station, public address system blaring, crowds heaving. Later that day, I was unable to take it, apparently: when I left the office in mid-afternoon, I felt strange. The canal towpath at King's Cross was closed and along the detour I felt suddenly lost: all sound ceased apart from a huge power drill excavating foundations for pricey 'waterside dwellings' where lovely Victorian warehouses once stood – VARRR-OOM! I panicked, my vision became mono-chrome apart from the colour green before I found a wall over-looking the closed towpath. If I can just get down there, I thought, I'll know where I am. When I landed, my clean-broken fibula and tibia were sticking out of my left shin, jellied matter on the tarmac. The brain is a strange thing: 'Hold on,' it said, 'I've got a call to make.' I phoned 999 and next thing I knew, several hours later, I was on a stretcher heading through the dark for University College Hospital.

I came to next morning after five hours of surgery on a 'complex, multiple fracture' to find a heavy steel structure around my leg, from the heel to just below the knee, held in place by five metal rods screwed into, and thirteen wires running through, what remained of the bones. Some hours later, the estimable consultant surgeon James Youngman arrived to introduce me to my Ilizarov 'external fixator' frame. I was then a month in various hospitals, subject to four further operations, on a cocktail of both intravenously dripping and oral morphine, gabapentin, and God knows what else. When I was high on pain and morphine, music of all kinds became unbearable. A lovely Italian friend spent money on a state-of-the-art iPod onto which I transferred Mozart, Verdi, Traffic and Dylan – but the sound of all of it terrified me.

A few days before discharge, the work of the Ilizarov frame began: to lengthen a leg that had lost five centimetres of bone and encourage the growth of bone tissue. This was done by turning dials on the frame to stretch the bone by a millimetre a day, though in my case this had to be increased to an excruciating three millimetres, then five, as things went wrong. The premise is basically that of the Inquisition rack – it worked well for them, and it worked on me. The 'pain management' team used to ask me to rate the pain. I could only express it in terms of musical instruments: there's 'piccolo pain', which is shrill and piercing, usually from plastic surgery; then there's 'double-bass pain', deep in the bone when and after it is stretched, on another level entirely.

Eventually I was discharged, only for things to keep going more wrong, and require five more operations – ten in all, two without anaesthetic, by my own choice, I've no idea why – and two years of acute pain. I mostly recall the pain I would wake to at night, and that made me burst into tears like a child. After the first year, much of it spent on my back to 'elevate' the leg, watching the rain, I began listening to a limited range of music, mostly jazz, drones by John Cale, Bach preludes for piano, Shostakovich comedies or Verdi operas. And to read: a strict diet of Beckett, Camus and Zola. Thanks to Mr Youngman I now walk again, though in pain when it is damp and cold, and I asked him whether this would improve with time. 'It'll start hurting less,' he replied, 'when you start getting younger every day.'

But why did I jump? The hospital psychologist had diagnosed some kind of 'dissociative episode', of the kind that made John Kennedy Jnr partially black out when flying a plane to his cousin's wedding: he thought up was down and left was right, and crashed to his death; I had thought the wall above the towpath shoulder-high – a condition brought on by stress. A visit to another psychologist two years later established that the jump was in part connected with the drill – VARRR-OOM! – which I had mistaken for shellfire; the leap had been a 'jump for cover'. And yes, I had shell shock – PTSD. Later, on fireworks night in 2015, the displays so beloved by the British to celebrate the burning at the stake of a Catholic plotter brought on such a fit of panic I ended up in handcuffs, then in a police cell, charged with assault, under a blanket on which the previous occupant had wiped his backside.

But shell shock was only part of the story. My first five years back in the UK from 2003 after Iraq were dominated by two things that implanted incurable and stressful rage, and a changed relationship to both music and the world: my father's death from cold, and my elder daughter's ordeals with bullying – encouraged by teachers – at a self-satisfied primary school, and the ensuing complex curse of anorexia. Thus the wars came home, 'inside ourselves', as Hendrix said.

There was a voyage around my daughter's music about the time of her suffering and eventual defiant recovery: via rage-rock, and Goth bands that we would go and hear together in dingy clubs around the country – Elsa, the youngest in the audience by several years, me the oldest by decades. Elsa went on her own tough journey and I learned a lot, about her and Goth, its intelligence, humour and dark places.

Parallel to this was the other battlefield, different from those in Bosnia and Iraq; the war you cannot return home from, because home is where it is. In March 2007 my father died from cold, and stress at the hands of those who had kept him cold through an entire winter. His death has since defined for me – and will forever define – Britain; not so much the vaunted 'banality of evil' with which Hannah Arendt described the Nazi Klaus Barbie, but the evil of banality.

In November 2006, the perfectly adequate boiler at the home of my then eighty-eight-year-old father and eighty-year-old mother was replaced under a scheme operated by the local authority, the Royal Borough of Kensington and Chelsea, and a company called Powergen, a subsidiary of E-on, and the company to which it had in turn 'outsourced' its operations, First Response. For four winter months, we pleaded to no avail into a black hole of silence or else apathy, ineptitude, incompetence, management-speak and squabbling over funds. For four winter months, I would return to my parents' house to find them sitting, freezing, by an open oven, with blankets on their laps. Dad, retired architect, had provided all callers with fastidiously accurate diagrams of the piping system and an explanation of what he thought should be done. He was elderly but in good health, ready to live a good while yet, and his hopes were high for a speedy solution. But all along, he had been right about the pipework that needed fixing, the 'experts' worse than wrong – he died the night they finally fixed the boiler.

(Powergen held an internal inquiry, and the parent company E-on did not return calls for comment for this book.)

Life forever changed after this lesson in Britain, but went on: this was my home again, and I felt trapped long before the outrage of 'Brexit'. I'd grown thin-skinned – or rather, lost what skin I had. Not tough enough to think of tannoy announcements that shriek across the London Underground as normal. On London's subway, one is a 'customer', never any longer a 'passenger' – until one is dead: that is, there is never an announcement about delays due to a 'customer under a train', but always a 'passenger under a train' – when someone has responded rationally to all this and jumped under the fucking thing.

Skin not tough enough for the police sirens; nor for the shrieking stag and hen gatherings drinking on trains, nor for 'customer information' like 'All services to Scotland will terminate at

Preston' . . . 'The 12.30 service to Cardiff is delayed due to congestion caused by other delays', ad nauseam. 'Transforming Travel' was the slogan of the Great Western Railway on which I was enduring too much of my life – and transform it they did. In the march of mediocrity people tended not to mind, for instance, that the wonder of Stonehenge – after millennia of being wrapped at night in still darkness – should be permanently bathed in a sickly-yellow sulphur light emanating from the vast sprawl of the 'Imperium at Solstice Park' distribution centre boasting 'A Million Square Feet To Let', and 'Solstice Services' with its Holiday Inn, Pizza Hut and Kentucky Fried Chicken a couple of meadows away.

But I did mind, especially when the government announced that it would build a tunnel beneath the stones, in the face of archaeological evidence emerging from an ever-expanding area soon to be devastated. I began to wonder: Am I mad, or is this country mad? Both, perhaps. Then the 'accident' to my leg inevitably happened, then Britain's nasty and gormless vote to leave the European Union – for me, not a matter of politics or economy, but existential.

What has this got to do with music? Answer: *Everything*. For a start, at the far end of this tunnel the sounds I could listen to were changed: gone was my favourite road music to rock the miles away: U2, Springsteen, the Allmans. Time needed measuring now in a different way from the Edge's driving rhythms or Springsteen's hop: by listening to Coltrane, Art Tatum or Thelonious Monk. Jazz – which often considers itself 'progressive' – was a way of escaping the unbearability of linear time in an awful world. I listened to music by the jazz balladeer Paolo Conte, whom I had met and heard play in Milan just before my accident. In a voice of gravel and silk, Conte sang what he described to me as '*la canzone perduta, e ritrovata*' – the song lost and found again. I played and replayed his finest song,

'Madeleine' – the sound of a way of living and loving lost in what Conte called 'the superfluity of vulgar, bad taste'. He had nibbled, backstage, from a bowl of fruit that looked like a Cézanne still life, and wanted, he said, 'to pass on a last breath of the romantic spirit' by defying time – with jazz.

The only man who came up with an apt phrase to describe the political world was Dmitri Shostakovich, who knew a thing or two about feeling lonely in, besieged by, the public mood of the moment. As we have seen, he was not a man to explain his work, but he did say of *The Nose* that it was about 'the appalling tyranny of the majority'. That kind of sentiment is politically incorrect, undemocratic perhaps, but its time had come in stupid times.

But there was also this: I do not have a bad singing voice – among the last things I did before my accident was to be gratefully whisked by a bookseller from a literary fair in Metz, France, to guest on vocals for a good electric blues band, Dr. No, in a nearby château. And now I was awoken musically from this stasis not by listening to, but by *playing*, music. My friend Paul Gilroy turned sixty in 2016, and for the occasion we reassembled a band from our schooldays (with absent friends substituted), calling ourselves Age Against The Machine – Paul on guitar, me on lead vocals. When we convened to hammer out the set, and slammed the soundproof door of the rehearsal room shut for a good few hours, it was like putting a stopper into an effluent pipe. All that mattered was in that room – music – and the world could go to hell, where it belonged. We rehearsed a song I love by Tom Russell, about the world going to hell since the days when Frank Sinatra played Ciudad Juárez.

15

Drones over Wasteland

John Cale, Barbican, September 2014

A burst of machine-gun fire crashes into shimmering half-sound, a drone like a penumbra connecting two songs. It's a deafening rasp from the electronic arsenal on a bank of keyboards and synthesized guitar. Then a second fusillade while, centre stage, John Cale remains motionless. Then silence. Not a long one, but it felt like those interminable intervals that follow real gunfire, during which one tries to figure out whence it came, where it went, how long until the next one.

Silences I know well, working out whether it is safest to run or take cover. There's no correct answer – it's all about hunch; like snowflakes or DNA, every burst of fire is different. But this isn't warfare, it's music, at the Barbican in London, autumn 2014, forty-four years since Hendrix played 'Machine Gun' on the Isle of Wight – and here is Cale's 'Machine Gun Redux', in a way – only now I know what the real thing sounds like. Here, I'm transfixed by what is unfolding on stage; in my mind's eye I'm back in Sarajevo, running up the steps behind the music academy, as we used to, dodging fire, back to our digs, scared stiff.

We've just heard Cale's recitation of a song called 'Santies', and its invocations of places we associate with war: '. . . Leipzig . . .

Leningrad . . . Phnom Penh' – now this, whatever it is. Cale, as usual, subjugates familiar material to his restless innovation, and lately to a vast electro-symphonic scale, so it's hard to know what's coming up next until way into the song. He plays a high lyrical chord on the organ, like a retort by peace or beauty against these detonations, or a craving for them.

The chord reminds me of swallows flying over the meadows in Bosnia, back to winter in Africa at the end of a bloodstained summer of which they were (hopefully) oblivious. But the organ chord does not migrate, it perseveres, stubborn peace, and at last there's a vocal incantation to hallmark the song: 'Wasteland'. It fills my middle and inner ears, sends shivers down the spine and across the skin, and runs a film-reel of memories: Sarajevo, Fallujah, Baghdad – fingers gripping the arms of the Barbican's seat, digging my nails into the black plastic. 'A black sea / A wind blows . . . Nothing could be done / You Comfort me' sings Cale. But does *anything comfort me? My guest, a teacher over from Derry, she's lovely, but she doesn't comfort, as the sardonic edge to Cale's lyric implies. Perhaps all this talk of 'comfort' is wishful thinking, maybe even the beautiful chord too.*

Cale and his band are making music-theatre tonight: the sound is amplified not only from the stage but also from flying drones, things that usually spy and bomb people. Tonight, however, drones are appropriated for music, and one is now launched, whirring above us, delivering the sound from around and above our heads. Cale had talked about this idea for months, during periodic visits to London, telling me about a man he'd met named Liam Young. Young calls himself a 'speculative architect', whose adventures aboard a cargo ship sailing across the Indian Ocean – reported on a website called Tomorrow's Thoughts Today – involve such things as 'tracing the supply chains of contemporary technologies from the point of distribution, in the mega-ports of Asia, through the world's largest wholesale market, the endless factory floors, the raw materials refineries and back to the rare earth mineral mines of inner Mongolia'. In other words: questioning the premises upon which our mass-consumerist society functions – something Cale has done with every song, directly or diagonally, for decades.

Tonight, Young is the situationist co-director, with Cale, of the spectacle that transforms these machines – associated with, in Young's words, 'protocols of surveillance and terror' – into purveyors of music and beauty, a metamorphosis and a transgression. Young and Cale thus contest with pastiche the video-game warriors beneath the Nevada Desert mass-murdering real people on screen, by taking Cale's music – the bitter, poetic beauty of tonight's performance – airborne. (Significantly, the Daily Telegraph failed to understand this claim for drone technology in its review of this concert – jeering boorishly at Young's 'bumf' on surveillance and terror in the excellent programme notes. Which tells you more about a stupid society's media than it does about Cale's music and Young's drones.)

The idea of music moving physically through the air 'goes back to a time in the seventies,' explained Cale later, 'when I had a job mixing albums at CBS, learning little tricks. It was like the hanging gardens of Babylon there, synthesizers in the walls, loudspeakers underneath you, loudspeakers over the heads of the audience. I wanted to find a way of getting vocals that would travel across the room – it cut me loose. That's where the idea for the Barbican began, and these things gestate – then I met Liam Young and it happened.'

Cale's own drone on the viola is different tonight – more metallic. He once called his original drone sound, influenced by collaborations with John Cage and La Monte Young, 'a bleak tapestry of unholy noises, searing into the listeners' ears and with any luck transporting them to a place they'll not want to leave for a long while'. And tonight's drone was carried by drone, a play on words and ideas as well as sound. The evening had begun with an overture: low chords from the depths, like the beginning of sound and time in Wagner's Das Rheingold; Cale crouched over, playing an acoustic Spanish guitar, then reaching for his viola to play the famous drone. He then laid the viola aside to begin his first song from the piano, voice morphed, distorted like a communication from *afar. This was 'Mercenaries (Ready For War)', about soldiers, but sung – like all Cale's songs about war – at a diagonal. 'It's all subliminal,' he had once said of the Velvet Undergound, 'it's all implication.'*

The drones rise, three of them, purple-and-pink-striped, answering back to the stage. It's hard to work out exactly which sound is coming from where. 'Say hello, you may never see them again,' sings Cale's voice, at once detached and committed. A huge chord sequence announces the next song, without pause: 'If You Were Still Around', but you'd be forgiven for not recognizing it yet. There's a gloaming before Cale comes in, voice unleashed – declamatory but incorporeal, somehow, yearning with every pulse of the heart for the departed, for someone missing. And another drone rises: dressed in a costume of pheasant feathers, lifting the sound skywards, playing back to the band that plays what it carries, and to us from above our heads, right to left, over and beyond. There's a safety net, which feels rather a shame – because during rehearsals a drone crashed into row M.

Then, terrifying 'Letter From Abroad', another war song: 'Afghanistan, Afghanistan whatever happened to you' – prescient, and more cogent with every turn of the rack in that country, since its release in 2003. Tonight, it is more assertive than on the HoboSapiens *album whence it came: music further forward, a more strenuous vocal presence, which on the record is sung as though along the inside of a pipe, to achieve understatement. There's nothing understated about the exasperation in one verse, for which Cale changes the line to 'Palestine, Palestine' – it's not been long since televised pictures of infanticide in Gaza. But again, this is not poster art, 'it's all subliminal' – by implication. Then into the trauma of 'Wasteland' . . .*

Being with John Cale is not unlike listening to his music, only funnier – same animation, same exhaustive range of references. His life, like his songs, is carpet-bombed with information gleaned through insatiable curiosity. He cruises the Internet for trinkets among the world's 'intelligence' (wrong word) communities –

Artificial Intelligence is the title of one of his albums. 'Don't believe most of what's out there,' he counsels. 'I realized early on that secrecy is based on nonsense. That you have to learn to read patterns until you understand things. If I get a book on medicine, I will read it and read it until it becomes clear and sinks in.'

I had first met Cale at his apartment a few blocks from Ground Zero in New York, not long after 11 September 2001. Only a musician could have an aural memory, above all, of that morning: 'I went down to the street door, and watched crowds rushing past in flight. Hundreds of people whose feet made no sound at all on the street, the dust was so thick. A stampede, in almost-silence.'

Fifteen years later, in summer 2016, we were having breakfast in Cardiff the morning after a concert for which his band had been supplemented by two choirs and a chamber orchestra. With a mix of bad taste, black humour and disgust, we were discussing a radio report on the takeover of Mosul University in northern Iraq by Islamic State, Daesh, and the syllabuses then banned, of which music had been first. 'This is how debased man can get,' said John. 'Ban music, take away all the record players and boom boxes. This really is a death cult. We can't live without music.'

He's right of course, but why not?

'What music does,' Cale answers, 'is to map your memory. People can have the same manipulated memory of the same event, and reach different conclusions. That is the political management of memory. But musical memory is not subject to political manipulation – with music, we can say: "Let's get to the bottom of this." I think music is tied in with a sense of identity. It's like going home. It doesn't have to be a mother who sings you to sleep, it's more like an accent, a language. The mind has various layers of expression, and this is one of them, perhaps the most important. When you are up against the wall, you turn to one of these means of expression – what means do I have? Music is the beginning of those means, music is the beginning of language.'

He illustrates the point from his own songwriting: 'Whenever I come to write, I start with the melody, then there's the steps from melody towards the finished song. You go through the stages, the first of which is onomatopoeic. What's the emotion here? Who are we this time? When you cast a song, you're method-acting. You're a character in your own song, and the characterization begins with the onomatopoeic *sound* of the emotion you're trying to convey. 'That's the value of the music, you can be who you want. Who are you? Where are you? You decide. The songs are my inventions, for nefarious purposes. I'm allowed to, I'm a musician.'

Onomatopoeia as foundation stone is a variation on Magma's theme or, again, a musical adaptation of the poetic principles of Mallarmé or Velimir Khlebnikov – the *feeling* of the sung sound, as foundation for content. Only gradually do melody and onomatopoeia become a song: 'It all begins with sound; then you find linkages between the words that the onomatopoeia has established. From the onomatopoeia, you find the words and join them up. You complete sentences, stitch and stick them together, cleaner and closer. The one thing I've learned is that the first words you come up with on that basis are the best you'll get. Lou Reed taught me that with what he did to [his song] "Heroin" – for which the original was "I *know* just where I'm going", not "I don't know just where I'm going". He ruined the sense of the song. Trust your instinct on the basis of the mood. You may not know what you're talking about, but leave it there.'

I ask John Cale about 'Wasteland', the song not the place. 'There is a machine-gun loop in that song, yes. It's a reaction against war in that way, yes.' And that line 'You comfort me,' I say – it had sounded hollow in my head, uncomforted. Cale replies: 'There's a yearning for satisfaction – for the kind of peace Zen taught me; that approach to things I learned from John Cage, who had a serenity about him. However, that's as good as it gets.

In "Wasteland" you've reached that point when you just want comfort from another person. I never saw "Wasteland" as a solution – it's more an explication of what can happen if you're not careful.'

Cale was born in 1942, the son of a miner and a schoolteacher. His father had come 'from an English-speaking home in Taff's Well; my mother was Welsh and he moved into her house, where my grandmother ... banned the use of English – only Welsh could be spoken, so he learned it in order to marry her. She dealt me the same card, and it did a number on my head, it drove me away from the Welsh language. I speak it and love listening to it, but all that really did my head in.' Words having thus failed, there was a place to hide from the language hex, a zone of study and music: he 'really liked school – I liked learning', made it to grammar school, and decided he wanted to be a conductor. Music, he says, was the language that transcended Welsh and English, 'a comfort I found nowhere else ... Music gave me a stronger sense of who I was.' Cale was glued to the BBC Third Programme, listening to Schoenberg and Stockhausen. 'The viola came to me by sheer chance, it was the only instrument in the school orchestra with a vacancy, and I found that I could play it.'

As the family hit crisis after crisis, first his mother's breast cancer, then the death of a favourite uncle, he 'retreated into the luxury of my interior universe, which was filled with music'. And there he has remained. His road to America was via Goldsmith's College, London, a meeting with Aaron Copland, and winning a Leonard Bernstein Scholarship to the prestigious Berkshire Music Center at Tanglewood, Massachusetts. Once in New York, Cale famously changed gear: after consulting Bernstein, he cashed in his return ticket to London for the deposit on a loft apartment, pairing up with Lou Reed; then friendship with Andy Warhol, love and music with the German singer-songwriter Nico, and the Velvet Underground adventure: innovation, heroin, eventual fragmentation – then the trajectory of a more interesting and solo career.

Cale's drone is the id of this music, with origins in early solo work before the Velvets. 'The drone,' Cale says in conversation, 'is a hypnosis. It puts your brain in a form of stasis. It's a dreamlike state. La Monte Young wanted to get into the duration of music, long duration. We'd play a drone for an hour and a half, and something is definitely going on, to do with time. La Monte's point was an adaptation of Stockhausen: he used the twelve-note scale, but took it a step further – he was not going to use pitch, he would instead use the duration of the notes. Stockhausen was always lecturing about how we must calculate change into the music, everything was organized to the point of absurdity, telling everyone how important it was to exactly calculate change. "No, you don't," said La Monte – "*length* is essential to the feeling, not calculation." I just nodded and went along.'

Those early experimental adventures were gathered on record as the boxed set *New York in the 1960s*, of which the most demanding piece was the album *Sun Blindness Music* – a long excursion in sound and time, a single chord played with varying dynamics and shifting timbres that accumulates critical mass. The viola had gone, but not the 'classical' training, which struck out into realms of atonal, minimalist sound. The drone drove two albums Cale produced for Nico, *Desertshore* and *The Frozen Borderline*, and opened the Velvet Underground's 'Venus In Furs' – a low pulse, pregnant with ominous anticipation, lust and lure. Recently, the drone propels more symphonic material to convey what Cale calls 'the things we have to understand about what time and sound do to our senses', and 'the organic entity' of music 'at that particular moment . . . All that stuff I couldn't do on the viola, that I'm doing now. I thought: I'll go back to classical music and see what's there. You find a sound that works, and you think: Hmm, it could go nicely into "Child's Christmas in Wales", so I'll adapt a song to work in the sound. The thing is to keep going back to the *mood* you are trying to communicate.'

He illustrates the point by recalling: 'I saw Ornette Coleman once in Munich, with a group of Moroccan drummers. He came out in a gold lamé suit with a baritone sax. They were drumming away and he took the microphone and just put it into the baritone and blasted. It was so strong, so loud, as if he was afraid of not being heard. I sat there thinking: How do you forge that sound in your brain? How did you put that together? And I realized: Ornette is an abstract kind of guy who happens to be a musician. It's not just in the doing, it's in the thinking, the mood, the thought process. It's a kind of Zen, actually.' So Monet was an 'abstract kind of guy' who happened to be a painter? 'Exactly,' says Cale. 'The idea was in his mind, the context was on the canvas.'

During my final week in New York, packing up, the city was plunged into darkness by a power failure. It was an eerie and fitting way to bid farewell, even a throwback to 9/11 in some weird way, dusk falling without electric light to punctuate it. I joined Cale, his lady friend and daughter Eden for the evening at his place round the corner, and sat there on the steps in the pitch-black night. John is teetotal but his daughter, his beloved and I wanted wine. Where to get it, with everything shut? Wonderful Johnny's Bar was of course defiantly open, candle-lit and one over the eight. I bought a couple of bottles and that's how my life in America ended: on those steps, drinking cheap Chilean Cabernet, with Cale and the women he loved.

John packed his bags soon afterwards, moving to Los Angeles, but toured Britain often around that time with an expert band from his newly adoptive hometown. Not many rock and roll shows feature songs about Magritte and Helen of Troy, and the kernel of these performances was a song called 'Gun', played long, and attacked with a blend of adventure and control by the

guitarist Dustin Boyer, Cale's longest-standing musical partner.
'Gun' is not an anthem like Hendrix's 'Machine Gun', but a
personal drama that invokes the lines 'When you've begun to
think like a gun /The days of the year have suddenly gone.' As
such, it had come to mean more to me than Hendrix's cry, by
virtue of the fact that I was exposed now to that different kind
of warfare that Hendrix called 'war within', the wasteland of
the mind.

When Cale tired of 'Dirty-Ass Rock 'n' Roll' (as one song was
entitled), he played a pair of concerts unrepeatable even by his
own standards: a full orchestration of his solo album *Paris 1919* of
1973, about the mood of ennui that followed the First World War
and the Treaty of Versailles. The score, by Cale himself, was
lyrical but with edges and layers of influence from Berg, Martinů
and others. The music was premiered, fittingly, at Cardiff Coal
Exchange – a homecoming – before moving to the Festival Hall
and ending with an encore from beyond the album's tracks, a
song about Henrik Ibsen's heroine Hedda Gabler, played and
sung as though it were Messiaen. The orchestrations 'needed
doing,' says Cale long afterwards, 'starting with *Paris 1919*. There
were certain things about those songs that required an orchestration and I realized: it's something I've never done – worked
live with an orchestra.

'What is the core element in *Paris*? It's that bass-line riff, a
stated presence from which one waits for things to happen. I
wanted to get that out of the studio, and do it with an orchestra
on stage.' Cale once said: 'I've no business in rock 'n' roll. I've
said it over and over, I'm a classical composer ... I'd love to
conduct a Brahms or Mahler cycle.' As is clear from his soundtrack for the film *Paris s'éveille* or his piece *Sanctus: Four Études
for Electronic Orchestra*, which paint a horizon of sound, some
passages like the climax to a Bach organ fugue, some like *pizzicato*
strings during, indeed, a Mahler symphony. There were other

soundtracks, like that to Andrés Vicente Gómez's *Antártida* (1994) – sparse as Sibelius and, at stolen moments, cantabile – or to Patricia Mazuy's *Saint-Cyr*, with twists and turns, at once quirky and ominous, à la Bartok. But when one quotes the 'no business in rock 'n' roll' line back at him, Cale shrugs, adding: 'I love rock and roll. I'm still not sure which one I want in the forefront. If any.'

Cale returned to rock and roll for a tour I caught in Hamburg, based around an album called *Shifty Adventures in Nookie Wood* (2012), a park in Tokyo where young people go to commit suicide – not a well-trodden niche. We convened in Paris for a fiftieth-anniversary performance of *The Velvet Underground & Nico* album with multiple guests, which included a revelation from the American singer and 'Slam poet' Saul Williams, who wrought an extraordinary version of 'Heroin', entirely appropriated and repositioned from Lou Reed's lugubrious original: sung and played at Cale-gale force, with a political edge to the delivery that made the song not so much about the opiate as about monstrosities in a world that would drive someone to want to 'nullify my life'. It just shows what a generation can do to a song.

Cale sang 'Sunday Morning', during which he was obliged to fight back a frog in his throat. Next day, we had lunch at a bistro – Le Gymnase, frequented by Beckett – and walked through Montparnasse Cemetery to say hello to Susan Sontag, who'd been here twelve years now. A track called 'People Who Died' is one of the most important on the *Antártida* soundtrack, and speaking of the departed, I asked Cale about Lou Reed's 'Sunday Morning' the night before. He replied: 'I had never sung that song. Did you catch the choking? The thing about music is that you never know when your subconscious is going to jump up and bite you on the back of the neck. I was back there, in that loft on the Lower East Side, Sunday morning indeed, at the harmonium – playing that song.'

Cale played the same music again, a year later, on the dockside at Liverpool, audience facing the Irish Sea into which my grandfather jumped off the Dublin ferry when Mum was five – my turn for the bite on the back of the neck. In November 2017 Cale brought the album home, to New York. Over two nights at Brooklyn Academy of Music he stripped it bare – dronier than ever, a raw, metallic but ethereal sound that felt like having an exposed nerve stroked smoothly, sometimes a little too roughly. By the time of these anniversary concerts, Andy Warhol, the guitarist Sterling Morrison, Nico and Reed had all passed way, and Cale said he felt their presence in the auditorium. The video to a revived song of yore, 'If You Were Still Around', features them; it was re-released in two versions on an album called *M:Fans*, the first of which follows an overture featuring recordings of telephone conversations between Cale and his mother back in Wales which, whether intended or not, seems to recast the song as a requiem for her, and for home.

The second is a studio version of a live performance during summer 2016, again back in Cardiff, for which Cale introduced a choir made up of local classically trained singers and a gospel chorus from London, adding a chamber string section. The result was a fusion reactor of music that seemed to bring together Harlem soul, the Welsh National Opera and the traditions of chapel, coalmine and rugby oratorio. The song opened with an a cappella choral line that could have come from Alfred Schnittke's Concerto for Choir, and proceeded as a gospel anthem driven by the band and the sophistication that Cale can bring to an orchestra – sometimes dense, sometimes icily sparse. The voice was eerier and more vehement than ever – perturbed and entropic; a place where ennui and power collide, in music dense with swirling subliminal warning.

Cale is still fascinated by what he calls 'the emotional curve of my journey from Wales to America'. He describes himself as 'very sensitive to the idea that I've betrayed my heritage. I'm over here, in America, and I wonder whether what I did has turned me into a traitor. If you reject something you grew up with, does that mean that you have the DNA structure of a traitor? I'm very interested in traitors these days.' Cale released an EP which included a song called 'E Is Missing', about Ezra Pound, a master of poetic onomatopoeia. 'Pound is full of chatter,' says Cale, 'extremely learned and elitist.' But it has a greater significance: 'It's a song about a traitor.'

There is unlikely to be a political slogan in a line by John Cale. 'The word "didactic",' he says, 'is the word I hate most of all, the word I am afraid of more than any other . . . Claiming to know, claiming to have the answer. I write and play into the political background of what [people] are talking about. You will miss getting to the point of things if you lean on a lectern, banging your fists. I deal with mood, with indeterminacy, with the mood of uncertainty. That's why there's so much improvisation. I haven't necessarily made up my mind. There's no trusted politics, there's no single, final argument.' Listening again – live – to the *Velvet Underground & Nico*, in Paris, Liverpool and Brooklyn, one realized: this music was written half a century ago at a time of relative assurance and assertion among our generation. How different Cale's diagonal vision was – and is: a counter-vision of incertitude, ambivalence, and how much more enduring for that.

And this is because his work applies better to the world of now than does the idealism of music discussed in the first chapters of this book. It addresses what the writer Rob Nixon and other academics call the 'slow violence' of a nightmarish twenty-first-century kind: climate change and species extinction, on which Nixon writes, but also violence in every human exchange, the commercialization of every encounter, the commodification of every endeavour and activity; the language of politics as mere cliché, as self-interest or that of party; the blitzkrieg of technology that claims to know what you want next before you do, and tells you – all masquerading as gratification, even 'freedom'. And there lies its final, awful victory. It's all there, in the slow throb of Cale's music, measured by the drone, a violence more akin to the advance of cancer through the cells of the social fabric and the slow but sure asphyxiation of nature than to that rasp of automatic weapons in 'Wasteland'. Every generation thinks it has witnessed the end of an era, but mine may just be on to something. With climate-change denial now effectively the official policy of the US government, Cale concluded his run of concerts in Brooklyn with a new song, arguably among his more 'didactic' to date, entitled 'What Is The Legal Status Of Ice?'

The critic Joanna Demers wrote a book called *Drone and Apocalypse*, about the primality of drone music, a sound, she says, intrinsic to Platonic philosophy on how to live life, rather than 'obsession with how long we live'. She also posits drone music as 'the sound of death . . . Consider drone works named with death in mind, *Trilogie de la Mort* [Éliane Radigue]; *Ravedeath 1972* [Tim Hecker]; and more abstractly *The Disintegration Loops* [William Basinski], where disintegration means the death of magnetic tape, the World Trade Center, the American empire.' On the other hand, Demers continues, 'there is also the fact that the sounds of the beginning of life in the womb consist of low hums and heartbeats, an enveloping sonic blanket undergirds experience and sensation.'[1]

Measurement by drone is the measurement of disintegration. It's there in the melancholy of baroque music and in the *Trauerspiel* plays that so intrigued Walter Benjamin; in the baroque 'cult of fragments' (great name for a rock band!) whereby artists of that era would collect fragments of broken Greek and Roman statues – sometimes to litter around their studios, sometimes to incorporate and remake into a part-copy of the original – in recognition of both destructive passing time and the durability of ancient stone. The Palazzo Altemps, my favourite museum in Rome, is full of such works – part-Greek, part-Roman, part-baroque – which in turn inspired the cult of depicting ruins, obsessively observed by the French artist Hubert Robert. The drone is part of that.

The Mexican poet Homero Aridjis wrote of his grandmother: 'Her room creaked and the world threatened to collapse – although it was her body that trembled and her days that were numbered. For according to her, everything advanced towards its destruction and contributed to its own defeat.'[2] Aridjis's poem was translated by his daughter Chloe, who echoed the sentiment in her prose, writing her novel *Asunder*: 'I had always been drawn to decomposition,' says one character, observing damage to a Van Eyck painting, 'and the knowledge that everything in the universe tends from order to disorder.'[3] And when touring a ruined chateau: 'Everywhere I looked, I saw signs of deterioration and decay, of wondrously indifferent dilapidation.'[4]

Drone time is a counter to the proliferation of contemporary apocalyptic culture: be it mass-market entertainment in disaster movies, or real literature, like the outrageous vision of Cormac McCarthy's novel *The Road*, or Stephen King's *The Stand*. The apocalypse now, an echo of Leverkühn and 'Go Down Moses', is wishful thinking – the hope that it will all end with a bang, quickly – and, I think, an eschatological extension of the personal hope we all share for a quick death, the corollary of which is our common dread of a slow, painful one. It is Odysseus's first, primal question to the ghost of his mother when he meets her in Hades: 'What death overtook you? Did you have some lingering illness? Or did Artemis the Archeress visit and kill you with her gentle darts?'[5]

In the end, the drone has it: environmental degradation, and what Charles Bowden called 'the great dying' of species, tell us very clearly – though in vain – that *Homo* supposedly *sapiens* faces not apocalypse, nor quick death by Artemis's darts, but a terrible, 'lingering' and painful one – as suggested and measured by drone music.

Cale's drone and the ennui of *Paris 1919* register the end of the idea of 'progress' on which my generation was reared and on which much of the music in this book is founded. That idea, common to monotheist religions, the socialist left and the capitalist right, that there's 'a better world a-comin'', as the gospel song promises. That somehow Tuesday is by definition an improvement on Monday. Why should it be? Progress is just nostalgia in reverse, a lie, I had by now come to acknowledge, in defiance of and in spite of so much of the music discussed earlier, especially that of my youth in the 1960s, brimful with hope and promise. So that drone becomes the musical equivalent of Shelley's dedication – to Leigh Hunt – of his verse-drama *The Cenci*, wherein he wrote that his poems hitherto had been 'visions which impersonate my own apprehensions of the beautiful and the just . . . dreams of what ought to be, or may be. The drama which I now present to you is a sad reality.'

I ask Cale: What are the politics of the drone? He replies: 'Draw a straight line and follow it. Prove or disprove Einstein's theory of relativity. It's about the power of music, and about human fragility. It's like that stone in your shoe. It's about how long you can keep going with that stone in your shoe. Keep going long enough, and you'll find out in the end.'

But where, if anywhere, does the journey lead?

16

When Words Fail

Schubert: Die Winterreise,
Paul Lewis and Mark Padmore, Wigmore Hall, London, 2012

From the very first notes, a phantasmal feeling descends like a mist from up there, where golden Orpheus holds his lyre above the stage. What other voyage, or piece of music, begins by bidding us 'Good night'? But this is how we set out on Winter Journey *with Franz Schubert. As one of Schubert's most ardent fans, Samuel Beckett, wrote: 'Sometimes it is all over, for the day, all done, all said, all ready for the night, and the day not over, far from over, and the night not ready, far, far from ready.' I'd been writing out those lines since adolescence, to post on walls and place on desks without ever having been to the place they described, and this is now the zone we enter, as Paul Lewis plays the opening notes of Schubert's* Die Winterreise, *and Mark Padmore sings the opening line: 'I arrived a stranger, a stranger I depart.'*

This is the first of twenty-four song episodes through a snowscape, the strangest existential voyage in music. Schubert introduced Die Winter-reise *to his friends as 'a cycle of horrific songs'. The poet Wilhelm Müller who wrote these verses never heard them set this way, and although his words do not in themselves fail, in the Beckettesque sense, the Wanderer's isolation lies in Schubert's score rather than on the page. Schubert is not setting the poetry – he is realizing it. We do not know why the Wanderer must venture as he does, only that he is heartbroken. The repetition in this opening song – a relatively gentle gateway to the rest, which can only get worse – establishes a sense of endlessness, as any true wanderer's journey must. In the second song, 'the wind is playing with the weather-vane' just as time plays with human endeavour.*

Each song is introduced by a musical idea on the piano, which the voice joins, and the one with which 'Frozen Tears' opens is played with poignant bleakness. The tick-tock beat of Lewis's left hand traces the Wanderer's footsteps, while Padmore's tone, as the poem demands, turns the tears that emerge warm from the breast, once spilled into the cruel air, into ice. In his book Winter's Journey *the singer Ian Bostridge finds in the third song, 'Estarring' (Numbness), a 'deep, repressed, sexual energy' – palpable in tonight's performance as, frenzied, the Wanderer seeks to kiss the ground and pierce the ice 'with my burning tears, until I see earth'.*[1]

Next is Schubert's most famous song, 'Linden Tree', a symbol of magic, played and sung as such; then 'Flood', which Padmore sings with menace while Lewis picks out the phrases with a mysteriously non-committal air, at once dreamlike and engaged. The song breathes with difficulty, like its composer – dying of syphilis when he wrote it – as Lewis seems to make the silences between phrases interminable, each step more painful than the last.

This is a voyage, but shot through with stasis. A stream is usually a flowing thing, in nature as it is across music (including Schubert's own 'Trout' Quintet) – its current, like our preferred view of time, purposeful towards the ocean. But not here: in a song called 'On the River' the current is 'cold and motionless', it 'gives no parting greeting' – a terrify-ing metaphor for marmoreal paralysis. Water, usually mellifluous, is trapped by its own 'hard, rigid crust' – as are we, in a place without entry or exit, to which Godot never comes; and here Lewis gives the music a mouldering, leaden langour. The alienation of this Wanderer, who in the nineteenth-century cult drew from Coleridge's Ancient Mariner,

Byron's *Manfred* and the accursed Wandering Jew, feels now more prescient of their twentieth-century descendants, in Beckett, Kafka and Camus.

Padmore and Lewis deliver 'Dream of Spring' as more akin to a nightmare – leaping dissonances – then, almost a relaxation into despair when it becomes clear that spring is unattainable, illusory. Lewis's visions on the piano recall Caliban's dreaming, through clouds that briefly part in his sleep, so that when he awakes he cries to dream again – in vain. The Wanderer too realizes that his reveries of flowers and 'love returned' were just that, vaporous unreality.

Paul Lewis can make anything lyrical, even this incertitude, and seems to stretch the tempi during the hallucinations, to hold us back in that sweet sleep from which the real world rudely awakens and banishes us. On, then, towards 'Loneliness', during which that mist over the audience seems to thicken; even the suited bankers have stopped yawning and appear to focus, their wives no longer flicking the programme pages to browse advertisements for jewellery and private schools. Lewis and Padmore have the hall in the palm of their hands, yet seem entirely oblivious of us, engrossed as they are in this music-making like a frozen waterfall, crystalline like Coleridge's line: 'Quietly shining to the quiet Moon'.

Soon follows the eeriness of 'The Crow'. The opening on piano conveys wary wonder at the mystery of the bird, and when the vocal line joins it Padmore allows the notes to swoop like its wings: the crow is Noah's messenger, Odin's thought and memory, the exorcised spirit, aboriginal trickster, thief of fire. In lore of the Pacific First Nations, this bird is a primal jester who stole the sun by way of a prank, and hid it in a box. The song understands and expresses a degree of delirium on the part of the prankster, but also panic at the darkness caused by the prank – full of foreboding and impending betrayal for the Wanderer. In the Arab world a crow signals regret, and the bird our Wanderer sees above him is a carrion crow: 'Strange creature, will you not leave me?' To the Wanderer the crow is, like death, a joker.

In Bostridge's book, the leaf on the tree in Schubert's next song, 'Last Hope', is a metaphor for 'all blind chance'. And Lewis plays the song as though it were life's throw of the dice, the difference between what happens – but only just – and the history of what nearly happened – but not quite – on the flip side of time. The Wanderer gambles his last hope on whether the leaf will fall; and if it does, with it falls his – and our – ability to believe in anything.

This music Lewis plays, and Padmore sings, as though it were entirely suspended on that zephyr of serendipity: we feel as though the next note may happen, or it may not; and when it does, we feel the same about the next. On which side of history will the next thing happen, but only just – or nearly happen, but not quite?

Lewis's part in the next song, 'In the Village', contains a nether 'rumble' as though from an underworld abyss, which Schubert would deploy in the opening of his final piano sonata, D960. This song finds the Wanderer 'finished with all dreams'; hope is now locked in a realm of fools, while the pianist and the singer now take us instead along a rambling path, away from barking dogs and towards a song called 'Illusion' – which affords a moment of lyrical indulgence, a glimpse of dancing light on the piano, a hallucination – or perhaps not, for the respite is forbidden; there is no turning off our road of 'ice, night and terror'. A signpost on that road is 'pointing towards the towns'; they are of no interest, yet the Wanderer asks: 'Why do I avoid the roads / That other travellers take?' And it is with painful beauty that Padmore sings, and Lewis plays, the resolve with which our Wanderer follows – we follow – whatever it is that propels us along this 'road from which no man has ever returned'. There was once a Procol Harum song called 'Homburg', about the time when the hands of a clock turn backwards and signposts point nowhere – and Schubert duly follows them, signs that point nowhere.

The graveyard presents itself as a 'cool inn' where the weary might find rest, but all the rooms are taken – no peace, even at the cemetery. Lewis picks at notes as though they were razor blades; and without even a tomb to rest on, a 'trusty staff' is all we have. So courage, then! And Lewis plays what feels like a drinking song gone awry: 'If there are no gods / Then we be gods ourselves!' But the inebriated moment is short-lived; Lewis returns to hallucinogenic mode, and a primal vision akin to the one in Aztec myth where the history of the universe is counted by the lives of five suns, four of which have already perished. Here we have three 'mock suns', two of which have set – and in our madness (or our wisdom?) we long for the third to do so too. Lewis plays this with uncanny measurement of the notes and silences to encapsulate the suns' pale light, and the gloaming that surrounds them. We do not know when or whether this third sun sets, for now the evening reaches its ghostly conclusion: an encounter with the hurdy-gurdy man.

Lewis announces his presence with the left hand, before the hurdy-gurdy man's desolate, tinkling motif comes in, and Padmore sings with tortured resolve. The player of the instrument, turned by a crank, is the first to enter what has until now been a monodrama. For this song, the piano part is entirely separated from the verse, and Lewis gives the accompaniment an apparitional feel, the sonority is weightless, immaterial. The hurdy-gurdy man is barefoot on the ice, his plate empty of coins. Otherwise, he is Charon the boatman, who does accept an obol to ferry your soul. Dogs growl at the hurdy-gurdy man, yet 'he lets everything go on / As it will'.

And now, at this unbearable moment, Lewis does something quite extraordinary: with the piano pedals he makes the notes whirl, like the hurdy-gurdy; the notes shudder, and make us shudder ('The purists will crucify me,' says Lewis afterwards). Padmore cries the Wanderer's pleading 'Strange old man, shall I go with you?' and Lewis picks the notes that vanish into oblivion.

Samuel Beckett's favourite composer was Schubert. It must be significant that the writer who asked what we should do when words fail should love Schubert above all. According to the literary critic Miron Grindea (who was married to a pianist): 'The composer who spoke most to [Beckett] was Schubert, whom he considered a friend in suffering.'[2] Beckett was himself an accomplished pianist, and there is music in his writing: sonority, sometimes guttural, sometimes fluid. The musicologist Deborah Weagel cites the composer Luciano Berio saying: 'I've always thought . . . that Beckett's writing was very musical, but it's very difficult to describe what this "being musical" means.' In a chapter on *Waiting for Godot*, Weagel considers 'the relationship between a performance of the play and the performance of a musical composition'. She examines, for instance, Beckett's directions on how actors should deliver their lines: *agacé* (irritably) – perhaps *agitato* on a musical score. Or *avec force* (violently) – *forzando*.[3] Beckett's television play of 1982, *Nacht und Träume*, is overtly inspired by Schubert, and Beckett was immersed in Matthias Claudius's poem *Death and the Maiden*, which Schubert set as a string quartet.

In Beckett as in Schubert, there are wanderers: Murphy, Molloy and his pursuer – wanderers, renouncing kinship, like those in Schubert's *Winterreise* and 'Wanderer' Fantasy. When Beckett insists that 'The artist who stakes his being is from nowhere, has no brothers', he describes the protagonist and maybe the composer of *Winterreise*. But the crucial element in Beckett that Lewis finds in Schubert is the way in which the movement, the motion, is not towards a destination but towards what John Cale calls 'incertitude'. It is the inconsequentiality of what the critic Declan Kiberd described in a lecture at the Beckett festival at Enniskillen in 2014 as Beckett's 'setting up camp in the void'. Beckett loved *Winterreise* above all; he called it Schubert's 'masterwork' and wrote to his cousin John in 1975 to say that he was 'shivering through the grim journey again'.[4] It's that zone again – 'all over for the day . . . the night ready to fall', but 'not ready, far, far from ready'.

Paul Lewis – leading interpreter, from his generation, of

Schubert's music for piano – grew up in Huyton, a desperately poor suburb on the outskirts of Liverpool – thus neighbour of the England football captain Steven Gerrard, master of a different craft. Lewis's father was laid off from Merseyside's docks after a famous strike in the mid-1980s, and his mother worked in the housing benefit office of the local Knowsley District Council.

There was no music in the family, but from the age of eight Lewis learned by borrowing LP records from Knowsley public library (it's questionable whether, after the recent successive library cuts, his career could happen now). 'It was an unusual way to start a life with music,' he reflects. 'It was all me – going to the library round the corner, taking out the three LPs I was allowed, taping them illegally, returning them and getting three more.' The music in the house 'was John Denver. My parents were never anything other than supportive but didn't themselves know about music – nothing to guide them, which was both an advantage and a disadvantage. At first, I expected everyone to feel like I did. There was a moment listening to that opening of Beethoven's Fourth, when the thing just takes off: dada-WOOOSH! I called my mother and said: "Listen to *this*!" and she did, and said: "Oh yes, very nice," and I felt like shouting "No Mum! It's, it's – like nothing else in the world!"'

Lewis's primary school had no piano teacher, 'which is why I started by learning the cello, at which I was not good at all.' After he switched to the piano, Lewis's parents arranged for him, aged eleven, to try for a place at Chetham's School of Music in Manchester. He was turned down, 'so I went to the local comprehensive, which was OK, but there were no kids interested in the same sort of things as me'. His talent had been spotted at Chetham's, however, by the piano teacher Nigel Pitceathly, who took Lewis on. 'So that every Wednesday, my father would drive me to Stockport for a lesson, which was quite a thing for him to do.'

It paid off. When he was fourteen, Lewis was accepted by Chetham's, and his course decided. 'For the first time, I was surrounded by people who shared my interest, who I could talk to about music, and that saved me, I suppose.' Saved from what? Lewis laughs: 'I never got to find out what exactly I was saved from.' After leaving school he was admitted to the Guildhall School, in 1994 he won the London International Piano Competition, then progressed to become a pupil and protégé of Alfred Brendel.

How did it happen? 'I've thought about it. I don't know. I wanted to discover things for myself; and everything I found on those records seemed new and exciting, although you have to know what you are looking for, and I learned how to do that at a very young age. Nowadays everything is online, and there's no physical search, and that's one thing. Another is, of course, whether a place like Knowsley will have a library with classical music for people like me to borrow. But this music was a whole new world for me, reflecting different things than those around me. When my mother said that about Beethoven's Fourth I had to ask myself: Are we listening to the same thing? This isn't about Mum or Beethoven, this is about what is happening when we listen, to do with the emotion when it hits us, and this is the most difficult thing of all to explain. You can break it down, analyse it, but in the end it's about a complex set of emotions and instincts, responding to what is written in the music and how it is performed, in ways that no amount of explaining gets you any closer . . . I will never get to the point of being able to explain exactly what this music is about, and why that meant so much to me at that age.'

Lewis, now a performer on the world's stages, says: 'The best I can do is carry what I feel with and in the music for other people to hear it. Do we ever get to the core of a piece? I don't actually think I'm best placed to judge that – I'm playing it, I'm not really hearing it in the way the audience is. Everyone else out there has the luxury of not knowing what you are trying to do, and hearing what emerges from that. I feel hugely responsible for what I am doing – to the composer and the audience – and sometimes you get a feeling that something happened … I get a suspicion occasionally, and say to a colleague "I don't think I can play any better than that." But the musician knows he can never really get to the bottom of a piece, because if you did, why bother carrying on?'

Lewis plays Schubert like no one else. His interpretations have an eerie lyricism, at odds with his personality: a more open-hearted, down-to-earth young man you could not hope to find. This concert in the Wigmore Hall was part of a series of a kind never before undertaken, upon which Lewis set out in 2011: to perform, over two and a half years and across four continents, every work Schubert wrote for piano during the six years between 1822, the year he learned he had syphilis – 'after which everything changes completely in his music' – and his death in November 1828. The project was divided into eight cycles of solo music, plus the song series. I followed its progress in the UK and the USA, prevented from hearing the very last concert, in Germany – though I had planned to – by my accident.

Before Lewis began this odyssey, I went to talk to him about it; heavy snow had cancelled many trains that day to outer London, where he lives, and I had to walk five hours through snowdrifts to his hometown of Amersham, where we sat and talked in a coffee shop while ice accumulated against the window. I made the obvious bad joke about *Winterreise*.

The date was 18 December 2010 – and Lewis remembered something: exactly two years previously we had both been in Vienna for Alfred Brendel's valedictory concert, so we raise paper cups of coffee in tribute. Recordings by Brendel were among those Lewis would borrow at the library, before he became

Brendel's star pupil. 'It was astonishing to see at close quarters what he was doing. We talked about his ideas and the sounds he was trying to achieve; for me, that was when the light went on. It was all about message – yes, we talked about pedals, timbres and colours, but you can talk about sonority and technique until you're blue in the face – the real point is how to get the message across. With someone like Schubert, there are many layers, many things being said at the same time, shedding different light. The tricky thing is to get the delicate balance that conveys the message – and Alfred was master of message.'

This fidelity to the composer's intentions propels Lewis's music-making; it's a mixture of mastery with modesty. 'Sometimes, I go to a concert and focus on the performer more than on what they are playing. I enjoy them putting on a show, I understand it, but it's not what *I* try to do . . . Yes, it's wonderful to walk onto a stage and have everyone applaud, and applaud again when I've finished. But that's not what this is about. It's not about me, it's about the composer and the music, the message of the music, the feelings and emotions it's trying to convey. The music is more important than me – Schubert is much more important than me.'

Schubert is the quintessential bohemian artist, the romantic's romantic. But we must, says Lewis, get away from the 'old stories' about Schubert, 'of the shy schoolmaster's son who wouldn't say boo to a goose' and the libertine that Schubert is supposed to have become. 'It's too interesting and complicated for all that,' says Lewis. 'It is elusive, and complex, but there's also something immediately comprehensible about it – Schubert is unusually clear about his understanding of things, and the way he feels. He is strong in himself, even if in the life he led he was shy and retiring and found that the best way to convey what he felt was through music.'

The fact that only a fraction of Schubert's music was published during his lifetime – and even less was performed – has forged the posthumous image of a 'rejected' genius; but Schubert had, says Lewis, a 'fierce awareness of his artistic worth'. The bohemian myth is fuelled also by Schubert's circumstances and private life. His music was mostly performed at *Schubertiade*, evenings of music, drinking and dancing with his devoted circle of students and political radicals opposed to the stifling repression of Metternich's Austria.

Schubert's romantic and sex lives have fascinated posterity: there've been treatises on his possible homosexuality, and he appears to have preferred heterosexual relationships 'on the side' with working-class girls – a chambermaid called Pepi Pöckelhofer in particular – rather than with ladies of his artistic circle. Meanwhile, his passions were unrequitedly reserved for an aristocratic pupil, Countess Caroline Esterhazy, who was beyond reach yet associated with creative spells that produced some of his greatest music. The countess once complained that Schubert dedicated no work to her, to which he replied: 'What's the point? Everything is dedicated to you anyway.'

There are descriptions of Schubert having 'drunk too much' and smelling strongly of tobacco; opium use is speculated upon. One of his friends, Wilhelm von Chézy, noted that 'when the juice of the vine glowed within him, he did not bluster ... but liked to withdraw into a corner and give himself contentedly to silent rage'. He was known, on account of his short stature and wild sticky-out frizzy hair, as *Schwammerl*, 'little mushroom'. Schubert's appearance was certainly unkempt, and he suffered bouts of depression – possessed, said a friend (and a regular at his *Schubertiades*), Eduard von Bauernfeld, by 'a black-winged demon of sorrow and melancholy' – disappearing from his circle for long periods that could also be his most productive. What is certain is that Schubert was uncompromisingly uninterested in a bourgeois lifestyle and bourgeois values, family life, marriage and toadying to the classes and circles that would have made for lucrative patronage. Von Bauernfeld wrote of his 'suffering from genuine dread of commonplace and boring people, or philistines, whether from the upper or middle classes ... Goethe's cry "I would rather die than be bored" was and remained his motto.'[5]

Part of Schubert's mystique lies in the simple fact that most of his work was little known outside these circles until long after his death. In a fine study of the piano music, Ernest Porter observes: 'Schubert had not the wide fame of other composers and much of his piano music remained unpublished for many years. The stature of Beethoven was such, and his work so quickly published, that no one could afford to be ignorant of his works, whereas it was quite possible for many musicians to be comparatively unaware of Schubert's main contributions to music.'[6] Dualities of sorrow and joy – and a fine calibration of sentiments in between – entwine and juxtapose with unique intensity in his music and, argues Paul Lewis, 'Schubert's very elusiveness lies in this intense communication. We want to identify with the person behind the music, and with Beethoven this is less complicated. With Schubert, it's all much hazier. Everything is on a smaller scale than Beethoven; he is not in search of the big effect, but something more graded and intimate.'

Schubert lived and worked in the shadow of this man he adored and whose influence was unavoidable in early-nineteenth-century Vienna. Although Beethoven and Schubert died within a short time of each other, the latter was a generation younger, and Beethoven's death bequeathed a mantle of sorts that Schubert is credited with having taken on, perhaps consciously, during the twenty months he outlived his idol. There's a famous story: after attending Beethoven's funeral, Schubert and some friends drank until late at a tavern, where a toast was made to the lost genius, and to whoever would follow him next to the grave – which in the event was Schubert.

Lewis forms part of a heredity after Brendel, in which the link is found among the finest Schubertian of *her* generation, Imogen Cooper, who studied under Brendel in Vienna when eighteen years his junior. Cooper's Schubert wrestles with every contrasting mood, so effectively that she was the subject of an editorial in the *Guardian* for putting 'the music before technique', and for possessing 'a rare ability to negotiate the composer's change of moods between flippancy and tragedy'.[7]

Lewis took on this mantle of 'music before technique' and after years of playing mostly Beethoven, began to formulate – in contrast to the wonderful muscularity of Cooper's Schubert – this spectral feel, which gives us a clue as to something Beckett too may have heard in this music. 'I never take much notice of Beethoven's shadow so far as Schubert is concerned,' says Lewis. 'A lot is made of the influence, but what strikes me are the differences.' Differences which militated against his professional career, as Percy Young writes: 'Schubert's originality was against him.'[8] 'We're all supposed to think that the Viennese classical era produced one tradition of music,' says Lewis. 'But no: Beethoven always seems to find a way through, even to triumph. Schubert never does. He never finds a solution. At least, not after 1822 when he was diagnosed with syphilis. Everything then changes in the music, it becomes so bleak. Beethoven takes you through the shadow of the valley, but there's resolution in the end. Schubert not so – he takes you on a journey, and leaves you nowhere.'

An example: 'There is no piece like Schubert's later A Minor Sonata, nothing so bare, so sparse: long unharmonized passages, a single repeated note going through the piece . . . there is stark resignation, rather than a will to win through.' In the C Minor Sonata, says Lewis, 'we've been on this journey, seen things along the way, but there is no accumulated wisdom – it has no end, there is no way out, we are still there. It's interesting to wonder,' he says, on reflection, 'what it is in the mind that conjures up that idea of inconsequentiality. How much do we *ascribe* that meaning to it, and how much of it is in the music? I think it must be there, in the music.' Much of this is achieved by Schubert's use of discord, Ernest Porter writes: 'Not only were Schubert's harmonies very free but discords which had before been used as passing chords were used in a much more pronounced manner.'[9]

Lewis argues that the incertitude reaches a level of acceptance in the A Major Sonata, D959, the penultimate. 'There is the terror of the slow movement,' says Lewis, 'and no resolution as such, but it's as close as Schubert gets – this is what we are left with, in the end.' The sonata 'concludes with a movement that is fourteen minutes long, as though he is wanting to work and rework these ideas with as much time as he has got left, like stolen time – the coda, so resigned, as if saying goodbye for the last time. But there is no sense of "I'll be all right."' Schubert knew he was dying; in an important letter to his friend Leopold Kupelwieser he said, 'my most brilliant dreams have perished'. And with his final sonata, D960, says Lewis, 'Schubert writes something that comes from another planet. I'm not a religious person, but it is something beyond—' Lewis leaves his point hanging in the cold air, his breath and his coffee giving off steam, snow against the café window. 'As though it's: Well, after all our trouble, this is what comes next.'

One of Schubert's hallmarks was the number of 'unfinished' masterpieces he left, not least the 'Unfinished' Symphony and the two-movement 'Reliquie' piano sonata which formed part of the first round of Lewis's two-and-a-half-year tour. One can either take these works as set out in shorthand or see them as very much 'finished'; or rather, deliberately unfinished like

Michelangelo's 'unfinished' statues of prisoners wresting their way free from their stone blocks. Their struggle to be free from – yet entrapped within – what Michelangelo saw as the material of eternity *is* the theme of the statues.

The same applies to the man who brought Michelangelo's methods into the modern era, Auguste Rodin, in works such as his *Meditation* (later called *The Inner Voice*), which uses 'unfinishedness' to thematic effect just as 'Schubert's supposedly "unfinished" pieces are extraordinary as they stand, precisely because they appear incomplete,' says Lewis, 'and may well be as finished as he intended them to be. The "Reliquie" is the most difficult of all his work to play; a piano redaction of an unfinished orchestral score, much of it unharmonized, so you have to realize the implied symphonic harmonies – those are colours you have to realize. The second movement has a mix of menace and a sense of dance. Maybe Schubert just felt there was nothing significant to add, and left them as they were.'

Some of the eight rounds of concerts in the Schubert tour began, appositely, in Lewis's native Liverpool before setting out around the world, and I travelled there to hear the launch of the third, which included the most lyrically beautiful of the late sonatas, D894 in G Major. Among the audience were Lewis's father, mother and aunt, and Ted Kirk, under whose baton Lewis first played – on cello with the Knowsley Youth Orchestra. Schubert's posthumous champion Robert Schumann rated the G Major Sonata above all the others, and Lewis navigated its contrasting colorations and opaque beauty with a perfect balance between dexterity and deep feeling, empowering the simple but almost painfully beautiful mellifluousness of the melodies with his phrasing and sonority of touch.

Next day was 'Ladies' Day' at the Aintree racecourse outside Liverpool, and the town was filled with groups of girls wearing not very much, perched on heels and drinking in preparation for drinks on a day out. We wound our way through them as far as Greggs the bakery, to talk about 'those beautiful, longing tunes in the G Major, but then in the piece written soon afterwards, D899, you get this repeated note figure: there it is, relentless, throughout. It's a beautiful and rather melancholy pulse, it has this feeling of loneliness; I see it in the context of *Winterreise*, where the repeated note also keeps appearing – frozen tears, frozen water, the signpost to nowhere. It's just a slow repeat, always present ... it just goes on and on. And it's the main narrative, one is unable to escape, it's background, it's not the melody, but always there, no matter.' Very much like Cale's drone.

Later in the tour, I caught Lewis playing the same programme at the Metropolitan Museum in New York, after which we adjourned to the Village Vanguard jazz club to hear the guitarist Bill Frisell. Lewis appeared to enjoy this music, of a kind he doesn't hear much. I asked him over margaritas if he himself got lonely wandering the world playing very solitary music, far from his Norwegian wife Bjørg, a cellist, and his children. 'Not in the least,' he replied. But 'Schubert's music does feel different after playing it around the world. Things become more prominent with time spent playing them, to a point which is so revealing. When I performed the song cycle in 2001–2, it was all new to me. It was like having a new, strong and volatile person in one's life. The first time I heard his music, I thought of Schubert as a tortured Romantic. But now I've realized there's this inconsequentiality, and in the end this acceptance, that sheds a different kind of light on the whole thing.'

The tour done, we convened at Lewis's home and tried to focus on Schubert throughout our day, but spent most of it exchanging tirades in complete agreement over 'Brexit', spitting rage. Lewis said that if his wife received 'so much as an enquiry about her status here, that's it – I move to Norway and become Norwegian. I won't stay in a country like that, whatever the outcome.' This was, actually, not a digression, but a conversation about limbo on the winter's journey, and the loss for me of what my father had loved in Beethoven. 'Beethoven,' Lewis reflects, 'is the most complete composer of all, because of this sense of resolution. But in my own life, I don't feel that I've arrived anywhere that is a culmination. I'm not sure there ever is such a place, and that is what makes Schubert the most human of all composers. The fact that there's no escape means it does not have to be as bleak as it appears. In real life, what do we escape from? Very little, and it's possible to come to terms with that.'

But how did he convey such thoughts, that night playing *Winterreise*?

'We're talking about details here,' he says, 'the way I try to convey spaces between notes and notes between notes, and I'm thinking primarily of the chord that announces the last passage of the *Winterreise*, the hurdy-gurdy man.' Lewis is about to share his secret. 'It's a bare fifth, an open fifth,' he says, 'it's the most ambitious thing a composer can write – let me show you.' We go to the back of the house, where he lifts the lid of an upright piano and plays three notes, making a discarnate, shadowy sound. 'They are B, F-sharp and a grace note of E-sharp. It's not major, it's not minor. There is as little harmonic information here as it's possible to play. It's open to any direction. Playing them together, you get this discord, this clash, and you are left with just the starkness of the open fifth.' So how does it work to such effect at the close of *Winterreise*? 'I apply the right pedal, so as to get a slow release. I play all three notes with the pedal down, and the slow release means that the bare open fifth doesn't come into view suddenly – it infuses the music that follows like a kind of echo, it's like the turning of a knife, to introduce the ghostly, grotesque vision of the hurdy-gurdy man, and bleed it into what follows.'

The Mexican poet Homero Aridjis coined this phrase: 'the ghost or sun of the instant just ended'[10] – seeping into, and infusing, the next. Lewis's idea is a variation on that idea as pure musicianship, on the premise that 'notation can only take you so far. In this open fifth, the lack of information is the purest information. It has the least amount of information possible; the information is in its very bareness, and in that it is very like Beckett.'

As Beckett implied across his work, as Lewis now demonstrates, as we come to learn in life: when even words fail – when the real world fails, dammit – we have the music.

7" Single: Postcard from Amsterdam

The sound builds, and builds, to bursting. A bath of noise, vast, loud but beautiful. Electronic thunderclaps crash into and around the room – this should be terrifying, especially to me, but for some reason it isn't. The music has no key or apparent direction, but heaves like the inhalation and exhalation of some huge celestial lung, breathing winds of creation and destruction. A vertical cinema screen shows a desolate landscape, land blessed by the absence of people, which looks like some distant planet but is actually Iceland, shot from a camera fixed to a drone. The music grows, accumulates, within and without one's outer, middle and inner ears, through one's pores . . .

This is the fifteenth edition of the Sonic Acts Festival, entitled 'The Noise of Being' – a three-day electro-sound fest, a cinema–seminar–light blitz, centred on the Paradiso in Amsterdam. Other events take place between 23 and 05 hours at a former school on the city outskirts, others again at the Stedelijk, the modern art museum; it's the kind of occasion the Dutch are cool enough to pull off intelligently without trying. The audiences, mostly from Holland, Germany, Italy and America, are earnest but fun: one man has his hair tied up in a spiral like a beehive;

a lady with electric-purple hair wears a tiger-print jumpsuit and military boots.

The core of the festival is this performance of Third Law *by Roly Porter from Bristol, the most interesting man and musician on this contemporary scene and, for me, doorman to a weird and wonderful Europe the existence of which I'd had no idea about. Porter is accompanied by the German artist Marcel Weber, a sculptor in light and maker of films with cameras fixed to drones, doing with film what Liam Young does with sound. This is Porter's programme note, defining his project:*

> *Mankind will never travel to the stars. Too long the journey, too weak the body. But our drones will. Satellites will become our eyes and ears in the most remote places. The Oculus Rift of the future is a mental connection between the traveller, whose body remains comfortably on Earth, and its avatar – a drone in deep space. While drones roam the skies the traveller dreams the journey. Each outward step into space becomes an inward one, into the mind, the home of the Self. Once the avatars venture into unthinkable realms, how will the traveller's mind make sense of the sensory input? If our senses are stimulated by solar storms, gamma ray blasts and supernovae, how will deep space dreaming feel? The stage performance for Third Law aims to construct this experience. It alters the reality of the concert venue with video projections, stroboscopic lights and intense stage fog. An epileptic warning is mandatory.*

I'm not sure I believe this, much as I'd love to. The last thing I would wish on any 'remote place' is a lot of clutter assembled by a failed species that has already cluttered its own habitat to death. I'm not even sure I want my home to be my Self. But none of this matters: here is music intended to come from – and aimed at – as far from the real world as possible.

On the screen, there's what looks like a star-storm, like when you shake a sparkler, only bigger and brighter. The pressure of Porter's sound intensifies – if there was an aural needle in your head to measure decibel, kilohertz, megahertz and impact, it would be pushing against the outer edges of the red zone. The music reflects itself, inexplicably, between both mind and brain – Oliver Sacks take note – echoing from one to the other, between the ears. The head is full, but nerves inexplicably intact. Then there's an instruction on the screen: 'For the next part, please close your eyes until the blinding light fades. Don't be afraid, you will see with your eyes closed.'

I watch the light show with eyes wide shut, but then of course disobey the instruction and half-open them to behold the forbidden sight. I have never seen anything so bright. Where beams of white light cross, there is a lilac colour. The air is thick with dry ice, but I can just about make out shadowy figures standing there, like that scene in Steven Spielberg's Close Encounters of the Third Kind, *when the alien spacecraft door opens and its passengers emerge. I get a squint of something ritualistic, like a space-mass. One man stretches his arms heavenwards, a woman weeps.*

Porter has his eyes open, but lowered towards his console. The music reaches almost-breaking point, a high plain, a chord held. Then, gradually, it settles, the explosions fade, the thunder abates, and into the aftermath a sparse melody rings – a note and its echo, really – the first attempt at melody this evening, progressing into a simple, beautiful six-note tune – reminiscent of the five-tone sequence 're-mi-do-do-so' (the second 'do' an octave below the first) and accompanied by Kodály's hand signals for teaching music to the deaf with which man communicates with the aliens in Spielberg's film. Here is music reaching through time and space, further than the eye or mind – but not the ear – can perceive.

What is this, and why is it not terrifying?

On the night of a winter sunset in early 2017, through freezing temperatures under an emergent new moon, I drove through

Dorset and played, as loud as my car stereo could manage, *Third Law*. Although this electronic symphony contains moments of beauty, it is, as even reviews from its own alternative musical scene acknowledge, uneasy listening. And especially for me and others who know war, let alone have been diagnosed with shell shock: there are explosive convulsions of what sounds like shellfire, while other passages are assailed by the kind of electronic machine-gun fire Cale unleashed at the Barbican. This music should be fearsome at best, wall-jumping-dangerous at worst. But it felt oddly serene, apposite to the glory of oncoming night and the first stars. Why? 'I often wonder,' Porter says, 'why is thunder not frightening? Was thunder frightening to people before they knew what it was?

'Thunder was never frightening to me as a child – and when I found out what it was, I was half sad and half in wonder: trying to get my head around the fact that this is air exploding from temperature and pressure. And when these mysteries are explained, they become even more mind-boggling.' Porter had written this music to try and capture, among other things, the sound of thunder, a natural phenomenon, not that of shellfire. His intentions had turned what could have been a menacing, even traumatic, sound into something beautiful – and this reaches the ear of the beholder.

In conversation back home in Bristol, he asks himself the question: 'What is it that I call music?' He begins his answer: 'I believe every idea has a sound. And that all the input I need exists in sound, only you do not know what that sound is.' Porter recalls his days as a 'committed junglist', playing dance music, and explains how 'most dub tracks have their bass line in G. But I preferred – and still do – an E-flat, which is not within reach of most systems. So you are not hearing the sub-bass of *Third Law* on the system in your car, or even most clubs, but your brain is backwards-calculating to tell you it is there, because we inherently understand the harmonic series so well.'

These considerations led him to replay a series of lectures given by Leonard Bernstein at Harvard in 1973, named after Charles Ives' strangest and finest piece, *The Unanswered Question*. Bernstein talked about 'overtones' that accompany a note and a sound simultaneously even though they are not played – 'harmonics' in music. 'And I wondered,' says Porter, 'what is the harmonic series? What is this relationship between music and sound? I've tried to explain this fundamental concept to myself, I've spent my life deliberating it.'

Then comes his striking idea: 'There was a moment, listening to Beethoven's Piano Concerto No. 5, the "Emperor". It's in the second movement. There is one fall in there, one sequence of notes, and it was a life-changing moment for me. In that phrase is a mathematical and spiritual truth about the universe. It isn't a truth about which notes are made physically in the universe, or even a truth about music. I realized . . . that within those notes is encoded a truth as fundamental as that one plus one equals two. There was no musical engagement in this realization; but it is a mystery and a truth that are only conceivable on a musical scale. This is my belief,' Porter says boldly: 'that the harmonic series is essential to the human experience. It is not a by-product of evolution. It would lessen my life and philosophical beliefs if I did think that this experience of music is a by-product of evolution. I am convinced it exists in a different form, in a different place, because it has to, because it's a universal truth. Something that is permanent, that is revealed to us who are impermanent.'

Porter recalls a scene in 'that awful film *The Day the Earth Stood Still*', when an alien meets a professor, played by John Cleese, and completes his calculation on the blackboard. 'But,' he says, 'then the alien hears a passage of Bach, and realizes that mankind already has the intelligence to comprehend all these mysteries.

In the same way that physicists are obsessed with celestial bodies, I am obsessed with that sequence of notes in Beethoven. That is the point at which Pythagoras began, and we haven't got much further, really.'

7" Single: Postcard from the Night Train

John Cale has a song, my favourite of his, I think, called 'Half Past France' from *Paris 1919*. At the Barbican, it had started with a vast electronic-orchestral sound, then the line: 'I suppose I'm glad I'm on this train.' The song strikes a balance between detachment and immersion, quirk and epic, understatement and thrust. It has apparent elegance, wherein lie fragmentation and collapse, like the royal palace of Versailles before the Revolution, and the treaty signed there 130 years later. At the Brooklyn concert in November 2017, Cale tore his own song apart – he almost emasculated it – into dissonant shards of sound just about held together by a huge musical undertow; as if bits of the train were falling off as it hurtled, reminiscent of the close of the second movement of Mahler's Ninth Symphony where 'he allows his orchestra to fall apart like a machine shedding its parts one by one', as the programme note to a performance of the symphony, conducted by Esa-Pekka Salonen, read.[1]

And here I am on a train, half past vast France, rattling south from Paris to Italy through plains, hills and forests, with a bottle of wine, staring out at passing Dijon: empty station platforms, sulphur-yellow lights, factory yards, then darkness again. Some time later, houses along the shores of Lake Geneva in the dark, like necklace-beads of light along the water's edge. Dawn breaks over Chiasso and Domodossola, where in the old days Italian customs would wake you – young and eager for the south, as again now – demanding passports. No longer – only Britain needs to do that, while over 450 million others criss-cross real Europe without hindrance.

I love the purgatory of a long train ride. It's like inhabiting a drone; watching a long film unfold through the window, distance travelled and time passed in harmony with one another, unlike the weirdness of aircraft. I have myself become a spoiled Wanderer of sorts, more physically comfortable than Schubert's but with no idea where I belong or live, or which signposts to follow. In his biography of Shelley, Richard Holmes uses the expressions 'the encroaching condition of exile' and 'the process of self-exile' to describe the poet – something I have felt all my life, and feel more than ever now. By the time he left the stifling England of 1818 to live in Italy, Shelley had become 'a complete exile, both geographically and spiritually', writes Holmes. To date, I'd achieved only the latter. For me, exile is home and vice versa.[2]

If Cale is a heavy-hearted traitor to his homeland, I am a proud one to mine. I'd spent much of my professional life writing about the importance to people of home, homeland, homestead and hearth: Bosnians who'd watched their homes burned but returned to rebuild them; Mexicans reflecting on the villages they had left, to migrate to *el norte*; Irish songs about distant mountains never to be seen again. But I'd reached a point at which I had wandered myself out of a home. Perhaps the loveliest piece by the Greek composer Mikis Theodorakis – another musician to be imprisoned for his art and beliefs – is entitled 'What Homeland Do You Want to Go To?' – but I had no idea what or where my homeland was.

Not the deserts of Arizona to which I tried a move in 2011, only to lose two thousand vinyl LP records and a thousand books, 'released for destruction' by US Customs – 'to a landfill called eBay,' joked a friend. Replacing the collection has been a major endeavour since – while I lost a further $200,000 on the value of the house there, due to the contortions of an inept real-estate agent and a criminal tenant.

This continent across which the train now speeds is home, but one from which I may be excluded by the curse, stigma and humiliation of my nationality once Britain has 'negotiated' itself into isolation; the other difference with Shelley therefore is that he – like Byron and Keats, also in flight from belligerent reaction back home – had no obstacle to his right of abode in Europe. Yet home is certainly not where I was born and raised, and this is hard: I'd become worse than uncomfortable in the city – now a demolition and construction site – to which I ostensibly belonged, and worse still in Notting Hill. While people I interviewed in Colombia dreamed of returning to the fields from which they had been displaced by violence and poverty, my own *Heimat* (a good German word for which we have no quite equivalent translation) had been contrarily ravaged by money. I feel differently dislocated – from a place that bears no resemblance to the one in which I grew up.

Then, on the night of 14 June 2017, a tower block I had watched go up, splitting the horizon from my bedroom window towards Shepherds Bush, caught fire. No one will ever know how many people asleep in Grenfell Tower that night died a fiery death one dared not imagine, but now must. All that is for certain is that the Royal Borough of Kensington and Chelsea, richest in the land, had been warned over and over by these tenants at the poor end of its fiefdom that the building was an inferno waiting

to happen – and did nothing. That same 'authority' that squab-
bled with the various utility companies about who should fix
Dad's heating while he froze. After the Grenfell fire, Mum and I
would pause in what was my bedroom, now her studio, to stare at
the outrageous crematorium in the sky.

I was unable to keep away from the site around which those
heartbreaking notices went up, as they had done in New York in
2001: 'Missing', with smiling faces, and desperate numbers to
call. Flowers and tributes, as in Washington Square. I played Rage
Against the Machine, as I had back in New York. And Radiohead,
as we had done back in Johnny's Bar – that song about 'How To
Disappear Completely'. I hosted a discussion with survivors of
the fire – 'survivors', that word I'd used for twenty-five years
since Bosnia – now within two minutes' bike ride from where I
was born. All that – now come 'home', viscerally local, but no
home of mine.

What a funny life I've led, unable to separate journalistic privilege from curiosity-killed-the-cat. Since that first trip to Northern Ireland as a student: cursed and blessed by specializing in
what the news calls 'hot spots', unable to leave it at that and
determined to join the dots, figure out what is really happening,
explore what Italians call *dietrologia*, the science of what lies
behind things. Needing to be in Berlin that night, needing to go
back and back to Bosnia during and after the carnage, trying in
vain to understand Why? Needing to go to Auschwitz under
snow with a survivor on the anniversary of the day he left on the
Death March. Needing to risk my life in Mexico to understand
narco traffic because I know that only by understanding narco
traffic can one understand capitalism. Needing also to set all this
to music, in some way. Trying to figure out how the music and
musicians fit in, or don't.

Since we left Gare de Lyon I've been reading two books, by

Shelley and Albert Camus. Shelley provides a literary way of helping us navigate the dilemma that has haunted this book: how far to separate music from context, and vice versa. The most 'political' of the Romantics, Shelley makes a point with regard to what we are trying to say – differently – about the circumstances of Hans Krása or Karel Ančerl or Shostakovich, about what Paul Kantner thought he was doing: Shelley, writes his biographer Holmes, 'did not say that great literature actually produced great revolutions or vice-versa. He seemed rather to feel that the two ran a mysteriously parallel course – "unfailing companion and follower"', as Shelley himself put it. He called the great poets 'the hierophants of an unapprehended inspiration, the mirrors of the gigantic shadows which futurity casts upon the present'. 'There is nothing here', adds Holmes, 'about the conscious intention of a writer in predicting new inventions or social institutions, nor about the writer as some kind of clairvoyant. It is rather that in what the writer produces naturally, the future pressures and contradictions and achievements of his society are *unconsciously expressed*' – and Holmes applies a musical analogy: 'the writer is a kind of tuning-fork for a melody yet to be composed'.[3]

This is what we are trying to say about music, and we can invert that: these composers' pieces and songs are pens for a poem yet to be written.

This journey down through France and Italy lasts thirteen hours, and I've also been re-rereading, in between scenes from the movie outside the window, my credo novel since schooldays, *La Peste* (The Plague) by Camus (like Shostakovich, a football fanatic – also a semi-professional goalkeeper). It's a book we should all read every five to ten years, and it makes it impossible to remain in Schubert's limbo with his repeated note through *Winterreise*, or with the long-time count of the drones.

To explain: Beckett was born seven years before Camus, and

was actually less indifferent towards the world than his character Molloy was towards his fictional world, as was Camus himself compared with his anti-hero of *La Chute* (The Fall). Both writers were active in the French Resistance – presumably, for a reason. And in *La Peste* absurdity becomes a source of value, values, and even action. Camus wrote elsewhere about 'the wine of the absurd and the bread of indifference which will nourish [man's] greatness'.

The group of men (Camus was never very good at women) inhabiting *La Peste*'s narrative variously represent all human response to real-world calamity. Each takes his turn to tell it, although it is the doctor, Rieux – the hidden narrator – who battles the pestilence with his work, medicine, just as Camus tried to battle injustice in Algeria, later fascism, with his labour in words. Rieux and his friend Tarrou demonstrate that, although they know they are powerless against plague, they can bear witness to it, and struggle against it, if only as Sisyphus struggled against the gradient (theme of a philosophical essay by Camus) – and this is in itself of value. When he accepted the Nobel Prize for Literature in 1957, Camus' magnificent speech urged that it was the honour and burden of the writer 'to do so much more than write' – implying that words alone fail, or lack meaning, unless they lead to or convey something else. Most of the musicians discussed in this book feel the same about music.

Camus saw no dichotomy between the emptiness at the heart of *L'Étranger* (The Outsider) or *La Chute* and the purposeful endeavours of *La Peste*. The fact of absurd powerlessness is no reason not to act: Camus offers us a way of abandoning our pointless quest for 'oneness' with ourselves while urging us to carry on fighting nevertheless, for some ill-defined moral justice, even though we have long ceased to be able to define it or even believe in its attainability.

At the conclusion to *La Peste*, Rieux – whose wife has died of illness elsewhere, unconnected with the pestilence – watches families and lovers reunite when the gates of Oran are finally opened. He wonders – in the wake of so much suffering and pointless struggle – whether there can be peace of mind or fulfilment without hope, and concludes that yes, perhaps there can, for those 'who knew now that if there is something one can always yearn for, and sometimes attain, it is human love'. These are the people 'whose desires are limited to man and his humble yet formidable love', and who 'should enter, if only now and again, into their reward'.[4] But Rieux has already qualified these words before he has written them, a few lines earlier: 'But for those others, who aspired beyond and above the human individual towards something they could not even imagine, there had been no answer.'

So for anyone accursed by 'aspiring beyond', no answer. No description, not even of what that 'something' might be. And yet it nags, it makes demands of us, and those who identify with Rieux know what it is, though we have abandoned a definition. Pointless, but imperative; political to a degree, but impatient with politics; religious, whether with a God or without; moral, certainly, but uneasily – and with serious regard to that vastness in nature against which – Camus reminds us throughout his work – our mortality measures itself. Surrounded by that mortality, Rieux strives against the plague, because he cannot do otherwise.

The Irish band U2 put the same idea differently in their famous song 'I Still Haven't Found What I'm Looking For', sung by a character who climbs mountains, crosses fields and scales city walls in search of 'what' – not 'who', note – he's looking for, which eludes him.

Back in Paris, I had surprised myself: by taking my place among a vast throng on *la pelouse* of the Stade de France for the ultimate night of stadium rock: U2 playing a thirtieth-anniversary tour of their *Joshua Tree* album, to which I'd listened while driving along tens of thousands of miles of road. There was poetry across a vast screen while we waited – 'even in heaven they don't sing all the time', from Lawrence Ferlinghetti's 'The World is a Beautiful Place'. Bono doffed a learned cap to Paris as the city to which Joyce and Beckett had come, and to a long shared history between the republics. His discourse from the stage set the album and its life into his own, and ours. 'Where are we now?' he cried during 'Bad' – since you ask, my mind's eye was back in the Lakota badlands, listening to the song on headphones at dawn one morning there, but also here, in France, in 2017. He said that after thirty years the band was 'still trying to figure out' what each song was about, 'it had changed so much over all these years'.

It was monstrous in some ways, but magnificent. By the time we got to 'Miss Sarajevo', performed against a backdrop of camps for refugees from Syria, from my war to this one, I became aware that I was crying. 'Where you're going was never really there,' said Bono. 'And I still haven't found what I'm looking for,' he sang.

I was so taken aback, I went again the following night, mostly to concentrate not on myself but on The Edge, one of the few guitarists who can claim to have invented a 'genre' – that long-chord wall-of-sound. I remembered complaints about U2 moving part of their business from Ireland to Holland for tax reasons; I heard the voices of friends who loathe this group's claim to righteousness, and that of the man in a record shop in London: 'I saw them in 1987, and I'm still embarrassed.' And I didn't care. When did we complain about the way Diego Maradona or Alessandro Del Piero would score a goal? Maybe we need stars to remind us that they too can speak what we think: 'There's no end to grief,' he said after another dose of 'Miss Sarajevo', 'that's how we know there's no end to love.' Something must be bugging him. I wondered: the second song of the second evening was 'A

Sort of Homecoming', after which he asked: 'Where's home?' Good question, I thought. Then he said: 'Maybe it's here!' I don't think he meant the Stade de France; I inferred that he meant the song was home.

I'm aware that U2 is not everyone's music, even if they are the biggest band in the world. But this book has been about my music – some of it, I've left out more than I've included. And perhaps some of these ideas may connect to whatever you listen to. Most music, after all, comes and goes without us noticing or knowing. One group that had passed me by was the Eagles of Death Metal: not bad, not much good either – and I find their all-American views on Donald Trump and frontman Jesse Hughes's dictum that 'everyone has to have guns' execrable. This latter stance made the band's appearance in the history of this country through which my train had taken me all the more ironic, on the night of 13 November 2015, when the Eagles of Death Metal took the stage at the Bataclan theatre in Paris.

Finale: 'We Can Change the World'

Graham Nash, Paris, 2015–2016
Marianne Faithfull, Bataclan theatre, Paris, November 2016

There was something creepily untrodden about the floorboards. The red velveteen seats showed no sign of wear, the same mint material as the curtains that framed the stage and skirted the parapet at the front of the balcony. The wood along the bar had been hewn uncomfortably recently, the metalwork factory-fresh. Even the pastel paint in which the Alphonse Mucha reproductions had been executed was pristine. But this is not a new theatre – this is the Bataclan in Paris, entirely refurbished, defiantly reopened. A year and a few days after 'Islamic State' gunmen burst in and opened fire on a crowd of young people, killing eighty-nine and wounding many more. There exists a picture of the audience, taken from the stage two minutes before the attack: poised but not posed, to watch a band. Daesh described them in its claim of responsibility as 'hundreds of idolatrous sinners at a festival of perversion'; as their faces show, they are my children and anyone's.

Stéphane and his girlfriend Corinne were 'holding hands, when this incredible noise filled our ears and made everything else silent. Neither of us were hit, but we fell to the floor out of instinct.' We meet, the three of us, at a café by the St Martin Canal, not far from the Bataclan and even nearer to restaurants and bars also victim to Daesh's murderous rampage – 130 were killed in all, that night, and hundreds wounded, one hundred seriously. 'We lay,' continues Corinne, 'and the gunmen started shouting. In French, though I cannot recall what they said. It was panicky, screaming, insults, shouting about Allah. There was an awful smell – I can't place it, gunpowder maybe, a deadly smell. And there was moaning, sobbing, cries of pain.'

Stéphane remembers: 'We were like a blanket of people, on the floor. It was wet, from spilled drinks. If anyone screamed or panicked or pleaded for mercy, the reply was a gunshot. I whispered to Corinne, "Play dead. If we are going to live, we have to play dead."' 'I tried to lie as still as possible, with my eyes open, staring,' says Corinne. 'I imagined those people who sit or stand completely still outside the Beaubourg, wearing masks or painted gold. I tried to be one of them.'

Sandra, whose parents are from Latin America but who lives in Paris, found herself able to run up a stairwell, towards the balcony, and to text her father Mauricio. 'Papa, I'm at a concert. They are killing people.' 'My treasure, stay still. Oh God, you are alive.' 'Papa, I'm alive. I'm scared.' Now, she says, 'I find it hard to remember the sounds in there. The shouting of the men. The screaming of the people. The guns, they were so, so loud.'

'When the police came in,' continues Stéphane, 'the noise was deafening. Guns firing everywhere. I thought: That's it – we're all dead. But no. One of the men, dressed like a Ninja warrior, grabbed Corinne and shouted at me to follow him into a corridor. We passed dead people, lifeless on the floor. I saw them only for a moment, like in a nightmare. Then we were safe, and Corinne began sobbing – out of gratitude I think, that we were alive – and disbelief.'

The theatre had reopened with a concert by Sting, to which survivors of the attack were invited, and those with connections obtained tickets. A second concert was given, poignantly, by a band called Tinariwen, from the mainly Muslim country of Mali, itself assailed by Islamist violence. The band played wall-of-sound guitar music, combining major chord *lifts with chromatics from their native land. And at a certain point, the wave of sound across the crowd invoked a howl, and seemed like an exorcism, a purging, a reclaiming.*

Two nights later Marianne Faithfull took the stage, a survivor of a different kind – muse and fashion accessory to the Rolling Stones, she had rebelled against her role as an adjunct to that man's world and turned instead towards an odyssey through heroin, rage, Kurt Weill and a new role in Paris as Grande Dame. She remains the great beauty, but now needs a cane to reach the front of the stage.

Marianne reclined into an armchair, lit a cigarette and poured herself a whiskey. 'Oh, I know, I know,' she said sardonically, in her plummy, gleefully debauched Catholic-girls'-school voice. Then she addressed a spellbound audience: 'It's impossible for us to imagine what happened here a year ago, or to find the right words to say. So we'll try and say it with music, listen to these lovely, talented young men play for you; I don't know why music manages that, but it just does, somehow.'

During the days and nights after the attack on the Bataclan and elsewhere in the city, citizens of Paris, France and all Europe placed tributes along the railings outside, stretching for hundreds of metres along the Boulevard Voltaire. Flowers, candles, flags, football scarves and messages of grief and remembrance, like a rock-and-roll version of Washington Square after 11 September 2001. Among them, a suspended vinyl disc on which someone had written: 'Rock will kill you', and a black boot with roses stuffed into it, and on the side, in silver ink: 'Rock in Peace'.

In May 2017 there was another appalling attack by an Islamist on a pop concert, this time in Manchester at a performance by the American star Ariana Grande. One difference from the Bataclan attack was that because of Ariana's fan base, the twenty-two people killed – by a suicide bomb – were mainly much younger, children and teenagers: the youngest was aged eight. Another was in the response of the emergency services:

although Daesh murdered scores at the Bataclan, the quick response of the French police saved hundreds more, whereas in Britain two fire crews that were within earshot of the attack were sent speeding away from it to a location three miles away.

Marianne Faithfull had been among the first artists to contact the Bataclan and register to perform. 'The drama touched a wide circle of musicians, directly or indirectly,' says Jules Frutos, co-founder of Alias, the company that manages the theatre. But within a year of the reopening, though the Bataclan could now accommodate two hundred more people than the fifteen hundred of before the attack, the number of concerts had been reduced by a fifth. During refurbishment, 'we weren't exactly overwhelmed by calls from producers wanting their artists to play here,' laments Frutos. One of those who did return to play was the singer Zazie, but only after having worked hard to persuade her band, one of whom lost a friend in the attack. Some musicians even criticized the reopening, Nicola Sirkis saying that it should become a sanctuary.[1] For Frutos, such a notion would entail 'an intolerable victory for those who committed those crimes'.

It was the Bataclan massacre – the idea that people should be killed for listening to music – and my partial escape to Paris that hauled me from limbo and *Die Winterreise* and back to Camus' Dr Rieux. There was something about the Bataclan that, in the spirit of Camus' doctor, made it impossible to end this book and leave you with the infinite ennui of the drone or of Schubert's hurdy-gurdy man in the snow. Something that made me need to hand the denouement over to someone else, whose art and essence resist stasis.

There were two concerts in Paris spanning the Daesh attacks of 13 November 2015: the first, two weeks before, by Crosby, Stills & Nash at the Olympia theatre, and another – more rewardingly intimate – soon afterwards by Graham Nash at the

Cigale, playing his own music with the accomplished session guitarist Shane Fontayne.

Foreseeing 'Brexit', in pursuit of somewhere to call home, and with terrible debts paid by selling all I had in London, I elected to spend what remained on a little flat in Paris, in the hope that payment of property tax in the European Union before the referendum might decrease my chances of getting stuck on the British island. I quickly found my local *café du coin*, Bar Naguere, a block away from Montparnasse Cemetery, where I gratefully made the acquaintance of regulars at *apéritif* hour. One of them asked me on my third night there, out of the blue: '*Et qu'est-ce que vous avez fait, monsieur, avec la fraîcheur du jour cet après-midi?*' Since he kindly asked, I replied, I had been to visit the poets and writers in the cemetery, as every day: Beckett, Baudelaire, de Beauvoir, Sartre and Susan Sontag, whom I helped bury *là-bas*. '*Ah*,' he said wistfully, '*ce sont nos voisins.*'

Another regular was an Englishman, Ronan Hyder, with whom I became friends, a film editor frustrated that he has to earn a crust by working for a curtain company. Among his recent commissions was to arrange for the new red velveteen curtains and balcony frontage at the Bataclan. Ronan talked about the commission casually. 'We got the specs – lengths of rod and pieces of velveteen. And they still had bits of human tissue on them. Jelly on the rods, bits of brain on the material. Globules of flesh on everything. I did wonder: Don't the police want this stuff?' He sighed, and ordered another beer, saying that his work entitled him to a free ticket to the Bataclan reopening night with Sting. 'Nah,' said Ronan, 'I never want to see those things again.'

If John Cale's music had helped rescue me from a vain hope in broken ideals, Graham Nash's rescued me from despair in the limbo of incertitude – and, accordingly, this book from ending rudderless in the doldrums. If there was one man whose songs could pull my mindset and music out from the dark lure and brilliance of 'Wasteland' and *Die Winterreise*, it was Nash. We met after each of his performances in Paris and arranged to talk further in America – conversations that brought the wheel full circle to what a therapist I consulted calls 'the undamaged core'. It was in part because of Nash's song 'Chicago' that I'd felt summoned to that city in 1971: 'Won't you please come to Chicago,' he'd sung, 'no one else can take your place' – I took that personally. He also promised: 'We can change the world,' which I believed then, believe no longer, but Camus had dealt with that; and Nash can too.

'You want to learn about the power of music?' he asks rhetorically. 'ISIS made the point themselves, right here at the Bataclan. It's strategy on their part to disturb the safety of every day . . . But on a primal level, far deeper: killing people because they were *listening to music*? Are you kidding me? This has been going on, of course, for centuries in one way or another, right up to burning Beatles records in America. But the Bataclan was music's *Kristallnacht*. So, ISIS, you can't tolerate music? You can't take music? In that case music must be doing something right!'

So: Music, what's going on? – he's recalling his thought at the Hendrix concert in London half a century ago, making a very English cup of tea in his small apartment on Manhattan's Lower East Side. 'We're supposed to be getting through the day, figuring out how to eat, procreate, preferably not get killed. But there's always this need for music, or there's a tune you heard this morning that you can't get out of your head, like an earworm, it takes over everything! We're human, and it's always music, for some reason.' As a songwriter, he says, 'I'm an imbecile on the page; I couldn't read or write music on a stave if I tried. Music happens in my head, and songs get written on the back of a napkin. I have to really feel what I'm writing, it has to affect me, I have to please myself with whatever it is I am hoping to please others with – I don't want to waste your time with a shitty song.

'It starts with melody, and rhythm and bits of poetry, going around my head. I've a couple of dozen songs in my mind at any given time, things I've forgotten but which stay on as songs, that need to marinate before they drop off the conveyor belt as a song. It's like a muscle, songwriting – if you're curious enough and keep it exercised, you keep the blood going. If not, it atrophies.' But, says Nash, 'when you get to typing words for a song, you become those words, you are the words you type.' As with Cale's method-acting: 'I have to become the pen, I have to *be* the song. It's hard to hide from yourself; writing songs is like the Wizard of Oz, tearing down the curtains to see who's there – who are you?'

Nash can look back at hundreds of songs with one of the world's leading ensembles: 'We were good at it, at our best, understanding what the others were doing, echoing it, sending it back, having a conversation in sound. This is not Bach, Mozart or Beethoven, but I do believe we've brought happiness and even inspiration – and if we have ... People have said we're the soundtrack to their lives – it's an easy thing to say, but think about it: our music means so much to someone they call it "the soundtrack to their lives"! It's a fantastic compliment, and pretty terrifying!'

Of his time with Crosby and Stills: 'There's a certain special beauty, when you take a song, work it out melodically and lyrically, but sing it with three voices, not one – make the three voices one voice. When good lyrics are put to music, it's like a double arrow to your heart, and when it comes out together as three or more voices, there's a mysterious gift, a magic in that.' But there's more to it than this: 'I do believe,' says Nash, 'that music is for the good.' He insists: 'Take music in schools. It's always the first thing to be cut. But it should be the last thing ... It's been shown over and over again that children who have learned music to a certain standard have a better view of themselves, are less likely to get into a fight, less likely to become a bully, more open, aware of the rest of the world. You have to be an insane and insensitive institution to want to cut music, let alone ban it, like ISIS. You think people can grow without learning about music? It goes back to the blackboard jungle in Salford where I grew up, when I was "slippered" for bunking off school to go and buy tickets for Bill Haley and the Comets playing in Manchester. It's all backwards – music should be the one thing that's *kept in*.'

The most striking thing about both of Nash's concerts in Paris is that they were entirely beyond cynicism or despair. In the first, Crosby sang the impatient 'Long Time Gone'; Nash, his anthem 'Teach Your Children'. There was a twist to the second, at the Cigale: 'Shane Fontayne', who had played with the bigger band in October but now accompanied just Nash, is the stage name of a man with whom I was at school, Mick Barakan: he was a good guitarist then, with a band called Byzantium, and used to play in concerts during lunch hour – now he plays with the best.

And something happened: the song after the interval was 'Military Madness', Nash's seething lament for just that, and the 'solitary sadness' it generates, about which I know too much. Before the song, Mick Barakan approached the microphone, and said: 'Ed Vulliamy is a very brave man. This is for him.' If relating that constitutes showing off, I apologize – but I do so only because I don't think I've ever been more gratefully proud.

On both nights, Nash sang 'Chicago' with as much passion for the generic Chicago of now as he did for the city in revolt in 1968–9. 'We can change the world' had rung out through the crowd at the Olympia, in harmony with Crosby and Stills, and it did a few months later with Barakan – even louder, perhaps. Whether true or not, this is the credo of the man behind the song: 'I have to think we can change the world, and that music is a driving force towards that end. I have to believe that truth and song can change the world, but that people have been taught not to think that nowadays – in fact, not to think at all. They can change the world, but they've been told they can't . . . The major corporations are saying: Lie down, be quiet, don't rock the boat. Let us sell you another gadget or pair of sneakers – that'll make you happy. So you have mass consensus . . . Isn't there that saying back in England that ignorance is bliss? Well I don't believe that and I never did.'

In his memoir Nash describes Crosby, Stills & Nash as 'flame-throwers in the best democratic sense'. 'Politics', he writes, 'has always been a staple of any CSN show.' Now, speaking for himself, he insists: 'Music was the essence of that movement in the sixties, and I have to believe that it can be again . . . Walter Cronkite was telling us the American [Vietnam War] death count all through dinner every night, and the changes that resulted from that had a musical soundtrack.

'Nowadays, the one thing they don't want is music that rocks the boat in Uranus – pun intended. Times are harder, for sure, but as an artist I have a duty to try my best to express what I believe with the means I have . . . and I have to convince others that they can too. Sometimes, when I'm singing to an audience, a feeling comes back that is real passion, real love, real yearning. There's a conversation with the audience . . . whatever energy I give out comes back from the audience, there's a cycle of giving and taking, emptying and filling. And with just Shane, that emptying and filling cycle is that much more intense, really communicating with people. I can see into their eyes, and they can see into ours. It's been very interesting, an exchange not just about the music but the state of the world, what happened in Paris, the spectre of Donald Trump. I can feel a real hunger out there for some kind of peace, but no one seems to be sure how to go about getting there.

'Sometimes,' he says, 'a song can turn out to be more than you intended.' He cites his best-known, 'Teach Your Children': 'It started out totally simple, about looking after kids on the road, and ends up being about the future of us all.' His song 'Cathedral' tiptoes into the territory of music and religion, written after a visit to Winchester Cathedral where, intimidated by the architecture, Nash looked down to see he was standing on the grave of a soldier who had died on his birthday in 1799. He responded with a complicated song about lying and dying 'in the name of Christ'. 'One of the reasons that song took me so long,' he says, 'is that it's about someone else's beliefs. It's not an attack on Christianity, I'm just pointing out a few things we should be thinking about, especially after what was done in the name of a perversion of religion at Bataclan.'

Nash was a war child of sorts: born at a maternity hospital in Blackpool to which women approaching childbirth were evacuated from areas under nightly bombardment by the Luftwaffe. His native Salford, part of Manchester, was one of them, and like me, Nash grew up playing on bomb sites. 'Salford, our neighbourhood, was a pile of rubble ... streets blown apart, huge craters in the landscape', he wrote in *Wild Tales: A Rock & Roll Life*.[2] His family was poor, and his father was arrested and jailed for receiving stolen goods (it turned out he was hiding the goods for his brother). The change jail wrought on his dad remains with Nash always. 'I came to the conclusion there was no such thing as true justice. And I began thinking that if this was the way things worked, then fuck justice ... I didn't need their rules and regulations.'[3]

Once in California, living with Joni Mitchell, Nash never came back, except to visit; his song 'Cold Rain', written when back in Manchester for his mother's funeral, speaks my own feelings.

Nash has a mission. 'What I want to do with these songs is to try and get little people to do big things.' We discuss an article we've seen about the guard who opened the gate in the Berlin Wall, letting the first crowd through it, East to West. Crosby, Stills

& Nash were part of all that, singing Nash's song 'Chippin' Away' right by the Wall days after it came down.

'Everyone knows you can't build a wall against ideas and aspirations. It was amazing to chip that wall down. People were getting shot down by Checkpoint Charlie, but when these kids in East Germany heard the music, and the ideas conveyed in the music emanating from the other side, no wall was going to stop them. The day before we got there, there was a radio interview. And I thought: OK, we don't have any equipment, let's make this simple. I said: "At 3.35 p.m., when the radio station plays the song, bring your little transistor sets, everyone, and we'll all sing it to accompaniment by all the radios." It was fantastic.'

Nash's most overt song about war and peace is 'Military Madness', as played at the Cigale in Paris. It connects his father's service in the Second World War and the bomb sites of his childhood with the war in Vietnam, as well as those in our mind's eye as we listen now: Iraq, Syria. 'When I first arrived in America, my eyes were opened to so many things: my own father going off to war, what was happening over there in Vietnam and what it was doing on the streets back here. As an artist, I thought: I have to respond to this. I'm proud that it is still as relevant now as it was then. But also depressed – what a nightmare to have to keep singing that song *for a reason*.'

His song 'After The Dolphin' takes his peace lyrics into our time, with its nightmarish visions of drone warfare, charting 'the "progress" from war that involves hitting someone over the head with a rock to sitting in Nevada playing a video game that kills innocent people far, far away, for nothing. What kind of "progress" is that?' I wonder whether anyone but Nash could have written a song as specific as 'Barrel Of Pain', about barrel bombs charged with chemical agents that make children 'glow' – as used by Syria's President Assad against his own entrapped people in Aleppo and Homs, as we speak. 'I wrote this in anger,' says Nash,

'I really want people to cry at the end of that song, if they get it. You have to try and impart this kind of information. Dammit I'm seventy-four, and we're losing a lot of people recently among the musicians and songwriters who want to communicate this stuff. Nowadays, the music industry throws any shit against the wall that happens to stick.'

Nash's songs take his views full circle, to his belief that music began with man trying to imitate the sounds of nature; and he entwines his songs about wars men fight against one another with those about the war fought by humankind against nature. 'Wind On The Water' is about the last whale, and Nash played it with Barakan at both Paris concerts. He is among the few to sing about 'not just changing the world, but changing it enough to save it' – although, he points out, 'If every single human being died this instant, the earth . . . would keep evolving and other life forms would emerge to replace us. When we say: "Save the Planet," we are saying: "Save Ourselves." We may not realize that yet, but we will do when the water rises above Miami, we lose Florida, Bangladesh long gone. People will ask: "What did we do to stop this?" "Did we stop every city from blazing all night?" "Did we cut back on our consumption?" If we can change the world, this is no longer because we want to, but because we have to . . .'

Nash pours another cup of tea and asks *me* a question, for once: 'Where and when would you like to have been in history?' I mumble something about Paris during the 1890s. And you, Graham? He does not hesitate. 'The premiere of Beethoven's Ninth Symphony, which he conducted but heard nothing of, stone deaf, and couldn't hear how the audience reacted afterwards either. It was all in his head . . . What is it about the human race?' he ponders. 'What would happen if someone found the violence gene in the human race and removed it?' What indeed, I reply – but what if they don't? 'Well,' he said, 'maybe music is part of its antithesis. When an audience sings "Chicago" and "Teach Your Children" like they do, it's moving, it's primitive, it's primal chant. We're all together at that point. When I see a conductor moving an orchestra with body language, getting the sound right, I'm watching a miraculous event. I'm touching an energy that comes through you, and must surely go somewhere. The music is saying something, it's saying: "Wow, this world is so fucked up, and so fantastic."'

We'd been talking for about five hours now, trying to figure out what it is that music does. 'But,' says Nash, 'we haven't quite got it have we? We haven't quite answered the question "What on earth is going on?" It's still a mystery isn't it?' And he had one final think. 'Maybe it's a kind of celestial id. You tend to play the blues in E, but I read somewhere recently that the universe resonates at a pitch of D. The celestial sound of the universe, going through its motions, it does its thing in D. Tell you what, are you free tomorrow? Do you want to come back, and we can talk a bit more and . . .'

Notes

1 Hendrix Comes East

1 See Jimi Hendrix, *Starting at Zero: His Own Story*, ed. Alan Douglas and Peter Neal (London: Bloomsbury, 2013).

2 Ibid.

3 Paul Gilroy, *Darker than Blue: On the Moral Economies of Black Atlantic Culture* (Cambridge, MA, and London: Harvard University Press, 2011), p. 130.

4 See Hendrix, *Starting at Zero*.

5 See ibid.

2 What on Earth Is Going On?

1 Homer, *The Odyssey*, trans. T.E. Lawrence (London: Collector's Library, 2004), p. 213.

2 Homer, *The Odyssey*, trans. E.V. Rieu (London: Penguin, 1946; rev. edn 1991), pp. 161–2.

3 Ibid., p. 158.

4 Arthur Schopenhauer, *The World as Will and Representation* (1819), 2 vols, trans. E.F.J. Payne (New York: Dover, 1969), vol. II, p. 163.

5 Richard Wagner, *Wagner on Music and Drama*, ed. Albert Goldman and Evert Sprinchorn, trans. H. Ashton Ellis (New York: Da Capo, 1964), pp. 179–80.

6 Ibid., pp. 234–5.

7 Hector Berlioz, *The Memoirs of Hector Berlioz*, trans. David Cairns (London: Gollancz, 1969; New York: Everyman's Library, 2002), p. 165.

8 Frances Densmore, *World of the Teton Sioux Indians. Their Music, Life & Culture*, ed. Joseph A. Fitzgerald (World Wisdom, Bloomington, 2016), pp. 83–4.]

9 Berlioz, *Memoirs*, p. 166.

10 Quoted in Alfred Einstein, *Mozart: His Character, His Work* (London: Cassell, 1946), p. 35.

11 Ibid., p. 39.

12 Paul Griffiths, *Olivier Messiaen and the Music of Time* (London: Faber and Faber, 2009), p. vii.

13 Thomas Mann, *Doctor Faustus*, trans. John E. Woods (New York: Knopf, 1997), p. 161.

14 Ibid., pp. 255–65.

15 David Evans, 'Goin' up the Country: Blues in Texas and the Deep South', in *Nothing But the Blues: The Music and the Musicians*, ed. Lawrence Cohn (New York: Abbeville, 1993), p. 49.

16 Robert Darden, *People Get Ready! A New History of Black Gospel Music* (London: Bloomsbury, 2005), p. 213.

17 Wolfgang Hildesheimer, *Mozart*, trans. Marion Faber (Original German, Frankfurt: Suhrkampf Verlag, 1977; New York: Farrar, Strauss, Giroux, 1982), p. 13.

18 Ibid., p. 9.

19 Ibid., p. 11.

20 Ibid., p. 18.

21 Ibid., p. 37.

22 Giacomo Leopardi, *Zibaldone: The Notebooks of Leopardi*, ed. Michael Caesar and Franco D'Intino, trans. Kathleen Baldwin et al. (London: Penguin, 2013), p. 2841.

23 Oliver Sacks, *Musicophilia: Tales of Music and the Brain* (New York: Picador, 2007), p. 15.

24 Ibid., p. 162.

25 Ibid., p. 165.

26 Daniel J. Levitin, *This Is Your Brain on Music: The Science of a Human Obsession* (New York: Dutton, 2006; London: Atlantic Books, 2008), p. 173.

27 Ibid., p. 127.

28 Sacks, *Musicophilia*, p. 51.

29 Bob Dylan, quoted in Ron Rosenbaum, 'The Playboy Interview: Bob Dylan', *Playboy* (March 1978).

30 Leopardi, *Zibaldone*, p. 1401, paragraphs 3422–4.

31 Ibid., p. 1402, paragraphs 3425–6.

32 Dr Alexandra Lamont on *Child of Our Time* (BBC, 11 July 2001).

33 Sacks, *Musicophilia*, p. 305.

34 Ibid., pp. 329–30.

35 Francis Newton (aka Eric Hobsbawm), *The Jazz Scene* (London: Penguin, 1961; London: Weidenfeld & Nicolson, 1989), p. 2.

36 Leopardi, *Zibaldone*, p. 806, paragraph 1781.

37 From Samuel Beckett, *Molloy* (London: Calder and Boyars, 1959), p. 168.

38 Tom Service, 'Symphony Guide: Mahler's First', *Guardian* (12 November 2013), online.

39 Leopardi, *Zibaldone*, p. 785, paragraphs 1721–2.

3 Double Entendre: Shostakovich Goes West

1 Elizabeth Wilson, *Shostakovich: A Life Remembered* (London: Faber and Faber, 1994), pp. 5, 7.
2 From Dmitry Shostakovich, *Story of a Friendship: The Letters of Dmitry Shostakovich to Isaak Glikman*, trans. Anthony Phillips (London: Faber and Faber, 2001), p. xix.
3 Ibid., p. xxii.
4 See Wilson, *Shostakovich*, Op. Cit. .
5 Quoted by Dmitri and Ludmilla Sollertinsky, *Pages from the Life of Dmitri Shostakovich*, trans. Graham Hobbs and Charles Midgley (New York: Harcourt Brace Jovanovich, 1980; London: Robert Hale, 1981), p. 83.
6 Ibid., pp. 92, 96.
7 Shostakovich, *Story of a Friendship*, p. 35.
8 David Rabinovich, *Dmitry Shostakovich, Composer*, trans. George Hanna (Moscow: Foreign Languages Publishing House, 1959), pp. 27–8.
9 Ibid., p. 31.
10 Ivan Martynov, *Dmitri Shostakovich: The Man and His Work*, trans. T. Guralsky (New York: Greenwood Press, 1947), pp. 45–7.
11 Victor Ilyich Seroff, *Dmitri Shostakovich: The Life and Background of a Soviet Composer* (New York: Knopf, 1943), pp. 169–71.
12 Ibid., p. 156.
13 Sollertinsky and Sollertinsky, *Life of Dmitri Shostakovich*, pp. 93–4.
14 Quoted by Richard Taruskin, 'Shostakovich and Us', in *Shostakovich in Context*, ed. Rosamund Bartlett (Oxford: Oxford University Press, 2000), p. 12.

7" Single: Viva Verdi! Una Vita Italiana

1 Max Bruschi, *Giuseppe Verdi. Note e noterelle* (Palermo: Sellerio, 2001), p. 3.
2 Mary Jane Phillips-Matz, *Verdi: A Biography* (Oxford: Oxford University Press, 1993), pp. 239–40.
3 Ibid., p. 191.
4 Ibid., p. 230.
5 Quoted in Giuseppe Verdi, *Verdi: The Man in His Letters*, ed. Franz Werfel and Paul Stefan, trans. Edward Downes (New York: L.B. Fischer, 1942), p. 345.
6 Quoted in Anthony Valerio, 'The Dante Society of Westchester', in *From the Margin: Writings in Italian Americana*, ed. Anthony Julian Tamburi et al. (West Lafayette, IN: Purdue University Press, 2000), p. 123.

5 'No Time for Love'

1 Christy Moore, *One Voice: My Life in Song* (London: Hodder and Stoughton, 2003), p. 89.

6 Floating Anarchy Radio: 'You Can't Unring the Bell!'

1 Newton, *The Jazz Scene*, pp. xi–xii.

2 Joe Boyd, *White Bicycles: Making Music in the 1960s* (London: Serpent's Tail, 2006).

7" Single: Dvořák in Iowa

1 Michael B. Beckerman, *New Worlds of Dvořák: Searching in America for the Composer's Inner Life* (New York: W.W. Norton, 2003).

2 Patricia Hampl, *Spillville* (Minneapolis: Milkweed Editions, 1987), p. 82.

3 Ibid., p. 85.

4 Beckerman, *New Worlds of Dvořák*, p. 151.

7 Fuck the Wall!

1 Leoš Janáček, *Leaves from His Life*, ed. and trans. Vilem and Margaret Tausky (London: Kahn and Averill, 1982), p. 36.

2 See Barry Miles, *Frank Zappa* (London: Atlantic, 2004).

8 Through the Wire

1 See Niklas Frank, *In the Shadow of the Reich* (New York: Alfred A. Knopf, 1991).

2 John le Carré, 'Why We Should Learn German', *Observer* (2 July 2017), p. 29.

3 Mann, *Doctor Faustus*, p. 183.

4 Misha Aster, *The Reich's Orchestra: The Berlin Philharmonic 1933–1945* (London: Souvenir Press, 2010), pp. 176–7.

5 Mann, *Doctor Faustus*, pp. 69–70.

6 Bryan Magee, *Aspects of Wagner* (London: Alan Ross, 1968), p. 29.

7 Bryan Magee, *The Tristan Chord: Wagner and Philosophy* (New York: Henry Holt, 2000), p. 84.

8 Robert Donington, *Wagner's 'Ring' and Its Symbols* (London: Faber and Faber, 1963), pp. 32–3.

9 Quoted in Laurence Dreyfus, *Wagner and the Erotic Impulse* (Cambridge, MA: Harvard University Press, 2010), p. 37.

10 George Bernard Shaw, *The Perfect Wagnerite* (London: Constable & Co., 1923), p. 53.

11 Barry Millington, 'Nuremberg Trial: Is There Anti-Semitism in *Die*

Meistersinger?', *Cambridge Opera Journal* 3.3 (November 1991): pp 247–60.

12 See Theodor Adorno, *In Search of Wagner*, trans. Rodney Livingstone (London: New Left Books, 1981).

9 Symphony Under Siege

1 See Harrison E. Salisbury, *The 900 Days: The Siege of Leningrad* (New York: Harper and Row, 1969).

2 Quoted in Wilson, *Shostakovich*, p. 158.

10 Radio Wall: Rock Under Siege

1 Joan Baez, 'Song of Sarajevo', *Washington Post* (16 May 1993), online (https://www.washingtonpost.com/archive/opinions/1993/05/16/song-of-sarajevo/971e2230-f184-4efc-bdd0-9901015e3c86/?utm_term=.9315442fef14).

12 Please Step into the Next Hall, Comrades!

1 Esti Sheinberg, *Irony, Satire, Parody and the Grotesque in the Music of Shostakovich: A Theory of Musical Incongruities* (Aldershot: Ashgate, 2000), p. 139.

2 Taruskin, 'Shostakovich and Us', p. 13.

3 L. Mazel & K. Sporamo, *Shostakoviche, Sovetskaya musyka*, 5. (1991), pp. 30–5, quoted in Taruskin, 'Shostakovich and Us', p. 21.

4 David Fanning, *Shostakovich: String Quartet No. 8* (Aldershot: Ashgate, 2004), p. 6.

5 Ibid., p. 10.

13 Strauss Is Cooler Than Salsa

1 'Venezuela violinist Wuilly Arteaga featured in a video discussing battle against regime', *Guardian*, 23 July, 2017.

7" Single: Beethoven in Juárez

1 See Roberto Saviano, *ZeroZeroZero*, trans. Virginia Jewiss (New York: Penguin, 2015).

15 Drones Over Wasteland

1 Joanna Demers, *Drone and Apocalypse* (Alresford: Zero Books, 2015). pp. 8–9.

2 Homero Aridjis, *The Child Poet*, trans. Chloe Aridjis (Brooklyn, NY: Archipelago, 2016), p. 109.

3 Chloe Aridjis, *Asunder* (London: Chatto & Windus, 2013), p. 61.

4 Ibid., p. 138.

5 Homer, *The Odyssey*, trans. E.V. Rieu, p. 144.

16 When Words Fail

1 See Ian Bostridge, *Schubert's Winter Journey* (London: Faber and Faber, 2015).

2 See Miron Grindea, 'Beckett's Involvement with Music', in *Samuel Beckett and Music*, ed. Mary Bryden (Oxford: Oxford University Press, 1998).

3 Deborah Weagel, *Words and Music: Camus, Beckett, Cage, Gould* (New York: Peter Lang, 2010), pp. 53, 62–3.

4 Quoted by Paul Lawley, '"The Grim Journey": Beckett Listens to Schubert', *Samuel Beckett Today/Aujourd'hui* 11 (2001): pp 255–66.

5 See George R. Marek, *Schubert: A Biography* (London: Robert Hale, 1985).

6 Ernest G. Porter, *Schubert's Piano Works* (London: Dobson Books, 1980), p. 13.

7 'In Praise of Imogen Cooper', *Guardian*, 11 December 2009.

8 Percy M. Young, *Schubert* (New York: David White, 1970), p. 121.

9 Porter, *Schubert's Piano Works*, p. 15.

10 Homero Aridjis, from 'The Horse That Comes Like Fire', *Eyes to See Otherwise: Selected Poems*, ed. Betty Ferber and George McWhirter (Manchester: Carcanet, 2001), p. 21.

7" Single: Postcard from the Night Train

1 Julian Johnson, Concert Programme, Philharmonia Orchestra Season 2007–8.

2 Richard Holmes, *Shelley: The Pursuit*, 2nd edn (London: HarperCollins, 1994), pp. xiv, 60.

3 Ibid., pp. 584–5.

4 Albert Camus, *The Plague*, trans. Stuart Gilbert (London: Hamish Hamilton, 1948), p. 245.

Finale: 'We Can Change the World'

1 'Un Bataclan Encore Convalescent', *Le Monde*, 13 December 2017.

2 Graham Nash, *Wild Tales: A Rock & Roll Life* (London: Viking Penguin, 2013), p. 10.

3 Ibid., p. 28.

Recommended Recordings

Here is a soundtrack to the book. I'd urge you to listen to almost all the LPs and CDs crammed onto my shelves, but to list them would take almost as many pages as this book despite the loss of those records to the American 'landfill called eBay'. (The help of friends in replacing the vast majority – especially Patrick Wintour, Paul Gilroy, Edin Ramulic and John Clews – is a debt I shall owe them for ever.) So what follows is a list of recommended recordings of works of direct relevance to the text, leaving out many that would be candidates for my *Desert Island Discs*.

There is no question in my mind that at home music is best heard on vinyl, the revival of which during the era of download and Spotify bears out the argument. Some new 180-gram vinyl editions are excellent, and if you want the original wooden sound, second-hand copies are widely available; for classical music these remain cheap, though for rock, blues and jazz they can be more expensive.

So where easily available, vinyl recordings are usually the best, but of course, if you want portable music or don't have the apposite equipment for vinyl, all of the following are available on CD – some on CD only – and almost all for download. Having made your choice, search around the Web if necessary, but ideally try your local record store, and shops you find in places you visit (my own favourites are listed in the Acknowledgements). There are few pleasures like browsing for music with your fingertips rather than in cyberspace.

Allegri/Palestrina
Miserere/Missa Papae Marcelli
Tallis Scholars
Gimell
1980

Amira Medunjanin
Rosa
Snail Records
2004

Amira Medunjanin/Merima Ključo
Zumra
Gramofon
2008

Amira Medunjanin
Amulette
World Village
2011

Anne-Marie O'Farrell
My Lagan Love
CMR Recordings
2000

Art Blakey and the Jazz
   Messengers
New Year's Eve at Sweet Basil
Paddle Wheel
1985

Art Tatum
His Rarest Solos
Saga
1973

Aswad
Aswad
Island
1976

B.B. King
Live at the Regal
Ace
1965

B.B. King
Blues Is King
Bluesway
1967

B.B. King
Completely Well
Bluesway
1969

B.B. King
Indianola Mississippi Seeds
Probe
1970

B.B. King
Live in Cook County Jail
ABC
1971

B.B. King
L.A. Midnight
Probe
1972

B.B. King
Live at San Quentin
MCA
1990

The Beat
I Just Can't Stop It
Go-Feet
1980

The Beatles
Sgt. Pepper's Lonely Hearts Club Band
Parlophone
1967
and 50th anniversary remixed
    boxed set, book etc.
Apple
2017

Beethoven
Symphonies 5 and 7
Simón Bolívar Youth Orchestra of
    Venezuela/Dudamel
Deutsche Grammophon
2006

Beethoven
The Complete Piano Sonatas
Daniel Barenboim
Warner/EMI
1998

Beethoven/Mozart
Symphony No. 5/Sinfonia
    concertante, K297b
West–Eastern Divan Orchestra/
    Barenboim (*Live in Ramallah*)
Warner
2006

Beethoven et al.
Wilhelm Furtwängler
Recordings 1942–1944 Vol. 1
Deutsche Grammophon
2001

Beethoven et al.
Wilhelm Furtwängler
*RIAS Recordings, Live in Berlin
    1947–1954* (14-LP boxed set)
Audite
2009

Berlioz
Symphonie fantastique
West–Eastern Divan Orchestra/
    Barenboim
Decca
2013

Bessie Smith
The Bessie Smith Story vols. 1–4
Columbia/CBS
1951–6

Billie Holiday
The Golden Years
Columbia/CBS
1962

Billie Holiday
The Billie Holiday Story Volume I
Columbia/CBS
1969

Billie Holiday
The Billie Holiday Story Volume II
Columbia/CBS
1973

Blind Lemon Jefferson
The Immortal Blind Lemon Jefferson
Milestone Records
1967

Bob Dylan
Bringing It All Back Home
Columbia/CBS
1965

Bob Dylan
Highway 61 Revisited
Columbia/CBS
1965

Bob Dylan
Blonde on Blonde
Columbia/CBS
1966

Bob Dylan
John Wesley Harding
Columbia/CBS
1967

Bob Dylan
Blood on the Tracks
Columbia/CBS
1974

Bob Dylan
Bob Dylan at Budokan
CBS/Sony
1978

The Wailers
Burnin'
Island
1973

Bob Marley and the Wailers
Natty Dread
Island
1974

Bob Marley and the Wailers
Exodus
Island
1977

Borodin/Shostakovich
String Quartet No. 2/String
  Quartet No. 8
Borodin Quartet
Ace of Diamonds
1962

Brahms
Violin Concerto/Double Concerto
Menuhin/Furtwängler
EMI
1990

Bruce Dickinson
Alive in Studio A
Castle Communications
1995

*Brundibár: Music by the Composers in
  Theresienstadt*
Nash Ensemble
Hyperion
2013

Bukka White
Mississippi Blues
Takoma
1963

Bukka White
Sky Songs vols. 1 and 2
Arhoolie Records
1965

Bukka White
Aberdeen Mississippi Blues: The
    Vintage Recordings 1930–1940
Document
2007

Charles Ives
Symphony No. 3/*Decoration Day*/
    Central Park in the Dark/*The*
    Unanswered Question
New York Philharmonic/Bernstein
CBS/Columbia
1966

Charlie Parker
Now's the Time
Verve
1957

Chet Baker
Chet Is Back!
RCA Victor
1962

Christy Moore
The Christy Moore Collection 81–91
Atlantic
1991

Christy Moore
At the Point Live
Frontline
1994

Christy Moore
Collection Part Two
Columbia
1999

The Clash
London Calling
CBS/Epic
1979

Composers from Theresienstadt: Hans
    Krása
La Roche Quartet
Channel Classics
1992

Crosby, Stills & Nash
Crosby, Stills & Nash
Atlantic
1969

Crosby, Stills, Nash & Young
4 Way Street
Atlantic
1971

Crosby, Stills & Nash
CSN [boxed set]
Atlantic/Rhino
1991

Graham Nash
Reflections [boxed set]
Atlantic/Rhino
2009

Graham Nash (with Shane
    Fontayne)
This Path Tonight
Blue Castle
2016

Diana Ross
Diana Ross' Greatest Hits
Motown
1976

Duke Ellington
Ellingtonia: Reevaluations: The
*   Impulse Years*
Impulse!
1973

Dvořák
Symphony No. 9 in E Minor,
    'From the New World'
Czech Philharmonic/Ančerl
Supraphon
1963

Dvořák
String Quintet in E Flat Major
Josef Suk, Jan Panenka et al.
Supraphon
1977

Dvořák/Borodin
String Quartet in F, Op. 96 [No. 12]
    'American'/String Quartet in D
Quartetto Italiano
Philips
1968

Dvořák
Violin Concerto
Josef Suk/Czech Philharmonic/
    Ančerl
Supraphon
1960

Edith Piaf
The Best of Edith Piaf
Capitol
1969

Elmore James
To Know a Man
Blue Horizon
1969

Elmore James
One Way Out
Charly R&B
1980

Elmore James
The Best of Elmore James
Ace
1981

Gesualdo
Tenebrae Responsories for Holy
*   Saturday*
Tallis Scholars
Gimell
1987

Gong
Camembert Electrique
BYG
1971

Gong
You
Virgin
1974

Planet Gong
Live Floating Anarchy 1977
Charly
1978

Gonzalo Rubalcaba
Fé
5Passion
2010

Grateful Dead
Live/Dead
Warner/Grateful Dead Records
1969

Grateful Dead
Workingman's Dead
Warner/Grateful Dead Records
1970

Grateful Dead
Shakedown Street
Arista
1978

Grateful Dead
In the Dark
Warner/Grateful Dead Records
1987

Hawkwind
Doremi Fasol Latido
United Artists/Atco
1972

Hawkwind
Warrior on the Edge of Time
United Artists/Atco
1975

Hawkwind
Blood of the Earth
Eastworld
2010

Haydn
Complete Piano Trios [incl. Trio Op. 8 No. 6] [boxed set]
Beaux Arts Trio
Philips
1996

Herbie Hancock, Dexter Gordon et al.
Round Midnight
Columbia/CBS
1986

James Brown
Sex Machine
King Records
1970

Janáček
String Quartets 1 & 2
Janáček Quartet
Supraphon
1964

Janáček/Haas
'Intimate Letters'/String Quartet No. 2
Pavel Haas Quartet
Supraphon
2006

Janáček/Haas
Janáček String Quartet No. 1/Haas
    String Quartets Nos 1 & 3
Pavel Haas Quartet
Supraphon
2007

Jefferson Airplane
Surrealistic Pillow
RCA
1967

Jefferson Airplane
Volunteers
RCA
1969

Jefferson Starship
Red Octopus
Grunt
1975

The Jimi Hendrix Experience
Are You Experienced
Track Record
1967

The Jimi Hendrix Experience
Electric Ladyland
Polydor
1968

Jimi Hendrix
Band of Gypsys
Polydor
1970

Jimi Hendrix
Isle of Wight
Polydor
1971

Joan Baez
Joan Baez
Vanguard
1960

Joan Baez
Joan Baez, Vol. 2
Vanguard
1961

Joan Baez
In Concert
Vanguard
1962

Joan Baez
In Concert, Part 2
Vanguard
1963

Joan Baez
David's Album
Vanguard
1969

Joan Baez
Diamonds & Rust
A&M
1975

Joe Boyd
*White Bicycles: Making Music in the
    1960s*
Fledg'ling Records
2006

John Cale
Paris 1919
Crazy Warthog
1973

John Cale
Music for a New Society
Domino
1982

John Cale
Sun Blindness Music
Table of the Elements
2001

John Cale
Black Acetate
EMI
2005

John Cale
Circus Live
EMI
2006

John Cale
M:FANS
Double Six
2016

John Coltrane
Blue Train
Blue Note
1957

The Red Garland Quintet with
    John Coltrane
Dig It!
Prestige
1962

John Coltrane with the Red
    Garland Trio
Traneing In
Prestige
1982

John Coltrane
*The Complete 1961 Village Vanguard
    Recordings*
Impulse!
1997

John Kay
Forgotten Songs and Unsung Heroes
ABC/Dunhill
1972

John Kay
All in Good Time
Mercury
1978

John Kay and Steppenwolf
Feed the Fire
CMC
1996

John Mayall and the Bluesbreakers
A Hard Road
London/Sundazed
1967

John Mayall
The Turning Point
Polydor
1969

Johnny Winter
Second Winter
CBS/Columbia
1969

King Crimson
In the Court of the Crimson King
Island
1969

Krása
Brundibár
Disman Radio Children's
    Ensemble, Prague
Channel Classics
1993

Krása
Verlobung im Traum
DSO Berlin/Ashkenazy
Decca
1998

Leadbelly
*Easy Rider: Leadbelly Legacy Volume
    Four*
Folkways
1950

Leadbelly
Rock Island Line
Folkways
1953

Leadbelly
The Saga of Leadbelly
Melodisc
1958

Led Zeppelin
Celebration Day
Atlantic
2012

Jimmy Page and Robert Plant
No Quarter
Virgin/EMI
1994

Robert Plant
Fate of Nations
Virgin/EMI
1993

Robert Plant
Band of Joy
Decca
2010

Leonard Cohen
Songs of Leonard Cohen
Columbia/CBS
1967

Leonard Cohen
Songs from a Room
Columbia/CBS
1969

Leonard Cohen
Live at the Isle of Wight 1970
Columbia/Legacy
2009

Leroy Carr
Blues Before Sunrise
Columbia/CBS
1962

Louis Armstrong
The Very Best of Louis Armstrong: 20 Golden Greats
Warwick Records
1981

Magma
Mekanik Destruktïw Kommandöh
Vertigo
1973

Mahler
Symphony No. 3
Vienna Philharmonic/Abbado
Deutsche Grammophon
1982

Mahler
Symphony No. 4
Popp, Tennstedt
EMI
1983

Mahler
Symphony No. 5
Simón Bolívar Youth Orchestra of Venezuela/Dudamel
Deutsche Grammophon
2007

Mahler
Symphony No. 6
Philharmonia Orchestra/Salonen
Signum Classics
2011

Mahler
Symphony No. 8
Harper, Popp et al., Chicago Symphony Orchestra/Solti
Decca
1972

Mahler
Symphony No. 9
Columbia Symphony Orchestra/ Walter
Columbia/CBS
1962
or
Czech Philharmonic/Ančerl
Supraphon
1967

Mamou
Mamou
ReverbNation
1988

Marianne Faithfull
Marianne Faithfull
Decca
1965

Marianne Faithfull
No Exit
EarMusic
2016

Martinů
Viola Concertos, Rhapsody
    Concerto
Josef Suk/Czech Philharmonic/
    Neumann
Supraphon
1994

McCoy Tyner
Nights of Ballads & Blues
Impulse!
1963

Miles Davis
Kind of Blue
Columbia/CBS
1959

Miles Davis
In a Silent Way
Columbia/CBS
1969

The Miles Davis Sextet and the
    Thelonious Monk Quartet
Miles & Monk at Newport
Columbia/CBS
1963

Mostar Sevdah Reunion
Šaban
Snail Records
2006

Moving Hearts
Moving Hearts
Warner
1981

Mozart
Così Fan Tutte
Schwarzkopf, Ludwig, Kraus,
    Taddei et al./Böhm
HMV
1962

Mozart
Don Giovanni
Ghiaurov, Ludwig, Berry, Freni
    et al./Klemperer
EMI
1994

Mozart
Mitridate, Re di Ponto
Banks, Persson, Classical Opera/
    Ian Page
Signum
2014

Mozart
Le Nozze di Figaro
Siepi, della Casa, Vienna
    Philharmonic/E. Kleiber
Decca
1959

Muddy Waters
Muddy 'Mississippi' Waters Live
Blue Sky
1979

O'Connor, McCartney, Stone
    Roses et al.
Help
Go! Discs
1995

The Oscar Peterson Trio
Night Train
Verve
1963

Oscar Peterson and Ben Webster
Ben Webster Meets Oscar Peterson
Jazz Wax Records
1959

Patti Smith
Horses
Arista
1975

Patti Smith Group
Radio Ethiopia
Arista/BMG
1976

Patti Smith Group
Wave
Arista
1979

Patti Smith
Trampin'
Arista/BMG
2003

Pete Seeger
We Shall Overcome
Columbia/CBS
1963

Pete Seeger
Pete Seeger's Greatest Hits
Columbia/CBS
1967

Pink Floyd
The Dark Side of the Moon
Harvest
1973

Pink Floyd
Wish You Were Here
EMI/Pink Floyd Music
1975

Planxty
Planxty
Polydor
1973

Plastic People of the Universe
*Egon Bondy's Happy Hearts Club
    Banned*
Invisible Records/Kissing Spell
1978

Plastic People of the Universe
Beefslaughter
Kissing Spell
1997

Plastic People of the Universe
Man with No Ears
Kissing Spell
2002

Quicksilver Messenger Service
Quicksilver Messenger Service
Capitol
1968

Rachmaninoff
Symphonic Dances
London Symphony Orchestra/
   Gergiev
LSO Live
2012

Radiohead
OK Computer
EMI/XL
1997

Radiohead
Kid A
EMI
2000

Rage Against the Machine
The Battle of Los Angeles
Sony
1999

Robert Johnson
King of the Delta Blues Singers
CBS/Columbia
1961

Roly Porter & Cynthia Millar
Fall Back – Live at Aldeburgh
Subtext
2012

Roly Porter
Third Law
Tri Angle
2016

Schubert
Piano Sonatas D.784, 958, 959, 960
Paul Lewis
Harmonia Mundi
2014

Schubert
Piano Sonatas D.840, 850, 894
Paul Lewis
Harmonia Mundi
2011

Schubert
Piano Sonata D.845,
    Wandererfantasie D.760, 4
    Impromptus D.935, *Moments*
    musicaux D.780
Paul Lewis
Harmonia Mundi
2012

Schubert
Death and the Maiden
Jerusalem Quartet
Harmonia Mundi
2008

Schubert
Winterreise
Paul Lewis, Mark Padmore
Harmonia Mundi
2009

Seamus Heaney, Liam O'Flynn
The Poet & The Piper
Claddagh Records
2003

Shostakovich
Symphony No. 5
Leningrad Philharmonic
    Orchestra/Mravinsky
Melodiya
1938
or
Berlin Symphony Orchestra/
    Sanderling
Berlin Classics
1992
or
London Symphony Orchestra/
    Rostropovich
LSO Live
2005

Shostakovich
Symphony No. 6 (and Symphony
    No. 9)
Oslo Philharmonic/[Mariss] Jansons
EMI
1992

Shostakovich
Symphony No. 7
Leningrad Philharmonic/
    Mravinsky
EMI
1962
or
Czech Philharmonic/Ančerl
Supraphon
1960
or
Concertgebouw/Jansons
EMI
1988

or
New York Philharmonic/Masur
Teldec
2000
or
National Symphony Orchestra/
    Rostropovich
Apex
2001
or
Mariinsky Orchestra/Gergiev
Philips
2003

Shostakovich
The 15 String Quartets
Beethoven Quartet
Doremi
2007

Shostakovich
The Bolt
Royal Stockholm Philharmonic/
    Rozhdestvensky
Chandos
1995

Shostakovich
The Film Album [incl. *The Silly Little
    Mouse*]
Royal Concertgebouw/Chailly
Decca
1999

Shostakovich
*The Girlfriends (Complete)/Salute to
    Spain/Rule, Britannia!/Symphonic
    Movement (1945)*
Polish National Radio Symphony
    Orchestra/Fitz-Gerald
Naxos
2009

Shostakovich
The Golden Age
Royal Stockholm Philharmonic/
    Rozhdestvensky
Chandos
1994

Shostakovich
Lady Macbeth of Mtsensk
Vishnevskaya, Gedda, London
    Philharmonic/Rostropovich
EMI
1979

Shostakovich
*Moskva, Cheremushki [Moscow,
    Cheryomushki] [CD]*
Kisselev, Baturkin, Residentie
    Orchestra The Hague/
    Rozhdestvensky
Chandos
1998

Shostakovich
The Nose
Mariinsky Soloists, Orchestra, and
    Chorus/Gergiev
Mariinsky
2009

Simón Bolívar String Quartet
Ginastera, Dvořák, Shostakovich
Deutsche Grammophon
2013

Simón Bolívar Symphony Orchestra
    of Venezuela/Dudamel
El Sistema 40: A Celebration
Deutsche Grammophon
2015

Smetana
Má Vlast
Czech Philharmonic/Ančerl
Supraphon
1968

Son House
Raw Delta Blues
Not Now Music
2011

Sonny Terry and Brownie McGhee
In London
Marble Arch Records
1958

Sonny Terry and Brownie McGhee
At the Second Fret
Prestige
1962

Steel Pulse
Handsworth Revolution
Island Records
1978

Steeleye Span
Time
Park Records
1996

Steppenwolf
Steppenwolf
ABC/Dunhill Records
1968

Steppenwolf
Monster
Stateside
1969

Steppenwolf
Live
Stateside
1970

Tallis
Spem in Alium
Tallis Scholars
Gimell
1985

Thelonious Monk
Les Liaisons Dangereuses 1960
Saga/SAM Records
2017

Tinariwen
Emmaar
Wedge
2013

UB40
Present Arms
DEP International
1981

UB40
UB40
DEP International
1988

The Velvet Underground and Nico
The Velvet Underground & Nico
Verve
1967

Verdi
Aida
Callas, Tucker, Gobbi/Serafin
EMI
1956
or
Ricciarelli, Domingo, Nucci/Abbado
Deutsche Grammophon
1983

Verdi
Don Carlo
Domingo, Caballé, Verrett, Milnes/
　　Giulini
EMI
1971

Verdi
Otello
Domingo, Scotto, Milnes/Levine
Sony
1978

Verdi
Il Trovatore
Domingo, Plowright et al./Giulini
Deutsche Grammophon
1984
or
Callas, di Stefano et al./La Scala/
    Karajan
EMI/HMV
1960

Verdi
I Vespri Siciliani
Domingo, Arroyo, Milnes et al./
    Levine
RCA Red Seal
1974

Vivaldi
Le Quattro Stagioni
Stuttgarter Kammerorchester/
    Münchinger
Decca
1986

The Voices of East Harlem
Right On Be Free
Elektra
1970

Wagner
Der Ring des Nibelungen [Complete:
    Das Rheingold, *Die Walküre*,
    Siegfried, *Götterdämmerung*]
Modl, Suthaus, Konetzni, Frantz/
    Furtwängler
EMI
1972
or
Nilsson, Hotter, Windgassen,
    London/Solti
Decca
1967

The Weavers
At Carnegie Hall
Vanguard
1957

*Woodstock: Music from the Original
    Soundtrack* [incl. Jimi Hendrix,
    'Star Spangled Banner']
Rhino
1969

Bibliography

The small spaces in which I've lived have been, and still are, almost suffocated (thankfully) by vinyl LPs, CDs – and books. What follows is not a definitive bibliography in an academic sense, but an arrangement – in accordance with the chapters in this book – of volumes on music that have accumulated over decades, all mixed in with fiction, poetry, warfare, history, philosophy and so on. These books have survived the occasional cull for Oxfam shops, been pored over and annotated, and flowed like tributaries, often subliminally, into *When Words Fail*. I'm indebted to them all, and recommend most. The essentials are marked with an asterisk, the absolute must-reads with two. Not everyone's words have failed when writing about music:

> *No, Music, thou art not the 'food of Love',*
> *Unless Love feeds upon its own sweet self,*
> *Till it becomes all Music murmurs of.*
> Percy Bysshe Shelley, 'Another Fragment to Music'

Overture
Beckett, Samuel. *Happy Days*. London: Faber & Faber, 1966.

1 Hendrix Comes East
* Allman, Gregg, with Alan Light. *My Cross to Bear*. New York: HarperCollins, 2012.
Cross, Charles R. *Room Full of Mirrors: A Biography of Jimi Hendrix*. New York: Hachette, 2005.

Dyer, Geoff. *But Beautiful: A Book About Jazz*. New York: North Point Press, 1996.

Etchingham, Kathy. *Through Gypsy Eyes: My Life, the Sixties and Jimi Hendrix*. London: Victor Gollancz, 1998.

Foulk, Ray, with Caroline Foulk. *The Last Great Event: When the World Came to the Isle of Wight*. Surbiton: Medina, 2016.

Giddins, Gary. *Visions of Jazz: The First Century*. New York: Oxford University Press, 1998.

* Gilroy, Paul. *The Black Atlantic: Modernity and Double Consciousness*. Cambridge, MA: Harvard University Press, 1993.

* —. *Darker Than Blue: On the Moral Economies of Black Atlantic Culture*. Cambridge, MA, and London: Belknap Press/Harvard University Press, 2010.

* Gioia, Ted. *The History of Jazz*. New York: Oxford University Press, 1997.

Hendrix, Jimi. *Starting at Zero: His Own Story*, ed. Alan Douglas and Peter Neal. London: Bloomsbury, 2013.

Murray, Charles Shaar. *Crosstown Traffic: Jimi Hendrix and Post-War Pop*. Edinburgh: Canongate, 2012.

Paul, Alan. *One Way Out: The Inside History of the Allman Brothers Band*. New York: St. Martin's Press, 2014.

2 What on Earth Is Going On?

Ball, Philip. *The Music Instinct: How Music Works and Why We Can't Do Without It*. London: Vintage, 2011.

** Baudelaire, Charles. *Œuvres complètes*, ed. Claude Pichois. Paris: Gallimard, 1975.

—. *Complete Poems*, tr. Walter Martin. Manchester: Carcanet, 1997.

** Berlioz, Hector. *The Memoirs of Hector Berlioz*, tr. David Cairns. London: Gollancz, 1969; New York: Everyman's Library, 2002.

Brophy, Brigid. *Mozart the Dramatist: The Value of His Operas to Him, to His Age and to Us*. London: Libris, 1988.

Cairns, David. *Berlioz, Volume One: The Making of an Artist, 1803–1832*. London: André Deutsch, 1989.

Cooke, Deryck. *Gustav Mahler: An Introduction to His Music*. London: Faber & Faber, 1980.

Dent, Edward J. *Mozart's Operas: A Critical Study*. London: Oxford University Press, 1947.

Feder, Stuart. *The Life of Charles Ives*. Cambridge: Cambridge University Press, 1999.

Fischer, Jens Malte. *Gustav Mahler*, tr. Stewart Spencer. New Haven, CT: Yale University Press, 2011.

Gay, Peter. *Mozart*. London: Weidenfeld & Nicolson, 1999.

Griffiths, Paul. *Olivier Messiaen and the Music of Time*. London: Faber & Faber, 2009.

Harley, John. *Thomas Tallis*. London: Routledge, 2016.

Heyworth, Peter, et al. *Mahler, Vienna and the Twentieth Century*, festival programme. London: London Symphony Orchestra, 1985.

Holmes, Edward. *The Life of Mozart*, ed. Christopher Hogwood. London: Folio Society, 1991.

** Homer. *The Odyssey*, tr. E.V. Rieu. London: Penguin, 1946, rev. edn 1991.

Ivry, Benjamin. *Maurice Ravel: A Life*. New York: Welcome Rain, 2000.

Jensen, Eric Frederick. *Debussy*. New York: Oxford University Press, 2014.

Jeppesen, Knud. *The Style of Palestrina and the Dissonance*. New York: Dover, 1970.

Kennedy, Michael. *Mahler*. London: J.M. Dent & Sons, 1974.

** Latham, Alison (ed.). *The Oxford Companion to Music*. Oxford: Oxford University Press, 2002.

** Leopardi, Giacomo. *Zibaldone*, ed. Caesar and D'Intino, tr. Baldwin et al. London: Penguin, 2013.

Levitin, Daniel J. *This Is Your Brain on Music: The Science of a Human Obsession*. New York: Dutton, 2006.

** Mann, Thomas. *Doctor Faustus*, tr. John E. Woods. New York: Knopf, 1997.

Mann, William. *The Operas of Mozart*. London: Cassell, 1977.

* Mauclair, Camille. *Charles Baudelaire, sa vie, son art, sa légende*. Paris: Maison du Livre, 1917.

* —. *The French Impressionists (1860–1900)*. New York: Bibliolife (reprint), 2008.

* Newton, Francis (aka Eric Hobsbawm). *The Jazz Scene*. London: Penguin, 1961.

Radcliffe, Philip. *Mozart Piano Concertos*. London: Ariel Music/BBC, 1978.

Ratliff, Ben. *Every Song Ever: Twenty Ways to Listen to Music*. London: Penguin/Allen Lane, 2016.

Ross, Alex. *The Rest Is Noise: Listening to the Twentieth Century*. London: Fourth Estate, 2007.

Sacks, Oliver. *Musicophilia: Tales of Music and the Brain*. New York: Knopf, 2007.

Schopenhauer, Arthur. *The World as Will and Representation* [1819], tr. E.F.J. Payne, 2 vols. New York: Dover, 1969.

Steptoe, Andrew. *The Mozart–Da Ponte Operas: The Cultural and Musical Background to Le nozze di Figaro, Don Giovanni, and Così fan tutte*. Oxford: Clarendon Press, 1988.

Swafford, Jan. *Charles Ives: A Life with Music*. New York: W.W. Norton, 1996.

Wagner, Richard. *Wagner on Music and Drama*, ed. Albert Goldman and Evert Sprinchorn, tr. H. Ashton Ellis. New York: Da Capo, 1964.

Walter, Bruno. *Gustav Mahler* [1957]. London: Severn House, 1975.

Watkins, Glenn. *The Gesualdo Hex: Music, Myth, and Memory*. New York: W. W. Norton, 2010.

3 Double Entendre: Shostakovich Goes West

Ardoin, John. *Valery Gergiev and the Kirov: A Story of Survival*. Portland, OR: Amadeus Press, 2001.

Ardov, Michael. *Memories of Shostakovich: Interviews with the Composer's Children*, tr. Rosanna Kelly and Michael Meylac. London: Short Books, 2004.

Bakst, James. *A History of Russian-Soviet Music*. Westport, CT: Greenwood Press, 1977.

* Bartlett, Rosamund (ed.). *Shostakovich in Context*. Oxford: Oxford University Press, 2000.

Bely, Andrei. *Petersburg*, tr. John Elsworth. London: Pushkin Press, 2009.

Brown, Malcolm Hamrick (ed.). *A Shostakovich Casebook*. Bloomington: Indiana University Press, 2005.

Clark, Katerina. *Petersburg, Crucible of Cultural Revolution*. Cambridge, MA: Harvard University Press, 1995.

Edmunds, Neil (ed.). *Soviet Music and Society under Lenin and Stalin: The Baton and Sickle*. London: Routledge, 2004.

Fairclough, Pauline (ed.). *Shostakovich Studies 2*. Cambridge: Cambridge University Press, 2010.

Fanning, David (ed.). *Shostakovich Studies*. Cambridge: Cambridge University Press, 1995.

* Fay, Laurel E. *Shostakovich: A Life*. New York: Oxford University Press, 2000.

— (ed.). *Shostakovich and His World*. Princeton, NJ: Princeton University Press, 2004.

Grigoryev, Lev, and Yakov Platek. *Dmitry Shostakovich: About Himself and His Times*, tr. Angus and Neilian Roxburgh. Moscow: Progress Publishers, 1980.

Ho, Allan B., and Dmitry Feofanov (eds.). *Shostakovich Reconsidered*. London: Toccata Press, 1998.

Ivashkin, Alexander, and Andrew Kirkman (eds.). *Contemplating Shostakovich: Life, Music and Film*. Farnham: Ashgate, 2012.

Krebs, Stanley Dale. *Soviet Composers and the Development of Soviet Music*. London: George Allen and Unwin, 1970.

Lesser, Wendy. *Music for Silenced Voices: Shostakovich and His Fifteen Quartets*. New Haven, CT: Yale University Press, 2011.

Lukyanova, N.V. *Shostakovich: His Life and Times*, tr. Yuri Shirokov. Neptune City, NJ: Paganiniana Publications, 1984.

MacDonald, Ian. *The New Shostakovich*. London: Fourth Estate, 1990.

Martynov, Ivan. *Dmitri Shostakovich: The Man and His Work*, tr. T. Guralsky. New York: Greenwood Press, 1969.

Morton, Brian. *Shostakovich: His Life and Music*. London: Haus Books, 2006.

Norris, Christopher (ed.). *Shostakovich: The Man and His Music*. Boston, MA: Marion Boyars, 1982.

Rabinovich, D. *Dmitri Shostakovich: Composer*, tr. George H. Hanna. Moscow: Foreign Languages Publishing House, 1959.

Reichardt, Sarah. *Composing the Modern Subject: Four String Quartets by Dmitri Shostakovich*. Aldershot: Ashgate, 2008.

Riley, John. *Dmitri Shostakovich: A Life in Film*. London: I.B. Tauris, 2005.

Rostropovich, Mstislav, and Galina Vishnevskaya. *Russia, Music, and Liberty: Conversations with Claude Samuel*, tr. E. Thomas Glasow. Portland, OR, Amadeus Press, 1995.

* Seroff, Victor. *Dmitri Shostakovich: The Life and Background of a Soviet Composer*. New York: Knopf, 1943.

Shostakovich, Dmitri. *Testimony: The Memoirs of Dmitri Shostakovich*, ed. Solomon Volkov. London: Faber & Faber, 1981.

* —. *Story of a Friendship: The Letters of Dmitry Shostakovich to Isaak Glikman*, ed. Isaak Glikman, tr. Anthony Phillips. Ithaca, NY: Cornell University Press, 2001.

* Sollertinsky, Dmitri and Ludmilla. *Pages from the Life of Dmitri Shostakovich*, tr. Graham Hobbs and Charles Midgley. New York: Harcourt Brace Jovanovich, 1980; London: Robert Hale, 1981.

Taruskin, Richard. *Defining Russia Musically: Historical and Hermeneutical Essays*. Princeton, NJ: Princeton University Press, 1997.

Volkov, Solomon. *St. Petersburg: A Cultural History*, tr. Antonina W. Bouis. New York: Free Press Paperbacks/Simon & Schuster, 1995.

—. *Shostakovich and Stalin: The Extraordinary Relationship Between the Great Composer and the Brutal Dictator*. New York: Knopf, 2004.

** Wilson, Elizabeth. *Shostakovich: A Life Remembered*. London: Faber & Faber, 1994.

4 State and De Soto: 'Down to the Crossroads'

Beaumont, Daniel. *Preachin' the Blues: The Life and Times of Son House*. New York: Oxford University Press, 2011.

Cohn, Lawrence. *Nothing but the Blues: The Music and the Musicians*. New York: Abbeville Press, 1993.

Dixon, Willie, with Don Snowden. *I Am the Blues: The Willie Dixon Story*. New York: Da Capo, 1989.

Gordon, Robert. *Can't Be Satisfied: The Life and Times of Muddy Waters*. Edinburgh: Canongate, 2002.

** King, B.B., with David Ritz. *Blues All Around Me: The Autobiography of B.B. King*. New York: Avon, 1996.

Lemann, Nicholas. *The Promised Land: The Great Black Migration and How It Changed America*. New York: Vintage Books, 1992.

Oakley, Giles. *The Devil's Music: A History of the Blues*. New York: Da Capo, 1976.

* Oliver, Paul. *Blues Fell This Morning: The Meaning of the Blues*. London: Cassell/Jazz Book Club, 1963.

* —. *Conversation with the Blues*. London: Cassell, 1965.

Palmer, Robert. *Deep Blues: A Musical and Cultural History from the Mississippi Delta to Chicago's South Side to the World*. New York: Penguin, 1981.

Sullivan, Mary Lou. *Raisin' Cain: The Wild and Raucous Story of Johnny Winter*. New York: Backbeat, 2010.

Wald, Elijah. *Escaping the Delta: Robert Johnson and the Invention of the Blues*. New York: Amistad, 2004.

7" Single: Viva Verdi! Una Vita Italiana

Beales, Derek, and Eugenio F. Biagini. *The Risorgimento and the Unification of Italy*. London: Pearson, 2002.

Bruschi, Max. *Giuseppe Verdi. Note e noterelle*. Palermo: Sellerio, 2001.

Illiano, Roberto (ed.). *VIVA V.E.R.D.I.: Music from Risorgimento to the Unification of Italy*. Turnhout: Brepols, 2013.

Martini, G. (ed). *Giuseppe Verdi, benefattore e politico*. Fidenza: Mattioli, 2014.

* Phillips-Matz, Mary Jane. *Verdi: A Biography*. Oxford: Oxford University Press, 1993.

Verdi, Giuseppe. *Verdi: The Man in His Letters*, ed. Franz Werfel and Paul Stefan, tr. Edward Downes. New York: L. B. Fischer, 1942.

5 'No Time for Love'

Coogan, Tim Pat. *Ireland in the Twentieth Century*. London: Arrow Books, 2004.

FitzGerald, Desmond. *Desmond's Rising: Memoirs 1913 to Easter 1916*. Dublin: Liberties Press, 2016.

Kinsella, Thomas (ed.). *The New Oxford Book of Irish Verse*. Oxford: Oxford University Press, 1986.

Moloney, Ed. *A Secret History of the IRA*, 2nd edn. London: Penguin, 2007.

Moore, Christy. *One Voice: My Life in Song*. London: Hodder and Stoughton, 2003.

Moylan, Terry (ed.). *The Indignant Muse: Poetry and Songs of the Irish Revolution 1887–1926*. Dublin: Lilliput, 2016.

Townshend, Charles. *The Republic: The Fight for Irish Independence, 1918–1923*. London: Penguin, 2014.

6 Floating Anarchy Radio: 'You Can't Un-ring the Bell!'

Boyd, Joe. *White Bicycles: Making Music in the 1960s*. London: Serpent's Tail, 2005.

Briggs, John. *Pete Seeger: The People's Singer*. Guilderland, NY: Atombank, 2015.

Denning, Michael. *Noise Uprising: The Audiopolitics of a World Musical Revolution*. London: Verso, 2015.

Didion, Joan. *Slouching Towards Bethlehem*. New York: Simon and Schuster, 1968.

Herr, Michael. *Dispatches*. New York: Knopf, 1977.

McNally, Dennis. *A Long Strange Trip: The Inside History of the Grateful Dead and the Making of Modern America*. New York: Three Rivers Press, 2002.

Olsson, Ulf. *Listening for the Secret: The Grateful Dead and the Politics of Improvisation*. Oakland: University of California Press, 2017.

Seeger, Pete. *Pete Seeger in His Own Words*, ed. Rob Rosenthal and Sam Rosenthal. Boulder, CO: Paradigm, 2012.

Tamarkin, Jeff. *Got a Revolution!: The Turbulent Flight of Jefferson Airplane*. New York: Simon and Schuster, 2003.

7" Single: Diamonds and Rust: Joan Baez and Bob Dylan

Baez, Joan. *Daybreak*. New York: Avon, 1968.

—. *And a Voice to Sing With: A Memoir*. New York: Summit Books, 1987.

Dylan, Bob. *Tarantula*. New York: Macmillan, 1971.

—. *Chronicles: Volume One*. New York: Simon & Schuster, 2004.

** —. *The Lyrics: 1961–2012*, ed. Lisa Nemrow. New York: Simon & Schuster, 2016.

—. *The Nobel Lecture*. New York: Simon & Schuster, 2017.

Heylin, Clinton. *Behind the Shades*, New York: Summit Books, 1991.

Ricks, Christopher. *Dylan's Visions of Sin*. New York: Ecco, 2004.

Shepard, Sam. *The Rolling Thunder Logbook*. London: Penguin, 1978.

7" Single: Dvořák in Iowa

Beckerman, Michael B. *New Worlds of Dvořák: Searching in America for the Composer's Inner Life*. New York: W.W. Norton, 2003.

— (ed.). *Dvořák and His World*. Princeton, NJ: Princeton University Press, 1993.

Butterworth, Neil. *Dvořák: His Life and Times*. London: Omnibus Press, 1980.

Clapham, John. *Dvořák*. Newton Abbot: David & Charles, 1979.

Hampl, Patricia. *Spillville*. Minneapolis, MN: Milkweed Editions, 1987.

Mellers, Wilfrid. *Music in a New Found Land: Themes and Developments in the History of American Music*. London: Faber & Faber, 1987.

Škvorecký, Josef. *Dvořák in Love*, tr. Paul Wilson. New York: Alfred A. Knopf, 1987.

7 Fuck the Wall!

Crump, Michael. *Martinů and the Symphony*. London: Toccata Press, 2010.

Ewans, Michael. *Janáček's Tragic Operas*. London: Faber & Faber, 1977.

Havel, Václav. *The Power of the Powerless*, ed. John Keane. Armonk, NY: M.E. Sharpe, 1985.

Hutton, J. Bernard, and Liam Nolan. *The Life of Smetana: The Pain and the Glory*. London: Harrap & Co., 1968.

Janáček, Leoš. *Janáček: Leaves from His Life*, ed. and tr. Vilem and Margaret Tausky. London: Kahn and Averill, 1982.

Symynkywicz, Jeffrey B. *Václav Havel and the Velvet Revolution*. Parsippany, NJ: Dillon Press, 1995.

Vogel, Jaroslav. *Leoš Janáček: A Biography*, rev. and ed. Karel Janovický. New York: W.W. Norton, 1981.

8 Through the Wire

Adorno, Theodor. *In Search of Wagner*, tr. Rodney Livingstone. London: New Left Books, 1981.

** Améry, Jean. *At the Mind's Limits: Contemplations by a Survivor on Auschwitz and Its Realities*, tr. Sidney Rosenfeld and Stella P. Rosenfeld. Bloomington: Indiana University Press, 2009.

Aster, Misha. *The Reich's Orchestra: The Berlin Philharmonic 1933–1945*. London: Souvenir Press, 2010.

Beckett, Lucy. *Richard Wagner: Parsifal*. Cambridge: Cambridge University Press, 1981.

** Borowski, Tadeusz. *This Way for the Gas, Ladies and Gentlemen*, tr. Barbara Vedder. New York: Viking Press, 1967.

* Browning, Christopher R. *Ordinary Men: Reserve Police Battalion 101 and the Final Solution in Poland*. New York: HarperCollins, 1992.

Burbidge, Peter, and Richard Sutton (eds.). *The Wagner Companion*. London: Faber & Faber, 1979.

Chancellor, John. *Wagner*. London: Granada, 1980.

Deathridge, John, and Carl Dahlhaus. *The New Grove Wagner*. London: Macmillan, 1984.

** Delbo, Charlotte. *Auschwitz and After*, tr. Rosette C. Lamont. New Haven, CT: Yale University Press, 1995.

* Donington, Robert. *Wagner's 'Ring' and Its Symbols*. London: Faber & Faber, 1963.

Dreyfus, Laurence. *Wagner and the Erotic Impulse*. Cambridge, MA: Harvard University Press, 2010.

Fantlová, Zdenka. *The Tin Ring*. Newcastle upon Tyne: Northumbria University Press, 2010.

Jacobs, Robert L. *Wagner*. London: John Dent & Sons, 1965.

* Karas, Joža. *Music in Terezín, 1941–1945*. Hillsdale, NY: Pendragon Press, 1985.

Lee, M. Owen. *Wagner: The Terrible Man and His Truthful Art*. Toronto: University of Toronto Press, 1999.

** Levi, Primo. *If This Is a Man*, tr. Stuart Woolf. London: Orion Press, 1959.

** —. *The Drowned and the Saved*, tr. Raymond Rosenthal. London: Abacus, 1989.

* Magee, Bryan. *Aspects of Wagner*, rev. edn. Oxford: Oxford University Press, 1988.

—. *The Tristan Chord: Wagner and Philosophy*. New York: Henry Holt, 2000.

McSpadden, J. Walker. *Stories from Wagner*. London: Harrap & Co., 1910.

Millington, Barry. *Wagner*. London: John Dent & Sons, 1984.

Newman, Ernest. *Wagner Nights*. London: Putman & Co., 1949.

Prieberg, Fred K. *Trial of Strength: Wilhelm Furtwängler and the Third Reich*. London: Quartet Books, 1991.

Sabor, Rudolph. *The Real Wagner*. London: André Deutsch, 1987.

* Shaw, Bernard. *The Perfect Wagnerite: A Commentary on the Niblung's Ring*. New York: Dover, 1967.

** Shirer, William L. *The Rise and Fall of the Third Reich: A History of Nazi Germany*. New York: Simon & Schuster, 1960.

Skelton, Geoffrey. *Richard and Cosima Wagner: Biography of a Marriage*. London: Victor Gollancz, 1982.

Wagner, Gottfried. *Twilight of the Wagners: The Unveiling of a Family's Legacy*. New York: Picador, 1997.

Wagner, Richard. *Wagner on Music and Drama*, ed. Albert Goldman and Evert Sprinchorn. New York: Da Capo, 1964.

von Westernhagen, Curt. *Wagner: A Biography*, tr. Mary Whittall. Cambridge: Cambridge University Press, 1978.

9 Symphony under Siege

* Akhmatova, Anna. *The Complete Poems of Anna Akhmatova*, ed. Roberta

Reeder, tr. Judith Hemschemeyer. Somerville, MA: Zephyr Press, 1998.

Berggolts, Olga. *Daytime Stars*, tr. Lisa Kirschenbaum and Barbara Walker. Madison: University of Wisconsin Press, 2018 (forthcoming).

* Conquest, Robert. *The Great Terror: A Reassessment*. London: Pimlico, 2008.

Feinstein, Elaine. *Anna of All the Russias: The Life of Anna Akhmatova*. London: Weidenfeld & Nicolson, 2005.

Glantz, David M. *The Siege of Leningrad, 1941–1944: 900 Days of Terror*. London: Cassell, 2001.

* Grossman, Vasily. *Life and Fate*, tr. Robert Chandler. London: Harvill Press, 1985.

* —. *A Writer at War: Vasily Grossman with the Red Army 1941–1945*, ed. and tr. Antony Beevor and Luba Vinogradova. London: Harvill Press, 2005.

—. *Everything Flows*, tr. Robert and Elizabeth Chandler with Anna Aslanyan. London: Harvill Secker, 2010.

Jones, Michael. *Leningrad: State of Siege*. London: John Murray, 2008.

Reid, Anna. *Leningrad: Tragedy of a City Under Siege, 1941–44*. London: Bloomsbury, 2011.

* Salisbury, Harrison. *The 900 Days: The Siege of Leningrad*. New York: Da Capo Press, 1969.

Snyder, Timothy. *Bloodlands: Europe between Hitler and Stalin*. London: Bodley Head, 2010.

10 Radio Wall: Rock Under Siege

Carter, Bill. *Fools Rush In*. New York: Doubleday, 2004.

Cohen, Roger. *Hearts Grown Brutal: Sagas of Sarajevo*. New York: Random House, 1998.

Rieff, David. *Slaughterhouse: Bosnia and the Failure of the West*. New York: Touchstone, 1996.

Sullivan, Kevin. *The Longest Winter*. London: Twenty7, 2016.

Vulliamy, Ed. *The War Is Dead, Long Live the War: Bosnia: the Reckoning*. London: Bodley Head, 2012.

7" Single: La Louisiane

Longfellow, Henry Wadsworth. *Evangeline: A Tale of Acadie* [1847]. New York: Nimbus, 2004.

12" Extended version: 'I Think You'd Better Wake Up, the World Trade Center's on Fire!'

* Smith, Patti. *Babel*. New York: G. P. Putnam's Sons, 1978.

—. *Early Work*. New York: W.W. Norton, 1994.

—. *Just Kids*. New York: Ecco, 2010.

* —. *Collected Lyrics*. London: Bloomsbury, 2015.

* —. *M Train*. New York: Knopf, 2015.

—. *Devotion*. New Haven, CT: Yale University Press, 2017.

11 Al-Malwiya – the Spiral

Anderson, Jon Lee. *The Fall of Baghdad*. New York: Little, Brown, 2005.

12 Please Step into the Next Hall, Comrades!

As for Chapter 3, plus:

Bakhtin, Mikhail. *Problems of Dostoevsky's Poetics*, ed. and tr. Caryl Emerson. Minneapolis: University of Minnesota Press, 1984.

Bertensson, Sergei, and Jay Leda. *Sergei Rachmaninoff: A Lifetime in Music*. Bloomington: Indiana University Press, 2009.

Fanning, David. *Shostakovich: String Quarter No. 8*. Aldershot: Ashgate, 2004.

Gogol, Nikolai. *The Overcoat and Other Stories*. New York: Dover, 1992.

—. *The Collected Tales of Nikolai Gogol*, tr. Richard Pevear and Larissa Volokhonsky. New York: Vintage, 1999.

—. *Dead Souls*, tr. Robert A. Maguire. London: Penguin Classics, 2004.

—. *Diary of a Madman and Other Stories*. New York: Dover, 2006.

Holquist, Michael. *Dialogism: Bakhtin and His World*. London: Routledge, 1990.

Mayakovsky, Vladimir. *The Bedbug and Selected Poetry*, ed. Patricia Blake, tr. Max Hayward and George Reavey. Bloomington: Indiana University Press, 1975.

Scott, Michael. *Rachmaninoff*. New York: The History Press, 2008.

Seroff, Victor. *Rachmaninoff* [1950]. New York: Books for Libraries Press, 1970.

Sheinberg, Esti. *Irony, Satire, Parody and the Grotesque in the Music of Shostakovich: A Theory of Musical Incongruities*. Aldershot: Ashgate, 2000.

La Discothèque

See the Cantos Cautivos website: www.cantoscautivos.org
or in Spanish: www.cantoscautivos.cl

Aguilera, Pila, and Ricardo Fredes (eds.). *Chile: The Other September 11: An Anthology of Reflections on the 1973 Coup*. Melbourne: Ocean Press, 2006.

White, Judy (ed.). *Chile's Days of Terror: Eyewitness Accounts of the Military Coup*. New York: Pathfinder Press, 1974.

Beethoven in Juárez

* Bowden, Charles. *Juárez: The Laboratory of Our Future*. New York: Aperture, 1998.

—. *Down by the River: Drugs, Money, Murder, and Family*. New York: Simon & Schuster, 2004.

—. *Murder City: Ciudad Juárez and the Global Economy's New Killing Fields*. New York: Nation Books, 2010.

— and Julián Cardona. *Exodus*. Austin: University of Texas Press, 2008.

Cacho, Lydia. *Slavery Inc.: The Untold Story of International Sex Trafficking*. London: Granta, 2012.

—. *Infamy: How One Woman Brought an International Sex Trafficking Ring to Justice*. New York: Soft Skull Press, 2016.

—, Diego Enrique Osorno, et al. *The Sorrows of Mexico*. London: MacLehose Press, 2016.

Rodríguez Nieto, Sandra. *The Story of Vicente, Who Murdered His Mother, His Father, and His Sister*. London: Verso, 2015.

Saviano, Roberto. Foreword Ed Vulliamy. *ZeroZeroZero*. New York: Penguin, 2015. Original Italian edition: Milan: Feltrinelli, 2013.

Vulliamy, Ed. *Amexica: War Along the Borderline*. New York: Farrar, Straus and Giroux, 2010.

14 Through the Wall

Barenboim, Daniel. *A Life in Music*. New York: Arcade, 2003.

* —. *Everything Is Connected: The Power of Music*. London: Weidenfeld & Nicolson, 2008.

— and Edward W. Said. *Parallels and Paradoxes: Explorations in Music and Society*. London: Bloomsbury, 2002.

Postcard from the Recovery Ward, 2013

Bowden, Charles. *Some of the Dead Are Still Breathing: Living in the Future*. New York: Houghton Mifflin Harcourt, 2009.

15 Drones over Wasteland

Aridjis, Chloe. *Asunder*. London: Chatto & Windus, 2013.

Aridjis, Homero. *The Child Poet*, tr. Chloe Aridjis. Brooklyn, NY: Archipelago, 2016.

Cale, John. *What's Welsh for Zen*. London: Bloomsbury, 2000.

Demers, Joanna. *Drone and Apocalypse: An Exhibit Catalog for the End of the World*. Alresford: Zero Books, 2015.

16 When Words Fail

* Aridjis, Homero. *Eyes to See Otherwise: Selected Poems*, ed. Betty Ferber and George McWhirter. Manchester: Carcanet, 2001.

** Beckett, Samuel. *Molloy*. London: Calder and Boyars, 1959.

* Beethoven, Ludwig van. *The Letters of Beethoven*, 3 vols., ed. and tr. Emily Anderson. London: Macmillan, 1961.

Biss, Jonathan. *Beethoven's Shadow*. New York: RosettaBooks, 2011.

Bostridge, Ian. *Schubert's Winter Journey: Anatomy of an Obsession*. London: Faber & Faber, 2015.

Cronin, Anthony. *Samuel Beckett: The Last Modernist*. New York: Da Capo, 1999.

Fiske, Roger. *Beethoven Concertos and Overtures*. London: BBC, 1970.

Gibbs, Christopher H. *The Life of Schubert*. Cambridge: Cambridge University Press, 2000.

* Knowlson, James. *Damned to Fame: The Life of Samuel Beckett*. London: Bloomsbury, 1996.

Marek, George R. *Schubert: A Biography*. London: Robert Hale, 1986.

Morris, Edmund. *Beethoven: The Universal Composer*. New York: HarperCollins, 2005.

Porter, Ernest G. *Schubert's Piano Works*. London: Dobson Books, 1980.

Sachs, Harvey. *The Ninth: Beethoven and the World in 1824*. London: Faber & Faber, 2010.

Solomon, Maynard. *Beethoven*. New York: Shirmer, 1977; rev. edn 1998.

Swafford, Jan. *Beethoven: Anguish and Triumph*. New York: Houghton Mifflin Harcourt, 2014.

Weagel, Deborah. *Words and Music: Camus, Beckett, Cage, Gould*. New York: Peter Lang, 2010.

Young, Percy M. *Schubert*. New York: David White, 1970.

7" *Single: Postcard from the Night Train*

** Camus, Albert. *The Plague*, tr. Stuart Gilbert. London: Hamish Hamilton, 1948.

** Holmes, Richard. *Shelley: The Pursuit*. London: HarperCollins, 1994.

* Shelley, Percy Bysshe. *The Complete Poetical Works of Percy Bysshe Shelley*. Oxford: Oxford University Press, 1948.

** —. *Shelley: Poetical Works*, ed. Thomas Hutchinson. London: Oxford University Press, 1970. (The best edition, if traceable.)

—. *Selected Poems and Prose*, ed. Jack Donovan and Cian Duffy. London: Penguin, 2016.

Finale: 'We Can Change the World'

Crosby, David, and Carl Gottlieb. *Long Time Gone*. New York: Doubleday, 1988.

Nash, Graham. *Wild Tales: A Rock and Roll Life*. London: Viking Penguin, 2013.

Young, Neil. *Waging Heavy Peace: A Hippie Dream*. New York: Blue Rider Press, 2012.

General

Arnold, Denis. *Monteverdi*. London: John Dent & Sons, 1963.

— and Nigel Fortune (eds.). *The New Monteverdi Companion*. London: Faber & Faber, 1985.

Ashley, Tim. *Richard Strauss*. London: Phaidon, 1999.

Bacharach, A.L. (ed.). *The Musical Companion*. London: Victor Gollancz, 1934.

—. *The Music Masters: From the Sixteenth Century to the Time of Beethoven*. London: Maurice Fridberg, 1948.

Beer, Anna. *Sounds and Sweet Airs: The Forgotten Women of Classical Music*. London: Oneworld, 2016.

Brahms, Johannes. *Life and Letters*, ed. Styra Avins, tr. Josef Eisinger and Styra Avins. New York: Oxford University Press, 1997.

Brown, David. *Tchaikovsky: The Man and His Music*. London: Faber & Faber, 2006.

Conrad, Peter. *A Song of Love and Death: The Meaning of Opera*. London: Chatto & Windus, 1987.

Craft, Robert. *Stravinsky: Chronicle of a Friendship* [1972]. Nashville, TN: Vanderbilt University Press, 1994.

Dean, Winton, and John Merrill Knapp. *Handel's Operas, 1704–1726*. Oxford: Clarendon Press, 1987.

Dromgoole, Nicholas. *Performance Style and Gesture in Western Theatre*. London: Oberon Books, 2007.

Ellen, Mark. *Rock Stars Stole My Life! A Big Bad Love Affair with Music*. London: Coronet, 2014

FitzLyon, April. *Lorenzo Da Ponte: A Biography of Mozart's Librettist*. London: John Calder, 1982.

* Giannaris, George. *Mikis Theodorakis: Music and Social Change*. London: Allen and Unwin, 1973.

* Harewood, Earl of (ed.). *Kobbe's Complete Opera Book*. London: Bodley Head, 1976.

Headington, Christopher, Roy Westbrook and Terry Barfoot. *Opera: A History*. London: Bodley Head, 1987.

Holden, Anthony. *Tchaikovsky*. London: Penguin, 1995.

—. *The Man Who Wrote Mozart: The Extraordinary Life of Lorenzo Da Ponte*. London: Weidenfeld & Nicolson, 2006.

Ivashkin, Alexander. *Alfred Schnittke*. London: Phaidon, 1996.

Jefferson, Alan. *Richard Strauss: Der Rosenkavalier*. Cambridge: Cambridge University Press, 1985.

Jensen, Eric Frederick. *Schumann*. New York: Oxford University Press, 2005.

Kaufman, Will. *Woody Guthrie, American Radical*. Urbana: University of Illinois Press, 2011.

Keates, Jonathan. *Handel: The Man and His Music*. London: Victor Gollancz, 1985.

Kennedy, Michael (ed.). *The Concise Oxford Dictionary of Music*. Oxford: Oxford University Press, 1980.

Kerman, Joseph. *Opera as Drama*. New York: Alfred A. Knopf, 1956.

Klein, Joe. *Woody Guthrie: A Life*. New York: Delta, 1980.

Landon, H.C. Robbins. *Haydn Symphonies*. London: BBC Music Guides, 1963.

Marlowe, Lara. *Painted with Words*. Dublin: Liberties Press, 2011.

Mitchell, Donald. *The Language of Modern Music*. London: Faber & Faber, 1963.

Morrison, Richard. *Orchestra: The LSO: A Century of Triumph and Turbulence*. London: Faber & Faber, 2004.

Mouyis, Angelique. *Mikis Theodorakis: Finding Greece in His Music*. Athens: Kerkyra, 2010.

Naughtie, James. *The Making of Music: A Journey with Notes*. London: John Murray, 2007.

Noble, Jeremy, Gustave Reese, Lewis Lockwood, James Haas, Joseph Kerman, Robert Stevenson. *The New Grove High Renaissance Masters*. London: Macmillan, 1980.

Osborne, Charles. *The Complete Operas of Richard Strauss*. London: Michael O'Mara Books, 1988.

Previn, Andre (ed.). *Orchestra*. London: Macdonald & Jane's, 1979.

Reich, Nancy B. *Clara Schumann: The Artist and the Woman*. Ithaca, NY: Cornell University Press, 1985.

Robertson, Alec, and Denis Stevens (eds.). *The Pelican History of Music*, vol. 2: *Renaissance and Baroque*. London: Penguin, 1963.

—. *The Pelican History of Music*, vol. 3: *Classical and Romantic*. London: Penguin, 1968.

Robinson, Harlow. *Sergei Prokofiev: A Biography*. Boston: Northeastern University Press, 2002.

Robinson, Paul. *Opera and Ideas: From Mozart to Strauss*. Ithaca, NY: Cornell University Press, 1985.

Rosen, Charles. *The Classical Style: Haydn, Mozart, Beethoven* [1971]. New York: W. W. Norton, 1998.

Sanders, Ronald. *The Days Grow Short: The Life and Music of Kurt Weill*. New York: Limelight Editions, 1985.

Service, Tom. *Music as Alchemy: Journeys with Great Conductors and Their Orchestras*. London: Faber & Faber, 2012.

Solti, Georg. *Solti on Solti: A Memoir*. London: Chatto & Windus, 1997.

* Theodorakis, Mikis. *Journals of Resistance*. London: Hart-Davis, MacGibbon, 1973.

Acknowledgements

My main thanks go to my employers at the *Guardian* and *Observer* for commissioning me to write about music as well as tribulations of the world, and for consenting to the reworking of some of the resultant material here. At both papers, I worked with colleagues and dear friends who facilitated my writing and encouraged me. The intelligent commissioning of John Mulholland, who urged me on persistently, and of Caspar Llewellyn Smith and Ruaridh Nicoll; the sagacity and talent of Alan Rusbridger, the judicious expertise of Ursula Kenny and Jane Ferguson, the support of Stephen Pritchard, Imogen Tilden, Tom Service and Tim Ashley – and Campbell Stevenson for knowing everything. Special thanks too to the book's co-dedicatee, Victoria Frances Edgar, for coming to some of the concerts and putting up with me.

To everyone mentioned in this text, my deep gratitude – without them there would be no book. They find their acknowledgements in the resulting volume. In addition to people featured and cited, I add my heartfelt thanks for all they have done to:

At Granta
Max Porter, for his faith in all this; wise editor, publisher, great writer himself; Pru Rowlandson for getting the book 'out there' to you and others; Christine Lo, for organizing everything; Dan Mogford for designing the cover and Mandy Woods for proofreading. And to Sue Phillpott, copy-editor *sans pareil*, for innumerable improvements to the text, and copious corrections.

At the Wylie Agency
Tracy Bohan, agent, friend, lifeline.

At Rocco Media
Luciano Ruocco, for friendship, for help with this project, and for hauling me into the world of technology.

In the family
My younger daughter, Claudia, for her inspiration in the visual arts. My elder daughter, Elsa, figures in the book, as do my brother, Tom, Mum and Dad. And my sister, Clara, and nephews and nieces, Paul, Adam, Alice, Leah and Martha.

From my childhood and youth
Patrick Wintour, Roger Cohen, Mark Pegram, Richard Astor, Simon Long, the memory of Dave Lund; Julia Fergusson, the memory of Kitty Fergusson; Johnny and Anne Roberts. Felix and Kitty Warnock, Meyrick Alexander, Melanie Jessop, the memory of George Melly, the memory of Robert Tear; Louisa Saunders, Paul Greengrass, John Blake, Karen Brown, Bernadette Wren, Joanna Robertson.

In the UK
Vron Ware, Marcus Gilroy-Ware, Cora Gilroy-Ware, Michelle Aland, Ginevra White, Katherine Cox, John Clews, Jon Lee Anderson, Elena Cosentino, Allegra Donn, Angelika and Peter Patel, Allan Little, Penny Marshall, Amelia Freedman, Connie Mayer, Jonny Greene; Arun Aggarwal, Mick Eve, Winston Delano, Wendy and Dave Clare, Mike Sumner, Carol Anderson and the memory of Ronnie Gordon.

At the London Symphony Orchestra:
Dvora Lewis, Kathryn McDowell, Lennie MacKenzie, Kenny Morrison.

In the Americas

The memory of Susan Sontag; David Rieff, Judith Thurman, Nita Scott, Marco Roth, Mark Dowie and Wendy Schwarz, Ange Turley Snr, Angela Turley, Thomas Turley Mooneyham, the memory of Jack Turley, the memory of Kate Turley; Sharon Delano, Meredith Parsons, Vince Stehle, Arabella Greene, Brigitte Neisa, Michael Zilkha, Lisa Hilton and Mimi and Antonia Doretti.

In Italy

Nicky Thomas, Paolo Petrocelli, the Ciolli-Foresta family, Milly Ruggiero, Clare Ireland; and all at *La Stampa*, Redazione di Roma, Via Barberini, Rome, 1990–4.

In Ireland

Kate Manning, Ciarán Crilly, Wolfgang Marx, Risteard Ó Domhnaill, Arthur and Mary Ó Domhnaill, Colm and Gabrielle Henry, Tony Conway and Erris FM Community Radio, Maura Harrington, Brian Maguire, Marty and Clare Melarky, Greta McTague; the Nerve Centre, Derry; Maurice Earls, John Waters.

In France

Florence Hartmann, Henri Peretz, Brigitte Lozerec'h, Françoise Ruffe, Eric and Beryl Mary, Olga Stanisławska and Jean-Gabriel Potocki, Florence Cestac, Simone Hisler and 'Dr No' Electric Blues, Rémy Ourdan, Elisa Perrigueur, Lara Marlowe.

Thank you for the music

Music and Video Exchange, Notting Hill Gate, London; Jazz House Records, Leicester; John Stapleton and Wanted Records, Bristol; Hairy Records, Liverpool; Second Hand Rose Music, New York; Vintage Vinyl, St Louis, Missouri; the music store at Buddy Guy's Legends, S. Wabash, Chicago; the Cheese and Grain, Frome, Somerset; The Constitution, St Pancras Way, London; the Marché des Puces, rue Marc Sangnier, Paris; Walrus Disquaire Café, Paris; Le Silence de la Rue Records, Paris; La

Bouquinerie (Oxfam), rue Daguerre, Paris; Mille Records, Rome; Claddagh Records, Dublin; All City Records, Dublin; LaRoma Records, Mexico City.

For the sustenance and welcome
The Ruocco family and all at Da Maria, Notting Hill Gate, London; the Russian Samovar, W. 52nd Street, New York; Al Pompiere, Via di Santa Maria de' Calderari, Rome; La Vela, Marechiaro, Naples; Walsh's Stoneybatter, Dublin; Wynn's Hotel, Dublin; all at Café Naguère, rue Daguerre, Paris; Gymnase, Boulevard Raspail, Paris; all Chez Karole, rue Boulard, Paris; all at Bar 61, rue de l'Oise, Paris.

In Memoriam
In London, all those specialist vinyl exchange shops in Notting Hill Gate, 'Classical', 'Jazz', 'Dance', etc.; Collet's Books and Music, Charing Cross Road; the Mountain Grill café, Portobello Road; All Saints Hall, Talbot Road; the Mercury Theatre and Ballet Rambert, Notting Hill Gate; Notting Hill Books and Mandarin Books, Notting Hill Gate; the Ark, Notting Hill Gate; the Kensington Park Hotel, Ladbroke Grove; the Prince of Wales, Princedale Road; the Portland Arms, Portland Road; the Patio, Shepherds Bush.

In Chicago, Rose Records.
In Glastonbury, Somerset, Tor Records.
In Sarajevo, the Nostalgija bar, now itself a subject of nostalgia.

Index